新竄起者

破解中國巧妙的霸權之路

Upstart
How China Became a Great Power

梅慧琳——著
Oriana Skylar Mastro
邱鐘義——譯

目錄

圖表一覽	
導　論　中國崛起，晉身強權俱樂部一員	004
第一章　竄起者策略	007
第二章　中國外交政策中的模仿與利用策略	033
第三章　中國外交政策中的創新作為	075
	115

第四章　中國軍事戰略中的模仿與利用策略	151
第五章　中國軍事戰略中的創新作為	195
第六章　中國在經濟政策上的模仿與利用策略	243
第七章　中國經濟政策中的創新作為	281
結　論　強權競爭的啟示	321
致謝	351
註釋	359

圖表一覽

圖0.1 三個E的定義……015

圖1.1 竄起者策略的各項要素……063

圖2.1 二〇〇六至二〇二三年中國從事國際調解活動的概略位置……081

圖2.2 一九九〇至二〇二二年美國與中國的軍售……103

圖3.1 與中國有戰略夥伴關係的國家數……123

圖3.2 中國的戰略夥伴關係協議數（雙邊與多邊協議）……123

圖4.1 一九九〇至二〇二〇年聯合國安理會五個常任理事國參與維和任務的總兵力……160

圖 4.2 中國人道援助與救災活動的概略位置	161
圖 4.3 各主要國家在二〇二〇至二〇二一年對聯合國維和預算的相對貢獻度	164
圖 5.1 美國與中國的國防支出對比	201
圖 7.1 二〇一〇~二〇二一年電動車生產量	298
圖 7.2 二〇〇〇~二〇一七年中國政府對外國政府的融資	312
表 1.1 不同的競爭策略	042
表 6.1 中國的經濟制裁行動記錄	257
表 6.2 人民幣國際化戰略的演變	276
表 7.1 中國主要產業政策推動項目一覽表	291

5　圖表一覽

譯者按：本書作者援引大量中國文本，引用文字部分保留中國文本的原始用語，例如：「集成電路」，而文章論述部分則譯為台灣習慣用語，例如：「積體電路」。又，本書探討「Great Power」的概念，基本上我們按照台灣慣用用法翻譯為「強權」，但中國為突顯其「和平崛起」的立場，通常以「大國」一詞表述 Great Power 的概念，後文若涉及中國方面的發言或意圖時，則按照其原始文本用詞稱為「大國」，作者論述部分則譯為「強權」。書末註釋之引用文獻，原始文獻名稱為簡體中文者，保留其簡體字；內文引用時，則轉換為繁體字。

導論

中國崛起，晉身強權俱樂部一員

三十年前，幾乎沒有人能夠想像中國可以在經濟、全球事務和軍事領域挑戰美國。冷戰結束後，美國不僅成為史上最強大的國家，還是全球最富裕的國家、世界上最大的經濟體，並在一九九二年至一九九九年之間達成經濟成長率年平均四％。美國建立了廣泛的軍事聯盟網路，其國內生產毛額（GDP）超過中國十六倍以上。美國並在第二次世界大戰後主導建立了一系列國際組織，並透過這些組織與盟友維繫全球主導地位。

相較之下，二〇〇〇年的中國呈現出完全不同的局面。當時，中國的經濟僅占全球GDP的三％，甚至低於法國。同一年，中國的手機用戶不到總人口的七％，而網路使用者的比例甚至低於二％。雖然中國擁有約四百萬人的龐大軍隊，但這更多反映了其「落後」的現狀，而非「實力」。由於裝備過時、訓練不足，中國幾乎不算擁有真正的空軍和海軍。當時，中國飛行員無法在海上飛行，更無法應對夜間或惡劣天氣。一九九九年，中國的第四代戰鬥機僅占總數不到二％，符合當代標準的攻擊型潛艇不到四％，水面艦艇也完全不具備現代化水準。事實上，中國海軍更像是一支「放大版的海岸警衛隊」，因為艦艇缺乏防空系統，巡邏時只能貼近海岸行動。中國的核武系統主要依賴固定式的發射井並使用固體燃料，極易在先制攻擊中就被徹底摧毀。冷戰結束後，北京在國際上依然處於孤

新竄起者　8

立狀態，無法參與像世界貿易組織（WTO）這樣的國際機構，也未與包括南韓在內的多個區域強權建立正式外交關係。

本書的敘述由此展開——中國領導人意識到中美兩國之間巨大的實力差距，並希望縮小這一差距。在當時，美國處於無可挑戰的「單極」優勢地位，尤其在一九九一年的波斯灣戰爭，1美軍的軍事表現令人驚嘆，充分突顯出強大實力。自波斯灣戰爭以後，從江澤民到習近平，每一任的中國領導人都希望提高中國的實力，重塑自身在國際體系中的地位，進而擺脫過去數十年來被強權壓制與羞辱的歷史。2然而，對實力與影響力的追求並非中國行為的唯一動機——中國共產黨（中共）堅持以強有力的國家控制來維持其國內權力。同時，這種控制也塑造出獨特的「中國式競爭」，對美國主導的國家秩序以及中國自身均造成一些困境。在新千禧年的開端，中國因國內因素，突顯出採取謹慎戰略的重要性。唯有如此，北京才能在美國主導的世界中競逐權力與影響力，且不至於因為威脅到華盛頓的利益而遭到強烈反制。3

接下來隨著時間演進，中國出乎意料地「脫胎換骨」。二○一○年，中國經濟超越日本，成為世界第二大經濟體，之後甚至已超過日本、印度和德國經濟的總和。從一九九〇

9　導論　中國崛起，晉身強權俱樂部一員

年到二○一○年間，北京擁有的國際組織會員總數翻了一倍，並在聯合國（UN）等組織中表現得更為積極主動。中國還在一九九○年代與二十八個國家實現了「關係正常化」。在接下來的三十年間，中國從外交孤立蛻變成在全球舞台上擁有與美國相當的外交和政治影響力（根據某些衡量標準，甚至略為超越美國）。截至二○二一年，中國已成為一百二十個國家的第一大貿易夥伴，當中包含美國所有的印太地區盟友。[4]

中國的軍事現代化同樣令人歎為觀止。這得益於從一九九二年到二○二○年間增長了七百九十％的國防預算，如今中國的軍事裝備多數已達到現代化水準，這意味著從戰鬥機到反衛星雷射技術的任何裝備都已足夠先進，足以對最尖端的技術構成威脅，中國現在能對世界上最先進的軍隊構成威脅，並有信心不會因技術與裝備上的劣勢而在交戰中失利。中國的核武力量現在具備生存能力，即使遭遇先發制人的攻擊，仍能保有足夠的核彈頭與投射系統以進行報復性核子打擊。二○一○年十月，中國測試了全球首枚高超音速核子飛彈，成為首個進行此類測試的國家，此舉促使前美國參謀長聯席會議主席馬克・麥利（Mark Milley）對外表示：「他們已經從一九七九年的一支龐大而落後的農民軍隊，成長為一支在所有領域都極具實力的現代化軍隊。」[5] 確實，中國目前的科學家人數

新竄起者　10

比美國多出約二萬人,且在過去二十五年內,每年平均的研發支出成長率達到十五%（相較之下,美國僅為三%）,因此,中國在許多與戰爭相關的新興技術領域被認為比美國更加先進,例如人工智慧、高超音速技術以及量子計算。

傳統軍事指標同樣顯示出中國人民解放軍的進步幅度之大。過去,中國飛行員無法飛越距中國海岸線僅約四十英里的台灣海峽中線,而如今他們幾乎每天都在進行此類飛行任務。從二〇二〇年九月至二〇二一年九月,中國軍機在台灣防空識別區（ADIZ）內進行了二百五十天的飛行活動,且入侵次數與參與飛機架數均呈現上升趨勢。6 早期,中國艦艇很少遠離本土海岸進行活動,但如今已在南海、東海和印度洋巡航。中國尚未擁有「藍水海軍」——即能在遠離本土的全球水域運作的海軍力量,但憑藉著位於吉布地的軍事基地及例行性的港口巡航,中國已經展現出一定的全球存在感。中國海軍目前是全球規模最大的海軍,擁有三百五十五艘各式艦艇（不過在總噸位上尚未達到美國海軍的水準）。中國還擁有全球最大且技術最先進的彈道飛彈和巡航飛彈工程計劃,包括一種能擊中海上移動目標的反艦彈道飛彈（ASBM）,這是美國目前尚未具備的武器。

為了縮小在外交、經濟和軍事實力上的相對差距,中國的戰略不僅需要具備效能,還

竄起者策略

二〇二一年三月，美國總統拜登的新任團隊前往阿拉斯加，首次與其中國對手會面。儘管會前雙方都抱持著高度期望，但此次會議的氣氛並不友好。中國方面無意聽取美國列舉中國在西藏、香港及新疆的人權以及外交政策上的一連串違反普世價值的行為。中央外事工作委員會辦公室主任楊潔篪更直接回嗆：「你們沒有資格在中國的面前以實力高人一等的姿態對中國說話。」

這場峰會中的表態雖然帶有一些表演性質，但楊潔篪的言論並非毫無根據。中美之間

必須極具效率。如果效率不足，中國將無法成功追趕，甚至可能面臨內部崩潰的風險。北京還必須設法避免引發美國的強烈反應，因為這可能摧毀其努力，抬高成本，甚至可能導致內部危機或觸發一場終結中國崛起的預防性戰爭。中國需要在實力最大化、霸主國（美國）的反應、國內穩定與繁榮之間找到平衡，並且必須靈活應對不斷變化的國際與國內環境。答案在於一種「竄起者策略」。

新竄起者　12

的相對實力差距已顯著縮小,甚至在某些領域,中國已經取得領先。如習近平在二○二二年十月的中共二十大報告中所言:「我國發展具備了更為堅實的物質基礎、更為完善的制度保證,實現中華民族偉大復興進入了不可逆轉的歷史進程。」[7]

在過去三十年中,中國是如何試圖建立實力和影響力的?是哪些因素決定了北京採取的策略?本書提出我的答案:「竄起者策略」。「竄起者」(upstart,在英文中同時也有暴發戶、新貴的意思)意指一個從低位突然迅速崛起,取得權力、財富或地位的實體。[8] 這一詞彙常帶有貶義,形容那些被認為自大、傲慢或咄咄逼人,最近剛開始從事某種活動並成功,卻未對前輩展現出應有尊重的人。[9] 然而,我所使用的這個術語並不完全是貶義,當「upstart」用來描述「新創公司」時,帶有中性意味。「竄起者策略」的靈感來自商業研究中的競爭理論。儘管在國際關係中新興勢力及重大衝突相對來說較為罕見,但在商業上以新興手法顛覆整個行業以及導致企業破產的案例卻屢見不鮮,因此商業研究中已有成熟的研究傳統,透過大量案例的測試與修正,探討新興企業如何擊敗並取代老牌成熟企業。

我的「竄起者策略」包括三個組成部分,以競爭領域和新興強權的行動模式來定義:

13　導論　中國崛起,晉身強權俱樂部一員模仿（emulation）、利用（exploitation）和創新（entrepreneurship），簡稱「三E策略」。

模仿是指一個國家在現有競爭領域中，用和既有霸權相同的方式進行競爭。大多數現有文獻關注這種競爭形式，認為有志成為強權的國家會以已被證明有效的方法建立和運用實力。第二個組成部分是利用，指新興強權在新的競爭領域採用類似於既有霸權的方法。例如，中國會在美國競爭力最弱的地方抓住機會──美國未積極參與或存在弱點的領域、國際秩序中的漏洞，或規範環境較弱的地方。最後一個組成部分是創新，涉及在新舊競爭領域中採取全新的方法。**圖 0.1** 中的維恩圖表示了這一策略的關係和區分。

探討商業競爭的文獻為每種方法的利弊提供了一些見解。例如，在某些領域，模仿可能是新興國家崛起最快且最有效的方式。模仿通常被視為「遵循既定規則」，這有助於新興國家在避免引發反彈或被其他強權制衡的情況下積累實力。然而，模仿也可能面臨高昂的成本且進展緩慢。在最壞的情況下，模仿可能因強權的競爭性反應而充滿風險。若新興國家在應對這些反應時欠缺競爭優勢，模仿策略可能最終成為徒勞的嘗試。

關於「竄起者策略」的第二個組成部分「利用」，商業領域中有些市占率低而企圖心強的競爭者，善加利用既有領導企業的盲點，擊敗他們而成為新的市場領導者。這樣的做

新竄起者　14

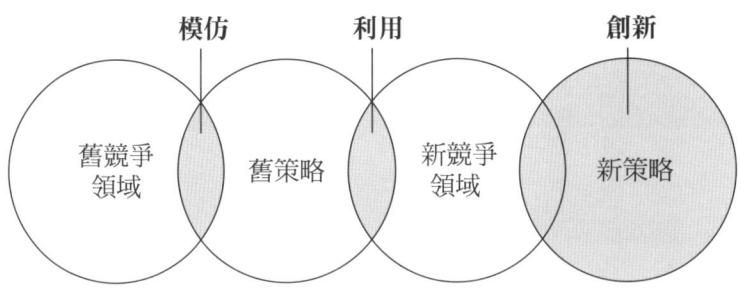

圖 0.1　三個 E 的定義

法正是新興國家效法的對象。10 這一策略的實行必須滿足以下兩個條件：①存在可利用的盲點——既有霸權因忽視、欠缺能力或認為該領域增長空間有限而未積極參與競爭的領域；②新興國家在這些領域具有一定優勢。11 此時，新興國家便可採用已被證明有效的方式，但無需直接與既有霸權競爭。若新興國家在相關領域擁有競爭優勢，這是一種相對高效的實力構建方式。

最後一個組成部分——創新，也有其優勢。一種全新的方法可能不會被視為對既有霸權地位的直接挑戰，因此不會立即引發其他國家的制衡行動。儘管創新可能比模仿（已被驗證的方式）更具風險，但若成功，其崛起速度和效率可能遠比模仿更快。12 更具創意的策略還可能使新興國家在新的戰略領域獲得「先

15　導論　中國崛起，晉身強權俱樂部一員

行者優勢」或充分利用其獨特的競爭優勢。成功挑戰領導者的競爭者往往能「以創意破壞根深蒂固的信念」,重新定義最佳建構與行使實力的方式。

這條道路並無明確的藍圖,採用不同尋常的策略也可能導致新興勢力的失敗。[13]然而,創新並非毫無風險,

從以上這項討論中,我們可以得出有五個主要因素會決定新興國家會採用「三E策略」中的哪一個:既有霸權策略的有效性、霸權對行為的最可能解讀、特定方法的效率(主要由競爭優勢塑造)、方法的侷限性以及是否存在差距與盲點。以中國而言,[14]

這意味著當中國評估美國的方法有效、模仿行為能使西方國家放心,且中國在相關領域具備競爭優勢以確保戰略效力時,往往會選擇模仿美國。例如,中國的外交推進、調解以及嘗試加入新的國際機構均屬於此類。當上述條件成立但中國因自身能力限制而無法直接參與競爭時,中國會意識到差距,並選擇在這些領域採行「利用盲點」策略。

新興策略的最後一個組成部分對中國的崛起最為關鍵。當中國認為美國的策略無效或是可能對黨造成風險,亦或採用美國的方法可能會引發強烈的負面威脅感時,中國便會尋求創新的實力建構途徑。在這種情況下,中國會設計出一種新的方式來建立某種類型的實力,這種方式能夠充分利用中國的競爭優勢,並降低其弱點的影響。例如,中國建設商業

新竄起者 16

港口設施，而非海外軍事基地，來保護其海外利益，或者訓練當地執法部門而非外國軍隊以謀求建立良好關係。

探討中國如何競逐強權地位

我們的敘述始於一九九〇年代中期，這一時期通常被認為是中國地緣政治崛起的起點。15 在此期間中國領導人做出關鍵的戰略決策，將目光從單純追求國內經濟成長拓展到國際舞台，著手構建政治、軍事和經濟力量。本書試圖透過深入分析二十二個案例，探討中國領導人如何在這些情境中做出決策，以實現特定的戰略目標。

這三十年（約從一九九三年至二〇二三年）也與中國對自身發展軌跡的認知相吻合。鄧小平曾將冷戰後的三十年稱為「追趕」的時期，並強調「抓住機遇」16 的重要性。知名中國學者鄭必堅在二〇〇〇年初提出中國「和平崛起」的概念，而在二〇〇三年溫家寶總理於哈佛大學演講後，官方文本和講話中開始公開討論中國的崛起。17 到新冠疫情爆發前夕，官方和學術界的評估已經普遍接受中國成功的縮小了與美國的實力差距，可以被視為

17　導論　中國崛起，晉身強權俱樂部一員

一個強權。

本書旨在闡述中國採取了哪些行動、為什麼選擇特定方式行事、這些做法為中國帶來了什麼，以及這些策略如何塑造了中國作為一個強權和具有影響力的國家的形象。透過詳細的數據分析和權威的中國資料來源，我將中國的選擇置於特定的背景之下，並以二十二個涉及中國經濟、外交和軍事策略的案例，描繪其在全球權力階梯上的崛起之路。在每個案例中，我提供了客觀的數據以及中國對其選擇「竄起者策略」組成部分的五個因素的評估——戰略效能、戰略效率、國內政治因素、美國可能的反應，以及漏洞或盲點的存在。

「竄起者策略」框架顯示，根據這些變數的不同，中國最有可能採取哪一種策略組成部分。由於「競爭力」是一個相對的概念，每一部分都將中國的戰略方法與美國戰略的主要原則進行比較。我分析並推斷，北京是如何透過資源的分配來選擇模仿、利用或創新，並進一步評估這些策略是否如預期的提升了中國的強權地位。

研究結果提供了詳細的解釋，說明中國如何基於模仿、利用或創新的優劣勢而選擇特定策略。若「竄起者策略框架」能捕捉中國實力累積的方法，我們應當能夠觀察到幾個關鍵數據點。首先，美國的戰略應是中國決策者在選用模仿、利用或創新的主要參考。我們

新竄起者　18

可以預期官方和權威的中國著作會評估中國相較於美國戰略的競爭優勢與劣勢,並且這些評估將直接影響中國的競爭方式。其次,我在案例研究中檢視中國選擇特定策略的邏輯是否符合竄起者策略的思維模式。數據應顯示,中國的策略選擇是基於成本效益分析,考量了戰略效能、效率、美國對此的看法、中國自身的競爭優勢與脆弱性,以及是否存在可供利用的空隙。儘管中國領導人可能因資訊不完整而無法每次都做出最佳決策,但我假設他們是理性的,至少會觀察中國的國內表現和外部環境,並在執行不力或戰略環境出現變化時進行調整和應對。[18]

我的研究方法有兩個主要特點。首先,它是以數據為導向的。本書的分析基於六個原創資料集和數十個現有資料集,這些資料集涵蓋中國的各項活動,並可在線上附錄中查閱。[19]其次,此方法依賴於中國的觀點和評估。本書的中文研究涉及數百個一手資料,包括政府出版物、領導人演講、媒體評論以及學術論文。在我檢視的八百五十六個資料來源中,有一百二十八本是由軍方相關出版社出版的書籍;三十七本是由共產黨相關出版社出版的書籍;六十九本是學術著作(包括領導人傳記、對波斯灣戰爭等事件的研究,以及由社會科學文獻出版社和世界知識出版社出版的其他書籍);一百五十本是政府白皮書及其

19　導論　中國崛起,晉身強權俱樂部一員

他政府出版物,如演講稿、新聞稿、報告、官方網站和資料集;四百七十二本是媒體報導和學術文章,其中大多數來自國家媒體機構和出版社。[20]

我的目標是闡明過去三十年來,中國如何構建實力,以及在何種情況下選擇模仿、利用或創新等方法。「竄起者策略」的一個延伸論點是:新興國家如何建立權力,取決於其所處的情境;如果條件有所不同,中國可能會採用不同的模仿、利用與創新組合。案例研究顯示,即使在相同時期(即在相似的國內與國際條件下),中國也會根據我之前提到的五個主要變數的變化,選擇不同的竄起者策略組成部分,這為「竄起者策略」理論奠定了堅實的基礎。我並不認為中國從未犯錯;相反,我納入了幾個案例,展示了其他動機如何使中國偏離竄起者策略,導致政策成本高昂、執行困難,或因不符合竄起者策略邏輯而引發重大反彈的情況。

新興論述的第二個可能延伸是:如果中國選擇模仿美國,它可能無法成功成為一個強權(換言之,竄起者策略是中國成功的原因)。本書中的資訊無法完全證明這一假設。從理論上講,中國可能透過採取不同的策略而成為強權。然而,進行一個簡單快速的思考實驗,就可以質疑這種可能性:如果在一九九〇年代或二〇〇〇年代,一位雄心勃勃的領導

新竄起者　20

人建立了遍布世界的軍事基地，與拉丁美洲和流氓國家結盟，甚至攻擊其較弱的鄰國，如約翰・米爾斯海默（John Mearsheimer）和其他戰略家所預測的那樣，美國很可能迅速採取行動進行反制，從而限制中國的發展。在這種情境下，中國今天可能無法成為一個強權，甚至可能無法以現有形式繼續存在。

使事情更加複雜的是，在國際政治中，評估「成功」這一概念的方法論挑戰，是一個長期存在的問題。我試圖透過兩種策略來應對這一問題。首先，我為每個案例研究提供了客觀且相關的成功衡量指標，並補充了中國對成功的評估以及其他觀察者的看法。這是因為對實力的認定有時與實力本身一樣重要。其次，雖然案例研究表明中國採用了「竊起者策略」，但下一部分進一步證明，中國至少在整體層面上成功地建立了強權的實力。

衡量成功的指標：中國作為強權

了解中國的戰略及其驅動因素的必要性，基於這樣一個前提：北京已在縮小與美國之間的相對實力差距方面取得了顯著成功，並達到了強權的地位。我沿用慣例，將「實力、

導論　中國崛起，晉身強權俱樂部一員

權力」(power)與「影響力」(influence)交替使用,來描述一種能夠說服、迫使他國採取其原本不會採取行動的能力。21 有趣的是,中國的文獻通常用「實力」來形容美國的做法,而用「影響力」來描述中國的方式。22 無論是實力還是影響力,它們既可以是壓制性的,也可以是促進性的;既可能是刻意行使的,也可能是潛在的;同時,它們既可以被視為一種性質上的特質或資源,也可以通過其結果來加以衡量。

雖然「強權」是一個常見的術語,但對於如何定義或衡量實力,並沒有一致的標準或指標。23 一些學者根據潛在特徵(如人口、土地、自然資源)來定義這一術語,認為國家規模決定了成為強權的潛力。24 較小的國家可能擁有高經濟成長率並具有重要的地緣政治影響力,但缺乏抵禦外部壓力或說服其他國家接受其偏好的能力。25 根據這些指標來看,中國無疑是一個強權。中國擁有世界第二多的人口(印度已於二〇二三年超越中國),其國土面積與美國相當,且擁有豐富的傳統礦產資源以及現代製造業所需的稀土元素等關鍵資源。

但這些條件充其量只是必要條件,而非充分條件。例如,俄羅斯雖然是世界上領土面積最大的國家,但沒有人會認為莫斯科能與美國或中國競爭(同樣地,即使加拿大的

新竄起者 22

面積比美國更大,也無法挑戰美國的地位)。若僅依據這一指標,那麼中華人民共和國自一九四九年建國以來就已是一個強權了,這顯然並不符合事實。最後,許多國家,如葡萄牙、英國和日本,在歷史上成為強權時,並沒有足夠的人口或領土,而是通過領土擴張和殖民活動逐步累積了這些條件。因此,僅憑人口和土地面積並不足以完全解釋或定義一個國家的強權地位。

軍事實力被現實主義學者認為是強權地位的關鍵必要條件。過去二十年間,「中國整合了資源、技術和政治意志……幾乎在各個方面加強並現代化了中國人民解放軍。」26 結果是一支與強權地位相稱的軍隊:符合保羅・甘迺迪(Paul Kennedy)所述「能與任何其他國家抗衡」的標準,也達到了傑克・利維(Jack Levy)對「強權相對於其他國家擁有高度軍事能力」及「相對安全的自足性」的定義,甚至接近米爾斯海默所謂「足夠的軍事實力,足以與全球最強國家打一場激烈的全面常規戰爭」的門檻。27 事實上,在某些領域如造船、陸基彈道及巡弋飛彈、綜合防空系統等,中國的能力如今已超越美國。28 一些人認為,核武器是強權地位的必要條件。29 而中國擁有世界第三大核武器庫,並正在進行重大的現代化更新。30

也有一些學者對過度側重軍事實力的觀點持批評態度，呼籲在強權地位的衡量上應更多地考慮經濟實力。經濟實力的衡量標準有各式各樣，從國內生產毛額（GDP）及其各種細化版本，到更抽象的指標，如管理組織能力、工業創新能力和科技工業優勢。[31] 但無論採用哪種測量方法，中國的經濟實力都是不容置疑的。中國是全球第二大經濟體，自二〇一〇年以來一直是全球最大的出口國。中國的教育水準和科技創新能力同樣表現出色（儘管在不同地域間存在一定的不平衡）。中國的識字率約為九十七％，而其國家知識產權局處理了全球約四十六％的專利申請。[32]

然而我們也需要小心，不可過度依賴經濟變量來衡量強權地位。統一後的德國和戰後的日本成為了其區域的經濟和政治領導者，但並未達到強權的地位（可以說這是出於主動選擇）。[33] 印度作為一個新興力量已有數十年，無疑擁有成為強權的資源，但「普遍被認為是一個無法完全發揮實力的準強權」。[34] 在中國崛起的這段時間，巴西也曾多次被視為一個新興力量，但「似乎至今仍未能將其龐大的經濟體量和政治活動轉化為實質性的區域和全球強權地位。」[35] 一個國家除了經濟實力外，還需要具備將經濟資源持續轉化為更廣泛政治利益的能力，並擁有成為強權的雄心。

新竄起者　24

外界的認定也起著至關重要的作用：實力和影響力不僅需要自身的積累，還需要來自其他國家的承認。根據曼賈里・米勒（Manjari Miller）的觀點，強權地位的全球認可，取決於兩種認定──外部認定（來自國際社會的關係和物質能力）以及內部認定（國內對於國際地位變化的支持）。36 在外部認定方面，二〇一七年美國的《國家安全戰略》將當代國際政治的主要特徵描述為與北京的強權競爭，這一表述基本延續至今。

中國的內部認定也表明，中國已成功崛起為強權。在二〇〇〇年代，多數中國學者專注於衡量中國的綜合國力（CNP），即實現其戰略目標的整體能力。37 約十年前，普遍共識仍認為中國尚未達到大國地位。38 然而，到二〇二〇年，在中國國內更常見的看法是，中國已是一個大國，無論是在多極體系中排名第二，還是在雙極體系中與美國平起平坐。39 在二〇二一年與美國同行會面時，中央外事工作委員會辦公室主任楊潔篪強調：「中美兩國都是世界大國。」40

本書不予討論的範圍

我的目標是探討中國如何建立實力與影響力,而非在不同時期精確地衡量中美之間的實力強弱對比。我的論點基於兩個關於相對實力的結論:①自一九九三年以來,中國已顯著縮小與美國的實力差距;②目前的差距已小到足以讓美國戰略家和思想家將中國視為強權競爭者。這些結論相對來說已經十分保守。

儘管本書聚焦於中國「如何」建立實力,但它也對中國目前的目標提供了一些見解。關於中國是否希望成為「全球性」或「區域性」強權的辯論,往往陷入一個假設的陷阱,即認為中國會像美國一樣有追求霸權的野心,並因此認為中國若擁有全球性野心,就必然會以類似於美國的策略來挑戰美國的全球利益。「竄起者策略」則假設中國希望擁有影響或決定結果的能力,特別是在對其利益至關重要的議題或區域上。

然而,中國無需在所有領域以相同方式競爭即可實現其目標。本書中的案例研究顯示,中國希望擁有全球觸角,但主要目的是鞏固其國內與區域地位。換句話說,中國不需要在全球展開全面競爭,就可以成為超級強權——事實上,試圖在全球每個領域競爭可

新竄起者 26

能反而會危及中國的強權地位。修正主義的觀點（通常指以某種方式改變或修改現狀的願望，通常伴隨著武力使用）在某種程度上是主觀的。41「竄起者策略」考慮到了這一事實。決定中國是否選擇模仿、利用或創新的一個因素，是美國將模仿行為視為對現狀的維持或是修正主義行為。

雖然我並未以實證方式將此方法應用於其他強權國家成功崛起的歷史，但我提供了一些例證，說明中國的戰略並非獨特。我推測，採用「竄起者策略」的國家在建立實力與影響力方面最為成功。例如美國在其崛起過程中經常選擇創新，選擇全球軍事存在、國際機構、軟實力與自由貿易體系，而非英國的殖民地、保護主義與佔領方式。但我並未嘗試證明這一假設。而中國的迅速崛起並非僅僅依靠模仿，這一點有力地說明了一個國家如何建立實力的方式，與其物質投入同樣關鍵。這表明，其他強權的歷史或許需要重新審視，去探討它們是否也曾運用過類似的策略。這一主題是我在本書結論中會進一步討論的內容。

最後，本書的目的並非要譴責中國，也不是為了讚揚中國。當我說某一項策略是有效或成功的時候，並不意味著我對該策略表示認同。我所關注的是中國在建立實力與影響力方面的效率與效果，而非對北京所採取的方法進行道德性的評價。歷史證明，創新既可以

27　導論　中國崛起，晉身強權俱樂部一員

本書架構速覽

本書闡述中國如何在競爭激烈的國際環境中崛起為強權。第一章中，我提出關於「竄起者策略」的主要論點，深入討論競爭理論的基本命題，並解釋為什麼行為者有時會採用與其主要競爭對手不同的戰術、行動和策略。我將「竄起者策略」分為三個主要組成部分——模仿、利用和創新，並探討了每種策略的優勢與劣勢。還分析了在何種條件下，每個組成部分可能成為構成實力與影響力的最佳途徑。

第二章和第三章集中評估了中國在建立政治與外交實力時，在多大程度上採用了「竄起者策略」。第二章特別探討了促使中國採取模仿策略的條件，例如在調解外交中的成功案例，以及像是軟實力這類相對失敗的案例。我還分析了導致利用策略的條件，並詳細討論了這些行為的具體實施方式。例如，中國在競爭壓力相對較小的領域採取了類似的策略，包括在軍售、外交接觸，以及操控國際機構運作中的行為。

第三章展示了五個主要因素如何促成創新策略的選擇，以及中國在外交領域中創新策略的具體表現。例如，美國通常致力於成為許多國家的外部安全夥伴，提供軍事保護和安全承諾，而中國則採取不同的方式，專注於成為內部安全夥伴，協助訓練執法人員並提供內部監控設備。另外，中國避免傳統的結盟模式，而是選擇建立「戰略夥伴關係」。這一策略使中國在組建以議題為導向的聯盟時擁有更大的靈活性，並避免因固定的結盟框架而疏遠任何國家或國家集團。北京的目標是努力成為所有國家的朋友，而無需將任何人視為敵人。

對任何新興強權而言，建立軍事實力而不激起既有霸權的強烈反應是一項極具挑戰且至關重要的任務。第四章和第五章探討了中國如何在不引發美國對其現代化進程強力阻撓的情況下，逐步建立與強權地位相匹配的軍事力量。由於全球軍事力量是美國實力和影響力的基礎，第四章聚焦於中國如何基於對美國可能的反應和戰略效能的看法，透過模仿的方式追求資訊作戰能力、進行「合法」的軍事活動（如人道主義行動和維和任務），以及參與軍備控制體制。本章還涵蓋了一個因不同動機導致中國偏離「竄起者策略」的案例——中國的航空母艦計畫。最後討論中國如何利用美國的弱點和漏洞，這一策略是中國軍事挑戰的核心，即其阻止美軍進入亞洲並擾亂中國行動的能力（即反介入／區域拒止能力）。

第五章首先探討美國如何利用其軍事力量進行海外干預和全球軍力投射來推動自身利益。我指出，與美國國防界內部一些擔憂聲浪相反，中國尚未採取類似的策略，這主要是因為中國認為這些策略既無效，又對美國過於具有威脅性。另外，中國在崛起的初期階段，通過推遲軍事現代化，成功在很大程度上避免了美國的強烈軍事反應。隨後，中國將重點放在創新方式上，以建立和行使軍事力量，包括：灰色地帶行動、獨特的核子戰略，以及不依賴海外基地或軍事干預的海外利益保護方式。透過避免對美國策略的直接模仿，中國成功度過了其崛起過程中最容易受到美國軍事壓制的時期。同時，中國建立了一支能夠在多數區域性緊急情況中對抗美國的軍隊。

儘管中國在建立軍事實力方面的表現令人印象深刻，但相比於過去三十年中國在經濟影響力方面的成就，仍稍顯遜色。第六章探討中國在自由貿易、使用經濟脅迫，以及推進人民幣國際化（部分失敗）的過程中，如何運用模仿與利用策略的實例。第七章則進一步分析中國透過創新方式獲取經濟實力的案例，包括產業政策的推行、對外經濟援助，以及

新竄起者 30

「一帶一路」倡議（BRI）。本章展示了中國如何運用這些經濟工具在全球主導標準制定活動，並有效獲取自然資源。在所有經濟案例中，中國根據美國策略、美國的感知，以及中國自身的競爭優勢，仔細權衡哪些方式在戰略上最具效能與效率，同時考量這些方式在國內外可能帶來的成本與風險。這些經濟策略充分展示了中國靈活應對國際挑戰並逐步提升其全球影響力的能力。

關於中國的未來，我們可以預見什麼樣的局勢？美國又應如何做出最佳政策回應？理解「竄起者策略」能夠為全球政策制定者提供了一個有力的框架，幫助他們預測中國的行為、評估潛在利益，並增加中國特定競爭方式的成本。本書的結論探討中國未來可能集中競爭力的領域，以及北京可能採用的方法。同時深入討論一些主要的理論和政策辯論，例如中國的實力是否已達頂峰、中國是否繼續採用其當前成功的模仿與創新策略的組合，或者是否會轉向更多直接競爭，部分答案取決於中國是否最終會超越美國（以及這種結果的實際意義）。我主張，中國可能採取更多模仿策略。最後，我提出了一些建議，說明美國可以如何借鑑並應用「竄起者策略」中的部分元素，以維持並增強其競爭優勢。

31　導論　中國崛起，晉身強權俱樂部一員

第一章

竄起者策略

不同形式的實力競爭,一直是國際體系的核心特徵。努力透過建立對他國的優勢來獲取或贏得實力、權力,本質上不一定會引發衝突或造成不穩定。例如,兩個國家理論上可以透過提供更多外援、推動更積極的環保政策,或實施更開放的移民制度來競爭影響力,而不涉及直接對抗。然而,新興強權與既有霸權之間的競爭,往往又具有零和博弈的特性。從歷史經驗來看,近代史上發生的十六次此類競爭中,有十二次最終演變成了大規模戰爭,顯示這種權力轉移通常伴隨著高度風險。[1]

雖然這類權力轉移戰爭在國際政治中並不常見,但能夠累積足夠的實力與影響力,進而躋身強權行列的國家也同樣稀少。打造堅實的國內資源基礎以成為強權本就不易,而要將這些資源轉化為國際舞台上的實質權力,難度更是有增無減。更具挑戰的是,新興強權必須在既有霸主國的密切注視下完成這一過程。作為現有的領導國,霸主國往往會警惕任何可能威脅自身地位的舉動,甚至主動設法削弱或遏制新興強權的發展,讓這場競爭變得更加艱難。

本章將闡述中國作為新興強權如何成功躋身世界強權俱樂部的戰略,以及影響其戰略選擇的關鍵因素。許多研究探討過歷史上的新興強權案例,並試圖將這些經驗套用到中

新竄起者　34

國際政治中的模仿

傳統觀點認為，國家選擇模仿，是為了讓自己變得更強大。其中，最早提出這一論點的之一是肯尼斯・沃爾茲（Kenneth Waltz）的「同質化效應」（sameness effect），他預

國，假設中國會像過去的新興國家一樣行事。有些人認為，中國將步上其他新興強權的後塵，最終無法擺脫「修昔底德陷阱」（Thucydides's Trap）2 的結構性限制，導致與既有霸主國（美國）發生衝突。另一些觀點則認為，中國和歷史上的新興強權一樣，會在實力達到巔峰前變得更具侵略性，以實現自身的野心。3 但問題在於，我們真的有理由認為中國會與歷史上的前例相同嗎？中國會循著相同的軌跡發展，還是會採取不同的競爭策略？這正是本章試圖回答的核心問題。

本章將探討為何新興強權可能會採取與既有強權不同的策略，以及這些策略可能包含哪些要素。同時，我將進一步闡述「模仿」在國際政治中的角色，並提供一個更清晰的概念框架，說明它如何影響國家競爭與權力轉移的過程。

35　第一章　竄起者策略

測國家會模仿那些成功的做法，以提升自身競爭力。4 這個概念其實並不新穎。早在十六世紀初，馬基維利（Machiavelli）就曾建議領導人應該仿效成功的榜樣，他寫道：「最重要的是，領袖必須學習過去那些偉人的做法，以他們為榜樣，時刻記住他們的事蹟與成就。」5 在政治學領域，模仿的理論被廣泛應用。軍事方面，國家經常複製對手的戰術與武器創新，例如許多國家在對手發展核武後，也開始發展自己的核能力，以維持戰略平衡。6 同樣地，在科技與醫學領域，各國領導者也傾向仿效已被證實成功的模式，以維持競爭力並縮小與先進國家的差距。7

模仿不僅會受到現實主義學派的青睞，在更廣泛的國際關係理論中也備受重視。國際政治中的威望、地位與正當性等概念本質上都依賴於模仿，因為某項行動只有在某類國家率先採取後，才會被賦予重要性並獲得認可。模仿源於國家之間對「成就與品質」的比較。8 國家可能會因此選擇發展某些軍事能力，例如核武或航空母艦；也可能透過派遣維和部隊或提供對外援助來提升自身形象。國家之間的競爭往往也呈現出模仿的特徵，例如軍備競賽、海軍擴張，甚至是非洲的殖民擴張，這些行為的背後動機，往往都是為了提升國際聲望。9 模仿也適用於較小國家。例如，小國可能會學習中等強權的行為模式，以獲

新竄起者　36

得「好國家」的名聲，進而提升自身在全球體系中的排名。10 同樣地，某些不屬於特定聯盟的國家，可能會模仿該聯盟的核心戰略，以展現自己遵循由霸權國主導的外交目標，從而獲取地位紅利。11 事實上，模仿甚至是抄襲，可以是一種理性的決策策略，尤其是在不確定性較高的環境下。這種做法能夠降低決策者蒐集與評估資訊的成本與時間，幫助國家更迅速地做出戰略選擇。12

社會科學中的其他學派強調，隨著國家的發展，彼此之間的差異將逐漸消失，這種現象被稱為「趨同性」（convergence）。當國家進行現代化時，通常會趨向同質化，或至少被限制在少數幾種發展選項內，迫使它們變得越來越相似。13 這種趨同性可能來自於競爭、壓力、模仿、仿效，或是國際規範的影響。許多學者認為，隨著國家進行工業化，推動不同社會趨於一致的力量，將逐漸超過維持多樣性的因素。14

社會學家提出了一種類似的模仿現象，稱為擴散（diffusion），用來解釋一種文化或群體的行為、信念、技術或制度如何傳播到另一個文化或群體。這類研究主要關注擴散的原因及其發生方式。例如，當兩個群體之間存在頻繁且緊密的接觸時，擴散更有可能發生。不過，如果兩個行為體在文化上更為相似，採納的可能性會更高。15 另一方面，組織

37　第一章　竄起者策略

領域的同質化可以透過強制（來自文化或組織所依賴的其他因素的壓力）、模仿行為（當組織模仿其他成功組織以應對組織技術、目標或環境的不確定性時）或規範行為（運用共同標準來定義工作條件、方法和合法標準）來解釋。

儘管模仿論是普遍而且有力的解釋，但這項理論的發展程度卻出乎意料地有限。首要問題是，對於何種行為可被視為模仿，尚未有明確界定。模仿可以用來描述一個國家的戰略，也可以指其競爭的領域。例如，中國參與國際機構可以被視為模仿（因為美國也參與國際機構），但中國建立獨立的國際機構同樣也可以被視為模仿（因為美國曾透過創建機構來擴展自身影響力）。事實上，一些學者認為，如果一個新興強權積極「有意識且謹慎地尋找成功典範，並仔細分析其成功的原因」，這本身就構成了一種模仿行為。[17]

其次，這種謹慎評估的目標是什麼？現實主義學派的論點明確指出，新興國家通常會模仿強權，但這可能指的是過去的強權，也可能是當代的強權。還可能需要區分既有強權在崛起過程中所採取的策略，與其維持霸權地位後所執行的策略，兩者的性質可能大不相同。對於那些關注國家如何透過社會化過程接受某些行為模式的學者而言，強權確實可能是主要的模仿對象，但一個國家是否採納特定的規範與做法，也取決於有多少國家採用該

新竄起者　38

行為,以及這些國家的類型為何。擴散理論則強調,社會之間的相似性是影響行為採納的關鍵因素。因此,一個國家在學習與模仿過程中,可能不僅參考國際上的成功案例,也可能從自身歷史中汲取經驗與教訓。

第三,採納的程度需要到多全面,才能被視為模仿?新興強權是否必須採納與既有強權相似的價值觀或國內政治運作模式,其實力累積策略才算是模仿?這種情況似乎不太可能,因為多項研究顯示,採納者往往需要對實踐或規範進行調整,以更符合當地條件。然而,這也引發了一個問題——要調整到何種程度,才會讓原本的模仿演變成完全不同的做法,從而不能再被視為模仿?

第四,僅以模仿來解釋競爭是不完整的。它無法全面掌握國家如何透過創新方式來獲取並維持強權地位。歷史上,一些極具影響力的國家,並未完全遵循當時主流的規範與做法,而是以獨特的方式建立與運用實力。羅馬帝國率先將征服的領土以道路連結,並提供基本社會服務,如引水道與排水系統。[19] 波斯帝國則透過允許被征服的民族保留其文化、傳統、語言與宗教,同時統一貨幣並建立區域治理,來鞏固統治。[20] 中國早期王朝利用戰車技術與青銅武器擊敗敵人,並最早建立了朝貢體系來管理周邊國家。[21] 大英帝國率先確

[18]

第一章 竄起者策略　39

立海軍優勢作為核心戰略，並重新定義「帝國」的概念，以招募當地人員管理官僚機構來擴展統治。22 蘇聯成為全球第一個馬克思主義共產國家，並積極輸出其意識形態，從而建立了一個盟國集團。23 美國選擇透過建立國際機構來保護自身利益，並非依賴永久占領，而是運用全球勢力投射與推動民主化來擴展影響力。24

最後，模仿論忽略了走上既定道路可能帶來的潛在缺點。許多學者雖然承認：「並非所有國家都會模仿既有強權的戰略」，但他們錯誤地假設：這種情況是一種次優選擇，需要額外解釋。25 然而，不選擇模仿其實可能是理性的決策。如果新興強權不需要強化特定領域就能獲得強權地位，那麼在該領域模仿既有霸權反而是浪費資源。在戰略領域，新興強權若明顯模仿霸權，其意圖將更難否認，尤其是當該行為被視為爭奪霸權地位的明確信號時。例如，德國在第一次世界大戰前試圖通過建造戰艦與爭奪殖民地來模仿英國的強權地位，這一舉動立即引起倫敦的高度警惕。作為回應，英國大幅增加海軍預算，建造無畏艦（dreadnought），從而阻止了德國在海上力量領域的競爭企圖。26 在中國的案例中，北京在冷戰結束後曾試圖直接與美國競爭全球領導地位，但中國高層很快意識到，這種戰略助

新竄起者　40

長了「中國威脅論」，增加其他國家聯手圍堵中國的風險。[27]因此，中國領轉向「社會創造力」（social creativity）戰略，在地緣政治框架之外尋找能夠發揮主導作用的領域。[28]

「竄起者策略」有助於我們理解國家如何累積實力，因為它清楚界定了何種行為可被視為「模仿」。在本書中，我為衡量標準提供合理依據，並在替代理論解釋的部分回應其他競爭性觀點。我也會更進一步擴展理論，將「利用」與「創新」納入框架，以全面涵蓋新興強權在國際舞台上的各種競爭方式。在清楚闡述「竄起者策略」的三個核心組成部分後，我將進一步探討影響這些策略選擇的決定因素，並具體說明在何種情境下，「模仿」對新興強權有利，以及在何種情況下，「利用」或「創新」才是更合適的實力累積途徑。

「竄起者策略」的組成要素

運用「竄起者策略」的領導人，會不斷在模仿與創新之間做選擇，以累積國家實力，同時平衡崛起過程中的成本與風險。「竄起者策略」包含兩大核心要素：即競爭的領域與競爭的方法。根據這兩個要素，競爭策略可分為三種類型：一、「模仿」：在既有的競爭

表 1.1　不同的競爭策略

		策略類型	
		模仿	創新
競爭領域	舊	策略一：模仿	策略三：創新
	新	策略二：利用	策略三：創新

領域，採用既有霸權的方法。二、「利用」：在新的競爭領域，採用既有霸權的方法。三、「創新」：不論競爭領域是舊或新，都採用全新的競爭方式。**表 1.1** 具體呈現了這些不同的競爭策略。

在中國崛起的案例中，「模仿」指的是在既有的競爭領域中採用既有霸權的做法。簡單來說就是當中國的行為模式和活動方式大致與美國相同，並且發生在相同的競爭領域時。舉例來說，中國和美國都在國際機構中爭取領導地位，試圖調解相同的國際衝突，同時也都打造擁有航空母艦的強大海軍，以及建立以本國貨幣為主導的金融體系。在模仿策略中，中國可能會根據自身的文化、政治環境和內部規範進行小幅調整，但整體戰略仍然與美國相似。因此，中國參與國際機構以及建立新的國際機構都可視為模仿，因為美國的競爭模式本身就包含這兩種行為。當既有霸權採取合作性戰略

新竄起者　42

時，模仿和合作之間可能會有重疊的地方。然而，也有許多情況下，中國模仿的是美國某些更具單邊主義或衝突性的做法，而非純粹的合作模式。

在「利用」策略中，中國在新的競爭領域採取與美國相似的策略，藉此利用美國的盲點或國際秩序中的空隙。國際體系的結構，以及國家在其中的地位，決定了不同實力建構方式的可行性與效益。29 過去三十年來，中國一直試圖塑造戰略環境以助長自身崛起，同時不斷尋找更有利的戰略位置。其中一種方式就是在美國未積極參與的領域尋找機會，這些領域可能包括：特定功能領域：國際規範、軍售、軍事力量投射、發展援助等。特定地理區域：亞洲、全球南方（Global South）、發展中國家，而非已開發國家。30 既有霸權的盲點，以及中國是否在這些領域擁有競爭優勢，是決定「利用」策略是否可行的關鍵因素。

盲點（blind spot）指的是既有霸權未曾關注的領域，也就是國際實力與影響力市場中的「未開發」區塊，在這些領域中，既有霸權並未積極參與。這些盲點之所以存在，可能有多種原因：美國可能低估某些區域的戰略重要性，例如貧窮國家或發展中國家，認為這些地方不值得投入過多資源。華盛頓可能認為某些全球公共產品的需求已經被滿足，例如

43　第一章　竄起者策略

透過支持世界銀行（World Bank）和國際貨幣基金組織（IMF）來提供國際金融援助，進而忽略其他替代方案的可能性。盲點也可能來自於既有霸權的注意力不足，或是因為政策執行不佳。

既有強權的忽視有時也是理性的選擇，因為新興強權與既有霸權的戰略「成本結構」不同，某個競爭領域對一方來說可能具有高回報，但對另一方來說卻不一定值得投入。例如：中國能夠以較低的成本在中亞擴展影響力，而美國則較難進入該地區。主要原因在於，中國作為鄰國，可以提供更好的基礎建設與交通連結，同時受到來自俄羅斯的阻力也相對較小。在這種情境下，中國並非真正「擊敗」美國，而是美國根本未積極參與競爭。

此外：不同國家對既有霸權及其國際秩序的滿意度有所不同，而中國更容易在對美國現行秩序感到不滿的國家中取得突破。既有霸權本身也存在可被利用的弱點，例如某些領域內在缺陷或忽略，為新興強權提供了機會。新興強權還可能「搭便車」，享受既有霸權建立並維持的國際體系所帶來的好處，而無需承擔相應的成本。

國際秩序中也存在可供新興強權利用的「漏洞」，這些領域的連結較為鬆散、非正式、不規則，而且相關規範和規則仍存有爭議（也就是說，各行為體對象徵與事件的解讀

新竄起者　44

不一致）。這些矛盾使國際體系內部出現結構性的空缺，從而在這些尚未完全確立的領域內創造出競爭空間。[31]當然，並非所有國家都參與所有國際機構，不同國家在現有秩序中的受益程度不均，部分國家與該秩序的聯繫較為薄弱。具有爭議的秩序與脆弱的國際網路，為中國這種新興強權提供了介入的機會。在這種情況下，新興強權可以扮演「議程設定者」（agenda-setter）與「規則制定者」（rule-maker）的角色，透過建立自己的國際機構，塑造新規則。在理念相近國家之間促成共識，影響國際決策方向。這樣中國就無需直接挑戰霸權國家的全球秩序核心，而是繞道塑造新的影響力，藉此延遲自身被視為威脅的時機。最後，新興強權還可以透過處理新的國際議題，或與某些在現有秩序中被邊緣化的國家互動，進一步強化自身在國際體系中的角色與影響力。

第三個組成部分強調一個成功崛起為強權的國家普遍具備的特徵：「創新」性行動。[32]當一個新興強權尋找新的權力來源，並且以有別於主要競爭對手的方式累積與行使影響力時，就可以被視為具備創新精神。[33]隨著歷史發展，權力的本質與國際秩序不斷演變，創新性行動的具體形式也隨之改變。真正具有創新精神的行動不只是做了什麼，而是怎麼做──關鍵在於如何發掘機會，並將創新轉化為現實。[34]創新性行動使國家能夠推動

45　第一章　竄起者策略

重大結構性變革，一方面打破過時的組織體系，另一方面為新體系的建立奠定基礎。35 許多類型的行動都可以被視為創新。一個國家可以用引入新型國際組織的方式向其他國家提供新服務或福利，或以不同方式使用外援等工具來創造價值。就像企業一樣，國家可以發現哪裡有供應短缺，並提供既有霸權無法或不願提供的新知識、產品或服務來做出回應。中國提供基礎設施建設融資，而不是像美國主要在醫療和改進治理領域提供援助的做法，就是一個例子。

美國的崛起就是一個很好的例子。學者們指出，美國透過建立政治秩序來限制自身行使權力的運作方式，是一種獨特的美式領導模式，這與英國帝國的統治方式截然不同。英國主要依賴威脅（threats）與利誘（inducements）來維持其主導地位，而不是要求其他國家自願服從。36 美國在累積實力的同時，成功延遲了來自英國的不利反應。到了二十世紀初，英國已經意識到，自己無法挑戰美國的崛起。正如當時的英國首相索爾斯伯利勳爵（Lord Salisbury）所言：「這確實令人遺憾，但我恐怕美國的崛起已經無法阻擋，我們之間的實力平衡再也無法恢復原狀。如果當初我們在美國內戰（南北戰爭）時干預，或許還有機會將美國的力量壓制在可控範圍內。」37

新竄起者　46

在「竊起者策略」中，「三E策略」（模仿、利用、創新）是以既有霸權目前採取的方式作為參照來定義的。這一點在本章稍後探討各種策略的成本效益分析時會進一步論證。不過，直覺上這樣的概念是合理的：在中國崛起的過程中，美國是國際體系中最強大的國家，因此對任何希望成為強權的國家來說，美國都是最具代表性的參考對象。中國若要成為強權，就必須縮小與美國的實力差距，這使得美國的應對策略對中國的成功與否產生極大影響。

新興強權的參照點是當代既有霸權的策略，而不是該霸權在自身崛起過程中所採取的策略。這是因為不同時期的國際環境有著根本性的變化，導致不同策略的相對成本與效益也隨之改變。這並不意味著中國不重視自身歷史經驗或其他國家的發展歷程，但在當前環境下，「竊起者策略」的每個組成部分的潛在成本與效益，都是相對於美國的策略來決定的。[38] 強權競爭是這一過程的核心驅動力。正如一位中國知名學者所言：「一個國家的崛起，本質上就是要超越世界上最強的國家，而這個最強的國家不可能成為它的支持者，只能是它的障礙。」[39] 美國之所以是中國主要的參考對象，原因在於：美國的行動與反應，將直接影響中國策略的效能與效率。中國的競爭策略必須在不引發過度反彈的情況下縮小

第一章　竊起者策略

與美國的差距，因此美國的應對方式對中國的成功與否至關重要。

案例研究提供了經驗性的支持，證明中國在制定戰略時，主要參考美國的做法，而非其他國家。本書也探討了一種替代假設，即中國的行為是否是模仿美國以外的國家。我特別關注以下兩種情境，因為這是中國可能從其他國家汲取靈感的最可能情境：①當中國戰略家認為美國的策略無效時。②當中國的政治體制不允許直接採納美國做法時。這兩種情境是中國最有可能轉向其他國家尋求模仿靈感的時機，特別是那些在特定領域表現更優異，或擁有與中國類似屬性的國家。

「竄起者策略」的決定因素

新興強權在推動戰略時，目標是提升自身的整體實力，但理想狀況下，這不應以犧牲其他更重要的目標為代價，即維持國內穩定與避免與既有霸權發生重大衝突。要實現這些目標，實力累積必須既有效，又高效，這涉及執政體制的堅強或脆弱的程度，以及國際體系的特性。新興強權透過選擇「竄起者策略」的不同組成部分來平衡這些權衡（trade-

新竄起者　48

offs），在模仿、利用與創新之間做出選擇。本節將探討影響新興強權決定採取哪種策略的五大關鍵變數：既有霸權（霸主國）的感知、戰略效率、戰略效能、國內政治考量以及國際體系的性質。

因素一：既有強權的感知

模仿理論或許能正確解釋某些國家如何提升自身實力，但它忽略了一些新興強權在追求大國地位時必須考慮的獨特因素。像中國這樣的新興國家，必須避免（或至少延後）與既有霸權進入激烈競爭的狀態，像是被圍堵或是被發起預防性戰爭。單純模仿既有霸權，可能會被解讀為意圖挑戰霸權地位的訊號，從而引發對方的警戒與反制。因此，最佳策略是選擇能夠累積實力與影響力的方式，但可以避免激起既有霸權的強烈負面反應。換句話說，新興強權必須在擴展全球影響力與降低霸權國安全壓力之間取得平衡。40

但這種平衡並不容易掌握。正如清華大學教授孫學峰所指出的，既有霸權對於任何挑戰其主導地位的勢力極為敏感，而這種敏感性對新興強權來說構成了重大的安全風險。41

歷史上，直接挑戰既有霸權往往會適得其反，挑戰國的海上霸權，最終卻引發英國的強烈反擊。例如德意志帝國曾試圖挑戰英國在大西洋東部的海上霸權，最終卻引發英國的強烈反擊。的一種挑戰，因此「現有秩序的受益者自然會提高警戒」。[42] 且新興強權在本質上就是對現行國際秩序反覆出現。例如中國必須面對西方資本主義強權的「冷戰思維」，[43] 這一點在中國的戰略思維中價高昂的衝突，最終削弱甚至終結其崛起的能力。[46] 事實上，中國領導人和戰略家一直認為，對中國崛起構成最大威脅的，就是來自其他國家的敵意，特別是美國。[47] 這正是鄧融入國際社會，並阻礙其公平參與建構更公正的國際秩序。同時，中國還需要應對「敵對勢力」的戰略意圖——這些勢力試圖「西化」與「分裂」中國。[44] 前中國外交部副部長傅瑩在二〇二〇年曾警告：「中美實力差距的縮小，必然會帶來緊張局勢。」[45]

理想情況下，新興強權應該盡可能延後讓既有霸權察覺其威脅的時機，直到對方已經沒有多少有效手段來應對。如果新興強權過早激起強烈的競爭反應，可能會被捲入代小平「韜光養晦」策略的核心邏輯——「避免四面樹敵」，創造有利於中國崛起的國際環境。[48] 二〇〇九年，中國國家主席胡錦濤強調：「中國努力避免成為重大國際衝突的焦點，避免陷入衝突與對抗的漩渦，以最大程度降低外部壓力與發展阻力。」[49] 中國領導人

新竄起者　50

與戰略家普遍認為，二十一世紀前二十年是中國追趕強權的關鍵時期，而美國作為全球霸權，必然會採取行動維持自身的優勢地位，這將使中國的崛起變得更加困難。50 因此，北京的戰略必須「削弱其他國家限制中國外交與經濟發展的能力。」並同時能夠「避免激起強烈的敵意，導致中國的崛起過程被徹底破壞。」51

這些考量突顯了影響新興強權選擇「竊起者策略」路徑的第一個關鍵因素──既有霸權如何看待特定戰略。在某些情況下，模仿可能會讓既有霸權感到放心。中國的模仿政策之所以「成功」，部分原因是其他國家對此感到安心，甚至希望其成功。美國及其「經濟合作暨發展組織」（OECD）盟國，樂見中國融入國際經濟秩序，因為發展中的中國總比貧窮、動盪的中國來得更可取。從既有強權的角度來看，模仿可能被解讀為合作或某種程度的安撫──「遵循我們的規則」。這種策略的好處是可以轉移注意力，讓既有霸權將焦點放在中國的「遵循國際規則」上，而忽略中國在其他領域更具挑戰性的行為。某些行為與合作本身重疊，如果中國選擇不參與這些行動，反而可能引發美國的疑慮。另外既有霸權很難將中國的模仿行為標誌為「非法」或「不可接受」（這是一種用於鞏固盟友和全球公眾意見的常見策略），因為這些行為與美國自己過去或當前的做法類似。

51　第一章　竊起者策略

然而，在某些情況下，新興強權如果以與既有霸權相同的方式累積實力，可能會被視為直接挑戰其核心利益，進而構成威脅。相反地，採取不同的方法反而可能帶來某種程度的不確定性──既有強權可能無法立即辨識新興強權的成就，因為其戰略與既有強權的競爭模式不符。這種策略相當於「跳脫大眾所認知的傳統競爭框架。」52

在個人層面上，確認偏誤(confirmation bias)也會發揮作用。領導人們傾向於將新資訊套入他們既有的理論與認知框架，因此當有跡象顯示本國實力正在衰退時，他們通常會抗拒接受這類資訊，尤其是當這些跡象模糊不清時。53 這種情況會導致各方無法對新興強權的意圖達成共識。新興強權的行動可能會被忽視、誤解，甚至根本不在既有霸權的關注範圍內。既有霸權還可能錯誤判斷競爭對手的行動，他們可能仍然沿用舊有的「成功標準」來評估新興強權，但卻忽略這些標準已經隨著國際局勢變化而過時。54

新興強權行動所帶來的不確定性越大，既有霸權做出回應的延遲時間就越長。55 只有當新興強權的意圖明確具有修正主義 (revisionist) 傾向時，既有霸權的領導人才能認知到威脅並制定應對策略。56 在國內政治層面，若既有霸權的國家內部缺乏菁英共識或政治凝聚力，可能會影響到該國制衡競爭對手的意願。57 中國的戰略家們清楚認識到必須避免給

新竄起者　52

外界一種「中國積極試圖削弱美國權力與影響力」的印象，因為：這類舉動可能加速美國及其盟友與中國進入公開對抗，而這將直接破壞中國累積權力的核心目標。58

因素二：戰略效率

新興強權的一個獨特特質在於，它必須以高效的方式在國際舞台上建立實力。59 如果要獲得同樣的實力增量，那就注定是虧本的生意，特別是因為新興強權相較於既有霸權，本來就擁有較少的資源。60 戰略效率可以來自內部或外部因素。例如美國的反國家主義政治傾向影響了其決策，使美國選擇建立全志願役軍隊，而非實施徵兵制，這樣的做法相較於蘇聯的軍事模式更為高效。61 邁可・貝克利（Michael Beckley）提出一種新的衡量標準，稱之為「淨實力」（net power），即在總體實力中扣除因建立財富與軍事能力所產生的內部負擔。62 而在外部因素方面，美國的「邀請式帝國」（empire by invitation）模式，其相對成本遠低於蘇聯的擴張型帝國模式，蘇聯面臨的是近代歷史上最嚴重的「帝國過度擴張」案例之一。63

53　第一章　竄起者策略

對效率的需求可能會促使一個國家採取更具模仿性的政策。競爭者可以在某種做法變得可行時，再來採用這些成功模式，這樣就能在不承擔初期投入成本的情況下獲取所有好處。64 透過積極的「搭便車」策略，一個國家可以避開試錯成本，直接跳躍至成功的戰略，繞過發展過程中的中間階段。65 一個新興強權可能由於其歷史、文化、政治或經濟特徵，特別適合在某個領域競爭。換句話說，它在該領域或競爭模式中享有競爭優勢。當這些特徵與既有霸權的特徵相符時，模仿者可以優化其「後發者優勢」，這指的是透過觀察先行者的成功與失敗所帶來的錯誤並改進現有策略。

此外，嘗試全新競爭模式的風險可能較高，讓模仿者能夠避免犯下致命的錯誤，甚至讓新興強權的崛起戛然而止。可能會被證明為低效甚至無效的方法可供參考，如果沒有成熟的方法可供參考，那麼新的策略可能會被證明為低效甚至無效，從而拖慢崛起速度。

相反地，激烈的競爭可能會促使新興強權選擇不同的做法。66 在美國已經將某種策略打磨至近乎完美的領域，模仿的邊際效益可能極低。事實上，新興強權在與資源豐富、實力雄厚的競爭對手對抗時，往往處於「明顯的競爭劣勢」，因為既有強權幾乎能夠應對任何競爭手段。67 因此，透過「利用」或「創新」來開拓新路徑，可能比單純的模仿競爭對手更為有利，因為這能讓新興強權更快速地縮小差距，甚至可以讓新興強權在新的戰略領

新竄起者　54

美國過去採取的策略，並不意味著中國今天也能夠以可負擔的成本複製類似的事情。國際體系不斷的在變化，當前某些策略的成本可能比既有霸權當初實施時高出許多。國際行為規範也在演變，一些過去被接受的做法如今可能變得不可行，甚至會帶來負面影響，使新興強權不再有動機去仿效。同樣地，技術創新可能增加或減少某些策略的成本。例如，長期佔領外國領土如今是一個效率較低的選擇，因為鎮壓的成本增加，領土本身的戰略價值卻下降。68 技術發展本身也有成本遞增效應，就像船舶的航速有物理極限，進一步提升的成本卻不斷增加。隨著其他國家發展出反制策略或不同的競爭方式，某些戰略的效益可能逐漸減少。

因素三：戰略效能

模仿理論隱含著一個前提——成功會吸引行為者去仿效。整體來看，既有霸權在實力

第一章　竄起者策略

建構方面確實是成功的，但這並不代表它所有的政策、做法和策略都是有效。如果某項策略被認為是有效的，那麼它更可能被新興強權模仿，或者至少被利用在新的競爭領域。但有時，新興強權會認為某些既有霸權的策略根本就沒有效果，甚至連既有霸權本身都未必能受益。例如，中國領導人就認為，美國的某些戰略從來都不是特別有效，或曾經有效但現在已經不適用了。美國軍方也認識到地緣政治與科技環境正在快速變化，因此需要進行調整，但在實際行動上卻舉步維艱。儘管許多美國海軍的高層將領不斷強調必須創新以應對新興威脅，且國防部的多場模擬兵棋推演也顯示，海軍的艦艇越來越容易受到攻擊，然而，美國海軍卻受限於政治與經濟因素，在艦艇採購上更關心「就業機會」而非適應性，這導致軍方難以擺脫舊有的造艦傳統。這種「對傳統艦隊的自負與執著」，反而阻礙了美國海軍的進步。69

美國為何仍然堅持某些低效的策略，這不是本書想要討論的範圍，但研究顯示，華盛頓可能因為自滿、制度的僵化，以及對從已知轉向未知的普遍抗拒，而難以改變方向。歷史上，強權的興衰通常是循環性的，其中一個重要原因是——讓一個國家崛起的因素，最終可能成為導致其衰落的關鍵。70 中國方面認為，美國習慣訴諸武力，頻繁介入國際衝

新竊起者　56

因素四：國內政治考量

戰略專家經常將美國與其挑戰者之間的競爭視為一場「制度測試」——一場檢驗哪種政治經濟模式最能有效動員資源、制定健全政策並在全球舞台上發揮影響力的較量。74 相關政治學理論普遍認為，一個國家的國內政治體系的堅強或脆弱程度會影響其戰略結果。自由國際主義的概念強調全球貿易在維護和平上的作用，並認為國際間的合作機制能防止直接衝突，同時主張「戰略克制」（strategic restraint）。這一理論基本假設民主國家最適

突，因此必須在全球保持軍事存在，這些因素正在消耗美國的實力並加速其衰落。71 美國還為了維持全球領導地位，過度依賴軍事力量，但事實證明，這種方式在許多戰爭中並未帶來成功，甚至面對阿富汗或伊拉克這類較弱的國家時，也未能取得決定性勝利。72 由中國的角度來看，美國的全球經濟戰略亦被視為低效，華盛頓要求各國遵守其偏好的經濟與政治發展模式。73 相較之下，中國沒有這類限制，因此能夠進入高風險、政治上較不受西方國家青睞的市場，填補西方企業的空缺。

57　第一章　竄起者策略

合在現有國際體系中扮演領導角色並維持運作。[75]研究顯示，民主國家贏得戰爭的比例普遍高於威權政權，可能的原因包括：民主國家在選擇開戰時更加謹慎，或其軍事體系的靈活性較高，加上軍隊士氣更佳，使得其整體戰力更為強大。[76]相較之下，威權政權的穩定性較低，因為內部威脅更容易被外部勢力利用來破壞政權。[77]

同樣地，威權體制的集中化與不透明特性，使其在外交決策上具備更高的速度與保密性，而資源動員能力以及領導層更替不頻繁的特色，則使專制政權相對可預測，甚至可能成為更可靠的盟友。[78]在科技競爭領域，有人認為美國的政治體系更有利於創新，因為其開放的市場環境與競爭機制能激勵科技突破；但也有觀點認為，政府的全面投入與龐大財政資源更關鍵，因此擁有強大國家動員能力的威權中國反而佔據優勢。[79]

我會在案例研究中探討這些論點的有效性，但目前最重要的結論是：不同的政治體系會產生不同的競爭優勢，而這些差異會影響一個國家選擇模仿、利用或創新策略的動機。[80]不同的實力積累策略適用於不同的國家，這取決於它們的意識形態與國內政治結構。因此，許多新興強權策略與既有霸權之間的競爭，往往是兩個體制本質完全不同的國家的競逐，這並不令人意外。例如雅典與斯巴達、新教的荷蘭共和國與天主教的西班牙，以

新竄起者　58

及冷戰時期的美國與蘇聯——這些國家各自擁有不同的競爭優勢，因此在建構與行使實力時，採取了不同的策略。

在中國的案例上，國內政治考量會從兩個主要方面影響其戰略選擇：競爭優勢與國內負擔。競爭優勢指的是一個國家獨特的屬性與優勢，使其能夠在國際體系中勝過競爭對手。這類似於企業在市場上的競爭力衡量方式，例如透過提供價格更低或品質更高的產品或服務來與競爭對手區隔開來。81 因此，競爭優勢也會影響新興強權策略的相對效率與效能，決定哪些方式最適合該國在國際舞台上提升自身實力。

一個國家的政治體制、官僚系統和軍事組織可能會限制其採納創新的能力，但「竄起者策略」強調，這些內部條件的差異同時也會創造不同的競爭優勢。82 其中一個不選擇模仿策略的主要原因，就是某個國家行之有效的方法，未必適用於另一個國家，這可能取決於地理環境、歷史背景與文化差異。決定一個國家競爭優勢的核心因素之一，也是該國如何將國內資源轉化為國際影響力的關鍵，就是其內部政治體系。事實上，擴散理論認為，當「模式的起源國」與「模仿者」具有類似屬性時，模仿的可能性最高；緊密的社會或文化聯繫也可能促使行為體趨於一致。83

第一章　竄起者策略

另一種影響戰略選擇的國內政治考量，是執政政權維持控制的動機。以中國為例，這種需求可能使模仿美國的做法變得不具吸引力，甚至不可行，特別是那些可能削弱共產黨地位的做法。習近平多次強調：「黨政軍民學，東西南北中，黨是領導一切的。」[84] 中共做出許多決策，認為這些措施對維持黨的控制至關重要，即便這些決策可能導致實力或經濟發展上的次優結果（近期在新冠疫情中的「清零政策」便是一個例子）。換句話說，中國希望崛起並提升其全球地位，但其領導層必須同時考慮某種做法是否會削弱黨國體制的掌控力。（對於民主國家而言，執政者爭取連任的需求，也可能影響某些戰略的相對吸引力。）

維持政權合法性的需求也可能促使中國採取「利用」或「創新」戰略，特別是當中國需要在內外部塑造與美國不同的形象時。習近平批評將改革等同於向西方價值觀和政治體系靠攏的觀點，對他而言，最好的道路是「中國特色社會主義」。[85] 習近平在二〇一五年一次高層會議上談及黨校教育時表示：

如果（中國）用西方資本主義價值體系來剪裁我們的實踐，用西方資本主義評價

新窺起者　60

體系來衡量我國發展⋯⋯不符合西方標準就是落後的陳舊的，就要批判、攻擊，那後果不堪設想！最後要麼就是跟在人家後面亦步亦趨，要麼就是只有挨罵的份。86

因素五：可利用的缺口、盲點或弱點

影響新興強權選擇模仿、利用或創新的最後一個因素，取決於競爭領域的性質，特別是國際秩序中是否存在缺口，或既有霸權的盲點與弱點可供利用。這類策略性利用可能帶來優勢，因為國家通常只有在認為某個行為削弱、補充或改變了現有秩序的明確原則、規則和制度時，才會將另一國的政治意圖視為「修正主義」。87

然而，在某些政治行為領域，國際秩序可能根本不存在，或處於薄弱、不穩定、模糊或不完整的狀態。如果新興強權能夠率先在這些領域建立影響力，同時積極參與並融入既有國際秩序的核心框架，它就能在不引發警覺的情況下鞏固自身的相對優勢。88 美國的戰

61　第一章　竄起者策略

略專家主要關注的是「明顯違反規則與規範的行為」。[89]在盲點領域,「競爭對手可能完全無法察覺事件的重要性,或者誤判其意義,甚至反應極為遲緩」。[90]這種競爭策略還具有效率優勢——在競爭較弱的領域採取行之有效的策略,能夠以較少的資源換取顯著的成果,相較於直接與既有霸權競爭,成本更低,收益更高。

竄起者策略與三E策略

在本節中,我將說明這五個因素如何相互作用,驅使中國在模仿、利用與創新之間做出選擇。中國可能會評估美國的戰略方式是否有效,並判斷某些策略是否會讓美國感到放心或威脅。對於中國共產黨而言,最關鍵的國內因素在於某種策略是否可能削弱黨的控制力(或者更理想的情況是,該策略能夠進一步鞏固其統治)。中國領導層還會考慮是否在競爭缺口,以及選擇這種實力建構方式的效率如何——也就是說,中國是否在這一策略上擁有競爭優勢。圖1.1描繪了這一決策過程。儘管這是一種簡化的分析方式,但最終的決策仍然取決於所有這些因素的成本與收益權衡。以下我將提供一些案例,展示哪些因素的

新竄起者　62

圖 1.1　竄起者策略的各項要素

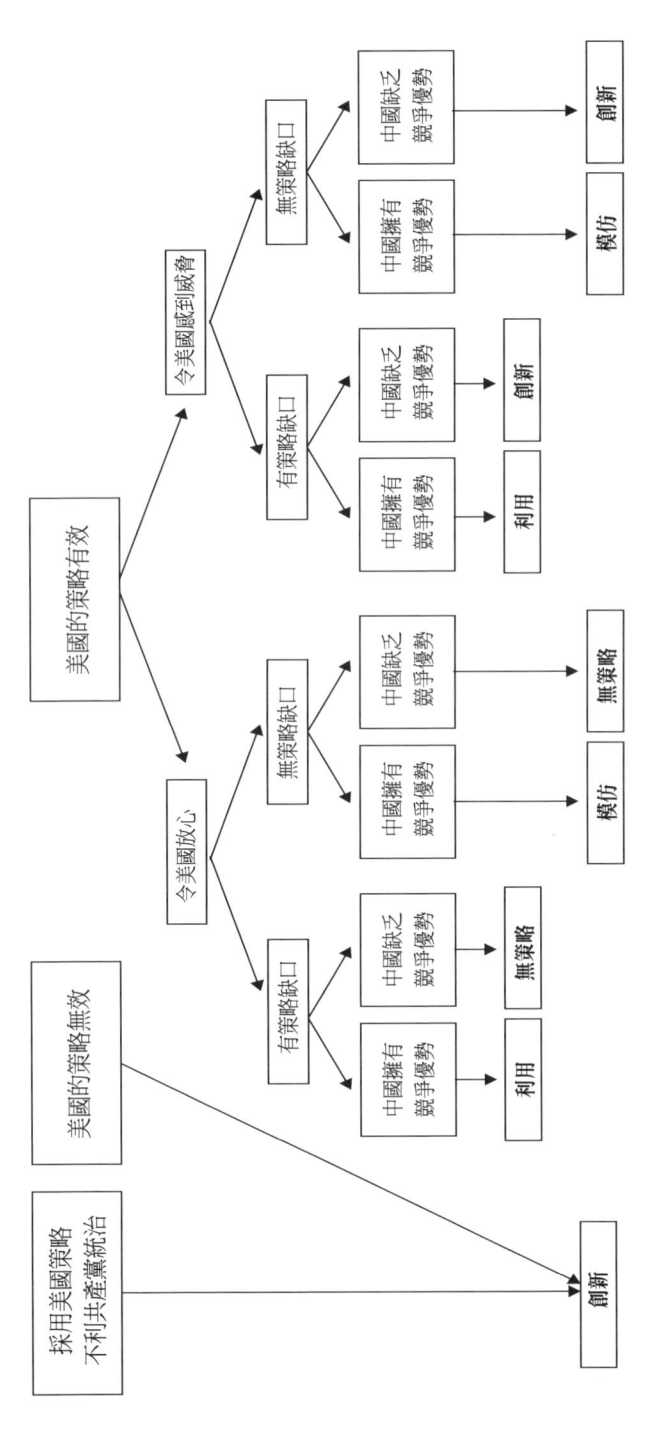

組合會導致中國選擇模仿、利用,或採取創新行動。

中國何時選擇模仿策略

一般的看法認為,模仿是獲取實力與影響力的關鍵。確實,中國有時會在相同領域以相同方式與美國競爭。北京設立大使館、參與大多數國際機構,並建設陸、海、空軍,這些行為都與美國類似。然而,模仿並非在所有情況下都適用。「竄起者策略」框架提供了一套標準,幫助判斷何時模仿能讓新興強權在建立實力的同時,管理來自外部與內部的風險。以中國為例,北京只有在評估美國的方式是有效的時,才會考慮模仿。如果中國認為模仿能讓美國放心(即該行為被視為負責任國家的合理做法),中國就更有動機對美國行為進行仿效。換句話說,當某項活動被認為在當代國際秩序中是「合法」且「適當」的,也就是所有國家都參與其中,且應當如此時,中國就最有可能選擇模仿。從中國的角度來看,參與這些行為可提升國際聲望與地位,特別是當中國模仿的行為是只有強權才能做到的事情。(當然,這一前提是該做法不會因中國在競爭上的劣勢而導致成本過高。)

戰略效能如何促進模仿

在某些情況下，戰略效能也可能促使新興強權選擇模仿策略。例如，當某種競爭方式的固定成本由既有霸權承擔時，新興強權就能以較低的成本建立實力──像是那些美國主導的國際機構。91 這也解釋了為什麼中國積極參與聯合國和世界貿易組織等國際體系。美國為這些機構的設立支付了高昂的前期成本，而中國則能在不激怒美國的情況下，利用這些機制建立自身的影響力。當中國優先在這些領域擴展影響力，並與既有國際秩序的關鍵部分互動時，它可以強化自身的國際地位，而不會立即引發警覺。透過模仿合作性行為，中國甚至成功地讓一些國家相信其和平意圖。92 另一方面，如果中國在某些競爭方式或領域擁有獨特的優勢，使其能夠更有效率地競爭，它也可能選擇模仿，即便這樣做會引發其他強權的安全疑慮。這是因為在這些情境下，相對實力的提升遠遠大於模仿所帶來的風險，使得模仿成為更具吸引力的選擇。

65　第一章　竄起者策略

中國何時選擇「利用」策略

如果美國的某種做法被認為是有效的，在滿足某些條件時，中國可能會選擇「利用」策略。首先是中國無法在直接競爭中有效取勝——當中國發現自己在某一競爭領域無法有效率地與美國正面競爭時，它會尋找那些競爭壓力較小的領域。若國際秩序中存在制度空白或美國在某些領域有所忽視，中國可以趁虛而入。在新的競爭領域運用已被驗證有效的方法，以此在較低風險、較小競爭壓力的情況下快速獲取戰略利益，同時降低引發直接對抗霸權的風險。

在不確定領域中進行競逐，充滿了收穫邊際效益的機會。國際秩序的建立通常涉及明確的界限、共同規則與慣例、共享的因果與規範性理解，以及足夠支撐集體行動的資源。93 然而，在某些領域或議題上，情況尚未穩定，邊界不明確，原則存在爭議，理解也存在分歧，導致對「適當行動」的模糊性。在美國主導的領域中競爭可能被視為一種挑戰，但在這些尚未確立明確規則的領域競爭，通常不會被視為對美國的直接挑戰，而是更像是「遵守國際規範的行為」。因此，中國選擇在國際秩序的競爭漏洞中建立影響力，是

新竄起者　66

一種在不激怒霸權的情況下建立實力的有效方式。[94] 雖然利用競爭中的不確定性和盲點不會立即引發劇烈的反應，但這種做法並非完全沒有問題。有時，在邊緣地帶、利基市場或國際秩序中的空隙中競爭可能並不高效，或者仍有可能會引起既有霸權的不滿。在這種情況下，新興強權可以採取不同的方式來建立實力，透過創新策略來發揮其競爭優勢。

中國何時選擇創新策略

競爭可以促使新興強權選擇與既有強權區隔，而非與其他國家的行為趨同，以發揮自身的競爭優勢並降低外界關注的程度。[95] 中國採取創新行動主要有三種路徑，首先，如果美國在類似目標上的做法被認為無效，中國就會選擇不同的創新方式來達成目標。其次，如果該做法可能削弱中國共產黨的控制力，無論美國的策略在多大程度上被視為有效或高效，中國都會避免模仿，而是選擇創新策略。第三，當美國的策略被認為有效，但模仿可能會被視為具有威脅性，而中國又無法利用現有的競爭空隙，也沒有足夠的競爭優勢來讓

第一章　竄起者策略

模仿的風險變得值得時，中國將會採取創新策略來建立實力。理想情況下（從中國的角度來看），中國的創新做法應同時達成以下目標：加強中共的統治、發揮自身競爭優勢，並削弱美國在該領域的政策影響力，同時將美國的威脅感知和反應控制在可被接受的成本範圍之內。

可以觀察到的「竊起者策略」影響

如果「竊起者策略」具有強大的解釋力，我們應該會在案例研究中觀察到哪些現象？

首先，中國戰略與美國戰略之間應該存在核心關聯。從外部來看，美國是驅動因素。在所有案例中，我們應該能看到中國正在評估相關的美國戰略——其成本、效益，中國是否能競爭，以及美國可能如何回應。是否存在可利用的戰略不確定性、創新機會，或模仿的誘因，這些主要取決於美國。然而，中國最終選擇的具體行動，例如「一帶一路」倡議，則主要由中國自身的競爭優勢以及其對共產黨統治的影響來決定。

「竊起者策略」的關鍵決定因素與北京所選擇的策略組成部分之間應該存在強烈的關

新竊起者　68

聯，正如前一節所述。當中國選擇模仿策略，即便根據「竊起者策略」的成本效益分析顯示，另闢蹊徑會更有利，那麼我們應該預期這種選擇將導致次優結果——既引發對中國崛起的擔憂，又無法在實力與影響力方面獲得明顯的收益。

雖然「竊起者策略」的各個組成部分能夠解釋中國的行為，但當中國的思考方式反映出模仿與創新之間的利弊權衡時，其解釋力將進一步提升。因此，每個案例研究中都會有一部分用來評估中國對競爭策略的看法。儘管中國共產黨的內部決策過程一向不透明，但仍有跡象顯示中國領導層的思維方式與「竊起者策略」的邏輯相吻合。中國領導人認識到，中國在一九九〇年代開始競爭時，政治、經濟和軍事實力都相對薄弱。根據中國內部一項重要的衡量指標——「綜合國力」（CNP, Comprehensive National Power），中國在一九九〇年代的自評分數並不理想；當時中國的國力僅約美國的三分之一強，甚至還落後於加拿大和法國等國家。96 儘管如此，中國對於成為強權的野心已經十分明確。97 然而，單靠累積國力還不夠。中國領導人深知，必須在「單極世界」的嚴格限制下保護自身利益，而美國作為潛在的對手，將長期維持全球主導地位。98 正如一位高級軍官所言，中國必須不惜一切代價避免捲入一場大規模戰爭，因為「我國的經濟建設基礎仍然薄弱」。99

替代論點

我的論點認為中國透過「竄起者策略」累積起足夠的實力,達到了強權地位,這挑戰了傳統的觀點。100 在本書中,我還額外評估了主要的替代解釋,即:中國之所以成為強權,是因為模仿了美國。與這一說法相關的另一個推論則是:中國的主要模仿對象並非美國,而是其他國家。在我的框架中確實允許中國從其他國家(甚至自己的歷史中)尋找靈感,我也在案例研究中指出了這些情況。但我主張,美國仍然是中國主要的參照對象,原因在於美國的相對成功。101 與美國的強權競爭還塑造了許多關鍵因素,影響了中國選擇模仿、利用還是創新的相對吸引力。

第二種替代假設認為中國的戰略選擇基於「竄起者策略」之外的某些因素。或許,競爭決策完全由中國的能力所驅動:當中國擁有足夠能力時,就會模仿美國的戰略;而當能力尚未具備時,中國會先採取不同策略,直到發展出相應能力後再行模仿。然而,「竄起者策略」的基本前提是,對於新興強權而言,除了能力因素外,還有其他理由讓它們選擇不模仿既有霸權的作法,例如:擔憂霸主國如何看待這種挑戰,以及可能的回應。當然,

新竄起者　70

能力因素確實影響了「竄起者策略」的發展方向。美國的失誤界定出競爭較弱的領域，而中國的競爭優勢則決定了其開闢新權力途徑的方式。但我主張：不能簡單地說中國不模仿美國是因為「它做不到」。

或許，獨特的理念因素，如戰略文化或不同的偏好（例如對繁榮的渴望超過對實力的追求），才是解釋中國戰略決策的關鍵。我確實在某些案例研究中發現，從「竄起者策略」的角度來看，中國並未做出最正確的戰略選擇來積累實力。在這些情況下，影響中國決策的，可能是我所列出的五個因素之外的其他原因。然而，我的案例研究表明，在大多數情況下，我強調的這五個因素對中國如何建立實力與影響力的戰略決策具有最大的影響。

最後，有人可能會認為，對中國戰略的解釋已經足夠明確──它正在採取「不對稱策略」，也就是說，中國利用自身的優勢來對抗對手的弱點，而不是「試圖在所有能力上與對手匹敵」。102 就像加迪斯（Gaddis）提出的「不對稱策略概念」一樣，「竄起者策略」注重資源分配，並試圖「改變競爭的性質與戰場位置」，以發揮不對稱優勢。然而，「竄起者策略」更為複雜，因為它不僅關注如何競爭，還幫助崛起中的國家決定應該優先發展哪些能力。例如，中國往往同時採取多條戰略路線，如當美國成為外部安全夥伴時，中國則致力於成為內部安全夥伴。中國也會在競爭力較弱的領域採取類似於美國的戰略。舉例來說，中國透過高層訪問積極拉攏非洲國家，而美國的外交重點主要放在已開發國家。即使中國想要達成與美國相同的目標——例如保護其海外利益，它也可能選擇利用商業機會或依賴當地國的安全部隊，而非在海外建立軍事基地。

中國的「竄起者策略」並不能簡單歸類為不對稱策略。這並不是說中國沒有採取非對稱手段，而是這種說法不足以完整解釋中國的戰略選擇。一個國家可以在整體上模仿另一個國家，同時在特定領域採取不對稱策略來抗衡對手的影響。例如，在冷戰期間，喬治·肯楠（George Kennan）認為，美國應該與蘇聯展開軍事競爭，方法是「加強自身與盟友的優勢」，但不試圖複製蘇聯的武力配置。103 然而，美國的不對稱策略——發展核武器、建立聯盟、進行秘密行動和心理戰——並非美國獨有，蘇聯同樣也採取了這些手段。104

本章提供了一種理解中國如何競爭及其競爭策略受到哪些因素影響的方法。我主張，「竄起者策略」（包含模仿、利用和創新）最能準確描述中國如何競爭以獲取實力。這一策略也解釋了中國在過去三十年如何在維持內部穩定與避免霸權戰爭（或者至少確保在戰

新竄起者　72

爭發生前達到實力平衡）之間取得平衡。105 換句話說，中國的崛起並非只是美國應對不力的結果，而是中國精心設計了策略，讓美國的反應出現延遲，從而更有效率地積累實力並維持相對穩定。106

在接下來的章節中，我將探討「竊起者策略」如何體現在地緣政治、軍事和經濟等領域之中。我將證明，相較於模仿，差異化往往是中國競爭策略的主要驅動力。雖然本書主要關注「竊起者策略」如何解釋過去的中國行為，但這一策略對於中國未來的實力發展及競爭模式也具有重大影響。隨著中國實力的增長，其競爭優勢以及挑戰美國所帶來的代價都將發生變化。這意味著，中國在「利用、創新與模仿」之間的權衡組合也可能隨時間而改變。透過本書中的案例研究，讀者可以了解中國每一項競爭決策背後的邏輯，進而推測未來中國的競爭方式將如何演變。

73　第一章　竊起者策略

第二章

中國外交政策中的模仿與利用策略

一九九〇年代對中國的外交政策而言，是一個劇烈變革的時期。中國從六四天安門事件後的外交孤立中走出，決心透過深化雙邊關係，並積極參與國際機構，在國際舞台上擴展影響力。在一九九〇年代，中國與二十八個國家實現關係正常化，其中包括南韓等重要國際角色。從一九八九年到二〇二二年，中國對政府間國際組織（IGO）的參與程度增長了二十倍，而對非政府組織（NGO）的參與程度則增長了七倍。1 中國國家主席江澤民在中國崛起的初期，為中美關係制定了一系列指導方針，內容包括：增強信心、減少摩擦、加強合作、避免對抗。

中國學者早已意識到，中國的實力不如美國，但在冷戰結束後，中國仍然必須找到擺脫國際孤立的方法，同時在中美雙邊關係中爭取更多戰略迴旋空間。2 中國成功從一個外交上被孤立的國家，轉變為在國際舞台上擁有與美國相當（甚至在某些指標上更勝一籌）的外交與政治影響力。3 儘管美國在外交政策上投注的資源遠超過中國——駐外外交官數量是中國的兩倍，但到了二〇二二年，對國際組織的貢獻更達中國的二十倍，許多觀察人士認為，北京在全球影響力競賽中正處於領先地位。4

中國之所以能夠達成這一成就，正是因為採取了「竊起者策略」。中國通常會在美

新竊起者 76

國的方法被認為有效，且這種行為被視為正當、能讓外界放心的領域模仿美國，藉此以最低成本改善自身形象。本章探討了兩個符合這些條件的案例：調解外交（mediation diplomacy）和參與國際機構。我另外還分析了一個偏離典型模式的模仿案例——軟實力（soft power）。在這個案例中，中國領導人選擇了模仿美國，即使當時並不具備理想的模仿條件。我之所以納入這個異常案例，是為了說明中國並不總是完全依照竄起者策略的邏輯行事（可能是因為這個決策背後還有其他動機，而不僅僅是權力考量）。但當中國偏離竄起者策略時，往往會付出代價。這些案例進一步增強我們對竄起者策略在中國成功崛起過程中所扮演核心角色的信心。

當美國的戰略雖然有效，但並未涵蓋所有領域時，中國則採取利用策略，即在競爭力較弱的領域，運用與美國相同的戰略方式，但同時發揮自身的競爭優勢。透過這種方式，中國成功擴展了影響力，特別是在美國基本上忽視的國家之間。本章探討了兩個中國利用美國盲點與國際秩序缺口的案例：軍售和外交拓展。在這些領域，中國並非直接超越美國，而是填補了美國不積極參與的空缺，藉此擴大自身的影響力。

77　第二章　中國外交政策中的模仿與利用策略

扮演調解者

衝突調解一直是美國自二戰結束以來的重要外交工具，在終結暴力行為與促進穩定方面相當成功。5 從一九四五年至一九九九年，美國共調解了五十六起內戰衝突，6 其中最具代表性的成功案例包括《貝爾法斯特協議》，成功終結了北愛爾蘭共和軍（IRA）的暴力行動。以及一九七八年的《大衛營協議》，解決了埃及與以色列之間的領土與政治爭端。7 美國調解衝突的重點通常放在防止衝突失控，以避免危及美國與盟友的利益。除了認識到調解外交的有效性外，中國官員和戰略家也意識到，調解外交在很大程度上被視為促進或保障經濟利益和政治影響力的合法方式。8 採納這一策略將因此提升中國作為負責任大國的形象，同時減輕對其威脅的觀感。9

在這方面，中國擁有一些競爭優勢。與美國不同的是，中國通常與爭端各方（包括一些被視為問題國家的政權）保持良好關係，因此更有可能影響相關參與者，並將自己定位為一個公正的調解者。在某些重要情況下，美國甚至並未正式承認相關當事方（如伊朗、北韓、阿富汗的塔利班政權），這使得美國更難以介入。而中國則能夠接待這些國家的政

新竄起者　78

治菁英，而不會像美國那樣承受聲譽上的損失。美國官員似乎也意識到了中國在這方面的競爭優勢，據報導，他們曾要求中國官員介入，以協助阻止俄羅斯入侵烏克蘭。

有鑑於調解的有效性與正當性，以及中國本身的競爭優勢，「竄起者策略」促使中國模仿此一做法。事實上，中國已在多個備受關注的危機中將自己定位為和平推動者。例如，在一九九八年印度與巴基斯坦進行核試驗導致緊張局勢升級後，中國在聯合國安全理事會推動決議，敦促兩國簽署《核武禁擴條約》。二〇〇八年孟買恐怖攻擊事件發生後，中國積極展開穿梭外交，試圖在巴基斯坦與印度之間進行調解；二〇一七年，當阿富汗指控巴基斯坦庇護塔利班武裝分子時，北京也在阿富汗與巴基斯坦之間斡旋。自二〇一〇年以來，中國也斷斷續續參與緬甸的內部安全與和平進程的調解，並曾多次主持緬甸官員與八個少數民族武裝組織的會談。

中國在促成北韓與其他參與國重返談判桌方面發揮了關鍵作用，特別是在二〇〇三至二〇〇九年間的六方會談，這是一項旨在透過外交協議實現北韓無核化的多邊努力。（至今，中國仍持續呼籲恢復談判。）[11] 北京也曾多次介入蘇丹衝突，協助交戰各方遵守二〇〇五年的《全面和平協議》以及二〇一五年的《南蘇丹和平協議》。二〇二一年美國自

第二章 中國外交政策中的模仿與利用策略

阿富汗撤軍後，中國與塔利班政權會面，展示其在當地和平進程中的關鍵角色。二〇二三年，中國更成功促成沙烏地阿拉伯與伊朗恢復外交關係，並提出自己的俄烏和平方案。儘管這些舉措的實質影響仍有爭議，但中國官方媒體大肆宣傳這些努力的過程，將其塑造成中國在國際事務中的仁慈形象，並突顯其外交方式相較於西方國家的優勢。[12]

中國的調解外交方式是有計劃且具有戰略性的。自二〇一六年以來，中國已任命多名特使，負責處理北韓核問題、非洲事務、中東事務、阿富汗問題以及敘利亞衝突。二〇二二年十一月，中國外交部宣布將會成立一個新的專門負責調解衝突的國際組織。[13]不出所料，中國的調解努力通常集中於對自身具有戰略利益的區域，例如參與「一帶一路」倡議的國家。[14]以蘇丹為例，中國國有企業在蘇丹的一個油田專案中持有百分之四十的股份，[15]這使其在當地的調解行動顯得尤為重要。調解也是中國控制鄰國局勢的一種有效方式，特別是在阿富汗、印度、緬甸、尼泊爾、北韓和巴基斯坦等邊境國家，這些國家的衝突有可能會波及中國境內。

圖 2.1 顯示了二〇〇六至二〇二三年間中國最重要的調解活動地點分布圖。[16]

調解行動是否真正能解決衝突，在我們的討論中僅是次要考量。單單是中國願意參

新竄起者　80

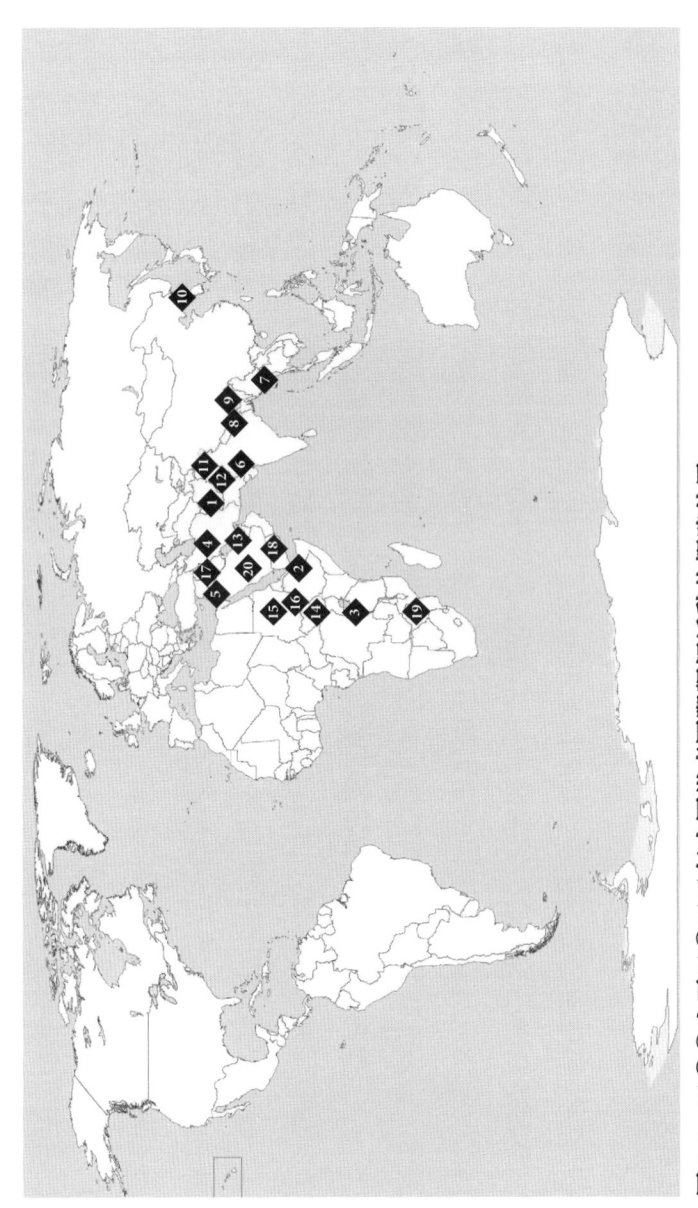

圖 2.1　二〇〇六至二〇二三年中國從事國際調解活動的概略位置

資料來源：Helena Legarda, "China as a Conflict Mediator: Maintaining Stability Along the Belt and Road," MERICS, August 22, 2018, https://merics.org/en/short-analysis/china-conflict-mediator；並根據本書作者的研究加以補充。

第二章　中國外交政策中的模仿與利用策略

與，就足以贏得好感、合法性及國際認可。川普曾公開表示，北京在北韓問題上「提供了很大幫助，比大多數人所知道的還要多」。17 二〇〇五年達佛危機期間，中國因向蘇丹政府施壓，促使其接受聯合國暨非洲聯盟維和部隊的部署，以及後續協助促成和平協議，因而受到讚譽。二〇一七年，中國試圖恢復聯合國與葉門胡塞組織之間的談判，該組織領導人感謝中國「在葉門問題上採取客觀公正的立場，並表示願意與北京保持密切溝通。」18

中國加入伊朗核協議《聯合全面行動計畫》（JCPOA）談判，被認為對達成協議具有關鍵作用。緬甸領導人翁山蘇姬也曾公開感謝中國在緬甸國內和解進程中的貢獻。

調解外交也幫助中國最大限度地降低與「流氓國家」進行貿易帶來的政治成本。中國因在蘇丹陷入種族滅絕爭議時向其購買石油、在伊朗發展核子武器時採購其天然氣，以及與北韓進行貿易而受到嚴厲批評。為了應對這些批評，中國在這三個案例中都積極斡旋，試圖將有關國家帶上談判桌。二〇二三年，北京更成功促成沙烏地阿拉伯與伊朗之間的協議，這兩個國家都是中國重要的能源供應國。

另一個讓中國選擇模仿的原因是，這些外交舉措不需要投入大量資源就能獲得回報，因此極具效率。正如一位中國外交官在談到中國在六方會談中扮演的角色時開玩笑地說：

「為了朝鮮半島的穩定，中國願意提供咖啡，這只花幾塊錢。」[19]這些很大一部分是公開的外交秀。中國偏好高調的外交手段，例如主辦外交、特使外交、高層訪問，而非使用多邊聯絡小組、文件外交、條件援助或穿梭外交等工具。透過這些手段，中國獲得的影響力通常受到歡迎，使得其他國家對中國的意圖感到安心，同時提升中國的國際形象。[20]中國也利用這些機會批評美國政策，並藉此與美國區隔立場。例如，二〇一一年五月，當中國提議主辦以色列與巴勒斯坦之間的會談時，中國外交部長王毅表示，這項提議展現了中國希望成為「建設性」的地區參與者，與美國「站在國際正義的對立面」形成鮮明對比。[21]

在外交手法上，中國試圖將採取調解外交所帶來的風險降至最低。為了維護中國共產黨在人權議題及西藏、香港、新疆和台灣等敏感問題上的立場，中國通常確保在相關國家正式請求中國介入後，才會採取行動，以此來維護其「不干涉原則」。[22]有許多文章討論中國的調解方式和美國有何不同，強調中國的調解是公正的、不具強制性、受到歡迎且不具其他意圖，顯示出中國希望確保自身外交行動不會無意間加強其他國家對中國的威脅觀感。[23]為了確保其戰略既有效又高效，中國也避免過度介入。正如著名學者王緝思所指出的：「中國必須在『創造性介入』與『像西方那樣被區域國家內部危機拖累』之間取得平

83　第二章 中國外交政策中的模仿與利用策略

衡。」24

操控國際機構

第二次世界大戰的毀滅性影響促使美國建立一系列國際機構，以促進國際合作並塑造全球政治格局。外交活動主要透過聯合國進行，該機構也負責編纂國際法的核心原則、維護國際和平與安全，並遏制侵略行為。關稅暨貿易總協定（一九九五年成立的世界貿易組織前身）旨在促進全球自由貿易。世界銀行最初是一九四四年成立的「國際復興開發銀行」，最初專注於戰後重建，後來轉向國際發展合作。國際貨幣基金組織自一九四四年成立以來，一直負責監管匯率及貨幣政策，包括資本流動等領域。而世界衛生組織則於一九四八年成立，專責國際公共衛生事務。另外還有設立了許多職能較為專門的國際機構，包括聯合國的附屬機構聯合國兒童基金會（UNICEF）和聯合國教育、科學及文化組織（UNESCO）等。

國際機構是美國以創新方式建立並行使權力的重要手段。透過這些機構，美國能夠設

新竄起者　84

定國際議程、規則、規範、原則與程序,讓其他國家遵循,同時促進資訊共享並降低國際合作的交易成本。正如國際關係學者約翰·伊肯伯里(John Ikenberry)所主張,這些機構為美國這樣的民主霸權提供了一種機制,使其能夠在有利的國際秩序中維持主導地位。部分原因在於,這些機構讓美國的權力更容易被較弱國家接受。[26]

美國對於國際機構能夠依照自身偏好約束國家權力充滿信心,以至於三十年前許多人認為,將中國納入國際秩序將迫使北京走向自由化,並建立更符合美國模式的國內政治與經濟體制。即便在一九八九年天安門事件之後,美國總統老布希在一九九〇年的《國家安全戰略》(National Security Strategy)中仍堅稱,中國與外部世界的聯繫對其重返經濟改革與政治自由化的道路至關重要。[27]這種認為制度嵌入(institutional enmeshment)會促使中國改革的邏輯,使美國在一九九〇年代決定授予中國「最惠國待遇」(Most-Favored-Nation, MFN),並支持其加入世界貿易組織。

換句話說,參與國際機構是一種有效的權力建構與行使方式。中國可以透過這種參與來擴展自身影響力,同時讓其他國家對其崛起感到放心。[28]根據胡錦濤時期的中共中央外事工作領導小組辦公室主任戴秉國的說法,中國在二〇〇〇年代中期的首要任務是透過積

85　第二章　中國外交政策中的模仿與利用策略

極參與國際體系,成為「建設性貢獻者」,以安撫華盛頓。29 這一策略也保證其高效性,因為美國仍需繼續負擔維護國際秩序的主要成本(截至二〇二一年,美國對聯合國的貢獻額仍約為中國的五點五倍)。30

到了二十一世紀初,中國已經加入五十個國際政府間組織以及一千二百七十五個國際非政府組織。31 相較於另闢蹊徑、採取更具創新性的做法,中國選擇模仿既有模式明顯是更好的權力累積途徑。正如北京大學國際關係學院副院長、國際關係理論學者王逸舟所說:

「西方主導的現行國際規則確實存在問題,其中不乏不公平與不公正之處。但對於弱勢的發展中國家來說,選項其實不多——他們必須先加入其中,然後在自身實力增強後,推動長期改革。所謂『另起爐灶』的想法並不現實,反而可能帶來更大的傷害。」32

中國戰略家呼籲在利用國際機構方面應該仿效美國,特別是要「聯合其他崛起中及發展中國家的力量,共同推動建立一個更加合理與公正的國際體系。」[33]

在這些國際機構內,中國隨後尋求類似於美國及其盟友的更高領導地位,目標是控制議程與決策結果,並推動體制改革。[34] 從中國在國際組織中當選的管理層與高級官員比例來看,中國透過兩種機制發揮相對的影響力:首先,是能夠成功安插中國公民擔任這些職位所需的對國際組織的影響力;其次,則是在掌控這些機構後,透過中國的官僚體系來決定機構的議程與決策結果。

根據我對二〇〇〇至二〇二一年間三十個主要國際與區域組織的數據分析,中國在過去二十年間大幅提升其公民在國際機構中的高階管理與高級行政職位的比例,特別是在標準制定機構中。[35] 二〇〇〇年時,在所調查的二十七個機構中,沒有任何一個由中國官員擔任最高領導職位,而二百三十二名高級管理人員中僅有八位是中國籍。到了二〇一五年,中國在高層領導中的占比提升至二十九個機構中有六個(其中兩個新機構為聯合國婦女署與亞洲基礎設施投資銀行,皆於二〇〇〇年後成立),佔比達到百分之二十一。

到了二〇二一年,中國在國際機構中的代表占比趨於穩定:在調查的二十九個機構中,四個由中國籍官員擔任最高領導職位,比同年美國所擁有的還多出一個。中國公民在

87　第二章 中國外交政策中的模仿與利用策略

這些機構中擔任高級管理職位的人數達到十九人，在三百零一個高級管理職位中佔百分之六點三。整體而言，中國在二〇〇〇至二〇二一年間，高層行政職位的佔比增加了百分之十三點八，高級管理職位的佔比增加了百分之二點八。截至二〇二一年，十五個聯合國專門機構中有四個由中國籍官員擔任最高負責人，分別是聯合國糧食及農業組織；國際電信聯盟；聯合國工業發展組織及國際民航組織。相較之下，僅有一個機構由美國公民擔任領導人。36

美國參與這些國際機構的減少，為中國影響力的提升創造了機會，這也帶有「利用」策略的特徵。在二〇〇〇年時，美國在國際機構中的高層行政職位佔比為百分之十五，高級管理職位則佔百分之十三，並在二〇一〇年達到最高值，高級管理職位的佔比增至百分之十七。然而，到了二〇二一年，美國的高級管理職位佔比下降至百分之十二，十一年間減少了約五個百分點。到二〇二一年，中國在高層行政職位的數量已經與美國相當，甚至在某些時候超越美國，但美國公民在高級管理職位上的數量仍然幾乎是中國的兩倍。歐洲作為美國的長期盟友，也是現行國際秩序的重要參與者，仍然在這些國際機構中佔據大量的領導職位。

新窺起者　88

另一個例子是國際海底管理局。該機構隸屬於聯合國，負責規範海底礦產開採。多年來，中國積極參與此機構，而美國僅是觀察員，並非正式會員。過去，美國的政策制定者可能對海底活動的規範不太感興趣，但現在情況已經發生變化。對於任何希望實現綠色轉型的國家來說，獲取海底豐富的關鍵礦產至關重要。例如太平洋的克拉里昂·克利珀頓區（Clarion-Clipperton Zone）富含大量的鎳礦，而鎳和其他材料是電動車電池生產的關鍵元素。目前，國際海底管理局正在討論海底開採的規範，但如果二〇二五年前無法制定出完整的法律框架，各國企業將開始自由開採。由於剩餘的時間不多，加上中國在該機構的影響力遠超美國，北京可能主導未來的法律規範，確保這些規則符合自身利益。這正是一個中國如何在「競爭縫隙」中行動的案例，即利用美國對某些領域關注不足的情況，趁機掌控規則制定權。[37]

中國在策略運用上有一些特性。例如，中國在外交運作中並不避諱使用賄賂和脅迫等手段。二〇一九年，在聯合國糧食及農業組織最高職位的選舉即將到來之際，出現了中國操縱選舉的指控。實際上，中國同時運用「胡蘿蔔與大棒」策略來建立支持聯盟。在胡蘿蔔（利誘）方面，中國免除了喀麥隆七千八百萬美元的債務，並據傳提供給投票官員

第二章 中國外交政策中的模仿與利用策略

頭等艙機票和其他奢華待遇。而在大棒（施壓）方面，中國威脅某些南美國家，如果它們不支持中國的候選人，可能會限制其農產品出口。據傳中國還要求投票官員拍攝投票給中國候選人的截圖，藉此繞過秘密投票程序。最終，中國的策略取得成功，如今它透過指導優先事項、制定國際標準和對全球飢荒的國際應對措施，對農業機構擁有了實質性的控制權。38

對於參與國際機構的模仿策略，確實提升了中國在國際體系中的影響力與權力。首先，中國利用其在國際組織中的地位來謀取自身利益（如同大多數國家所做的），但特別著重於增強黨在國內的控制力與合法性。例如，中國成功讓國際刑警組織主席一職由中國官員擔任，在二〇一六年由中國公安部副部長孟宏偉當選。39 在他任內，國際刑警組織投入更多資源，協助追捕中國的異議人士與貪腐官員，並與義大利、保加利亞、希臘、西班牙、匈牙利與法國等國簽訂的引渡條約，將這些人遣送回中國受審。40

中國在二〇〇六至二〇二〇年這十五年間，有十年擔任聯合國人權理事會理事國，主要目的是減少國內在人權問題上的負擔。41 一名外交官回憶道，中國在其他發展中國家的建議下，意識到爭取國際支持的最佳方式，不是直接辯論人權的實質內容，而是將焦點從

新竊起者　90

人權實質問題轉移到程序問題——也就是提出那些其他國家在美國壓力下也可能支持的決議。42 例如，中國提交了一系列提案，試圖重新定義人權，將其聚焦於經濟與社會權利，而非政治與公民權利。根據國家亞洲研究局（National Bureau of Asian Research）的一份報告指出：

透過經濟施壓、威嚇、恐嚇、誘因交易、動員關係網絡，以及精巧操作國際程序，中國如今已掌握足夠的選票與支持，得以在聯合國人權理事會推動自己的願景……在這個架構下，中國的價值觀、規範與話語權成為核心，而所謂的「雙贏合作」意味著：各國政府可以迴避國際審查，逃避對人權侵害指控的問責，受害者則無法獲得任何補償或申訴管道。43

二〇一九年，當美國、澳洲、德國、英國等二十二個國家聯合發表公開信，向聯合國人權理事會譴責中國在新疆大規模拘禁維吾爾族穆斯林及其他少數民族時，中國迅速作出反擊，發表了由二十三個伊斯蘭國家簽署的反駁信（其中包括三個駐有美軍基地的國

91　第二章　中國外交政策中的模仿與利用策略

家），稱相關指控「毫無根據」，並批評這些國家試圖對中國施壓。這顯示出中國已能有效運用國際機構來推動自身國家目標，包括維護政權穩定。二〇二二年十月，中國成功阻止了一項由美國和七個西方國家提交給聯合國人權理事會的提案，該提案要求針對「中國新疆維吾爾自治區的人權狀況」展開正式辯論。[44] 許多分析認為，中國這次的勝利顯示出中國在國際場合積極推動破壞西方「普世人權」概念的努力。[45] 一份二〇一八年的報告列出了一九九〇至二〇〇五年間，中國成功阻止十二次聯合國對其人權紀錄的投票，顯示中國長期以來在國際機構內運作的影響力。[46]

強勢推動軟實力

乍看之下，建立軟實力（Soft Power）——即透過吸引力與說服力而非脅迫或金錢交換來達成目標——似乎是中國可以模仿的一個領域，特別是考慮到這一策略在美國的成功。美國一直是軟實力的主要受益者，其全球知名品牌、流行文化、速食連鎖店、世界頂尖大學、自由政治價值觀以及道德權威在國際舞台上具有主導地位。[47] 軟實力被認為是美

新竊起者　92

國外交政策的一大創新,並且經常被認為是幫助美國贏得冷戰的重要因素。⁴⁸

然而,對中國而言,軟實力是一個不太適合模仿的領域,因為軟實力是美國實力的核心,中國若試圖發展軟實力,很可能被視為對美國的直接挑戰。考慮到中國的國內政治體制,中國在這方面並不具備競爭優勢,因為軟實力主要是透過公民社會自然產生的。不難理解,軟實力的主要競爭對手通常來自其他開放社會,如英國的英超足球聯賽(Premier League)、印度的寶萊塢(Bollywood)、南韓的韓流(K-Pop),以及日本的科技品牌等。在這種情況下,「利用」國際秩序中的空缺,即試圖在美國軟實力較不具優勢的領域建立影響力,會是更好的選擇。事實上,中國已投入數十億美元,在非洲建立媒體影響力,其科技品牌也逐步滲透該地區。⁴⁹ 同樣地,較貧窮或政治不自由的國家,也是北京獎學金計畫的主要受益者。⁵⁰

然而,中國並不僅僅試圖在國際秩序的空缺與盲點中發展軟實力。儘管存在不利於模仿的因素,中共仍在二〇〇七年正式宣布,要將軟實力作為綜合國力與國際競爭力的重要組成部分。⁵¹ 或許是因為中國的政策制定者認識到,中國作為威權國家在國際上的吸引力有限,官方文件中將中國文化視為最有潛力的軟實力來源,同時也強調社會主義價值體系

93　第二章　中國外交政策中的模仿與利用策略

以及「中華民族的團結」等概念。52 最高領導層也紛紛響應這一方針。例如，曾經聲勢顯赫的薄熙來（在他被指控貪腐被免除黨職之前）曾表示：「在國際競爭中，思想與文化的優勢更內在、更持久，且無可取代。」53 中國軍方的主要新聞機構則提出警告：「僅僅依靠軍事與經濟等硬實力，不僅消耗巨大資源，還會招致國際社會的譴責。」54 這一訊息促使中國戰略學者與學界開始關注如何衡量與構築軟實力。55

結果，中共試圖透過自上而下的強勢手段與笨拙的宣傳方式來提升自身的吸引力。56 二〇〇四年，中國政府成立孔子學院，旨在向國際推廣特定版本的中國語言與文化。在達到最高峰的二〇一七年，全球有超過五百所孔子學院，以及一千間孔子課堂（針對中小學的版本），遍及一百三十多個國家。57 中國官方媒體也開始走向全球化。例如，新華社在二〇〇九至二〇一一年間新增了將近四十個海外分社，截至二〇二三年，已在全球設有超過一百八十個海外分社，規模大約是美國CNN的五倍。58 二〇一六年，中國官方廣播機構中央電視台推出國際新聞部門：中國環球電視網。59 從那時起，習近平則敦促官員要「提升中國的軟實力，講好中國故事，做好對外宣傳。」60 習近平進一步強調這一方向，要求官員加強軟實力建設，以掌握敘事權，並將中國「真實、立體、全面」地呈現給

新竄起者　94

然而不出所料，這次中國的模仿嘗試最終未能達成預期目標。在長達十五年的軟實力建設後，中國在全球軟實力排行榜中仍僅位居第十，而美國通常位列第一。62 隨著北京加大對軟實力的宣傳，全球對中國的負面看法卻同步上升。從二〇〇二至二〇二〇年，澳洲、英國、德國、荷蘭、瑞典、美國、南韓、西班牙和加拿大等國對中國的負面觀感顯著增加。二〇二〇年，在十四個國家的調查中，百分之七十八的受訪者表示他們不信任習近平能夠「在國際事務上做出正確決策」。63 截至二〇二三年，美國人對中國的好感度降至歷史新低，僅百分之十五的受訪者持正面看法。64 二〇二二年的一項調查顯示，在四十三個國家中，全球對中國的觀感大幅下降，唯一的例外是部分非洲和太平洋地區的開發中國家，與已開發國家相比，對中國的看法仍相對較為正面。65 另一項二〇二一年針對東南亞國家協會的調查顯示，中國作為高等留學標的和旅遊目的地方面表現極為不佳，分別只有百分之三點三和二點九的受訪者選擇中國。66

中國經過審查且充滿官方宣傳色彩的流行文化，可想而知，吸引力相當有限。67 二〇二一年上映的電影《長津湖》，講述中國參與韓戰的故事，由中共中央宣傳部主導製作，

世界。61

投資超過二億美元，並創下中國國內最高票房紀錄。然而，該片在國際市場上反應冷淡，在新加坡的票房甚至低到無法統計。68 中國票房第二高的電影《戰狼二》則因對非洲人的形象刻畫充滿歧視而受到批評。這一點並不令人意外，畢竟中國曾在電視小品中安排女演員塗黑臉扮演非洲婦女，同時還誇張地加上巨臀，並帶著寵物猴子入場。69

中國在全球品牌方面也面臨類似的挑戰。中國企業在全球市場投入鉅額資金進行廣告宣傳。例如，二〇一八年世界盃足球賽的贊助商中，有一半來自中國。然而，這些努力並未成功提升中國品牌的吸引力。在全球十大最有價值品牌中，除了三星和LV以外，其他全部為美國品牌。中國品牌甚至未能進入前五十名──而這還是在二〇二〇年新冠疫情期間，美國經濟受創程度遠超中國的情況下所發布的排名。70 中國品牌在海外市場的辨識度極低。二〇一九年的一項調查顯示，近八成的美國人無法說出任何一個中國品牌的名字。71 美國在亞洲的軟實力優勢依舊明顯。二〇二三年的一項調查顯示，百分之七十五的受訪者對美國的軟實力持正面看法，而對中國持正面看法的比例僅為百分之三十三。72

中國模仿建設軟實力的努力甚至被視為直接威脅。例如，中國試圖利用歷史、經濟和文化聯繫來建立其在東南亞的軟實力，這引起了一些分析人士的擔憂。他們將中國的計畫

新竄起者　96

稱為「東南亞版的門羅主義」，認為這可能削弱美國在該地區的聯盟。[73] 然而，中國的孔子學院、文化展覽、全球媒體佈局及提供來華高等教育獎學金等措施，不但沒有改善國際社會對中國及其政府的印象，反而引發了全球的懷疑與警戒。[74] 在美國，超過九成的孔子學院已經關閉，而中國的國際媒體企業因操控內容、偏袒中國共產黨的立場而受到抵制。[75] 英國也出現類似的情況。二〇一九年，英國保守黨人權委員會進行的調查指出，孔子學院「威脅全球各大學的學術自由與言論自由，並成為中國共產黨用來傳播其宣傳、壓制異議的工具」。[76] 除了美國和英國，丹麥、芬蘭、瑞典及日本等國也已經關閉孔子學院。[77]

中國學者已意識到中國在軟實力方面的弱點。一些人認為這是中國國內制度的限制所導致，而另一些人則將其歸咎於全球的「反華政治勢力」。[78] 中國前大使傅瑩在二〇二〇年坦承，美國仍然「在國際輿論場上擁有更大的影響力」，部分原因是「中國仍然與西方的信息（資訊）生態系統隔絕」。[79] 換句話說，中國共產黨及其宣傳機器難以真正打動全球民眾的內心。或許正因如此，中國近年來在軟實力方面的戰略關注度有所下降。《人民日報》在二〇一二年曾發表約四百三十五篇與軟實力相關的文章，但到二〇二二年，這一數字已減少到不到一百五十篇。80

這個案例提供了幾個關於「竄起者策略」的重要見解。首先，它證實了一個觀點：模仿只有在適當條件下才能幫助國家累積實力，這些條件正是「竄起者策略」所定義的條件。當新興強權偏離這些條件時，模仿可能會變得具有威脅性，成為一種低效，甚至是無效的競爭方式。一個典型的例子就是二〇〇八年北京奧運會，這場規模龐大且精心策劃的活動確實提升了中國作為強權的形象，但其代價卻極其高昂。僅直接成本就高達二十億美元，而與體育無關的基礎建設投資則估計達到四百億美元，這與二〇〇四年希臘舉辦雅典奧運會的一百六十億美元支出形成了鮮明對比。81

這個案例還顯示了中國共產黨在國內強化自身合法性的需求，如何主導其他的戰略考量，並因此妨礙中國與美國競爭的能力。中共似乎試圖透過推銷中國文化與制度來向國內民眾解釋其政權的合法性，即便它並非民主政體。習近平曾強調，文化軟實力是實現「中國夢」的關鍵。82 如果以這個標準來衡量，也許中國的軟實力策略可以被視為一種成功。

雖然中國的激進媒體策略並未提升國際社會對中國的正面觀感，但它確實將東亞、東南亞及太平洋島國的媒體報導，從負面導向轉為中立。83 另外，中國龐大的電影市場甚至讓它能夠影響好萊塢對中國的刻畫方式。[84] 根據一名中國學者的說法，中國的「政黨外交」旨在將中共形象塑造為一個有能力且負責任的執政黨，這在某些外國政界人士中獲得了好評。[85]

在軍售利基市場的利用策略

各國，尤其是強權國家，往往利用軍售來鞏固與外國政府的正面關係，或達成某些政治目標，例如取得軍事基地協議或建立聯盟承諾。[86] 根據美國國務院的說法，軍售是美國外交政策的「具體工具」，可能對區域安全產生深遠影響。[87] 過去二十年來，全球軍火交易大幅成長，其中美國在二〇一五至二〇二〇年間占全球武器轉讓總額的三成以上，其中近一半流向中東地區。[88] 二〇二〇年，美國授權的武器出口總額達約一千七百五十億美元，主要銷往日本、摩洛哥、以色列、新加坡、埃及、法國和印尼。[89] 二〇二一年，銷售額有所下降，但仍然高達一千三百八十億美元。[90] 目前，美國也透過軍售來抗衡中國；美國對東亞及太平洋地區的軍售總額在二〇一八至二〇一九年間增加了二點五倍，二〇一九

99　第二章　中國外交政策中的模仿與利用策略

至二○二○年間又再增長百分之四十一。[91] 軍售更是美國對台灣政策的核心：從一九七九至二○二○年，美國提供了台灣超過七成五的武器進口量。[92] 簡而言之，美國利用武器交易作為「外交政策的延伸」來建立長期關係，並在外交場域中獲取影響力。[93]

中國分析家認識到，軍售一直是美國獲取權力的有效工具，特別是在冷戰期間。即使武器交易完成後，軍隊仍需要技術支援、零件補給和額外彈藥，這些因素確保了買家對供應國的長期依賴。中國專家也理解到，美國透過軍售獲取龐大的財務利益，不僅支持了國內軍工產業，還創造了就業機會。[95] 許多中國學者分析，美國透過軍售來確保對其夥伴國家的某種程度控制，甚至可能獲得軍事進駐權，因為這些國家高度依賴美國的武器供應鏈。[96] 值得注意的是，中國方面的相關論述中，對美國軍售的評價異常大方。許多中國學者指出，美國的軍售主要是為了維持區域穩定，而且美國在這方面大體上是成功的。[97]

儘管中國學者認可軍售對於外交影響力的重要貢獻，但他們認為模仿美國並不是明智的選擇，因為中國難以直接與美國競爭。首先，軍售具有「先行者優勢」。由於冷戰期間美蘇之間的影響力競爭，當今世界上大多數國家早已選擇從美國或俄羅斯獲取軍備。而且更換武器供應商的成本極高，因為不同國家生產的系統可能無法無縫整合，導致操作成本上升。許多國家在採購武器時，更傾向於從單一供應商獲取設備、武器與平台，以確保系統的整合性。

其次，如果可以選擇，大多數國家更願意購買美國的武器。雖然中國的軍事裝備價格較低，但在可靠性、維修性與品質方面存在問題。舉例來說，中國出售給孟加拉國和緬甸的潛艦故障頻繁，賣給肯亞和巴基斯坦的護衛艦也屢次出現故障，導致許多買家對中國軍備的品質產生懷疑。98 而對於那些需要較便宜替代方案的國家來說，俄羅斯的軍事設備仍然是更好的選擇。美國還會透過補助降低武器購買成本，特別是針對那些無力以市場價格購買裝備的國家。另外，美國的軍售主要涉及軍用飛機與引擎，而這正是中國較難與之競爭的領域。99

最後一個中國難以模仿美國軍售的明顯原因是：美國經常將武器賣給與中國有軍事競爭關係的國家或區域，如日本、菲律賓、印度與台灣。因此，中國的研究人員普遍憂心美國利用軍售來強化其亞洲盟友，並藉此與印度、印尼和越南建立新的夥伴關係。100 雖然中國可以選擇向美國的對手或戰略競爭者出售武器，例如巴基斯坦，但整體而言，中國認為增強自身軍事實力才是最有效的抗衡方式。

101　第二章　中國外交政策中的模仿與利用策略

確實，中國的軍售紀錄顯示，它並沒有仿效美國的模式。從數量上來看，中國的軍售與美國相比幾乎微不足道。在這段期間，美國的軍售數額大約是中國的九倍，占全球武器交易總額的百分之三十，而中國僅占不到百分之四。這並非因為中國早期的軍售數據拉低了平均值，即便到了二〇二二年，美國的軍售數額仍然是中國的七倍以上。[101]

中國也並未尋求與美國相同的客戶群體。在全球一百九十五個國家中，自二〇〇一年以來，美國已向一百六十九個國家出售武器，而中國僅向八十二個國家銷售。[102] 即使在發展中國家這一領域（這通常是中國試圖與美國競爭的地方），美國依然佔據主導地位。從一九九五至二〇一五年，中國向發展中國家出口的傳統武器總額約為四百億美元，同期美國則高達二千八百五十億美元。[104] 全球前五大武器製造商皆為美國企業。雖然已有四家中國企業進入全球前二十五名，但它們無法對美國在武器市場的地位構成挑戰。[105] 以下**圖2.2**顯示了中國與美國軍售規模的巨大差距。

鑑於軍售被美國視為外交政策的有效工具，而中國雖然也具備生產武器的能力，但無法直接與美國競爭，那麼依據「竄起者策略」，如果美國軍售活動存在空隙，則利用策

新竄起者　102

圖 2.2　一九九〇年至二〇二二年美國與中國的軍售

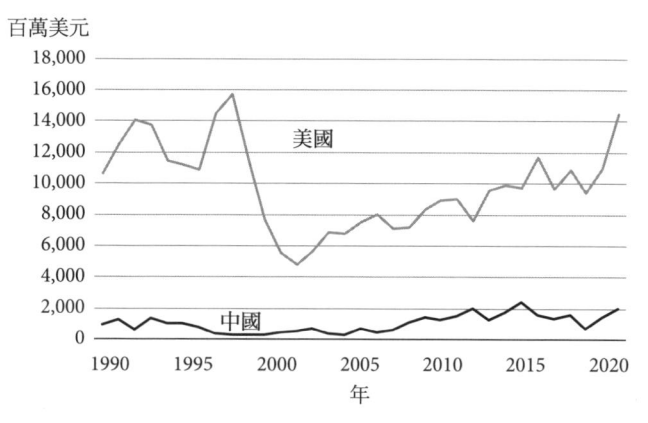

資料來源："SIPRI Arms Transfers Database," Stockholm International Peace Research Institute, https://www.sipri.org/databases/armstransfers.

是最佳選擇。在這方面，中國確實有機會，因為某些領域的競爭較為薄弱，使得中國製造的武器系統更具吸引力。首先，某些國家無力負擔美國武器，而且如果它們對美國的戰略重要性不高，就不太可能獲得美國提供的補貼、貸款、贈予或軍事援助。其次，市場會出現某些空隙是因為美國國內法限制向人權紀錄不佳的國家出售武器。最後，美國國內法也禁止出口特定類型的技術。

中國的軍售符合集中於競爭較弱市場的模式。孟加拉是全球最貧窮的國家之一，而其八成的武器進口自中國。其他買家，如巴基斯坦、緬甸和蘇丹，

103　第二章　中國外交政策中的模仿與利用策略

經濟狀況更為低迷。[107] 中國試圖利用這些軍售帶來的影響力,例如勸阻孟加拉與「四方安全對話」成員國合作——這個由印度、日本、美國和澳洲組成的聯盟,主要目的是應對中國在印太地區的擴張行為。[108] 中國也透過軍售來限制印度在該地區的影響力。

從一九九〇到二〇二二年,中國前四大武器買家中有三個:巴基斯坦、緬甸和伊朗,都不是自由國家。其中,美國對伊朗和緬甸兩國實施了某種形式的武器禁運。以緬甸為例,可以看出中國如何利用機會填補市場空缺。美國與歐盟在一九九〇年緬甸軍政府拒絕接受民主選舉結果,並將勝選的反對派領袖翁山蘇姬軟禁後,全面中斷與緬甸的國防合作。當年八月十日,中國第一批大型武器與彈藥就送達仰光。自此之後,中國逐步擴大對緬甸的軍售份額。二〇一四至二〇一九年間,中國供應了緬甸一半以上的主要武器進口。在拉丁美洲市場,中國百分之八十六的軍售流向一個國家:委內瑞拉,中國依賴該國的石油供應,同時委國也是美國武器禁運的對象。[109][110][111]

中國也利用了美國對某些技術出口的限制。根據《飛彈科技管制建制》(Missile Technology Control Regime) 的規定,美國對巡弋飛彈的出口有所限制,而長程無人飛行載具最初被美國法律視為巡弋飛彈的一種。然而,中國並未簽署該協議,因此不受這項

新竊起者　104

限制。112 即使美國在二〇〇二年修法放寬部分限制，但一系列國內法規、國際協議和先例仍然使美國難以向法國、日本、澳洲和英國等少數國家以外的市場出口無人機技術。113 這些限制為中國創造了一個絕佳的市場機會，使中國能夠向阿拉伯聯合大公國、沙烏地阿拉伯、埃及和塞爾維亞等國銷售無人機。二〇〇三至二〇一八年間，中國向十三個國家交付了一百八十一架無人機。115 在商用無人機市場上，中國企業大疆創新是全球領導品牌，二〇一七年時佔據全球市場百分之七十四的份額。116 俄羅斯和烏克蘭士兵都在戰場上使用小型消費級無人機進行偵察和監視，甚至投擲手榴彈攻擊毫無防備的敵軍。

透過這種利基市場的策略，中國成功取得一定程度的進展。從一九九〇到二〇二一年，中國的軍售額成長了百分之一百二十。117 中國與巴基斯坦、沙烏地阿拉伯、委內瑞拉和阿拉伯聯合大公國等國加強了關係，這些國家在其區域中扮演關鍵角色，同時也是中國主要的石油供應國。118 由於中國的手法較為謹慎，美國至今並未因此對中國施加重大制裁，儘管在某些情況下，美方有試圖減少中國銷售的效果。例如，歐巴馬和川普政府都曾放寬無人機出口管制，以便促進美方對外銷售。中國的這種方式尚未引發足以促使美國採取高代價應對措施的擔憂，可能是因為中國刻意避免觸發這類反應。例如，中國在美國對

105　第二章　中國外交政策中的模仿與利用策略

外部干預特別敏感的拉丁美洲市場，武器銷售比例僅約佔該地區軍購的百分之二一。（有趣的是，隨著中美競爭在近年升溫，中國銷往拉丁美洲的武器反而更少了。）儘管中國學者普遍認為中國在全球軍火市場上的影響力正在提升，並強化其地緣政治影響力，但他們對於公開討論這點依然相對保守與謹慎。120

中國的菁英階層也試圖將武器銷售政策在國內所帶來的成本降到最低。首先，中國並未在國內高調宣傳這項策略，部分原因是許多中國人將美國的軍售視為一種控制盟國、打壓對手、干預區域事務的工具——而中國共產黨有必要在國內與國際上展現出截然不同的形象。121 事實上，中國官方媒體經常公開批評美國是世界上最大的「戰爭販子」，並聲稱美國有強烈動機讓世界持續動盪，以服務美國國內軍工複合體的利益。122

出於國內政治上的考量，中國無法仿效美國在某些相關戰略上的做法，例如透過武器禁運來表達對特定政權及其政策（尤其是侵犯人權的政策）的反感。截至二〇二二年，美國針對八個國家實施武器禁運（白俄羅斯、中國、古巴、伊朗、緬甸、北韓、敘利亞與委內瑞拉），並對中國、俄羅斯和委內瑞拉實施三項與軍事用途及最終用戶相關的出口許可規定。123 相較之下，中國從未單方面對任何國家發起武器禁運，僅在某些情況下支持聯合

新窺起者　106

國對特定國家的武器禁運決議。¹²⁴整體而言，中國避免支持任何因人權問題而干涉內政視為正當化的政策，因為這類干涉若被視為合理，將會直接威脅到黨對國內的掌控。¹²⁵

總結來說，中國並未仿效這條美國建立權力的路徑，北京也尚未提出什麼創新的替代方案。相反地，中國採取的是「利用」策略，選擇在美國競爭較少的特定國家與特定技術領域中進行軍售。¹²⁶這種做法讓中國成為一個具有影響力、但仍屬次要的軍火供應者，並與那些對中國武器形成依賴的國家建立了某種影響力關係。

利用美國缺席的機會進行外交拓展

外交是建立國際實力與影響力的有效方式，這點幾乎無人能反駁。擴大與世界的外交往來，特別是雙邊互動，能支撐國家實力的各個面向；它既是實現外交政策目標的重要工具，也是一種和平解決「敵對利益衝突」的方式。¹²⁷相較於具威脅性的對外手段，外交較不具挑釁性。對中國而言，外交更有助於其戰略目標：降低美國對中國活動的反應程度。

不出所料，拓展外交關係成為中國在崛起過程中的首要任務之一。一九九六年，中共中央總書記江澤民宣示中國必須「走出去」，也就是要超越國界積極參與國際事務，以促進中國的經濟成長與發展。128中國的任務頗具挑戰性。從一九九〇到二〇一一年間，中國與三十四個國家建立了正式外交關係，其中包括像南韓這樣的重要國家。129中國在崛起過程中特別著重於投資建設外交網絡，尤其是在亞洲地區，如今中國在亞洲的外交網絡規模甚至已經略為超越美國。130

但故事不止於此。除了效能、安撫與效率這些因素之外，還有一個額外的因素促使中國超越模仿，轉向「利用」策略：那就是美國在外交接觸方面存在空隙。具體來說，中國將外交重點放在發展中國家，並且比起美國更頻繁地運用「主場外交」以及次國家級的接觸。

首先，中國積極拜訪周邊地區與發展中國家，這些地區往往被美國忽略。131舉例來說，美國領導人至今僅拜訪過非洲五十四個國家中的十六個（其中小布希總統造訪的國家最多，也僅有十一國）。相比之下，從二〇〇七到二〇一七年的十年間，中國高層領導人就對非洲的四十三個國家進行了七十九次訪問，其中包含非洲三十三個最不發達國家中的二十六個。133自二〇一三年以來，美國總統僅出訪南亞國家四次（其中兩次是印度，兩

新竄起者　108

次是阿富汗），而習近平除了三次訪問印度外，還去了巴基斯坦、孟加拉國與尼泊爾。[134]更明顯的是，從未有任何美國總統訪問過中亞地區，但習總書記多次造訪哈薩克、吉爾吉斯、塔吉克與烏茲別克。[135] 僅從二〇一三至二〇二〇年間，習近平就造訪了六大洲共六十九個國家，比他之前任何一位中國領導人都來得活躍。[136] 其中，四成的出訪地點是亞洲國家，而百分之三十三是與中國有海陸邊界的國家。相比之下，歐巴馬與川普總統百分之四十三點七的出訪是前往歐洲，主要集中在德國與英國。[137] 這樣的對比特別值得注意，因為在外交上，「出席」本身就代表了一種重視與承諾。

中國也更加重視主場外交。二〇一〇到二〇一九年間，來自亞洲、非洲、大洋洲、北美洲、南美洲與歐洲的領導人拜訪中國的次數，超過他們到美國訪問的次數。特別是在亞洲方面，亞洲領導人到中國的訪問達到二百八十七次，這是他們訪問美國次數的三倍以上。非洲領導人也訪問中國一百七十二次，遠高於訪問美國的八十三次。這代表一種中國在崛起過程中採取的新型實力積累手段。在二〇〇〇年代初期，情況還不是這樣，那時多數領導人仍偏好訪問美國。[140] 中國也建立了一系列區域論壇，來強化與那些在美國多邊外交中常被忽視的國家之間的協調合作。例如：與俄羅斯及中亞國家於二〇〇一年共同成立的上海合作組織；二〇〇〇年開始的中非合作論壇；二〇〇四年成立的中國—阿拉伯國家合作論壇；二〇一四年啟動的中國—拉丁美洲暨加勒比國家共同體論壇，以及二〇一二年與中東歐國家建立的多邊合作平台「十七加一」合作機制。

這些趨勢並非偶然，而是中國刻意部署的戰略，目的在於有效建立國力，同時降低外界的反彈。自二〇〇二年以來，無論是胡錦濤政府還是習近平政府，都提出了所謂的「全方位外交」，其外交方針可用一句話來概括：「大國是關鍵，周邊是首要，發展中國家是基礎，多邊是重要舞台。」141 習近平外交思想更是明確強調，中國應該轉向更專注與發展中國家的合作。142 根據一位中國著名的國際關係學者說法，中國選擇像中亞這類地區作為發展重心是明智的，因為這些地區不像傳統的戰略熱點（如東亞或中東）那樣已經被美國牢牢掌控，反而是「競爭規則尚未確立的地方」，143 更容易施展拳腳。中國戰略家普遍認為，聚焦於周邊與發展中國家，能削弱美國阻撓中國崛起的能力。144 前中國外交部長李肇星在二〇一四年就曾強調，非洲對中國的「長期政治支持」具有重大戰略價值。145

最後，習近平也重新強化了中國在另一個空隙領域的布局：次國家級外交，也就是在

新竄起者　110

中央政府以下層級所進行的外交活動。自二○一一年成立，但在二○二○年被美國基於「滲透疑慮」終止的中美省州長論壇，到中美省州立法機構合作論壇、中國與中東歐國家市長論壇以及中國官員與一帶一路沿線各城市、省、市長及州長的各種直接會晤。這些活動顯示，中國正大力發展次國家級的聯繫。無論是美國還是中國的評論人士都指出，這些次國家級外交往往能繞過與民主國家在中央層級上的意識形態分歧，轉而訴諸地方政府的經濟利益來建立合作。[146] 由於地方政府在決策上通常具有更多彈性、受到中央監管較少，中國因此更容易與他們打交道。例如，中國就曾透過與美國州長的交流，與多家美國大型太陽能公司達成合作，並逐步拿下了美國原本居於主導地位的太陽能市場。[147]

次國家級的交流也被用來推動北京的政治議程。這些交流往往隱含著政治上的期待與立場表態。舉例來說：所有與美國城市簽訂的姊妹市協議都包含一條款，規定雙方的活動應該要「根據美利堅合眾國與中華人民共和國建交的原則」來進行。這些原則可能會被用來阻止與台灣進行官方交流。又例如，澳洲維多利亞州州長簽署加入「一帶一路」協議，儘管該協議沒有任何具體的法律義務或契約責任，但也引發了爭議與關切。外界擔心，維州政府是否交換了一些「不透明的政治利益」，選擇支持中國共產黨的外交政策立[148]

111　第二章 中國外交政策中的模仿與利用策略

中國在次國家級外交上對於制度漏洞的利用起初確實頗為成功，但各國逐漸意識到這些手法，並開始設法限制北京的影響力。例如二〇二〇年，美國國務卿龐培歐終止了中美省州長論壇的夥伴關係，指控中方「直接且惡意地影響」美國各州與地方領導人。150 二〇二一年四月，由於內部審查警告該協議可能強化中國在當地的影響力，並削弱澳洲在該區域的戰略地位，澳洲聯邦政府撤銷了維多利亞州與中國簽訂的「一帶一路」協議。二〇二二年七月，一份美國情報報告指出，北京正利用這些次國家級的論壇，向州與地方政府官員施壓，進而在美國境內施展影響力。151

鑑於美國在某些地區的缺席，以及對次國家級外交缺乏關注，中國在過去幾年中，幾乎可以說是在毫無對手的賽場上進行公共外交，鞏固其影響力。152 這些區域的競爭相對薄弱對中國來說非常關鍵，因為中國的外交能力其實並不優於美國。在高層會談中，大多數中國官員仍嚴格遵守事先準備好的講稿，這樣的方式限制了坦誠的交流，也可能妨礙建立有效外交網絡的努力。153 儘管許多國家不願在北京與華盛頓之間選邊站，但中國在海外越來越大的存在感，也開始在一些國家引起反彈。以非洲為例，一份由美國智庫蘭德公司

場。149

發布的報告發現,「非洲的工會、民間團體以及其他社會群體批評中國企業存在勞工條件差、環境破壞嚴重以及造成當地就業機會流失等問題」。154 總結來說,多數國家對美國的參與持歡迎甚至偏好的態度。換言之,如果美國在這些外交領域能夠更積極的投入,中國將更難在這些空間與美國競爭。

但中國在外交實力上崛起的故事,還沒結束。光靠模仿和利用還不足以讓中國成為全球強權。但中國無法完全仿效美國,其實也並不想完全仿效。二〇一六年,國務委員戴秉國曾表示:「不管中國發展得多好,都不會取代美國⋯⋯沒有人能取代美國成為世界第一,也沒有人能阻止中國的和平崛起或復興。」155 中國的目標是取代(displace)而不是複製(replace)美國。而要達到這個目標,用新的方式、在新的領域展開競爭,正是關鍵所在。

第三章

中國外交政策中的創新作為

一九七四年四月,中國國務院副總理鄧小平在聯合國發表了一場頗具震撼力的演說,其中包含了一句出人意料的話:「中國永遠不稱霸。」接著他提出了一個問題:「什麼是霸權?」他的回答是:「霸權就是帝國主義國家,到處侵略、干涉、控制、顛覆、掠奪別的國家。」他接著表示,如果中國政府哪一天也幹出這些事,那麼其他國家完全可以聯合中國人民一起反對它。1 透過這種帶有標誌性的修辭風格,鄧小平清楚表明,中國的意圖是要走與美國和蘇聯不同的道路。

鄧小平的這番宣示顯示出,「走自己的路」早就是中國對外政策的一個核心元素,歷屆領導人也都延續了這個方向。江澤民的創新表現在於推動「戰略夥伴關係」的建立;胡錦濤則提出了「和諧世界」和「中國和平發展」的概念。2 到了習近平時代,他強調中國必須「明確表達出外交觀與行動模式有別於傳統西方強國」。3 根據中共官方的說法,中國「獨特的外交風格」是透過實踐來推動創新,不斷在國際舞台上做出新嘗試,開創新平台、解鎖新範式,並積極推動新的國際議程與倡議,倡導建立新的國際規則。4

這些並不只是中共為了在國內樹立形象而發表的宏大宣言。實際上,種種現實因素也促使中國嘗試用不同於傳統方式來建立外交實力。本章探討的正是這些具創新精神的外交

新竄起者　116

行動。具體來說，中國刻意避開了美國在外交上常用的幾條老路，例如結盟、成為各國首選的外部安全夥伴，以及推動他國採用美國的治理模式。北京認為，若沿用美國的這些策略，不僅會激起美國更高的威脅感知，還無法發揮中國自身的競爭優勢。雖然美國戰略本身也存在一些空白，但那些空白領域對中國來說未必能帶來實質回報。因此，北京選擇了另闢蹊徑來累積影響力，包括：打造「戰略夥伴關係」、成為他國首選的「內部安全」夥伴，以及在政體議題上採取中立立場。

這些具創新精神的外交策略，是中國能在外交實力上迅速追趕美國的原因之一。不可否認的是，中國在崛起的前二十年間，比較成功地避免引發外界的強烈反彈；相比之下，習近平時代常被稱為「戰狼外交」的外交風格，則引起了更多的關注與警惕。但即使如此，這些不安的情緒尚未轉化為實質性的阻礙。即便中國的外交強硬程度明顯提升，各國仍然不願意真正選邊站，公開與中國對立。美國也還沒有實施任何類似「圍堵中國」的政策；事實上，從二〇一一到二〇二〇年，美國對中國的對外投資與證券持有額還翻了一倍以上。[5] 即便許多國家對中國的國內政治提出批評，北京的影響力仍足以壓制具體行動。例如，儘管中國在新疆問題上遭到種族滅絕的指控，但最終真正對二〇二二年北京冬季奧

117　第三章　中國外交政策中的創新作為

戰略夥伴關係：中國對美國盟友體系的回應

運進行外交抵制的，僅有美國、英國、澳洲與加拿大四國，而且他們也只是拒絕派出官方代表，運動員依舊照常參賽。

美國的戰略家、學者與政府官員雖意見各異，但在一點上高度一致：美國的盟邦網路是美國國力的核心之一。多數人認為，這個同盟體系是「二戰以來美國外交政策中最持久、最成功的元素之一」。6 這套體系的好處並不僅限於軍事合作；盟友們會在國際機構中支持美國的立場、協調發展援助政策，並透過貿易與投資協助彼此經濟繁榮。7 美國的盟邦還會為駐軍「買單」，支付美軍駐紮在當地的相關費用。這讓美軍得以用遠低於英國殖民帝國或是蘇聯在鄰近國家多次被抵制的占領行動的成本來維持全球存在。8

既然同盟關係是美國權力的主要來源之一，那它似乎會成為一個值得中國仿效的目標。但事情沒那麼簡單，中國的學者與決策者的結論認為，尋求建立同盟體系，反而會讓北京在與美國的競爭中處於劣勢。首先，很多人質疑對中國而言建立同盟網路是否真的有

新竄起者　118

效。當前的戰略環境和美國二戰後所面對的局勢完全不同。當年,美國透過同盟外交成功崛起為強權,並擊敗蘇聯,但中國學界普遍認為,冷戰後的時代背景已經不再適合這種戰略。9 正如一位中國學者簡明扼要的闡述:「同盟外交已經不合時宜。」10 研究中國問題的學者亞當・利夫(Adam Liff)也同意這一點,他寫道:「美國的同盟體系起源於某些歷史上獨特的地緣政治條件,而這些條件很難再次出現。」11

第二,當前並沒有太多值得中國「鑽空子」的同盟缺口。鑑於中國的遠征軍力有限,且與亞洲多數美國盟友的歷史關係緊張,要挖角美國的合作夥伴根本不太可能。這使得中國可追求的同盟選項非常有限。12 像俄羅斯和印度這樣的大國,作為潛在夥伴其實並不理想,因為俄羅斯不願讓出主導地位,而印度對中國則充滿不信任與敵意。13 俄羅斯入侵烏克蘭更凸顯了與這種難以預測的國家建立緊密關係所帶來的風險。14 中國也可以嘗試對一群較小的國家提供安全保證,組成某種聯盟,但大多數中國分析人士認為,這樣的策略對提升中國的安全並沒有太大幫助。15 換句話說,去爭取那些美國沒特別經營的國家當盟友,對中國的整體國力提升幫助不大,反而可能帶來更多麻煩。

反對中國建立同盟體系最有力的論點之一,是這樣的做法將會疏遠美國及其盟友,特

第三章　中國外交政策中的創新作為

別是當中國與那些對美國懷有敵意的國家達成協議時。[16] 中國在過去幾十年的崛起，恰好必須強化與那些深度整合進美國同盟體系的國家的關係，因為這些國家往往是世界上最富有、最具影響力的國家。[17] 簡單來說，中國的崛起必須仰賴這些貿易與投資關係。[18] 如果中國一心一意想要打造自己的同盟網路，不但會破壞與非同盟國家的合作關係，也會讓中國更難處理那些在同盟體系內、卻對中國利益造成損害的國家。[19]

因此，中國並未模仿美國的同盟路線。相反地，中國領導人一直以來都自豪且有意識地拒絕建立軍事同盟。美國目前擁有超過五十項防衛協議，而中國只有一項符合傳統軍事同盟定義的防禦性協議──一九六一年與北韓簽署的《中朝友好合作互助條約》，而且這項條約的誕生是在中國崛起之前的時期。[20] 即使中國與俄羅斯關係密切，北京也無意被捲入俄國的境外冒險行動。為了讓立場更明確，中國外交部長在二○二三年一月稍微下調了與俄關係的定義，從「沒有止境、沒有禁區、沒有上限」調整為「不結盟、不對抗、不針對第三方」。[21]

鑑於缺乏可利用的缺口，加上建立自己同盟體系所帶來的負面影響，「竄起者策略」預期中國會採取創新的路徑：也就是運用自身的競爭優勢，既不疏遠其他國家、也避免引

新竄起者 120

發威脅感，同時又能確保北京在雙邊關係中建立足夠的影響力來保護其國內利益。22 北京的答案就是「戰略夥伴關係」——這是一條進入強權階層的新途徑。23

所謂的戰略夥伴關係，是「圍繞某種總體（安全）目標所建立的系統原則（例如倡導多極世界），而非針對特定任務，如嚇阻或對抗某個敵對國家……這類關係通常是非正式的，承諾成本低，而非透過某種正式的同盟條約來規範彼此必須採取的具體行動。」24 北京善用這類關係，來制度化、規範並緩解與重要全球角色的關係，同時協調外交政策，以推動中國偏好的國際準則，例如「不干涉內政」原則。25 依據前國務院總理溫家寶的說法，這種夥伴關係「超越了意識形態與社會制度的差異，不受偶發性事件影響。」26 從北京的角度來看，建立戰略夥伴關係代表「夥伴國願意承認中國崛起的正當性，管控分歧以持續提升雙邊關係，並在國際場域協調推進共同利益主張」。27

自從一九九三年首次達成此類協議以來，「夥伴外交」就成為中國外交中最具代表性的一個面向。江澤民在一九九〇年代末期首先與多數主要強權建立戰略夥伴關係；接著胡錦濤將重心放在對中國崛起具有不成比例影響力的國家，例如中東地區的國家。習近平則更進一步的把焦點放在中國周邊國家，特別是「一帶一路」倡議的參與國。28

中國並不是第一個使用「戰略夥伴關係」的國家——歐盟就與十個國家建立了此類關係。然而，中國的創新之處在於將「戰略夥伴關係」作為其外交政策的核心架構。根據一項對中國相關著作的回顧研究指出，中國把這一策略視為「管理對外關係的主導工具，以及代替競爭性聯盟思維的一種方式」。29 戰略夥伴關係並不只是換個名稱的準軍事聯盟，事實上，中國有多達百分之七十五的夥伴協議中完全不包含任何安全合作條款。30 中國還以前所未有的規模推行此項策略：截至二〇二二年，已有一百二十八個國家的經濟與政治目標，透過這類夥伴協議與中國掛勾。**圖3.1** 與**圖3.2** 展示了中國在過去三十年崛起過程中，對這個獨特外交架構的依賴程度不斷上升。31

這種創新的外交策略帶來了幾個優勢。首先，它讓中國能善用自身作為經濟強權的競爭優勢，來降低外界對共產黨的批評。戰略夥伴關係建立起一個明確的連結：若某個國家選擇在像是人權或台灣等敏感議題上對北京施壓，那它就有可能會損失與中國的貿易與投資機會。事實上，所有戰略夥伴關係協議都提到了貿易、投資與經濟合作，以及在聯合國中的合作；而除了三份協議之外，其餘全部都包含了支持北京對台灣立場的條款。32 正如一位中國學者所解釋的，這種外交策略讓中國能夠爭取那些希望從中國崛起中受益國家的

新竄起者　122

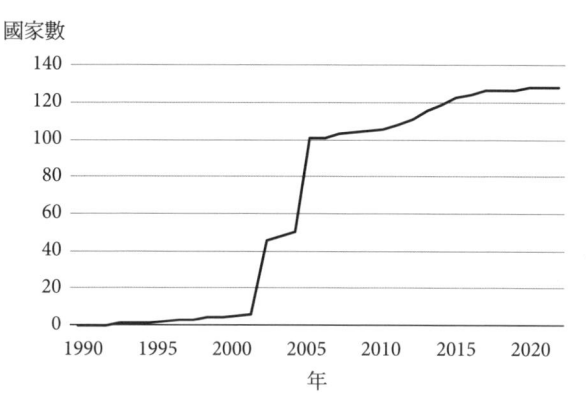

圖 3.1　與中國有戰略夥伴關係的國家數

完整數據見 www.orianaskylarmastro.com/upstart

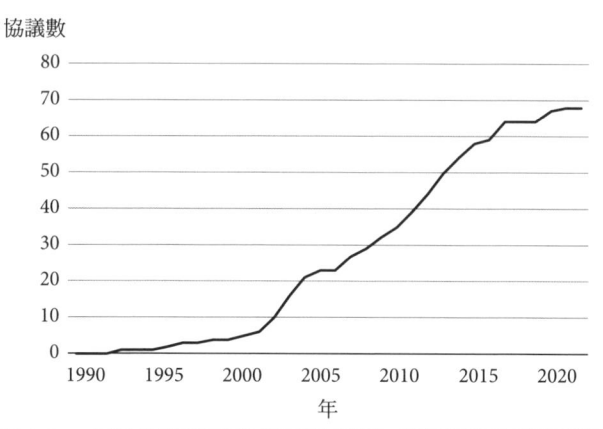

圖 3.2　中國的戰略夥伴關係協議數（雙邊與多邊協議）

完整數據見 www.orianaskylarmastro.com/upstart

支持，同時也削弱了美國的反制力道。[33]

戰略夥伴關係也讓中國得以在開發中國家中展開競爭，而中國領導人早就認定，這些國家是尚未被充分開發的政治實力與經濟機會來源。[34] 中國學者認為，北京所主張的「不結盟、不對抗、不針對第三方國家」的原則，相較於美國那種開發中國家來說更具吸引力。[35] 通過譴責助長「霸權主義、擴張主義與強權政治」的聯盟體系，中國得以與發展中國家形成共同立場，從而增強其全球影響力。[36] 例如，有一位中國學者分析指出，中國與阿爾及利亞、埃及、沙烏地阿拉伯、伊朗、阿拉伯聯合大公國、以色列與土耳其等國建立的戰略夥伴關係，客觀上「稀釋了其他強權在中東的影響力」。[37] 資料顯示，與非經濟合作暨發展組織（non-OECD）國家建立戰略夥伴關係後，雙邊貿易流量平均增長，這些國家在聯合國投票與中國的合作程度也顯著提升。[38]

或許最重要的是，戰略夥伴關係讓中國能夠與比傳統軍事同盟更多的國家建立緊密關係。這種關係不會限制中國的夥伴必須具備意識形態上的相似性，或擁有相同的政治體制、與美國的關係、或經濟發展水準。[39] 事實上，相似的國內政治特性、共同的威脅感知，甚至是意識形態的一致性，都不是中國建立戰略夥伴關係的關鍵指標。[40] 根據自由之

新竄起者　124

家（Freedom House）的分類，大約百分之三十八點五的中國夥伴國被評為「自由」、百分之三十二點六六為「部分自由」、百分之三十九點八四為「不自由」。41 中國甚至成功說服大約一半的美國盟國與其簽署戰略夥伴協議。中國也看準與中等實力國家深化關係的機會，例如紐西蘭、澳洲與芬蘭等，這些國家在安全領域上比較有彈性，也對加強文化與經濟聯繫持開放態度。42 透過這種方式，中國甚至能同時維持與敵對雙方的良好關係，例如伊朗與沙烏地阿拉伯、北韓與南韓、巴基斯坦與印度，以及以色列與巴勒斯坦。43

這並不是說中國的夥伴外交就完全沒有問題。中國與俄羅斯的「新時代全面戰略協作夥伴關係」，可說是中國最深厚的戰略夥伴關係之一，在俄羅斯入侵烏克蘭後，確實為中國的外交政策帶來了麻煩。但中國創新型的策略，比起傳統同盟更能靈活處理這些權衡。

在俄羅斯這個案例中，儘管美國對中國在這場戰爭採取的消極立場感到不滿，但中國與俄羅斯的友好關係卻仍未導致中國與歐洲夥伴的關係破裂。舉例來說，二〇二三年四月，法國總統馬克宏訪問北京，尋求加強法中之間的商業合作；而早在二〇二二年底，德國政府就表示，德國無意與其最大貿易夥伴中國「脫鉤」。相比之下，如果中國與俄羅斯結成軍事同盟，那麼歐洲國家的安全考量可能就會超過與中國維持良好經貿關係的需求。

中國的這項戰略有一個明顯的失敗，那就是無法說服美國同意建立全面戰略夥伴關係。一九九〇年代後期，柯林頓總統曾與江澤民討論過這個可能性，儘管小布希總統在二〇〇〇年競選時曾將中國定義為「戰略競爭對手」，他與江澤民仍在二〇〇一年達成共識，要建立「建設性的合作關係」。44 然而，在接下來的十二年裡，這段關係始終未能提升為全面戰略夥伴關係。

二〇一三年，習近平試圖重新推動所謂的「新型大國關係」這個概念。在加州陽光之地那個輕鬆、非正式的場域中，習近平試圖向歐巴馬總統推銷這個想法。45 儘管多位歐巴馬政府官員曾用「新型大國關係」來描述中美關係，但日本對華盛頓示警，認為中國的目的是透過這個框架來合理化自己與美國平起平坐的地位，藉此影響其他國家與中國互動的方式，同時幫助習近平在國內建立民族自豪感與政治資本。人們擔心這將助長中國美國在亞洲軍事上邊緣化、最終取而代之達成成為區域霸權的目標。46 中國也顯然試圖以類似手法來限制美國，就如同它對其他國家的策略一樣──將密切的政治與經濟關係與接受中國的「核心利益」掛鉤。47

有些人可能會提出另一種解釋，認為中國的做法純粹是由意識形態所驅動的⋯「中國

新竄起者　126

共產黨和解放軍對結盟的意識形態與歷史根深蒂固，這種反感在他們對當代國際發展的解讀中展現得淋漓盡致，也不太可能輕易改變。」48 中國與蘇聯的結盟經驗曾是一場失敗，主要源於赫魯雪夫與毛澤東之間的意識形態分歧，這讓許多中國領導人，尤其是鄧小平，對於透過結盟作為爭取全球影響力的路線產生強烈懷疑。49 不過，中國國內並不認為這是唯一、甚至是主導中國領導人思考的因素。中國領導人在過去也曾放棄長久以來的傳統做法，只要這麼做有助於增強國內與國際的實力。中國領導人在過去也曾放棄長久以來的傳統做法，只要這麼做有助於增強國內與國際的實力（例如在吉布地建立海外軍事基地、加入國際機構，都是典型例子）。而單靠意識形態的解釋，也無法有效說明中國接下來會怎麼做。從「窜起者策略」的角度來看，中國更可能選擇一條能發揮自身競爭優勢、降低威脅形象，並與美國路線形成鮮明對比的路徑。在這些條件下，建立以經濟連結為核心、而非安全同盟為基礎的框架是一個頗富吸引力的選項。

中國成為「內部安全合作夥伴」：中國對美國海外軍事訓練的回應

美國對外政策中有一個密切相關但又相對獨立的支柱，就是致力於成為各國「外部安全合作夥伴的首選」。50 美國透過各種手段，包括聯合軍事演習，訓練外國軍隊，這些被認為是「美國在安全合作領域稱霸的基石」。當初的目的是對抗蘇聯在歐洲的影響力，但隨著歐洲逐步復甦，該計畫的重心便轉向拉丁美洲、太平洋地區、中東和非洲。52

如今，美國在與中國的區域競爭中積極運用這項競爭優勢，透過加強與區域內國家的安全合作，不僅包括其傳統盟友如南韓、日本、菲律賓與澳洲，也涵蓋其他區域重要國家如印度，以及東南亞的合作夥伴，如越南、印尼和馬來西亞。根據統計，美國國防部與國務院每年共同編列約一百九十億美元的預算，用於訓練外國軍隊。53 藉由協助這些國家提升軍事素養與作戰能力，美國能夠在降低自身防務負擔的同時，也建立良好的外交關係，從而以更低成本保障其海外利益。54 有研究指出，美國的援助計畫也成功地將過去屬於華沙公約組織的國家「融入」美國主導的國際體系，不僅促進歐洲的穩定，也提升了這些國家的內部穩定性。55

儘管這種做法在美國外交戰略中至關重要且卓有成效，但有幾個因素讓中國卻步，避免進行仿效。首先，中國要取代美國的角色並不容易。中國人民解放軍自一九七九年以來

新竄起者　128

就沒有參與過實戰,這種缺乏實戰經驗的情況,使得解放軍在傳統軍事作戰的訓練與顧問角色上,相較於經驗豐富、戰場歷練完整的美軍,吸引力明顯不足。此外,針對依賴美國提供防禦保障的國家進行外交拉攏並不會奏效,因為中國既不會提供正式的防禦條約,也不具備延伸嚇阻的條件。若中國試圖直接與美國競爭這一角色,不但可能徒勞無功,還可能引發美國的反彈,一旦美國認為中國試圖取代其關鍵地位,或是發現中國在強化某些「錯誤」國家(即那些可能威脅到美國利益的國家)的軍力。

因此,華府成為「外部安全夥伴」首選的戰略並未遭遇來自中國的激烈競爭。儘管中國在二〇一九年的國防白皮書中自豪地表示,從二〇一二到二〇一九年共參與了二十場聯合演習,但單就二〇一八年而言,北約一個年度就進行了一百零三場類似演習。[56] 同樣在二〇一八年,中國參與了六十場軍事演習,並進行了三十一次港口訪問。而與此同時,美國海軍第七艦隊(負責印太區域)每年平均會參與約一百場雙邊或多邊軍演,並進行大約二百次港口訪問。[57] 即使是在非洲地區,美國在訓練交流與夥伴關係方面也遠遠超過中國。[58]

中國之所以未給人仿效美國模式的印象,不僅在於規模差異,更關鍵在於軍演本質的

129　第三章　中國外交政策中的創新作為

區別。北京運用這項工具的目的，與其說是推廣軍事專業能力或提升參演國戰力，不如說是為了傳遞安全保證。二〇〇三至二〇一八年間，中國與六十三個國家所舉行的三百一十場聯合軍演中，多數屬非戰鬥性多邊演習，且美國竟位列前五大參與國。[59] 解放軍於二〇一〇至二〇一九年間參與的聯合演習，主要對象更是美國在亞洲的五大盟邦。[60] 值得注意的是，中國在這些合作中從不提供作戰顧問支援、直接行動或防務體制建設，而是聚焦於融資與基礎設施建設、專業軍事教育、情報監偵等領域──特別是針對那些較少獲得美方支持的國家。[61]

因此，在這樣的條件下，中國採取創新路線是合情合理的。從中國的競爭優勢以及中國共產黨維持統治的需求來看，中國確實在一個領域上比美國更具優勢──那就是「內部安全」。這不令人意外，畢竟中國是一個壓制內部異議的威權國家，並投入了大量資源來強化其內部維穩系統。中國在內部安全上的支出比軍事支出還多約二成。[62] 中共打造了所謂的「防火長城」，透過網路封鎖來控制國內資訊流通，包括封鎖像是Facebook和Twitter這類可能威脅政權的外國科技平台。中國還建立了一個高度發展的監控國家，這個體系結合了人工智慧、臉部辨識技術、生物辨識、監視攝影機以及大數據分析，能快速

新竄起者　130

對個人進行資料建檔與分類、追蹤行動、預測活動，並對被視為威脅的人事物進行預防性打擊，無論是在現實世界還是網路空間。63 這種控制的程度幾乎到了荒謬的地步。舉例來說，二○二○年一月，蘇州市的官員就使用街頭攝影機與臉部辨識技術，公開張貼穿著睡衣外出的居民的照片與個人資訊，作為一項「公開羞辱」的宣導行動。64

中國在成為「內部安全合作夥伴首選國」這條創新型戰略路線上的做法十分廣泛。從排練正步的卡達士兵到中非共和國的總統衛隊，中國已經訓練了許多國家的內部安全部隊。65 為了掌握這些訓練行動，作者建立了一份原創資料庫，內容涵蓋了警務、鑑識、網路安全、軍事與海巡等訓練項目。其中，最常見的類別是軍事與警察培訓。迄今，中國已為一百一十個國家培訓警務人員、移民官員、總統衛隊等安全人員，範圍遍及近四分之三的非洲國家、超過三分之二的美洲國家，以及超過一半的亞洲國家，都曾接受中國的警察訓練。還有大約有四分之一的歐盟成員國也接受過某種形式的中國執法訓練，包括保加利亞、克羅埃西亞、法國、義大利、拉脫維亞與西班牙等國。66

中國於二○○二年開始制度化的推動相關建設，在北京附近的廊坊成立了亞洲規模最大的警察培訓基地「中國維和員警培訓中心」，專門為聯合國維和任務培訓安全力量。67

131　第三章　中國外交政策中的創新作為

截至二〇二〇年十月，該校下屬的中國維和警察培訓中心已舉辦八十八期國際警務培訓課程，並派遣師資赴多國開展培訓項目。68 公安部直屬的中國人民公安大學同樣設有外警培訓項目，二〇一九年即舉辦三十一期培訓班，培養六百七十七名外籍學員。69 二〇一七至二〇一八年間，河南警察學院、江蘇警官學院等較小的省級警察學校，以及鐵道警察學院等專業院校也相繼啟動國際執法培訓項目。70

中國海警是全球規模最大的海警部隊，正積極擴展與俄羅斯、法國、印尼、馬來西亞與巴基斯坦的合作夥伴關係，藉此打造區域性乃至全球性的海上執法網絡。例如在二〇一七年，中國與非洲、加勒比海與東南亞地區的二十六個國家推動海警合作。到了二〇二〇年，中國海警仍持續與菲律賓進行合作，舉辦了「海上搜救與消防聯合演習」，地點律賓的海警部門互訪，並舉行聯合海上訓練演習（雖然雙方關係近年來惡化）。71 中國也與菲在南海馬尼拉外海，旨在強化參與國在海上的協同作業能力。72 中國海警也積極參與「東協地區論壇災害救援演習」，並曾於二〇一五年與馬來西亞共同主辦。73 除東南亞外，中國海警也與南韓海警進行教育交流與聯合演習。74

在大戰略布局中，尋找有效又高效的方式來保護自身利益至關重要。美國訓練外國軍隊，部分目的就是為了降低自身的國防負擔；同樣地，中國訓練外國的內部安全部隊，也是為了用最低成本保護自己的利益。例如，二〇一一年十二月，因應毒品暴力事件，中國在雲南設立了「湄公河聯合巡邏指揮中心」，持續與寮國、緬甸與泰國共同展開沿岸聯合巡邏行動。75 至二〇二〇年十二月，四國已經在湄公河上合作執行了一百次聯合巡邏任務。76 這些反毒巡邏行動大多是出於中國自身的利益考量，目的是防止毒品與犯罪分子流入中國西南地區。若是其他國家也在採用類似的內部安全措施，他們就會更不容易對中國的相關政策提出批評。

中國也開設了一系列有關在「新媒體」上控制資訊（即網路審查）的訓練課程，已吸引來自至少三十六個國家的政府官員參加。77 相較於直接關閉網路，中共更偏好透過讓資訊變得難以取得的方式進行控制。這類隱性審查技術在很多情況下比起直接切斷資訊更有效，因為使用者往往不容易察覺。78 中共中央對外聯絡部也曾派遣來自新華社等國營媒體集團的代表，為其他國家的國營媒體提供訓練。79 中國也向其他國家提供關於如何制定網路安全立法的建議，藉此為推行其做法鋪路。80 二〇一四年，中國創立了「世界互聯網大會」，作為各國探討網路政策和實務的平台。到了二〇二二年，中國更進一步在北京創立

133　第三章　中國外交政策中的創新作為

了「世界互聯網論壇大會」，根據自由之家的說法，這個論壇可能讓中國政府有機會推廣其以國家為中心、帶有威權特色的網路治理模式。[81]

各國紛紛爭相尋求中國在內部安全這一新前線上的專業知識、技術指導與物資支援。[82]像華為與中興通訊這些中國企業——也就是美國長期制裁的對象——正是內部監控科技的領頭羊。[83]二〇一二年時，全球僅有二十個國家採用了中國的監控技術；但到了二〇一八年，這個數字翻了四倍。自二〇〇八年以來，已有至少七十五個國家採用中國的監控技術，主要用途包括：智慧城市／安全城市平台、人臉識別系統，以及智慧警務。[84]中國國有的軍民融合科技企業海康威視以及華為，則是領先全球的5G技術供應商之一。[85]超過一半的這些中國製的設備不僅吸引威權政權，連許多先進民主國家也紛紛導入。封閉型威權國家僅有百分之三十七使用，而選舉型／競爭型威權國家則有百分之五十。[86]雖然美國及其盟友如加拿大、南韓、澳洲、英國與日本並未採用中國的內部安全技術，但值得注意的是，美國的其他盟國：例如菲律賓、英國、法國、德國、西班牙和義大利卻都採用了這些技術。[87]

中國在監控科技領域擁有競爭優勢，部分原因是其龐大的國內市場（截至二〇一九

新竊起者　134

年，全球約七點七億支監視攝影機中，有超過一半設置在中國）。88 但有證據顯示，這些發展並不單純是出於商業考量。中國政府對提供內部安全支援的企業給予各種支持。例如，中國商務部會直接出資支付培訓計畫的費用，有時甚至會補貼中國企業，進一步提高它們進入小型、服務不足市場的意願。中國企業隨後會以大幅折扣價格向開發中國家提供設備，經常以數據存取權作為交換，從而換取優惠貸款條件。89 而所謂的「國家冠軍」企業，也就是那些被政府視為能推動更宏大國家利益的成功企業，往往能輕易取得融資與政府補助。例如華為在二〇一八年就獲得了二點二三億美元的政府補助。90

總的來說，中國透過成為各國「內部安全首選夥伴」，成功建立國際影響力。其培訓計畫不僅強化了外國執法機構保護中共海外利益的能力，更在更高層次上為中國的國家安全與執法立場爭取國際支持。91 中國不只利用這一策略來增強與民主國家及威權政權的政治、軍事與經濟關係，它在人工智慧監控領域的主導地位，更讓中國在這些關鍵領域的規範制定上，擁有比美國及其他民主國家更大的影響力。這種創新型的戰略，也讓中國得以主導該產業的發展方向，進而賦予中國企業經濟上的競爭優勢。92

135　第三章　中國外交政策中的創新作為

政權中立：中國對美國推動民主政策的回應

推廣民主，換句話說就是「旨在鼓勵他國轉型為民主或改善其民主制度的外交政策行動」，自二戰結束以來一直是美國外交政策的核心特徵。自冷戰結束後，「代議政府能回應人民的需求，較不可能對鄰國發動侵略行為」以及「民主制度更有能力支撐經濟自由並促進穩定」這類理念，已經成為美國對外政策的基本信念。93 老布希、柯林頓與小布希三位總統皆將推廣民主列為其外交政策的主要支柱。歐巴馬總統在其第一份《國家安全戰略》中，也強調推廣民主是美國重要的價值觀。而拜登總統則選擇聚焦於「強化民主」，優先協助已經是民主國家的鞏固體制，而不是鼓勵推翻舊政權的民主革命。

實際上，美國在冷戰結束後推動民主的作法，大多透過對外援助來進行。每年約有二十億美元透過美國國務院、美國國際開發署、國家民主基金會及其他機構投入民主推廣相關計畫。美國國防部的一些計畫也可被歸類為推廣民主的一環；在二〇二一財政年度，該部門編列了超過七十五億美元的相關預算。95 除了官方援助，美國還曾使用祕密行動、軍事干預以及選舉介入等手段來推動民主。根據統計，從一九四六到二〇〇〇年間，美國曾干預了八十一場外國選舉。96 從一九四八到二○一七年，美國共進行了二百三十四次軍事干預，其中部分是以民主的名義進行。97

推動民主的成效可以說是毀譽參半。美國國際開發署於二○○六年委託的一項研究顯示，其民主推廣活動對民主發展有顯著的正面影響。98 到了二○○○年，全球已有超過一半的人口生活在民主政體之下，這一比例為史上最高，許多人認為這歸功於美國的努力。99 然而，自二○○五年以來，民主開始出現倒退現象，政治權利與公民自由下滑的國家數量，超過了權利擴張的國家數量。100 自二○○六年起，「選舉型民主國家」的總數再無淨增長，一直在一百一十四至一百一十九個之間徘徊，約佔全球國家的六成。101 部分問題在於阿富汗與伊拉克戰爭後，民主推廣政策已與災難性的軍事干預產生聯結。

毫無疑問，中國不可能仿效民主化，因為這會對中共的統治構成直接威脅。但中國有自己的模式可供推廣。所謂的「中國模式」在過去十年間逐漸演變，主要是指一種威權資本主義，也就是「強勢政府與市場經濟之間的相互關係」。102 這個模式的關鍵組成包括：拒絕多黨制與政府三權分立制度，以及在政治上有利時可因地制宜地調整或與其他意識形態融合。103 在經濟層面上，遵循中國模式的國家可能會選擇性地融入全球經濟體系，同時

137　第三章　中國外交政策中的創新作為

推動以基礎建設為導向的發展策略。104

即使是在推廣自身體制這一方面,中國也面臨不小的仿效阻力。中國的戰略專家普遍認為,將中國模式強加於他國、甚至試圖推翻民主政權,將是一種既昂貴又適得其反的競爭方式。畢竟,相較於威權國家,民主國家通常更穩定、更繁榮。105 如果中國公開推行「推廣威權體制」的政策,勢必會立即疏遠那些富裕且強大的民主國家。中國十大貿易夥伴中有八個是民主國家;六成的中國戰略夥伴也是民主政體。106 正如中國問題專家黎安友(Andrew Nathan)簡明扼要指出:「試圖破壞一個外國民主政權,從商業角度來看,成本遠高於其可能帶來的利益。」107 更複雜的是,美國的戰略是建立在「民主世界更安全」這個前提之上,因此中國若刻意推廣威權體制,勢必會立刻被視為一種威脅。

除此之外,中國學界也普遍認為,美國推廣自身體制的方式並非建立與維持影響力的有效途徑。將經濟政治體制強加於他國,不僅成本高昂、執行困難,更難以真正贏取各國對其目標的支持。108 中國學者也指出,不論是美國的模式,或是中國自己的模式,都不具備普世適用性。109 正如一位學者所說,中國的「一黨領導體制」對於中國而言,是實現政策高效執行與連貫性的必要條件。110 但更廣泛的共識是,中國的威權資本主義體制難以被

新竄起者　138

其他國家複製,特別是那些政府控制力較弱、資源不足、又沒有類似共產黨這樣的執政組織的國家。111

由於在這種情況下,模仿策略不但具威脅性且成效不彰,「竊起者策略」預期中國會採取創新途徑來累積實力。事實上,中國確實並未試圖讓世界按照自己的樣貌重塑。政治學者賽瓦・古尼茨基(Seva Gunitsky)於二〇一八年指出:「迄今為止,中國是繼荷蘭黃金時代以來,第一個不進行意識形態傳教的強權。」112 中國領導人本身早就聲稱,無意輸出中國模式。鄧小平曾主張:「各國只能根據自己的實際情況來發展自己的發展戰略、方法和途徑……只有一種模式是行不通的。」113 雖然胡錦濤曾提出要向世界推廣中國模式,但他也表示接受不同的發展模式。與美國形成鮮明對比的是,習近平在二〇一七年明確表示,中國「不輸出」自身模式,也「不要求」其他國家「照搬」中國的發展方式。115 中國學者也經常強調,中國從未倡導自己的模式應被普遍接受,也未曾要求他國複製中國的做法。116

中國並未試圖推廣威權資本主義,而是透過推動「政權中立」的外交政策進行創新。中國所傳達的訊息是:每個國家都有權依據自身情況決定其治理方式,任何強加於人的做

139　第三章　中國外交政策中的創新作為

法,都是對該國作為國際社會平等一員的不尊重。[117]對中國領導人與學者而言,中國「獨特風格」的外交政策特色,就是反對僵化地套用某一種特定的哲學觀點,也反對強加偏好的發展道路與政治體系給他國。[118]北京主張,每個國家的發展路徑應當因地制宜,需要經過試驗與調整──就如俗語所說的「摸著石頭過河」。而更重要的是,國家應當享有免於大國干涉的自由。[119]

這樣的理念或許容易被認為是中國對外宣傳的一部分,但其實有相當多證據顯示,中國在外交上並未特別偏好威權政體。首先,必須承認的是,自毛澤東時代之後,中國已停止試圖輸出無產階級革命或顛覆民主政體。[120]中國的官方發展援助並不依據受援國的威權程度或貪腐程度來決定援助對象;像是南非、肯亞、坦尚尼亞、印尼與巴西等民主國家,都是中國的主要借款國。[121]中國也未曾藉由多邊經濟制裁或武器禁運,來促使他國採納自身的政治或經濟體制。習近平在二〇二〇年對全球幾乎所有四十場民主選舉的當選人都表達了祝賀。[122]而在祝賀拜登當選美國總統時,中國外交部也公開表示:「中方尊重美國人民的選擇。」[123]

中國的政權中立策略,尤其受到發展中國家的廣泛共鳴。儘管全球多數人普遍認為民

新崛起者　140

主制度具有吸引力，但國際調查顯示，近一半的受訪者認為由「非民選專家」來治理國家是「非常好」或「比較好」的選擇。124 中國在提供對外援助時所採取的「不附加條件」原則，也很受這些國家歡迎。許多國家對世界銀行和西方政府長期以來試圖透過援助誘因來強迫推動人權與民主改革的作法感到厭倦。他們傾向尋找那些能幫助建立穩定與繁榮社會、卻無需向民主進程妥協的非自由主義領導人作為合作對象。

雖然中國並未強行將「威權資本主義」制度輸出至他國，但其外交策略仍存在陰暗面：中國正在努力打造一個對威權政體（進而對中國共產黨本身）更為安全的國際環境。中國戰略家對美國的民主推廣抱持高度懷疑，認為這些行動是「西方勢力削弱對手、擴張自身影響力的手段」。125 尤其自從一九八九年天安門事件後，中共領導人深信，美國正試圖透過「和平演變」政策，即使用非武力手段促使中國走向民主化，以動搖中共的統治根基。126 為了能順利崛起為世界強權，中國積極致力於阻止這類民主化推動，以確保中共政權的穩定與延續。中國方面這樣的防禦行動日漸強勢，從公開的言語抨擊、國際規範的重塑，乃至於更具爭議性的政治干預行動，手段日益多元且激進。

首先，中國試圖在國際舞台上削弱民主化的正當性，轉而倡導主權、不干涉、文化多

141　第三章　中國外交政策中的創新作為

元與相互尊重等原則。[127]中國還積極致力於重新塑造國際社會對「人權」的認知及其在國際機構中的應用方式。例如，中國正積極推動改變聯合國相關程序，目的是減少該組織對中國自身及其他政府人權做法的監督與干預。[128]正如美國國防部南亞與東南亞事務副助理部長林賽‧福特（Lindsey Ford）所言：「北京並不需要在他國複製中國的政治體制來施加影響。它只需要推動各國採用有助於鞏固其權力的制度與工具即可。」[129]

其次，中國領導人日益公開批評美式民主。在二○二一年二月中美在阿拉斯加安克拉治進行的高層會晤中，中國外交部長楊潔篪明確列舉種族歧視、一月六日的國會山莊暴亂事件及美國抗疫失敗作為其制度缺陷的例證。[130]他宣稱：「我們要求美方徹底放棄干涉中國內政的霸權行徑，這個老毛病應該要改改了。」[131]中國國務院報告進一步強調：「美國政府不認真檢視自身糟糕的人權紀錄，卻不斷對別國人權狀況指手畫腳，充分暴露其人權標準的虛偽性。」[132]此類尖銳批判旨在迫使美國「降低民主與人權議題的聲量」，以維護中共統治的正當性。[133]

第三，中國在確保其他國家的偏好與自身一致方面，展現出高度的「創新精神」。與其試圖將他國塑造成自身體制的樣貌，中國更傾向於運用多面向的手段來影響政府、企業

新竄起者　142

和個人如何處理其所認為的「內政問題」。其方法在合法性、強制性和危害程度方面各有不同。在光譜的一端,中國運用主要屬於合法範疇的方式,如遊說、文化交流與付費新聞稿刊登。亦透過學費收入、現金捐贈與具聲望的合作項目,積極影響學術機構,特別是西方民主國家的學術機構。值得注意的是,在美國等地的中國留學生及學者若公開批評中國政權,往往會迅速遭到中國當局的報復。中國還透過「千人計畫」針對海外華人科學家與工程師,試圖吸引其參與合作研究。此計畫不僅涉及合法的研究交流,也牽涉非法的竊取智慧財產權行為。

控制中國在海外媒體中的形象,是中國對外宣傳戰略的支點。以中國國營媒體《中國日報》為例,該報投入數百萬美元,在《華盛頓郵報》、《時代雜誌》、《洛杉磯時報》與《華爾街日報》等美國主流媒體上刊登其宣傳專刊〈中國觀察〉(China Watch)。[134] 中國國營媒體已與境內外的華語媒體簽署超過二百項內容共享協議,[135] 並在三十多個國家的外國媒體插入新聞內容。截至二〇一八年,已有三十五個國家的五十八家廣播電台轉播中國國際廣播電台的節目。在非洲,中國的電視服務商「四達時代」(StarTimes)協助三十多個國家、超過一千萬名訂戶從類比電視轉向數位電視,藉此進一步影響當地民眾可接觸的媒體內容與資訊來源。136 近年來，中國的宣傳策略更進一步進軍社群媒體。中國國營新聞機構如今在推特、臉書與IG等平台上已累積超過一億名追蹤者。137 根據自由之家的報告，中國在二〇一九至二〇二一年間對全球的言論自由產生負面影響，並試圖影響超過三十個國家的媒體報導方向與內容。138

在這場全球形象與影響力競賽中，中國的手段不僅限於公開與合法的宣傳操作，也涵蓋了更隱秘、具威脅性甚至腐敗的行動，目的是削弱外界對中國共產黨的批評聲浪。中國試圖拉攏菁英與意見領袖，有時透過提供經濟援助與貿易協定來達成，有時則直接透過賄賂與利益輸送。139 例如，一名前中國軍官曾捐贈二百二十輛摩托車給柬埔寨總理洪森的私人武裝部隊，隨後便獲得興建一座價值五十億美元渡假村的許可。140 中共的統戰部門負責吸收那些「有用但不受信任」的境外重要人物與團體。該部門被揭露曾在紐西蘭與澳洲等地向親中或具中共背景的政治人物輸送資金。141 澳洲一位工黨官員後來被揭露收受中國資金，在任內曾反對美國的航行自由行動，並在移民決策上做出有利於中共關係人士的舉動，最終因此辭職下台。142

中國在這類國家主導的活動中具有競爭優勢。美國體系中並沒有與中國主要負責對外

新竊起者　144

影響的機構相應的組織，例如中共中央統戰部、中央宣傳部、國際聯絡部、國務院新聞辦、全國僑聯以及中國人民對外友好協會。143 與中國媒體不同的是，美國大多數具有影響力的媒體並非國有，也不受政府控制。即便是像美國之音這類隸屬於美國政府的媒體機構，其記者也都恪守新聞倫理守則，強調報導的準確性與透明度，並且「認知到自己對公共事務與政府監督的特殊責任」。144 相對而言，中國記者的職業道德則著重於維護社會穩定的重要性。145 中共試圖透過對海外華人的影響力擴張其全球勢力，在美國體制中也找不到類似的作法。

中國的「竄起者策略」，無疑比起強行將自身體制輸出到其他國家來得更有效，而且所需資源也少得多。正如柯特・坎貝爾（Kurt Campbell）和傑克・蘇利文（Jake Sullivan）在二〇一九年所指出的，中國「最終展現出的意識形態挑戰比當年的蘇聯還要強大，即使它並沒有明確地試圖輸出自身體制」。146 將近一半的墨西哥受訪者表示，他們更偏好由中國主導的世界秩序，儘管這樣的看法在開發中國家中較為罕見：像是巴西、奈及利亞和印度的受訪者則對美國持正面看法。147 對於那些優先考慮穩定與經濟成長的國家而言，中國模式似乎是一種高效率的「後民主」解方。148

145　第三章　中國外交政策中的創新作為

全球各國正變得越來越不民主（雖然中國奉行的「政權中立、不干涉內政」策略只是其中一個原因），而中國與這些國家的互動反倒比美國來得輕鬆。美國經常因為與某些問題國家關係有限，導致難以施加壓力。強烈的意識形態與政治分歧常常導致雙邊關係破裂，例如美國與古巴之間的關係就是一個例子。美國常常會因為抗議某些國家惡劣的人權紀錄、支援恐怖主義或發展大規模毀滅性武器，而限制其與這些國家的外交與經濟往來。例如美國與敘利亞、北韓與伊朗沒有正式外交關係，並且對這些國家，以及古巴、蘇丹和委內瑞拉施加制裁。諷刺的是，美國為了支持人權與民主，在對這些政權施壓，逼使他們在國內外表現得更負責任時，反而不得不依賴中國的協助。

中國也成功地削弱任何可能促進其國內政治體制自由化的因素。事實上，在習近平主政的過去十年裡，黨對國家的控制只增不減。中共已經逆轉了邁向自由市場原則的趨勢，打造出一個「加強版國家控制」的體制。150 國家監控系統變得越來越先進，運用的工具也越來越多樣化，包括手機應用程式、生物辨識數據蒐集、人工智慧和大數據等。151 中國也藉著新冠疫情加速推行各種追蹤系統，並持續打壓私人虛擬網路的使用。152 基於這些發展趨勢，過去五年中，中國在自由之家的評分持續下降，並且一直被歸類於「不自由

新竊起者　146

的類別。

中國的戰略並不是在各方面都取得成功。北京在一點上犯了嚴重錯誤，那就是低估了民主國家對中國觀感的程度。許多民主國家已採取重要措施，阻止中國的影響力操作。二〇二二年，美國聯邦調查局起訴了十三名人士，指控他們「涉嫌非法為中華人民共和國政府謀取利益，試圖在美國施加影響」。[153] 二〇一八年，澳洲議會通過了一系列法律，旨在限制外國對本國政治的干預。台灣也制定了類似的措施，讓政府能夠起訴中國的不正當遊說行為。歐洲議會則自二〇二一年起，拒絕執行與中國的投資協議，除非北京撤銷對歐洲議會議員的制裁（這些議員是因為指控涉及新疆人權侵害的中國官員而被制裁）。[154]

習近平的「政權中立」策略也正在演變，從一開始要求世界尊重中國的治理體制，到如今逐漸把中國模式呈現為一種「啟發」。中國的戰略家與領導人（包括習近平本人）越來越大膽地聲稱，其他國家可以從中國的做法中汲取經驗，儘管中國並不強求他們仿效。[155] 習近平曾毫不掩飾地表示，中國正在「為人類尋求更好的社會制度提供中國方案」，並且「為其他發展中國家實現現代化開闢了一條新路」。[156] 中國似乎正在利用其國內經濟上的成功來收割成果，畢竟「一個政權只要取得成功，本身就具有某種道德吸引力」。[157]

自一九九〇年代中期以來，中國就奉行一項旨在讓自己躋身世界強權俱樂部的外交戰略。和所有強權一樣，中國希望在國際舞台上擁有影響力，並在自己認為重要的議題上獲得他國支持。但如果要靠建立聯盟網路、塑造成為首選的外部安全夥伴，或把自身體制強加於他國來建立權力與影響力，對中國來說恐怕是事倍功半。在某些情況下，中國根本無法與美國競爭──尤其在美國具主導地位且經驗豐富的領域，模仿只會讓中國付出高風險卻收效甚微。在某些情況下，模仿美國的策略將會讓北京直接與當今國際體系中最富裕、最有權勢的國家發生衝突，並且提高被聯合圍堵的風險，使得這些路線並不明智。因此，中國選擇避開部分美國的核心戰略手段，改採有利於強化自身權力、同時降低挑戰風險並維護中共在國內控制的方式。

大約二十年前，中國問題專家梅艾文（Evan Medeiros）和傅泰林（M. Taylor Fravel）就曾警告，隨著中國影響力的拓展及外交手段的老練，它將會變得更善於維護自身利益──即使這些利益與美國相衝突。[158]中國近期的「戰狼外交」似乎證實了這一預測。如今

新竄起者　148

中國官員開始主動出擊，強硬捍衛中國及其利益。事實上，中國似乎已從過去那種「保守、被動、低調」的外交路線，轉變為「強勢、主動、高調」的與他國互動。[160]中國前外交部長唐家璇就曾形容，中國外交政策的演變歷程，從最初的「在國際舞台上找到一個位置」，到「改善國際環境」，再到如今「前所未有地積極參與外交事務」。[161]習近平則呼籲，外交事務應該以有助於中國重拾世界強權地位為目標，保護中國日益擴大的全球利益，並建立足夠的戰略自信，推動如全球治理體系改革以及深化夥伴關係等重大任務。[162]

但即便過去幾年中國在國際舞台上變得更加強勢，這三個案例仍顯示出中國依然維持其「創新」的戰略路線。中國的夥伴外交、將自身定位為「內部安全夥伴首選」，以及對政體的中立態度，正是中國如何發展出具有「中國特色的大國外交」的幾個例子──正如習近平所說，中國正在「提出新理念、新倡議」，打造具有自身特色的大國外交風格。[163]

149　第三章　中國外交政策中的創新作為

第四章

中國軍事戰略中的模仿與利用策略

二〇一八年，在又一輪針對台灣海峽衝突的美中兵棋推演後，美軍官員感到相當沮喪。一位參與者對時任空軍部長表示，再繼續進行兵棋推演也只是浪費時間，因為結局早已明確──美軍會輸。1昔日無人能敵的美國軍隊，不得不開始面對這樣一個新現實：中國已經針對美軍最不具優勢的領域，精準地推動了軍事現代化。事實上，二〇二一年三月，美國印太司令部司令的菲利浦‧戴維森上將警告道，中國的軍力在六年內將「超越」美國，並可能「以武力強行改變東亞的現狀」。2

十五年前，美軍無論在哪種情境下都能壓倒中國軍隊。中國也對此心知肚明，並且非常不滿意。事實上，當中國在一九九〇年代中期開始邁向強權地位時，台灣海峽的局勢正是中國領導人最關心的核心議題之一。當時，中國開始進行一系列飛彈試射，以表達對中華民國總統李登輝的不滿，一九九六年中國繼續進行飛彈試射，企圖影響台灣總統大選的選情。美國則派出一支航空母艦戰鬥群前往台海附近示警，隨後更增派另一支航母戰鬥群，明確警告中國不要輕舉妄動。

美國這次的武力展示確實奏效。中國隨即收斂對台的軍事挑釁，停止了飛彈試射行動。在外交上，中國轉而集中火力說服美國，讓其約束台灣，避免走向「台獨」。然而在

新竄起者　152

中國內部，戰略家和菁英們卻感到憤憤不平。中國誓言絕不再讓自己處於如此劣勢的局面。[3]

中國戰略專家針對美國的軍事優勢與弱點進行了詳盡的分析，以判斷中國應該在哪些方面仿效美國，又能在哪些領域利用美軍能力上的缺口來發揮自身優勢。本章將說明，中國在軍事戰略上的選擇，時常是基於戰略成效、效率、美方可能的反應、現有的空隙，以及國內政治因素等多重考量。例如，中國主動參與多邊軍事行動與軍備控制機制。在這些案例中，中國戰略家認為仿效美國的作法既能夠讓其他國家放心，又能透過限制美國軍力或增強中國軍力來縮小實力差距。這樣的策略甚至一度讓不少觀察家相信，中國軍隊未來可能成為一股有助於全球穩定的「正面力量」。

中國對美軍作法的仿效，並不全都遵循「避開挑釁、降低威脅感」的邏輯。發展「資訊化條件下作戰能力」——中國軍事思想家定義為「透過資訊、電磁與飛彈武器系統組成的『三位一體戰爭』」，以追求全域優勢的作戰模式」[4]——被視為戰略上極為重要，甚至是中國從「大國」邁向「強權」地位所不可或缺的關鍵。即使這種發展可能會引發美國更強烈的威脅觀感，中國也認為這是值得的權衡。[5]現代化軍力建設也直接支撐了中共的統治。正如胡錦濤所說：「國防和軍隊建設直接關係到中國特色社會主義的成敗。」6 北京雖試圖透過更具創新性的作法（第五章會詳細討論）來降低國際反彈，但中國在建構傳統軍事系統方面的突飛猛進，確實引起了美國的不安與強烈反應。

在多數情況下，為換取更強大的軍事能力而付出這些代價是值得的。但本章要論證的是，中國的航空母艦計畫卻是個例外──這個模仿案例並不符合上述邏輯。中國在航母計畫上投入巨資，雖然提高了周邊地區的威脅感知度，卻始終無法在品質或數量上打造出能與美國媲美的航母體系。這個案例顯示，當「竄起者策略」之外的因素（例如對國際聲望的渴求、意圖震懾周邊國家）主導決策時，會產生怎樣的結果。

本章也將探討五大因素──戰略效果、戰略效能、國內政治因素、美國可能的反應，以及是否存在戰略縫隙──如何促使中國在其軍事戰略上採取「利用」策略。我將說明，美國為了與中國抗衡，必須具備遠距離投射軍力的能力，而這正產生了獨特的弱點，中國則刻意透過「反介入／區域拒止」戰略來加以利用。所謂「反介入／區域拒止」戰略，就是專注於削弱美國的軍力投射能力、阻止美軍進入特定區域，並在限制美軍成功進入特定區域後的行動自由。

模仿以取得信任：追求「正當」的軍事角色

二〇〇五年，美國副國務卿佐立克（Robert Zoellick）公開呼籲中國成為一個「負責任的利害關係者」（responsible stakeholder），也就是不僅能從開放且以規則為基礎的國際體系中獲益，還應該對這個體系做出貢獻的國家。某種程度上，他這番話是在回應中國改革論壇主席兼中國領導人顧問的鄭必堅所提出的「和平崛起」理論。該理論主張中國不會尋求霸權，而是會把重心放在促進全體的經濟成長上。[7]在演講中，佐立克提到鄭必堅的觀點，但也明確表示，光說不夠：「世界將會看你實際的行動。」[8]

佐立克的演說反映了二〇〇〇年代美國戰略界普遍存在的一種觀點：中國若能更積極參與國際和多邊軍事行動，將能有效傳達其和平意圖。正如中國問題專家沈大偉（David Shambaugh）所指出的，倘若中國的軍事行動「是在聯合國或其他受認可的區域組織架構下進行」，西方國家政府和民眾不僅會接受，甚至可能「鼓勵中國展現更積極的國際角色」。[9]

「成為負責任的利害關係者」這項呼籲在中國一開始並未受到歡迎。舉例來說，胡錦濤就認為這是美國為了限制中國崛起而設下的圈套。10 他曾這麼說：

……並不是真的想讓我國在國際社會發揮更大作用，而是給我們戴高帽子，壓我們承擔超出我們能力的義務，要求我們按照他們的邏輯，來處理國際和地區重大問題，甚至企圖通過這種方式來影響我國對內大政方針。其真實用心是想向我國轉嫁矛盾，牽制我國發展。11

從中國的視角來看，「西方國家只想讓中國幫忙分攤其霸權的成本，卻不願分享全球領導地位。」12 用「竄起者策略」的語言來說，美國其實是在鼓勵中國犧牲戰略效能與效率，以換取更強的「讓外界安心」能力。

對像中國這樣的「竄起者」來說，若真要如佐立克所設想的那樣為全球公益做出相應程度的貢獻，其實並不符合其國家利益。但既然美國公開呼籲中國在國際事務中扮演更積極的角色，這反而為中國軍方創造了一個機會。中國軍方領導人很清楚，其他國家對於任何與軍事有關的行動都非常敏感；解放軍若過於活躍、過於高調，可能會引來國際社

新竄起者　156

然而，若能在某些層面仿效美國軍方在全球所扮演的角色，便有可能會的檢視與疑慮。[13] 向外界釋出善意，讓大家相信中國正在打造一支「和平之師」，同時又能在背後悄悄提升關鍵的軍事能力。[14] 長久以來，美國軍方持續進行大量的「非戰爭軍事行動」(MOOTW, Military Operations Other Than War)。根據美國智庫蘭德公司的分析，自一九一六年以來，美國空軍（含其前身單位）共執行了八百四十六次非戰爭軍事行動。[15] 這類行動涵蓋範圍很廣，從軍備控制、維和行動、打擊恐怖主義，到人道救援等都包括在內。

儘管美國已在二○○六年正式廢止了「非戰爭軍事行動」與戰爭行動之間的明確區分，改採「從和平到戰爭的衝突連續體」這種更具彈性的概念，美國現行的軍事戰略仍然視非傳統軍事行動為一種將軍隊轉化為「政治工具」的手段，用來塑造對美國有利的國際環境。[16] 對中國而言，美國的這種非戰爭軍事行動，正好是個可行的模仿對象——它可以幫助中國塑造和平形象，並在中國爭取國際組織領導職位時「累積資本」。[17] 值得注意的是，解放軍參與多邊維和任務，以及在國外進行人道救援與災後協助，這些行動不僅獲得中國民眾高度支持，也有助於鞏固黨的統治。[18]

國內政治上的考量也進一步促使中國思考是否應該仿效美軍在全球的角色。中國歷史

157　第四章　中國軍事戰略中的模仿與利用策略

上首次出現「擁有數百萬中國公民常駐海外」的情況，同時還有成千上萬的中國企業在世界各地設立據點。面對這樣的局勢，中國政府開始面臨越來越大的國內壓力，要求保護中國在海外的利益與公民安全。19 在二〇〇〇年代到二〇一〇年代初期，中國的海外投資版圖逐漸擴大，所面臨的威脅也逐步上升。20 二〇〇四年，有十四名中國公民在阿富汗和巴基斯坦喪生，這一事件讓中國外交部領事司面臨龐大壓力，要求設立專責單位來保護海外公民。21 這些日益增加的威脅，最終促使中國政府史無前例的在二〇一三年版的《國防白皮書》中加入了「保護國家海外利益」的專章。22

中共察覺到，若能在「被接受的領域」擴展中國在全球的軍事角色，將有助於在國內外強化其地位，因此下令解放軍參與「非戰爭軍事行動」。中國首次參與的重大行動是加入亞丁灣反海盜任務，這是聯合國安全理事會於二〇〇八年發起的一項國際合作行動，呼籲會員國共同打擊索馬利亞海域的海盜活動。23 這個時機點絕非巧合──就在同年稍早，索馬利亞海盜試圖劫持一艘中國商船，這在國內激起了強烈的民意壓力，迫使中國必須有所回應。自二〇〇九年起，中國海軍便開始派遣艦艇參與這項反海盜任務，至今已在亞丁灣執行超過四十次反海盜及護航任務，成功護送了超過六千艘商船。24

新竄起者　158

中國也開始積極參與聯合國維和行動。在二十一世紀初,中國僅有五十二人參與聯合國維和任務;十五年後,這個數字已突破三千人,是美國派遣人數的二十三倍。中國軍方至今已參與了二十五項聯合國維和行動,過去三十年間共派出近五萬名維和人員,其中約三萬六千五百人是在二○○○年至二○二○年間出任務的。25 目前,中國是聯合國維和任務的第八大出兵國,自二○○九年以來,中國派遣的維和部隊人數已經超越所有其他的聯合國安全理事會常任理事國。26 中國對維和行動的貢獻性質自二○一二年開始出現重大轉變——當年中國首次派出戰鬥部隊(過去的部隊主要為工程、運輸與醫療人員)。27 **圖4.1**顯示了一九九○至二○二○年間,聯合國安理會五個常任理事國參與維和任務的總兵力對比。

最後,中國也開始自主執行人道援助與災難救援行動,其中絕大多數任務是在二○一○年之後展開的。28 截至目前,中國已大約執行了四十次人道援助與災難救援任務,而其醫療艦「和平方舟」號則在二○○二至二○二二年間停靠了三十八個港口。二○一一年,中國軍方首次參與非戰鬥人員撤離行動,在十天內從利比亞撤出了三萬六千名中國公民,這是中國空軍歷史上已知最長的海外部署任務。四年後,中國海軍又被派往葉門,協助撤

159　第四章　中國軍事戰略中的模仿與利用策略

派遣軍事人員數

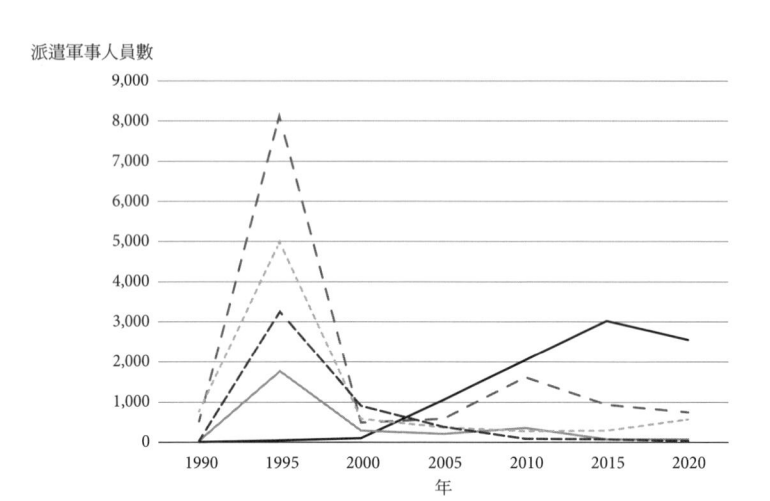

[圖表：1990至2020年聯合國安理會五個常任理事國派遣軍事人員數折線圖，縱軸0至9,000，橫軸年份1990、1995、2000、2005、2010、2015、2020，線條分別代表中國、法國、俄國、英國、美國]

圖 4.1　一九九○至二○二○年聯合國安理會五個常任理事國參與維和任務的總兵力

資料來源："Troop and Police Contributors," United Nations Peacekeeping, https://peacekeeping.un.org/en/troop-and-police-contributors.

離六百多位中國公民與另外二百七十九名外國人。[29] 二○二三年四月，隨著蘇丹局勢惡化，中國也自該國撤離了約一千名公民。[30] **圖4.2** 呈現了中國人道援助與災難救援活動的大致位置。圖中菱形符號上的數字對應於各別任務，其詳細資訊可參閱附錄；而圖中圓點則代表中國海軍醫療艦「和平方舟」號的各個停靠點。

中國致力於模仿美國的「非戰爭軍事行動」，透過多種途徑以極小的成本累積實

新竄起者　160

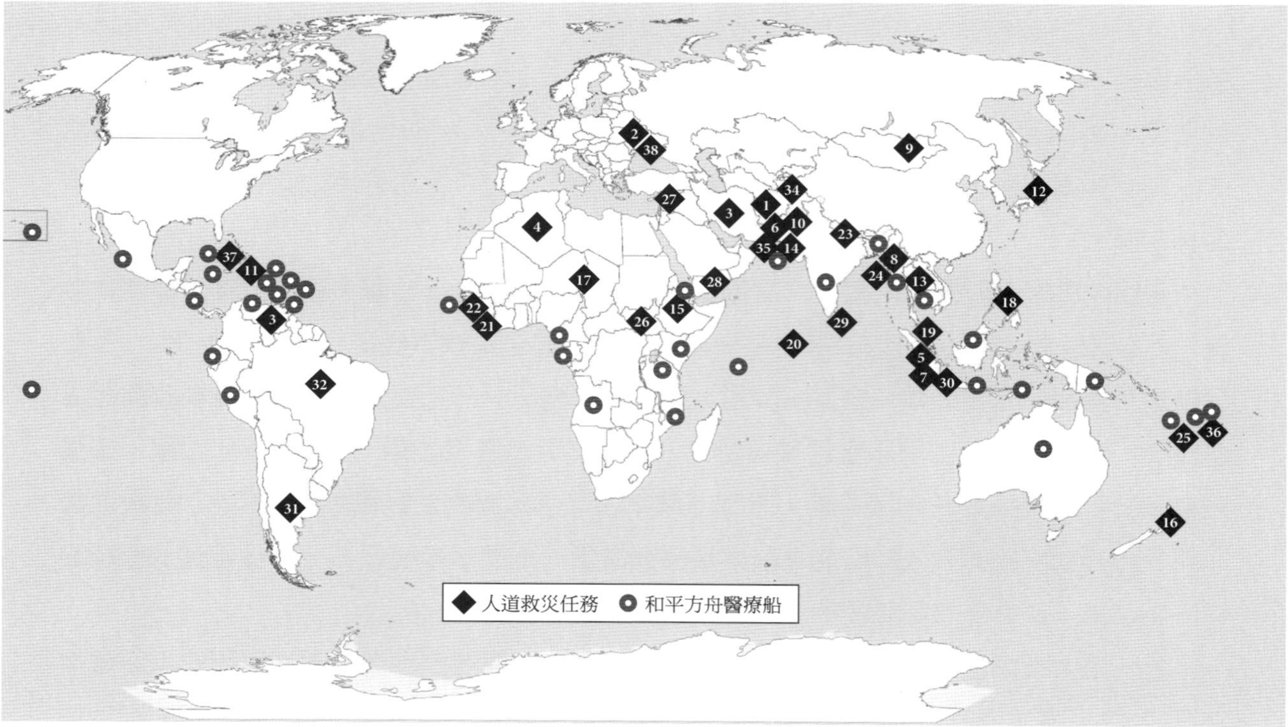

圖 4.2　中國人道援助與救災活動的戰略位置

資料來源：作者自行繪製

161　第四章　中國軍事戰略中的模仿與利用策略

力。首先，中國的參與使其軍事能力有所提升。根據一份美國國會報告指出：「在與美軍進行的人道援助與災難救援相關演習中，一再尋求之下，北京多次成功獲得一些訓練機會，這些訓練能直接或間接強化解放軍執行作戰任務的能力，例如進行兵力投射或對台灣實施封鎖。」32

中國分析人士認識到，透過「選擇性但積極的」參與和行動，中國既能改善自身形象，又能提升解放軍的全球行動能力，包括「發展新的軍事實踐和創新軍事理論」。33 中國確實從其他出兵國家身上學到了經驗，發展了外語和文化技能，讓中低階軍官接觸高風險環境，提升與遠征行動相關的規劃能力，並測試部隊戰備狀態。34 透過維和行動，中國還改進了在複雜環境中快速協調、遠程空運投射兵力和部署機動部隊的能力。35 此類行動也為中國贏得了影響力，有助於推動其他安全目標。不過也有人指出，中國的政治考量妨礙了解放軍有效參與這些活動。36

除了提升作戰能力和訓練水平外，中國參與亞丁灣反海盜任務，也為其在吉布地建立首個海外基地提供了正當性。當二〇一五年關於該設施的消息曝光時，中國謹慎地將其稱為「後勤保障設施」而非「基地」。北京官方宣稱，該設施旨在支援中國海軍護航任務及

新竄起者　162

人道救援活動。[37] 儘管許多分析人士擔憂國際社會對中國首個海外基地的反應，但由於中國以人道主義為理由，面臨的國際反彈比預期的少很多。事實上，中國增加參與維和、反海盜、反恐和人道救援任務，明確目的就是為了「常態化中國軍事力量在海外的存在、確保重要海上通道安全，以及保護國家海外利益」。[38]

中國官方媒體對這些行動的大幅報導顯示，北京認為這些行動有助於強化中共政權的正當性。官媒讚揚中國在葉門的非戰鬥人員撤離行動，稱這體現了「以人民為中心、外交為民」的理念，展現了政府保護海外公民的堅定決心與高效執行力。[39] 在蘇丹撤僑行動之後，中國政府則將該行動形容為習近平新時代中國特色社會主義的體現，認為這不僅展現了中國的實力與承諾，也彰顯了解放軍威武雄壯的形象。[40] 這種「中國是保護者」的形象也被搬上大銀幕，而且不只受歡迎，更在國內票房大賣──電影《紅海行動》和《戰狼二》分別在中國創下了五點七五億美元與八點五四億美元的票房佳績。[41]

為了確保此類模仿行為帶來的效益大過於代價，中國在這方面一向小心謹慎，從未投入與美國相當的資源。雖然中國有參與和聯合國在亞丁灣護航的任務，但行動上基本上是單邊進行，拒絕接受其他國家或國際組織的指揮。[42] 幾十年來，美國對聯合國維和行動

163　第四章　中國軍事戰略中的模仿與利用策略

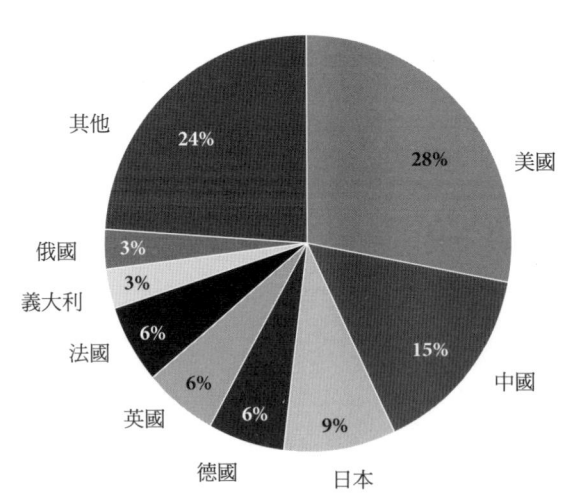

的資金投入遠遠超過中國。二〇一二年，中國僅提供了維和預算的百分之六點六，而美國則高達百分之二十八。雖然此後中國的比例上升到百分之十五，但仍比美國少了十二點六個百分點。[43]儘管中國曾高調承諾會投入更多部隊與資金，但實際上，自二〇一五年以來，中國的維和部隊人數反而下降了四分之一，而中國

圖 4.3　各主要國家在二〇二〇至二〇二一年對聯合國維和預算的相對貢獻度

資料來源："How We Are Funded," UN Peacekeeping, https://peacekeeping.un.org/en/howwe-are-funded, accessed June 26, 2023; "UN Document A/67/224/Add. 1: Scale of Assessments for the Apportionment of the Expenses of the United Nations Peacekeeping Operations," United Nations General Assembly, December 27, 2015, https://documents-dds-ny.un.org/doc/UNDOC/GEN/N12/665/78/PDF/N1266578.pdf?OpenElement.

新竄起者　164

對習近平設立的「中國──聯合國和平與發展基金」每年僅貢獻約二千萬美元，遠低於原本承諾的十億美元。⁴⁴ 中國在參與人道救援與災難應變方面的次數與投入金額也遠低於美國。⁴⁵ 部分差距當然是由於中國海外投送能力上的不足，但從資金投入也明顯較少這一點來看，顯示出中國是有意控制整體成本。以伊波拉疫情為例，中國提供的援助總額超過一點二億美元，但美國自疫情爆發以來對西非的援助金額則高達二十四億美元。⁴⁶ **圖4.3** 呈現了中國在二〇二〇至二〇二一年對聯合國維和預算的相對貢獻度。

總體而言，中國在參與「非戰爭軍事行動」方面一直是精打細算、審慎操作的。它的目的一是讓外界對中國的軍事崛起感到安心，二是在國內強化黨的正當性與掌控力，三是藉此逐步提升軍事實力。同時避免投入過多資源，以免破壞該策略的整體效能。

模仿以制衡：參與多邊軍備控制機制

中國參與軍備管制體系的歷程，往往被視為一個成功案例。⁴⁷ 一九八〇年時，中國幾乎完全沒有參加軍備控制協議；但到了一九九〇年代末，其參與程度已與其他主要強權不

48 這是一個典型的模仿案例,不過若從「竊起者策略」的角度來看,這個故事比相上下。「社會化理論」的樂觀說法更具現實考量。筆者主張,中國之所以選擇模仿,是為了達成兩個目的:第一,是藉此對美國形成不成比例的約束;第二,是讓外界對中國軍事發展的意圖感到安心。舉例來說,當中國在二〇〇四年加入「核供應國集團」時,獲得了布希政府與美國軍備控制人士的公開支持。49 中國在潛在收益方面也幾乎沒有犧牲——軍售並非其實力累積戰略的關鍵組成部分,且中國戰略家並不認為大規模殺傷性武器具有實戰價值。因此,中國致力於限制美國在這些領域的能力是合乎邏輯的策略。

事實上,中國一貫支持那些能夠限制華盛頓在其優勢領域發展的國際機制。在十七項多邊軍備控制機制中,有十三項主要關注核子武器,兩項涉及生物與化學武器,還有兩項則是用來規範常規武器的銷售。50 毫不意外地,中國特別支持《武器貿易條約》,該條約用以規範國際間常規武器的交易(正如第二章所述,這是美國實力的一大來源,對中國則影響較小),而中國在二〇二〇年簽署並批准該條約。相對地,美國則在二〇一九年退出該條約。51 中國在對太空軍事用途設限方面也採取了更積極的態度。太空是美國在全球投射軍事力量時相當倚賴的一個領域,而中國對此的依賴程度則相對較低。52 中國人民解放

新竊起者 166

軍國防大學唐永勝教授等專家更直言，中國應該「利用聯合國的軍控與裁軍機制來制約美國的軍備發展，並緩和中美軍備競賽」。53中國甚至進一步超越現行機制，主張全面禁止並銷毀核子武器。54

中國問題專家江憶恩（Alastair Iain Johnston）和麥艾文（Evan Medeiros）在各自關於中國參與國際軍備控制的研究中提出了不同解釋。麥艾文認為，中國立場的演變源於一九八〇至一九九〇年代持續接觸國際軍備控制議題，特別是透過美國的政策行動及美中之間非政府專家的交流。55江憶恩則指出，一九八〇年代中國在軍備控制方面話語方式的轉變，源自於參與聯合國裁軍談判會議等重要軍備控制談判的經歷——中國代表當時「模仿」並採納了國際軍備控制人士的某些行為習慣、專業術語和組織模式。56從這個角度來看，中國參與軍備控制協議的行為，可被視為它在國際外交共同體中被「社會化」的結果。

竄起者理論同樣認為，中國加入這些軍備控制機制是一個社會化的過程。也就是說，透過與其他國家的互動，中國認識到加入這些條約可能帶來的好處。然而，在竄起者策略框架下，這些好處略有不同：加入這些條約能夠安撫美國、改善中國的國際形象、降低國際社會對其崛起的負面反應，同時還能增強其相對實力。這種情況在冷戰結束後尤為明顯。正如一位中國戰略家所言：「美國將其軍備控制政策的重點從冷戰時期的限制和削減戰略武器，轉而朝向防止大規模殺傷性武器及其技術擴散」——而這需要中國的合作。[57]

中國學者對這段歷史的研究指出，北京參與美國主導的軍備控制談判，確實反映出其對西方主導國際秩序及國際機制態度的深刻轉變。[58]但中國的核心目標之一是透過談判建立與美國的互信，構建互惠的雙邊關係。[59]在中國眼中，美國無疑是當前國際體系的主導者，而加入該體系能表明中國無意對其發起挑戰。[60]換言之，若中國決策者認為採取不同的軍售政策或核子戰略可以在與美國的競爭中佔據上風，中國就不會簽署這些協議。

雖然反事實（counterfactual）難以證明，但「竄起者策略」比「社會化理論」更能解釋中國對軍備控制機制接受程度的差異。例如，一種更具競爭邏輯的觀點就能說明，為何中國在出口管制方面的表現並不一致。目前，中國只參與了八個出口管制與防擴散機制中的三個，分別是出口管制（核供應國集團，Nuclear Suppliers Group）、防擴散（贊格委員會，Zangger Committee）以及保障機制（國際原子能總署的保障措施）。至於中國未參與的另外五個機制：包括澳洲集團（Australia Group）、飛彈技術管制建制（MTCR）、

新竄起者　168

瓦聖那協定（Wassenaar Arrangement）、防擴散安全倡議（PSI）以及海牙行為守則（Hague Code of Conduct）——快速檢視一下就不難看出原因。中國在傳統飛彈技術方面比起美國更具優勢，並且更仰賴陸基系統作為其核嚇阻力的核心，而這些能力正是飛彈技術管制建制與海牙行為守則會加以限制的。舉例來說，簽署海牙行為守則的國家必須每年公開其彈道飛彈計畫的資訊，包括飛彈的數量、種類，甚至是試射活動的相關細節。61

江憶恩指出，中國雖支持《反彈道飛彈條約》與《中程飛彈條約》等軍控機制，但基於「明顯利己的搭便車考量」拒絕加入。62 為獲取戰略優勢並遏制美國影響力，中國透過有企業持續支持沙烏地阿拉伯、巴基斯坦、伊朗與北韓的軍備計劃，儘管中國已承諾遵守《飛彈技術管制建制》規範。63 簽署這些協議將使中國喪失用以經營與巴基斯坦、北韓及伊朗關係的關鍵手段。

中國雖然支持許多針對核武的軍備控制協議（這些協議因為美國擁有更大的核武庫存及更具侵略性的核政策，對美國的限制較大），但中國始終不願加入任何可能限制其自身核武庫的協議，特別是那些被視為讓美國維持主導地位的安排。64 中國外交部軍控司司長傅聰就曾明確表示：「考慮到中國與美國及俄羅斯之間在核武庫規模上存在巨大差距，

169　第四章　中國軍事戰略中的模仿與利用策略

中國對加入所謂的三邊談判毫無興趣。」[65]這種根深蒂固的不信任，也體現在《軍事戰略學》這本解放軍高階軍官的核心教材中，該書將軍備控制描述為「自私自利的大國的鬥爭」。[66]中國領導人對美國主導的軍備控制體系尤其懷有戒心，中國戰略學者普遍認為這是一種「陷阱」，其目的是鞏固美國在核武上的霸權，並削弱中國的核嚇阻能力。[67]事實上，更多時候中國是將軍備控制作為抗議其他國家發展與部署武器的一種手段。

仿效以競爭：「資訊化條件下的局部戰爭」

一九九〇年夏天，伊拉克總統海珊（Saddam Hussein）入侵鄰國科威特，引發聯合國譴責，並設定撤軍期限。在接下來的五個月裡，美國籌組了一支獲得聯合國授權的聯軍，成員包括北約與沙烏地阿拉伯、埃及與敘利亞等中東盟國，以解放科威特為目標。[68]在一場大規模轟炸行動之後，地面戰鬥僅持續了一百小時，一九九一年的波斯灣戰爭便以海珊的軍隊被摧毀收場。

這場衝突也向北京傳達了一個訊息：美國精通一種全新的作戰方式，而中國尚未準備

新竄起者　170

好應對這種方式。當時由江澤民擔任國家主席的中國領導層深受震撼，並召開了三場高層官員座談會，討論這場戰爭對中國軍隊的啟發與衝擊。根據官方出版的資料，江澤民認為波斯灣戰爭應當讓中國警覺，意識到發生衝突的可能性，以及中國在技術能力上遠遠落後於美國的現實。69

中國軍方立即著手重新評估在不斷變動的安全環境下的戰略。70 儘管決策者從未直接點名美國，他們卻反覆提到波斯灣戰爭展現出「因應在高科技條件下進行的局部戰爭與武裝衝突」的重要性，這明顯表示中國的優先戰略目標，是針對技術上佔據優勢的對手。71

這些「裝備優勢明顯的敵人」能夠發動所謂的「現代化戰爭」，涵蓋從外太空到深海等多個戰場，擁有能夠「大規模、不間斷、持久進行空襲」的空軍，以及「以指揮、控制與通訊網路為核心，先進且成熟的作戰體系」。72 在二○○三年目睹美軍戰力對伊拉克造成毀滅性打擊後，中國領導層得出結論：「美軍具備強大作戰能力的關鍵原因之一，就是它在資訊技術方面的領先地位。」73

美軍的作戰模式被視為極為有效，以致於中國必須發展出相應的競爭能力。74 軍事專家得出結論：未來戰爭將展現更高程度的「信息化、智能化與一體化」（譯註：「信息台灣稱為「資訊」，此處按照作者引用的中國文本用詞。以下同。）武器系統，因此解放軍需要完成「機械化與信息化的雙重歷史任務」。一九九三年，中國制定新戰略方針：「打贏現代技術特別是高技術條件下局部戰爭」。[76] 二〇〇四年，中央軍委調整方針，強調「打贏信息化條件下局部戰爭」（將資訊技術應用於軍事行動各環節），以應對中國國家安全面臨日益增長的非傳統威脅。[77] 二〇一五年方針再次調整，重點轉向「打贏信息化局部戰爭」、準備海上軍事鬥爭，以及有效管控重大危機。[78]

從那時起，中國便下定決心要「大力發展軍隊的信息化能力」。[79] 自二〇〇〇年以來，「信息化」成為中國每一版《國防白皮書》的核心主題，其中二〇〇四年版更是提及超過四十次。[80] 根據解放軍高層將領的說法，軍隊必須強化指揮與控制能力，打造一套統一的資訊系統，並將訓練重點放在網路的應用與實施上。[81] 二〇一七年，習近平明確指出，到二〇二〇年，解放軍應基本實現「機械化」，也就是以現代化裝備全面升級部隊，並在「信息化」方面取得重大進展，即讓資訊科技完全整合進解放軍體系。[82] 到二〇三五年，軍隊在理論、組織結構、人員、武器與裝備等方面，應大致實現現代化。[83] 為實現資訊化建設，中國需要建立天基指揮、控制、通信、計算機、情報、監視與

新竊起者　172

偵察（C4ISR）系統基礎設施，以滿足從導航通訊到精確制導與即時指揮控制等資訊化需求。[84] 千禧年初，中國軍事分析人員大量撰文，論述太空作為「終極制高點」的戰略價值。[85] 同樣地，中國學者認為太空已成為關乎國家安全與強權「生存發展競爭」的「戰略新疆域」。[86] 中國軍事思想家強調，強大的太空力量對實現戰場「制天權」與「制信息權」不可或缺。[87] 鑑於美國在太空領域的壓倒性優勢將嚴重惡化中國周邊安全環境並阻礙國家統一進程，中國必須採取相應對策。[88]

二○一○年，中國加快了太空軍事基礎設施的發展。從一九七○年到二○○九年間，中國共發射約一百三十枚火箭，將一百四十二個有效載荷送入軌道。而到了二○一○年，中國的年度發射量大幅上升，從二○一○至二○一九年間，共發射二百零七枚火箭、送出三百七十個有效載荷。[89] 如今，中國每年發射的火箭數量已超越其他國家（成功率約為百分之九十五，與美國和俄羅斯相當）。[90] 二○二○年六月，中國完成了「北斗衛星導航系統」的最後一塊拼圖。這個第三代導航系統是為了與全球定位系統（Global Positioning System, GPS）競爭而設計，由三十五顆衛星及全球超過五十座地面站組成，除了商業用途外，目的也是提升解放軍對地面目標的精準打擊能力。[91] 透過建構這個系統，中國希望擺脫對ＧＰＳ全球定位系統的依賴，這點至關重要，因為中方認為美國曾至少兩次關閉中國對全球定位系統的存取權，包括一九九六年台海危機期間。92

不可否認，中國在太空發展方面仍無法趕上美國，也未展現出特別高的效率。美國每次火箭發射能攜帶的有效載荷數量遠高於中國——以二〇一九年為例，美國僅用二十一次發射就將超過二百個有效載荷送入軌道，而中國則用了三十二次發射才送出七十九個有效載荷。截至二〇二三年一月，中國在軌的有效衛星數量約為五百九十顆，其中大約有五分之三是政府或軍事用途；相比之下，美國在軌有效衛星數量約為四千五百二十九顆，其中只有約百分之六是政府或軍事用途。93 美國的太空策略之所以更具成本效益，主要得益於與商業部門的合作。例如，太空探索技術公司（SpaceX）的「獵鷹重型火箭」與「獵鷹九號火箭」的每公噸發射成本分別約為一千四百美元與二千七百美元；而中國的「長征三號甲」與「長征二號丁」的發射成本則高達每公噸八千美元以上。94

為了在資訊化條件下打贏局部戰爭，中國也需要具備現代化的傳統武器平台，來實施「網絡中心戰」（network-centric warfare）。這種戰法的核心是「透過資訊優勢，將感測器、決策者與武器平台整合成一個整體網絡，藉此產生更強的戰鬥力」。95 因此，在進行反介入／區域拒止武器擴張的同時（下一節將詳細討論），中國也展開了一項大規模的現代化計畫，目標是打造一支擁有先進裝備的大型部隊。一九九九年時，中國的第四代戰機（具備有限匿蹤能力、較舊型的引擎技術與較差的機動性）佔比不到百分之二；攻擊型潛艦中僅有百分之四屬於現代化艦艇，而水面艦艇則完全沒有現代化型號。但如今，中國軍隊的多數裝備已經現代化。[96] 中國在這方面也有一些可供運用的優勢──例如，在二十一世紀初期，中國的造船工業就已非常強大，僅次於日本與南韓，佔全球總噸位的百分之五。[97] 這項造艦計畫在二○一五至二○二○年間達到巔峰，在那段時間，中國海軍的作戰艦艇總數首次超過了美國。[98]

北京方面試圖透過其他「利用」與「創新」策略（本書後續章節將會詳談），來降低外界對其軍事現代化產生的威脅感以及從而引發的反制成本。舉例來說，北京會刻意延後某些關鍵的現代化項目。就海軍實力而言，中國在崛起初期並未急於與美國艦隊在數量上較勁，而是採取策略性建軍的方式，先從小型艦艇開始實驗，再逐步推進到大型艦隊的發展。[99] 中國也得益於一些運氣：美國當時專注於「反恐戰爭」，可能因此對中國軍力擴張的反應較為遲緩。事實上，江澤民就在中國共產黨第十六次全國代表大會上大力宣傳「戰略機遇期」的概念，將二〇〇〇至二〇二〇年視為中國崛起的關鍵時期，部分原因就是美國分身乏術。[100]這套策略也包含了「耐心部署」的做法──也就是有計劃地、避免與潛在對手發生大規模正面衝突。[101]

最根本的一點是，中國的戰略思考者認為，具備打贏資訊化戰爭的能力，對中國打造一支能夠實現自身戰略目標的軍隊來說至關重要。[102]中國領導層明白，若要實現一些核心目標，就必須擁有一支更龐大、更先進的軍隊，即使這樣的軍備擴張勢必會引發外界強烈反應也在所不惜。正如習近平在中共第十九屆中央委員會第五次全體會議上所說：「過去我們比較落後，往往是去滿足別人的需求；現在我們發展起來了，勢必與別人產生更多競爭。」[103]

不太明智的模仿：中國的航空母艦計畫

或許沒有什麼比航空母艦更能象徵美國軍事實力了。從作戰角度來看，航母的主要任務是建立局部空中優勢，無論是確保海上交通線安全、保護船隊免於潛艦與空中攻擊，或是投射火力到岸上，例如美國在太平洋戰爭中對日本實施的跳島作戰。一九八〇年代，雷根政府提出「六百艘軍艦計畫」，當中規劃了共十五支航空母艦戰鬥群，作為盟軍對抗華沙公約組織勢力的主要海上投射與制海力量。104 美國多次在衝突中部署其航母戰鬥群，例如一九九一年的波斯灣戰爭；在外交上，也常用來展現姿態，例如在南海執行航行自由行動。105

換句話說，航空母艦一直是美國對外投射力量、因應危機、安撫盟友與嚇阻潛在對手的有效工具。除了實戰價值之外，航空母艦那種龐大的火力投射能力，也讓它成為國家威望與民族自豪感的象徵。106 然而，儘管航空母艦在戰略上極具效能，有很多因素讓中國不太適合跟進仿效。首先，航母是美國軍事實力的核心之一，建造航空母艦無異於向世界大聲宣告：「我們要挑戰美國的霸權！」其次，雖然航母在過去對美國至關重要，但它早已不再是當年的「海上堡壘」；隨著先進的情報、監控與偵察系統（ISR）以及精確導引武器的出現，航母在投射武力方面的效益已受到嚴重削弱。107 同時，這條通往強權之路的代價也非常高昂──美國最新的航空母艦「福特號」的造價高達一百三十三億美元，而接下來的三艘「福特級」航空母艦預計總共還要花近四百億美元。108

因此，在中國邁向強權的前十五年間，中國領導人決定不追求這個終極的強權象徵。這並不是因為航空母艦沒有用處。解放軍海軍前司令劉華清就曾回憶，早在一九八六年十一月的一場海軍戰略會議上，許多人就提到航空母艦在統一台灣、保護中國在南海的領土利益方面會非常有幫助。109 劉華清進一步指出，當時由於艦載防空系統的限制，中國水面艦艇無法在岸基飛機作戰半徑外行動。而擁有航母將能顯著延伸其行動範圍，且無需投入大量資源購買更多戰機。110

儘管中國公開的資料對於這項決策過程語焉不詳，但似乎可以看出，中國領導人一開始選擇不仿效美國建造航空母艦，是因為潛在代價遠遠高於那些有限的戰略效益。北京大學教授葉自成指出，在中國國防預算有限的情況下，更明智的做法應該是把資源投入到新一代戰機的研發上，並提升飛彈的性能。111 兩位專家程剛與張冕在二○○三年也主張，中國應避免建造航母，因為這只會強化「中國威脅論」，而且經濟成本與技術門檻都過高，實在不值得。112 事實上，早在一九九五年，劉華清就曾向中共中央政治局提交報告，建議建造航空母艦，但據說當時遭到否決，理由是這項提議與當時中國「對外展現和平崛起意圖」的大戰略不一致──特別是在北京血腥鎮壓天安門在國際上引起抗議之後，更需要安撫國際社會。[113]因此，中國當時選擇了一條更具創新性的路線（本書第五章會詳述），例如在南海運用灰色地帶戰術，一方面透過經濟與文化交流拉攏各方，另一方面發展反介入／區域拒止能力作為威懾工具，來防止台灣邁向獨立，並最終研發出像是紅旗九與紅旗十六這類具備中長程打擊能力的艦載防空飛彈系統。

二〇一二年，中國開始改變策略，以一種相當低調且不透明的方式正式加入航空母艦俱樂部。一九九八年，一位澳門商人購買了前蘇聯的廢棄船體「瓦良格號」。該艦隨後在二〇〇二年被拖至中國北方的大連造船廠。十年後，也就是二〇一二年，中國海軍終於宣布，這艘改名為「遼寧號」的航母正式服役，成為中國第一艘航空母艦。[114]

自那之後，中國又自行建造了兩艘國產航母：「山東號」（於二〇一九年十二月服役）和「福建號」（於二〇二二年六月下水）。與遼寧號相比，山東號配備了更先進的雷達系統，且飛行甲板面積更大，可停放更多艦載飛機。[115]而福建號則更為先進，採用了電磁彈射技術，能夠發射更大型、配備更重武器的作戰飛機。中國計畫在二〇四九年前擁有十艘航空母艦，其中包含六艘傳統動力航母與四艘核動力航母。[116]採用核動力的航空母艦將賦予中國航母近乎無限的航程、更快的航速，以及足以運作蒸汽彈射系統的強大發電能

179　第四章　中國軍事戰略中的模仿與利用策略

力。

儘管效能有限、效率不高,還會引發其他國家的威脅觀感,中國仍選擇模仿美國發展航空母艦,這樣的決定果不其然付出了代價。由於航空母艦長久以來被視為「美國軍事霸權最具體的象徵」,中國戰略上轉向發展航母,自然引起警覺。117 美國五角大廈在二〇二一年提交給國會的年度報告中,總共二十八次提及中國的航母計畫,卻鮮少提到人道援助與災難救援這類被認為較「正當」的中國軍事行動。118 拜登總統任內的國家安全會議中國事務專家杜如松(Rush Doshi)認為,中國發展航母象徵著北京意圖主導區域秩序。119 而二〇二二年六月福建號的下水,則更加強化了外界的觀感:中國正積極爭奪太平洋霸權,未來在投射軍事力量、奪取制海權以及執行兩棲作戰等方面,將會展現出更具對抗性的姿態。120

除了引發他國的威脅觀感外,中國在這一領域要有效率地與美國競爭也相當困難。中國的航空母艦在各方面都遠遠不及美國的黃金標準。美國的航母更大、可搭載的艦載機數量也更多,而且是核動力推進(也就是說,美國航母二十年都不需要加油),這和中國的遼寧號與山東號形成鮮明對比,後者每六天就需要加油一次。121 就核動力技術而言,中

新竊起者　180

國落後美國超過六十年——美國早在一九六一年就下水了第一艘核動力航母。[122]這並非因為中國沒有努力，許多評論者甚至形容中國目前正「不遺餘力」的追求核動力航母。[123]不過，由於在核子反應爐核心技術方面仍有所欠缺，中國在這方面的進展一直有限。[124]

若想打造美式航空母艦戰鬥群（包含航空作戰、水面作戰、水下作戰與後勤支援等完整編制），解放軍海軍很可能會處於競爭劣勢。美國擁有極豐富的航母操作經驗，其航母「每天能執行十餘波艦載機起降，每波達十至十二架次」。[125]雖然中國航母的相關數據並未公開，但中央電視台曾自豪的報導「遼寧號在十日內完成二百架次起降」，這仍是其明顯弱項，將構成後勤方面的重大挑戰。[126]儘管解放軍海軍正努力提升海上補給能力，可以窺見中國航母的起降能力上限。[127]

既然在戰略效益、實際效能與引發美國戒心等方面存在明顯弊端，中國為何仍違背「竄起者策略」邏輯，選擇仿效美國發展航母？第一種可能，是中國領導層的誤判——或許他們原本預期計劃成本會更低、成功率更高，或引發的威脅感更弱。中國在引進「瓦良格號」（遼寧艦前身）時，正好抓住了一個有利的戰略時機：當時美國需要中國支持全球反恐行動，因此未對此事表示強烈反對。[128]

中共領導層或許也認為能透過「重新包裝」航

母計畫來降低外界威脅認知。例如中國國防部曾聲稱改造瓦良格號是用於「科研試驗與訓練」，直到二○一九年才正式將其列為作戰艦艇。130 官方宣傳試圖將航母塑造成「中國願承擔大國責任、維護和平穩定」的象徵，131 強調中國航母僅會用於防衛目的，如救援任務，不會導致國防或海軍戰略轉向擴張。132

更可能的解釋是，中國發展航空母艦的決心，源自比五大強權競爭因素更強烈的其他動機。首要因素正是「國際聲望」──學者指出，這種追求往往促使國家甘願承受弊端也要跟進模仿。在中國領導人眼中，航母始終是真正強權不可或缺的象徵。一九七三年，身體已經抱恙的周恩來在接待外賓時坦言：「我搞了一輩子軍事、政治，至今沒有看到中國的航母，我是不甘心的啊！」133 二○一一年有解放軍軍官直言：「全世界的強國，包括聯合國安理會其他的常任理事國都有航母，這就像強國的『身分證』。中國人要走向世界，這關非過不可。」134 海軍上將劉華清更坦承：他曾因美軍軍官在酒會上綜合國力的象徵。」135「遼寧艦」艦長劉喆的經歷更耐人尋味：他曾因美軍軍官在酒會上評價其驅逐艦「小巧精緻」感到羞辱，暗自發誓總有一天要當上航空母艦艦長。136

中國共產黨領導人或許也認為，發展航母計畫可以在國內獲得更多民眾支持。事實上，早在多年以前，劉華清上將就曾表示，航空母艦在中國人民眼中象徵著綜合國力的提升，因此能夠增強國家的整體聲望。137 在習近平領導下的中國，航母幾乎成了「中國夢」的具體化身，不僅代表著國家的經濟成就，也是全民引以為傲的象徵。138

除了國際與國內的聲望考量外，還有一個關鍵因素促使中國最終推動航母計劃：區域競爭。139「山東艦」被部署至南海艦隊，肩負著「填補南海島礁防禦體系最後漏洞」的任務。140 雖然中國已在該爭議海域的人工島嶼上建立軍事據點，但這些固定設施容易成為敵方轟炸的目標。相較之下，機動性高的航母戰鬥群較不易受到空襲威脅，這將幫助中國在面對越南或菲律賓等較小國家時，有效保護海上交通線的安全。141

終極的利用策略：中國的「反介入／區域拒止」戰略

在中國崛起的最初十五年間，中國極易受到美國政策的左右。冷戰結束時，美國擁有世界上最大、最有實戰經驗、裝備最精良的軍隊。142 二十一世紀初，美國的國防預算遠高於其他國家，達到三千二百億美元（相較之下，俄羅斯為六百四十億美元，中國則為

183　第四章　中國軍事戰略中的模仿與利用策略

四百六十億美元）。即便到了二〇二二年，美國的國防預算仍接近中國的三倍。[143]

中國領導人從蘇聯的教訓中明白一件事：若試圖在軍費支出上「斤斤計較」地與美國競爭，可能會導致毀滅性的後果。為了與美國抗衡，莫斯科過度投入資源進行軍備擴張，結果反而拖慢了經濟成長，使得蘇聯更難擺脫僵化的史達林式體制。[145]蘇聯的經濟體系無法有效兼顧軍備與民生，因此根本不適合與美國進行軍備競賽。

中國的軍事無需全盤仿效美國軍力，因為北京的戰略目標主要聚焦在區域，在共產黨政權的正當性，與其能否在南海、東海爭端，尤其是台灣問題上推進領土主張密切相關。[146]從中國角度看，解決這些爭端意味著「洗刷百年國恥」——在經歷西方列強與日本憑藉軍事優勢侵佔中國領土、奴役中國人民的屈辱後，重新確立中國在亞洲的軍事主導地位。[147]

出於對戰略效能、效益與黨的控制等考量，中國在面對軍事競爭時，選擇採取不同的思維方式。正如江澤民所說，中國「要有所為、有所不為，有些地方要趕上，有些地方則不用」，清楚知道自己該把資源花在哪裡。[148]中國的軍事戰略家最後決定發展能夠利用美國弱點、產生不對稱效果的能力，用中國軍事術語來說，就是發展「讓敵人害怕的東西」，也被稱為「殺手鐧」能力。[149]前中共中央軍委副主席、解放軍上將張萬年曾說，中

新竄起者　184

國應該「緊跟高新技術，選擇重點先進武器裝備進行發展」，讓中國軍隊擁有「對敵人最具殺傷力的武器手段」。150

對中國而言幸運的是，美國存在可供利用的重大戰略弱點。這促使中國發展出被美國稱為「反介入／區域拒止」的戰略。所謂「反介入」，是指阻止敵方部隊進入某個作戰區域的能力。中國發展出一套能拖慢對手部署、限制美軍在特定區域（像是從日本南端延伸到印尼北部、涵蓋台灣與菲律賓的第一島鏈）活動，甚至逼迫美軍在離戰區更遠的地方運作的能力，使其無法在最理想的位置發揮作戰優勢。

相較之下，「區域拒止」的目的並不是阻止敵軍進入特定區域，而是要造成干擾──透過增加敵方自由行動的成本，迫使其做出中國所希望的行動選擇。中國建構的整體防空系統、反艦巡弋與彈道飛彈、海上轟炸機、搭載飛彈與魚雷的潛艦，以及高速巡邏艇，這些裝備全都是為了讓任何敢於靠近中國本土的國家付出難以承受的代價。中國愈來愈強的分層防空網，再加上戰機、軍艦與飛彈等戰力，足以打擊區域內的美軍基地與設備，從而對美軍的行動造成重大干擾。

美國的許多弱點來自於這個事實：美國並不是亞洲的「常駐強權」，因此不像中國那

185　第四章　中國軍事戰略中的模仿與利用策略

樣能夠直接在家門口投射軍力，而是必須跨越遼闊的距離才能介入亞洲事務。具體來說，美國必須依賴其他國家提供基地使用權，而中國則可以依靠國內本土的軍事基地。這點帶來諸多問題。冷戰結束後，美國的海外基地數量持續減少，而中國在幅員遼闊的國土上擁有許多基地可供選擇（目前美國在台灣作戰範圍內僅有沖繩一處的嘉手納一處空軍基地，中國則有三十九處）。[151]

但最嚴重的問題在於：美軍戰機可能連升空作戰的機會都沒有。二〇一五年蘭德公司的報告評估指出，包括嘉手納空軍基地在內的日韓美軍基地，戰時可能遭遇中國數千枚飛彈的飽和攻擊，就連關島安德森空軍基地也處於中國轟炸機與戰機數百枚飛彈的打擊範圍內。特別是二〇一七年部署的殲二十戰機，大幅強化中國打擊區域內空軍基地、後勤設施與地面基礎建設的能力。[152]同樣地，經過多次改裝的轟六型轟炸機，其打擊範圍已可遠及關島。[153]雖然實際破壞程度取決於中國的作戰策略，但美軍在遭受攻擊後於該區域的作戰能力將嚴重受限。美軍基地可能被迫關閉超過六週，且幾乎所有戰機都將受損或遭摧毀。[154]

中國的軍事戰略家非常清楚美軍在這方面的弱點，而中國發展龐大飛彈庫的結果也絕

新竄起者　186

非偶然；中國的軍事著作中明確討論美軍能力上的缺口，以及中國應如何「反介入」，也就是削弱甚至癱瘓美國的戰力投射能力。155 從中國的角度來看，這種「利用美方弱點」的策略特別有吸引力，因為中國的巡弋與彈道飛彈計畫（遠程精準打擊能力的核心）是全球最先進的。而且，中國飛彈庫的規模也大幅成長：從二〇〇五年約七百五十枚短程與中程彈道飛彈，到二〇二二年已增加到超過一千一百枚。156 同期中國的洲際彈道飛彈數量從四十五枚增加到三百枚，中程彈道飛彈則從二十枚激增到二百五十枚。雖然中國的對地巡弋飛彈與短程彈道飛彈的總數在這段期間有所下降，但這很可能是因為中國正逐步以更先進的系統取代老舊武器。157 不只在數量上有所增長，中國飛彈的品質也大幅提升。例如二〇一五年服役的東風十六型飛彈，其準確度是東風十五型及其改良型的近七倍。158

中國在針對美國的航空母艦方面，還擁有另外一項競爭優勢。美軍目前在印太地區部署了五艘航空母艦，其中兩艘母港設在聖地牙哥，兩艘設在華盛頓州，真正駐紮在亞太地區的，只有位於日本橫須賀的一艘航母。二〇二二年的電影《捍衛戰士：獨行俠》(Top Gun: Maverick) 也間接突顯了航空母艦在深度打擊行動中的關鍵角色：片中飛行員從部署在某個敵對國家外海的航空母艦起飛並順利返航，完全不用擔心航艦本身的安全。事實

187　第四章　中國軍事戰略中的模仿與利用策略

上，大多數國家都沒有能力從本土對海上移動的航空母艦進行打擊，尤其是像美國航空母艦這種有重重防禦網的目標。

但中國是個例外。中國人民解放軍所研發的末段導引型反艦彈道飛彈，就是專門為了打擊「海上緩速移動目標」而設計，而這些目標幾乎毫無疑問就是美國的航空母艦。159 以東風二十一D型的估算射程來看，在區域衝突中，中國很可能有能力讓美國航空母艦及其艦載機被迫停留在有效作戰範圍之外。160 即便美國戰機成功升空，也仍將面臨中國強大防空系統的威脅。161 而且，中國更在其於南海興建的人造島嶼上部署雷達系統，使得其預警範圍可以向太平洋方向大幅延伸。162

中國的防空系統能力將使美國難以用慣用手段（例如電子干擾、遠距打擊與匿蹤武器）突破中國的防空系統。中國的整體防空體系已經成熟到足以阻止美國第四代非匿蹤戰機在中國大陸及其周邊空域行動。前美國資深情報官員韓利（Lonnie Henley）曾向國會指出，若中國成功阻止美軍在台灣海峽進行空中作戰，中國就可能封鎖台灣並持續對台灣本島及美國海軍艦艇發動打擊，時間可以無限延長。163 雖然在像南沙群島這類距中國本土較遠的地區發生衝突時，美方可能佔據優勢，但中國的能力仍足以避免迅速潰敗。美國屆時

新竄起者　188

將不得不倚賴第五代匿蹤戰機（具備小型化、模組化、射程更遠、飛行速度更快等特性）以及遠距打擊武器，對中國本土目標發動攻擊。不過，中國在這方面也正在迎頭趕上，包括部署紅旗九B中程防空系統與紅旗十九反彈道飛彈系統。164 雖然目前尚不清楚中國的防空系統是否能持續鎖定美軍的先進匿蹤戰機，但可以確定的是，美軍勢必得在較高空域操作，並得先用遠程飛彈癱瘓或摧毀中國的防空設施，才能在區域內建立空優。165

由於美國主要是從關島、夏威夷，甚至美國本土投射軍力，因此其軍隊在行動上將高度依賴各種「支援單位」（enablers），也就是那些讓主要作戰平台或單位能夠運作所需的支援資產。而這些支援單位本身，也正是中國可以加以利用的弱點。例如，在執行遠距任務時，美國的轟炸機與戰機需要空中加油，這就必須仰賴空中加油機，而這些加油機本身幾乎沒有防禦能力。正如一位中國軍事研究人員所指出的，美軍的「空中預警機、加油機、偵察機與其他大型高價值空中目標將無法接近戰區，其作為作戰體系中支援性的角色將會下降」。166 換句話說，中國可以迫使美國在更遠的地點進行空中加油作業，這將進一步壓縮美軍戰機與轟炸機的有效作戰時間。167

中國軍事分析家深知美軍對太空系統的依賴程度——從部隊指揮、情報監偵數據傳輸

189　第四章　中國軍事戰略中的模仿與利用策略

到精確打擊定位,無不仰賴太空設備與服務。[168]中國戰略家認識到,若對通訊衛星實施反衛星作戰,或對敵方指揮控制系統發動網路攻擊,將可以有效破壞美軍的兵力部署與作戰執行。[169]事實上,太空威懾已被中國視為「未來威懾的首要領域」,因為太空戰力不受政治與地理疆界限制,具備「將威懾力量投射至地表每個角落」的潛力。[170]

中國戰略學者同時注意到,美國對網路能力的依賴正與日俱增。從一九九一年波斯灣戰爭到二〇〇三年伊拉克戰爭之間,美軍指揮官所能調用的頻寬與資訊流量增加了四十二倍,隨著自動化程度提升,作戰單位日益習慣資訊過剩環境,這個數字仍在持續攀升。[171]援引中國權威軍事文獻所述,網路作戰可以用來散布假訊息、模擬各種作戰行動以誤導敵軍、干擾敵方的資訊流通、癱瘓其指揮控制系統,甚至可以入侵對方的網系系統並破壞其資訊。[172]

有鑑於此,中國專家建議解放軍應強調「軍民融合」,同時發展攻防兼備的網路作戰能力。[173]正如一份中央軍事委員會出版社出版的文件明確指出:

「通過重點打擊敵方電子對抗系統、指管通情(C3I)系統等戰役體系重要節點，可破壞敵作戰力量整體功能，達成『四兩撥千斤』之效，實現以劣勢資源取勝之目標。」174

在此戰略指導下，中國已從一九九〇年代電子技術相對落後的狀態，發展到如今「能在境外實施大規模網路作戰，目標包括竊取智慧財產權、擴張政治影響力、進行國家級間諜活動，並在未來衝突中預先部署具破壞性的能力」的網路強權。175 如今，中國已躋身全球前五大發動阻斷服務攻擊及網頁應用程式攻擊的來源國。176

中國也利用了網路與太空等領域缺乏既定國際規範的空隙，積極推動符合自身優勢、限制美國行動的新規範。例如，中國提出的《禁止在外太空放置武器、對外太空物體使用或威脅使用武力條約》，主張限制外太空的進攻性武器，但對反衛星武器的約束卻相當有限。177 美國認為此類條約會限制自身的進攻能力，卻對中國與俄羅斯的反衛星飛彈毫無影響，因此持續反對該提案。178 中國也透過聯合國和「數位絲路」倡議，推動「網路主權」等概念。「網路主權」的意思是各國可以依自身情況自由規範其資訊科技產業，這項原則被中國用來合理化對其國內網路的嚴格審查與管控。179

總結來說，中國的軍事戰略家明確指出美國軍事能力中的漏洞，並認為「利用」這些弱點是戰略上有效且符合中國競爭優勢的選擇。就效率而言，只需一枚價值一千八百萬美元的中國東風二十一D型「航母殺手」飛彈，就可能癱瘓一艘造價達一百三十億美元的美國福特級航空母艦；或是用一枚價值二百萬美元的紅旗九型防空飛彈，就能擊落一架造價二千六百萬美元的F—16戰機。180 就效能而言，如前所述，中國如今在區域層級上，已具備與美軍抗衡的實力。經過十年的針對性軍事現代化改革，中國的「反介入／區域拒止」戰力已使美國軍方高層認為，美國已不再是全球無可挑戰的唯一強權。181 事實上，多次兵棋推演顯示，一旦美國被迫將軍力投入中國「反介入／區域拒止」的覆蓋區域（例如台海戰爭爆發時），美軍有可能會落敗。182

冷戰結束後，隨著中國進入我們現在所知的崛起初期階段，當時的中國領導人除了推行一系列新的外交政策戰略外，也開始重新思考軍事戰略方向。當時的中國必須在兩個看似矛盾的目標間取得平衡：既要增強軍事實力以抗衡美國，又要避免直接對抗；特別是在經濟基礎仍薄弱時，北京更需要避免與美國展開代價高昂的軍備競賽，尤其是防止爆發大規模戰爭。183

新竄起者　192

為了平衡這些需求，中國對外國的軍隊進行了深入研究，特別是美軍。[184]中國的戰略家們判斷，解放軍必須現代化，才能具備在資訊化條件下打贏局部戰爭的能力。因此，中國選擇讓軍隊扮演一些「正當」角色，例如人道援助與災害救援以及聯合國維和行動，藉此提升作戰能力，同時降低外界的疑慮。中國也加入軍備控制協議，以進一步限制美國的全球投射能力，同時向世界展示和平崛起的意圖。與此同時，中國更是毫不手軟、精準地利用美軍能力上的漏洞，推動其「反介入／區域拒止」戰略，儘管資源有限，卻仍顯著縮小了雙方的軍事差距。當然，並非所有中國的軍事路線都能以最小成本最大化軍力差距：例如，為了獲得國際聲望及威嚇區域內較弱的對手，使中國放棄了原本不發展航空母艦的決策——這個原本符合「竊起者策略」的方針。這種偏離也的確帶來了預測的各種代價。不過整體來看，中國的軍事決策大致仍遵循了這一策略邏輯。因此，如今的中國已經擁有足以讓美國在印太地區採取審慎態度的軍事實力。

第五章

中國軍事戰略中的創新作為

對於一個有志成為強權的國家而言，在不引發既有霸權強烈反應的情況下建立軍事實力，是最艱難且最關鍵的任務。就中國而言，這項任務或許從未像現在這樣艱鉅，因為美國的軍力是史無前例的強大──能以前所未有的速度、距離、精確度與殺傷力進行力量投射。然而，自一九九五年以來，中國在實現多項安全目標方面取得了進展，包括鞏固其領土主張，且在此過程中成功避免與美國爆發戰爭。這是一項令人印象深刻的成就，不僅因為中國推動領土主張已威脅到美國的重大安全利益，也因為各國在涉及領土與經濟利益（如自然資源控制）時，往往特別好戰。事實上，過去四百年間的大多數戰爭，特別是新興強權與既有霸權之間的戰爭，幾乎都是為了這些理由而爆發的。[1]

在本章中，我將列舉若干例子，顯示中國為了避免引發美國的反彈、出於對行動成效與效益的考量，以及因應共產黨本身的脆弱性，而在安全領域中採取了具創新精神的擴張策略。具體而言，中國刻意延緩軍事現代化的進程，選擇將重點放在經濟發展上。中國也大量依賴灰色地帶行動來擴張領土控制，尤其是在南海地區。最後，中國在核武政策及海外利益保護方面採取了一種獨特的策略──這種策略不需要依賴龐大的海外駐軍。

新竄起者　196

另闢蹊徑：推遲軍事現代化

軍事實力造就強權國家。強權國家至少需具備不依靠外援的自衛能力，而歷史經驗顯示，多數情況下強權國家還需要擁有足以將自身意志強加於他國的相對軍事實力。

因此，美國並非唯一強調軍事力量對其全球地位至關重要的國家。冷戰時期美國最重要的文件之一《國家安全會議第六十八號文件》指出，要維護自由世界的安全以及美國的領導地位，必須擁有「足以威懾（潛在的）蘇聯擴張，並在必要時擊敗蘇聯主導的有限或全面侵略行動的軍事力量」。[2] 即使在蘇聯解體近十年後，柯林頓總統於一九九九年發布的《國家安全戰略》仍然強調強大的軍事力量是維護美國安全的核心。[3] 在中國崛起期間，自布希政府以來的每一份《國防戰略》或類似文件皆主張美國必須維持全球第一軍事強權的地位。[4] 最近拜登政府的《國家安全戰略》也強調，美國強大的軍事實力是其整體影響力的關鍵，因為它能「支撐外交、對抗侵略、威攝衝突、展現力量，並保護美國人民及其經濟利益」。[5]

雖然追求軍事霸權對美國而言可能是有效的策略，但對中國來說，仿效這種做法並不明智。首先，想要提升軍事實力，往往會加劇他國對威脅的觀感。軍事競爭會形成一種明確的「追趕」態勢，因為軍事力量不僅取決於兵力規模，也取決於一個國家在軍事用途上所運用的技術。儘管中國在許多方面可以（且確實）偏離美國模式，但北京若要提升其軍隊的數量與品質，很難不被美國察覺並產生疑慮。事實上，各國在判斷對手意圖時，往往會高度依賴對對手軍力的評估，因此，一個崛起中的國家必須格外謹慎，以免引發警覺。那句經常被引用的鄧小平名言「韜光養晦」，正是暗喻此一動態。

盲目仿效美軍的發展模式還可能導致效率低下，甚至危及中國的崛起進程。正如前文所述，自鄧小平以降的中國領導人都認知到：單純增加軍費投入，並無法有效的讓中國縮小與美國的實力差距。蘇聯曾試圖與美國展開長期軍事競賽，最終因此拖垮經濟。[6] 即便到二〇〇〇年代初期，中國學者與分析人士仍不斷警告，應避免「重蹈蘇聯覆轍」——將過多資源投入軍事領域，可能導致國家其他層面的發展陷入停滯。[7]

最後，模仿永遠不足以讓中國趕上美國，而其他國家的模式也不一定能在中國發揮效果。對此，江澤民的一段評論值得在此詳細引用：

「創新也是軍隊進步的靈魂，一支沒有創新能力的軍隊，難以立於不敗之地。軍事領域是對抗和競爭最為激烈，因而也必然是創造多於模仿、創新最為迅速的領域。……世界上找不出兩場完全相同的戰爭，一味機械地模仿只能導致失敗。……我軍是黨絕對領導下的人民軍隊，必須保持政治本色和政治優勢，不能照搬外軍作戰原則。各國國情不同，我軍現代化建設模式也不能簡單複製外軍。對於外軍諸多優秀經驗與做法，不能生搬硬套，必須結合我軍實際消化吸收再創新，堅持走中國特色軍事現代化建設道路。」[8]

鑑於軍備擴張具有威脅性，以及效率與成效方面的考量，軍事現代化成為中國發揮創新精神的一個理想領域。其中一個創新的做法，就是中國選擇延遲軍事現代化，直到其建立起足夠的經濟與政治實力，能透過營造有利的國際氛圍來緩解來自美國的負面反應。[9] 例如，在鄧小平提出的「四個現代化」戰略中，國防現代化排在四項優先事項的第三位。[10]

因此，許多中國軍事建設的跡象都較晚才被觀察到，許多第一代現代化系統直到二〇一〇年代才投入使用，而量產加速更是之後的事。二〇一〇年的情況顯示，中國海軍當時沒有航空母艦、沒有〇五六型護衛艦、〇五二D型導彈驅逐艦數量有限，而先進潛艦可能僅有一艘。11 到了二〇二二年，中國已擁有三艘航空母艦、七十餘艘〇五六型護衛艦、三十多艘〇五二D型導彈驅逐艦，以及五十艘潛艦。12 同樣地，解放軍空軍的殲二十戰機（針對美國F—22隱形戰機開發，F—22起源於一九八〇年代，但直到二〇〇五年才初備作戰能力）也是過去十年才開始部署。13

中國在崛起過程中選擇延遲軍事現代化的做法相當罕見。從歷史上看，新興強權往往主要在軍事力量上展開競爭：第一次世界大戰前夕，德國和英國的軍事支出規模相當（德國多支出約百分之六）。14《凡爾賽條約》在一戰後限制了德國的軍事支出，但柏林顯然試圖急起直追，在一九三三至一九三九年間的支出是英國的兩倍。一九七〇年之前，美國的平均支出比蘇聯多百分之三十二，而一九七〇至一九八八年間，蘇聯反超美國平均百分之二十六。15 相較之下，中國的軍事支出是逐步增加的：一九九五年時僅佔美國國防總支出的百分之五；二〇〇〇年升至美國預算的百分之八點六；二〇〇五年達百分之十點五；二〇一〇年為百分之十四

新竄起者　200

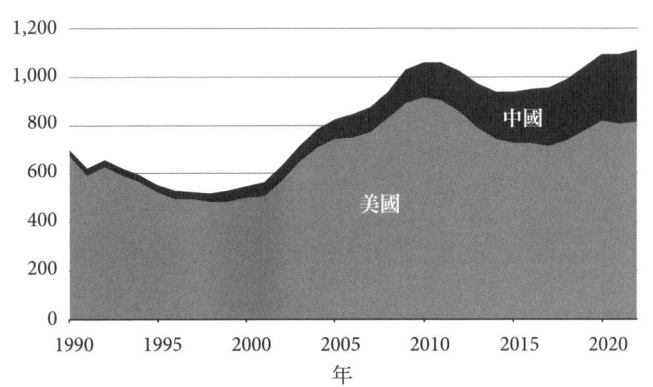

點九七；二〇一七年則躍升至百分之三十二（此後保持穩定）。[16] 如**圖5.1**所示，中國並未尋求全盤複製美軍的兵力結構。

需要釐清的是，中國有限的國防支出並不意味著其野心有限。相反地，這反映出一種更具創新性的策略──專注於「以更少資源達成更多目標」的方式，這種做法既能發揮中國的競爭優勢，又能在國家實力仍弱時，將軍事對抗的可能性降到最低。正如中國軍事問題專家傅泰林解道：「中國當時只能用有限資金推動軍隊現代化，這意味著作戰研究必須

單位：十億美元（按照2019年的美元計價）

圖5.1 美國與中國的國防支出對比

資料來源：Source: Data from "SIPRI Military Expenditure Database — 2022," Stockholm International Peace Research Institute, https://www.sipri.org/databases/milex, accessed August 25, 2023.

強調如何從劣勢地位打贏高科技戰爭。」[17]即便在展開重大軍事現代化後，中國仍持續依靠創新方法來平衡「實力最大化」與「可能適得其反」的風險——包括避免刺激美國出手遏制其崛起，或自身因過度擴張與超支而導致失敗。本章後續將探討中國創新策略的三個案例：透過灰色地帶活動擴張勢力、獨特的核戰略，以及保護海外利益的方式。

中國的灰色地帶行動

對一個強權而言，控制廣袤領土是其顯著特徵之一，而領土擴張往往是新興強權的核心目標。新興強權試圖擴張領土的行為，常常導致與既有霸權爆發戰爭。事實上，領土爭端是國與國之間衝突的主要原因：從一六四八年到一九九〇年間，約有八成的戰爭是因領土問題而起。[18]

中國目前有多項現在進行式的領土爭端。其中一些爭端位於南海，越南、台灣與中國皆聲稱擁有西沙群島（目前由中國實際控制）；這三方以及馬來西亞和菲律賓也主張對南沙群島的主權。中國對主權與專屬經濟區的大範圍主張，與汶萊、印尼、馬來西亞、菲律賓、台灣與越南的主張產生衝突。二〇一三年，菲律賓就南海爭議島礁（包括黃岩島、西沙群島及其他島礁）對中國提出仲裁案。二〇一六年，國際常設仲裁法院裁定不利於中國的結果——北京至今仍拒絕接受該裁決。[19]

中國戰略家將南海控制權視為確立強權地位的關鍵。每年約有五萬艘商船、百分之五十的油輪及百分之六十四的中國對外貿易需經過南海海域。[20]南海諸島不僅為中國大陸提供天然屏障，若加以佔領，更能支持中國將力量投射至麻六甲海峽與日本之間的廣闊海域。[21]但如前一節所述，若為領土控制目的發展傳統軍事力量，不僅成本高昂且具威脅性。這種軍事建設甚至可能引發中國無法取勝的戰爭，從而中斷其崛起進程。中國需要找到另一種領土擴張方式，而最理想的方式是能充分發揮中國的競爭優勢。

二〇〇九年三月八日，正在南海和西太平洋執行例行監視任務的美軍「無瑕號」（USNS Impeccable）海洋監測船遭遇特殊狀況。五艘中國船隻不僅尾隨該艦，更違反國際海軍慣例在近距離進行危險動作。其中一艘懸掛中國旗的拖網漁船上，一名脫到只剩內衣的船員開始干擾「無瑕號」的設備。儘管艦上配備水砲等標準防禦裝備，但面對如此怪異的挑釁行為，美軍官兵當下難以判斷是否該採取強力反制。

美軍最終決定降級衝突,「無瑕號」透過無線電通報將離開該海域,並要求安全通行。為了進一步複雜化美方的可能回應,中國政府強烈否認自己與這些中國船隻的行動有任何關聯,儘管參與事件的船隻中,包括一艘海軍情報蒐集船、一艘海洋漁業局的巡邏船,以及一艘國家海洋局的巡邏船。這些所謂的中國「漁民」還清楚的知道無瑕號的拖曳式聲納陣列的外觀與用途(即用來蒐集聲學資料以追蹤潛艦),這顯示他們事先受過專業訓練。

這起事件是我們如今所稱的中國灰色地帶行動最早的案例之一。灰色地帶行動是有組織、整合性高的行動計畫,透過主要非軍事或非武器的手段來逐步獲取利益,其特點是難以明確歸責,因此能避免引發全面的傳統衝突。22 灰色地帶行動不同於傳統戰爭,後者是軍事部隊在明確的交戰中運用暴力以取得具體勝利。以南海為例,中國船隻會騷擾目標船隻,包括:近距離航行、使用水砲、實彈射擊或警告射擊、發送威脅性訊息,甚至威脅撞擊對方。他們也會登船,有時會引發肢體衝突,並逮捕船員。23 在過去十年中,中國已針對台灣、日本、越南、印度與菲律賓使用了近八十種不同的灰色地帶戰術。24

中國方面從未直接談及灰色地帶行動,這主要是因為此類行動的目的即在於模糊行動

新竄起者　204

的責任歸屬與意圖。25但中國顯然正在利用自身的競爭優勢，在亞洲爭取軍事主導地位。共產黨掌控著一支中國海上民兵（People's Armed Forces Maritime Militia, PAFMM），這是一支由基層組織、國家武裝的漁民後備部隊。這支部隊在中華人民共和國成立初期即已存在，但其在南海的角色自二〇一二年開始擴大，並在二〇一六年後加速發展。26雖然難以估算具體數字，但據推測，每天約有近三百艘民兵船隻在南沙群島附近活動——而那只是眾多民兵活動區域中的一處。27海上民兵常被用來圍堵、衝撞並騷擾其他主張領土的國家及美國的船隻，使這些國家難以在其專屬經濟區及更廣泛的國際水域安全作業。中國的海上民兵體系具有獨特性：除了中國外，世界上唯一也使用海上民兵處理主權爭議的國家是越南（而其海上民兵的設立正是為了應對中國）。自那以來，中國的海警與海軍，協助鞏固中國對南海的控制，其中包括一九九五年從菲律賓奪取美濟礁，以及二〇一二年奪取黃岩島。28

此外，美國在該區域部署的執法力量極為有限，而中國則擁有全球規模最大的海警力量。這支海警部隊於二〇一三年由中國人民武裝警察部隊（武警）、邊防海警部隊及其他

第五章　中國軍事戰略中的創新作為

中國海上執法機構整合組建。數據顯示，在南海百分之七十三的重大事件當中，都至少有一艘中國海警船參與。2018年七月，中國海警局轉隸武警部隊，由中央軍事委員會直接指揮，同時保留民用執法機構的海事權益與執法權限。29

中國的列寧式一黨制傳統，也使其在塑造自身領土主張的敘事方面具有優勢。共產黨對全國所有媒體機構擁有絕對控制權，而統戰部則擅長影響海外輿論。30 中國的政治體制因此促成灰色地帶戰術的另一個面向，即所謂的「三戰」：輿論戰、心理戰與法律戰。「三戰」策略後來發展成一項更為全面的戰略構想，延伸至軍事訓練與作戰準備層面。31 中國將這種灰色地帶戰術視為一種手段，能在不承擔傳統戰爭代價的情況下，改變現狀、朝有利於自身的方向發展。32 倘若無法避免戰爭，「三戰」策略將確保中國軍隊能以最小代價贏得武裝衝突。33

輿論戰涉及塑造國內外對中國的觀感。正如毛澤東曾說過的，共產黨是「左手拿傳單，右手拿槍彈，才可以打倒敵人的」。34 在國內，共產黨認為民眾承受代價的意願是決定持久戰中勝負的關鍵變數，因此積極透過宣傳與國防教育來強化民眾的戰爭意志。35 在國際上，中國試圖動員海外華人，包括在大學校園中的中國留學生，來支持對中國友善的

新竊起者　206

政治菁英，並傳播官方敘事。海外中文媒體的擴張，以及對研究機構與國外學術機構的國家資助，也促進了中國的資訊戰行動。36

心理戰旨在影響決策者的觀點，進而左右其決策。中國解放軍國防大學戰役教研部前主任張玉良將心理戰定義為「特殊的綜合性作戰行動」，透過將資訊與通訊工具武器化，達成「以最小代價獲取最大勝利」的目標。其核心目的是「提升己方韌性與士氣，同時削弱敵方意志」。心理戰的攻擊對象涵蓋個人、組織、企業乃至國家。37而如美國等民主國家，在應對資訊戰方面往往準備不足。38

最後，法律戰旨在為中國的行動創造有利的法律環境。其目標是利用國內法、國際法，特別是戰爭法，來削弱對手行動的正當性，並確立中國的法律優勢。39在南海問題上，中國試圖透過錯誤適用國際法和利用國內法來影響國際法，為其行動建立法律依據。40為了削弱美國對其擴張行為的揭露與批評，中國指出美國至今仍未批准關於海洋權利的主要國際法框架——《聯合國海洋法公約》。二〇一六年七月，當菲律賓向常設仲裁法院對中國提起訴訟並獲得有利裁決時，中國官方媒體辯稱，由於美國本身不是《聯合國海洋法公約》的締約國，中國不會遵守該法院的裁決。41

美國並不擅長進行灰色地帶競爭。根據政治學者麥可‧馬札爾（Michael J. Mazarr）的說法，美國軍方通常將戰前與戰後的行動視為「他人的責任」。戰前行動通常僅限於「戰場準備」，也就是專注於提升美軍在主戰場上的表現的行動。42 在組織架構上，國務院與五角大廈之間政治與軍事的分工，也造就了一種人為割裂。而北京採取的漸進式策略，讓其他國家難以辨識具體威脅，因此也難以讓盟友與夥伴意識到威脅的存在。這種情況會導致聯盟與夥伴關係出現裂縫，從而降低彼此協調一致應對的可能性。

中國的灰色地帶策略能夠以遠低於傳統軍事手段的政治、經濟與軍事成本，鞏固對更多領土的控制。在過去十五年間，美國未能阻止中國的擴張行動，至今也仍缺乏有效因應中國灰色地帶行動的手段。44 為了應對這些危險行為，美國起初嘗試透過雙邊對話進行接觸，例如《海上軍事安全磋商協議》會談與隨後的《海上意外相遇規則》。這些論壇本可為雙方提供討論突發事件和商定行為準則的平臺。但中國拒絕讓其海警、執法和准軍事力量受這些協議約束，並持續否認中央政府指揮這些活動。作為反制措施，美國於二○二一年派出海岸防衛隊予以反制。截至二○二三年，一艘名為「門羅號」的美國海巡艦被部署在第七艦隊，並與日本海上保安廳與菲律賓海岸防衛隊協同作業。

美國對中國法律戰的直接回應也相對遲緩。華盛頓直到二〇一七年才開始例行性地執行航行自由行動，並且直到二〇二〇年才正式宣稱中國在南海的主權主張為非法。美國在反制中國法律戰方面也面臨困難，因為美國尚未批准《聯合國海洋法公約》。更複雜的是，過去漠視國際常設仲裁法院（海牙法院）裁定的國家，不光只有中國，也包括美國及其盟友（最近還包括台灣），這削弱了該法院的權威性。使情況更加複雜的是，有關航行自由的國際規範本身仍具爭議，一些關鍵國家主張在專屬經濟區內進行軍事活動須獲得沿海國的許可。美國也無法阻止中國在南海建造並軍事化面積多高達三千二百英畝的人工島礁。

儘管我認為，中國選擇以灰色地帶行動來擴張其領土控制，主要是出於與軍事上更強大的美國進行競爭時的風險管控考量，但仍有幾種其他觀點值得探討。首先，有人可能會認為，中國之所以選擇灰色地帶戰術，是源於其戰略文化。《孫子兵法》中最著名的一句話是：「不戰而屈人之兵，善之善者也」。但其實《孫子兵法》的大多數內容仍然關注如何以武力進行戰爭，而孫子所謂的「不戰」可能是指戰爭開始之前所做的各種準備工作。

45 正如江憶恩所指出的，「不戰而屈人之兵」或許更應該被理解為：「首先營造出對擊敗敵人最有利的條件，然後再開戰並擊敗敵人」。46另外，在中國崛起之前，當其「竄起者策略」尚未成形時，中國確實使用過傳統軍事力量進行領土擴張：一九六二年對印度發動戰爭、一九六九年與蘇聯爆發邊界衝突、一九七九年與越南的邊境戰爭，以及一九七四年從越南手中奪取西沙群島部分島嶼，一九八八年奪取南沙群島中的赤瓜礁。這些例子顯示，冷戰結束後，中國的行動邏輯出現了轉變，考量也有所不同。

另有批評認為灰色地帶行動不應被視為創新策略，因為其他國家（特別是弱國）也採用類似手段。但中國的特殊性在於，它並未面臨能力限制——中國擁有全球規模最大的海軍，本可直接動用海軍力量推進領土主張，卻仍選擇採取灰色地帶活動。這種選擇正好印證了「竄起者策略」的邏輯。更重要的是，中國擅長同時運用多種灰色地帶手段，範圍從在目標區域實彈射擊，到收購目標國媒體機構等。47最後需強調的是，創新策略不必完全新穎，只需不同於既存霸權（偏好傳統軍事行動且難以應對灰色地帶戰術的美國）的既有模式即可。

最後一項常見的批評是，中國的做法其實並沒有生效，應被視為一種在戰略上不明智的實力建構方式。中國的海上野心與具有侵略性的灰色地帶行動，已引發區域性的回應。

新竄起者 210

其他國家加強了其海上能力，並開始協調應對措施，包括與美國建立更緊密的關係。[48]可以說，中國在南海的軍事擴張促使歐巴馬政府對中國採取更強硬的行動。[49]但問題的關鍵在於相對成本——也就是說，如果中國採取的是更傳統的軍事擴張手段，是否會引發美國更強烈、更果斷的回應？答案顯然是肯定的。

中國的核子戰略

一九五〇年，由美國主導的聯合國軍似乎可能輸掉韓戰。十月十九日，中國軍隊跨過鴨綠江，並於十月二十五日發動首次攻勢，將聯合國部隊從北韓境內向南驅逐。為防止南韓遭共產主義軍隊佔領，杜魯門總統在記者會上公開表示，當局正積極考慮使用核武器。[50]

這次聲明是美國首次，但並非最後一次，以核武器威脅新成立的中華人民共和國。三年後，艾森豪總統威脅稱，如果中國拒絕談判結束韓戰，美國將動用毀滅性力量來迫使戰爭終結。[51]韓戰結束後，中美之間的敵意持續升溫。在首次台灣海峽危機期間，中國對金門和馬祖島進行砲擊。艾森豪政府則再次威脅要為這些島嶼發動「有限原子戰爭」。52

不出所料,中國領導人認定中國必須發展核子武器。

一九五四年九月,蘇聯領導人赫魯雪夫同意向中國提供技術支援,即便只是為了嚇阻核勒索。此一決定於一九五五年一月在國務院全體會議上受到周恩來的讚揚。53 周恩來在講話中明確地將中國發展核能的需求與美國的威脅掛鉤,表示:「美國人想要恐嚇我們,但他們不會成功。」54 一九五六年,毛澤東親自強調發展核子武器的重要性,以「防止中國被欺負」。55

雖然核威懾的邏輯迫使中國在發展自身核武計畫時模仿美國,但與美國的相似之處大致也僅止於此。在接下來的六十年中,中國對核子武器的態度——從理論學說、作戰規劃,到武力部署與現代化優先順序,都與美國大相逕庭,而這些差異,正是中國在崛起為強權過程中堅定不移的一些選擇。

核能政策是中國採取創新策略的領域,這主要是因為中國領導人認為美國的做法既無效(核武並不像美國所想的那樣有用),又低效(美國在建造與維持核武上浪費了大量資源)。在美國的主導下,中國幾乎沒有可以利用的機會。而大規模擴展核能對華盛頓而

新竄起者　212

毛澤東之後的歷任中國最高領導人始終質疑核子武器在實戰中的效用，強調「核武器不可能隨意使用」且「士兵比原子彈更有用」。56 一九七八年，鄧小平明確指出：「今後戰爭主要是常規武器的戰爭，不是原子戰爭。因為核武器破壞力太大，敵人不會輕易使用」──因此中國將「主要發展常規武器」。57 中國領導層普遍認為核子武器基本上無法投入戰場，且一旦達成相互威懾，「擴大核庫或參與軍備競賽不僅成本高昂、適得其反，最終更將自食其果」。58 基於這種思維，中國至今對戰術型核武器（專為戰場使用或有限打擊設計的小型核彈）的發展依然有所節制，而此類武器自一九五〇年代（美國）與一九六〇年代（蘇聯）起便成為美俄核武庫的標準配備。59 隨著中國對核戰爆發可能性的評估持續降低，其現代化建設明顯向常規軍力傾斜。60

對效能的考量也促使中國採取創新策略，因為中國領導人認為，他們能以比美國更低的成本達成威懾效果。當美國與蘇聯建造足以摧毀世界多次的核彈頭時，中國認為這種做法既不必要，又代價高昂。61 用鄧小平的話來說：「我們有一些核武器⋯⋯如果他們想摧毀我們，他們自己也會遭到一些報復⋯⋯有一點核武器，畢竟也是一種制約力量。」62 中

第五章 中國軍事戰略中的創新作為

國人民解放軍第二砲兵部隊（現改制為火箭軍）的軍事理論要求中國的核力量必須「小而精」，並且符合中國作為一個發展中國家的現實情況。根據這一理論，只要中國的核武器庫能滿足有效威懾的需求，就無需與超級大國在規模上看齊。

實際上，一九九八年美國在核武器上的支出高達三百五十一億美元，超過了中國當時全年國防預算總額。[63] 二〇二一年至二〇三〇年間美國核武計畫的總預算估計將達四千五百六十億美元。[64] 這筆預算中有很大一部分（百分之三十六）用於戰術核武器，而中國在這方面幾乎沒有投入。[65] 美國的「核三位一體」戰力，亦即透過飛機、潛艦與飛彈投射核彈頭的系統，形成過程更多是受到軍種間預算之爭的影響，而非純粹基於戰略考量。然而，這一架構也帶來了巨大的財政負擔：在冷戰時期，美國核武支出中有百分之八十六用來建設這些多樣化的投射系統。[66]

這些考量促使中國建造的核武數量遠少於美國。截至二〇二三年，中國人民解放軍火箭軍擁有約三百八十二個陸基飛彈發射器，其中約一百四十枚飛彈（搭載二百四十枚彈頭）具備打擊美國本土的能力。[67] 中國目前擁有四百一十枚可由飛彈、轟炸機與潛艦投射的核彈頭。當中七十二枚可由潛艦發射、二十枚可由飛機發射，這些都可能具備打擊美國

新竄起者　214

本土的潛力。剩餘的三百一十八枚彈頭則全數為飛彈型。相較之下，美國估計擁有四百枚洲際彈道飛彈、二百八十枚潛射彈道飛彈，以及近八百枚可由轟炸機投射的核彈頭。而這些僅是發射平台的數量──美國總共擁有超過五千枚核彈頭。69

中國還發展出獨特的核戰略以配合其有限規模的核武庫，選擇專注於「最低威懾」與「確保報復」能力，亦即「透過核反擊造成難以承受損害的威脅來威懾對手」。70 二〇〇六年中國首次官方闡述其核戰略時，提出「自衛防禦核戰略」，強調需要建立「精幹有效」的核力量作為「可信的核威懾力量」。71 該戰略部分內容包含「不首先使用」承諾：僅在遭受核打擊時進行報復性反擊，且僅針對核武國家。72 透過此承諾，中國成為唯一同時向無核國家提供「消極安全保證」與「積極安全保證」的國家。73 這項承諾也意味著中國不向任何國家提供核保護傘（而美國已將其核保護傘擴展至近三十個國家）。74 基於「最低威懾」原則與「不首先使用」承諾，新組建的戰略火箭軍唯一準備的作戰形態就是核防禦戰役。75

相較之下，美國既未承諾「不首先使用核武」，也未聲明核武器的唯一用途是嚇阻核攻擊。事實上，美國的核戰略聲明中常包含允許對非擁核國使用核武的條款。這些威脅

215　第五章　中國軍事戰略中的創新作為

的強硬程度不一,從小布希時期偏好單邊預防性行動的說法,到歐巴馬時期較為緩和的立場,即只要非擁核國是《核不擴散條約》(NPT)的成員並依規行事,美國就不會對其使用核武。[76] 川普政府的政策則更進一步降低美國動用核武的門檻,保留在面對「重大非核戰略攻擊」(包括對美國、盟國或夥伴國的平民或基礎設施的攻擊)時使用核武的權利。[77] 即便是拜登總統,也拒絕承諾核武的唯一用途是嚇阻性核攻擊。

中國與美國在核武戰略上的差異不僅止於數量與政策層面。由於基本戰略理念不同,中國的核子戰備與警戒等級明顯低於美國。中國人民解放軍火箭軍(前稱第二砲兵)的訓練原則是「遭受攻擊後發射」,而非美國自一九七〇年代以來持續採用的「預警即發射」政策。[78] 在和平時期,中國大部分核武處於非戰備狀態,發射器、飛彈與彈頭分開儲存;而美國則有百分之四十五的核武器處於「即時戰備警戒狀態」(hair-trigger alert),也就是可在數分鐘內發射升空。[79] 事實上,中國大多數的核彈頭是與發射載具分開儲存在固定地點,只有在準備攻擊時才進行組裝,這更進一步引發外界質疑中國是否具備可靠的二次打擊能力。[80] 美國在首次核子試爆後不久即部署了太空紅外線偵測系統以建立預警能力,而中國直到近年才開始建構天基洲際彈道飛彈來發射偵測系統,截至二〇二二年,僅有三顆

新竄起者　216

預警衛星在軌運行。[81]相較之下，美國國防部在二○二三年要求國會撥款建造用於太空飛彈預警系統的五十多顆衛星。[82]

中國的核威懾力量主要依賴陸基系統，而美國與俄羅斯則發展了「三位一體」核武體系。實際上，中國百分之七十六的核力量為陸基；相較之下，美國的核力量中僅有百分之二十二為陸基，百分之五十四為海基，百分之二十四為空基。[83]中國直到二○一五年才擁有三位一體中的「海基」打擊能力，當時搭載巨浪二型潛射彈道飛彈的「晉級」彈道飛彈潛艦首次展開巡航。據分析人士推測，中國的新型戰略隱形轟炸機轟二十可能於二○二五年前服役。該機型具有常規及核打擊能力，但中國是否能夠發展出空基核打擊能力尚未確定。[84]

基於戰略理念與部隊部署的差異，中美兩軍核武組織結構自然也有所不同。中國始終保持獨立建制的飛彈部隊，同時管轄常規與核武飛彈。[85]第二炮兵部隊原為中央軍事委員會直屬獨立兵種，二○一五年升格為獨立軍種並更名為中國人民解放軍火箭軍。二○一七至二○二○年間，火箭軍旅級單位從二十九個擴編至四十個，其中半數配備可攜帶核彈頭的彈道飛彈發射系統。[86]美國則於一九九二年成立統一指揮所有戰略核武部隊的「戰略司

217　第五章　中國軍事戰略中的創新作為

令部」，而陸基常規飛彈仍主要由陸軍管轄。87

儘管中國在其崛起的大部分過程中，對於核武戰略採取的是創新式的策略，但目前學界爭論的焦點在於，中國是否正放棄這一長期策略，轉而採用模仿美國的方式。二〇二一年，隨著中國核武現代化的進程加快，外界的不安情緒開始升高，衛星影像顯示中國在內蒙古、甘肅和新疆的核設施新建了約三百座飛彈發射井，引發外界擔憂中國可能進行計劃性擴軍。隨著六十枚東風五型、九十枚東風三十一型與八十四枚東風四十一型飛彈陸續服役，使中國具備發射九十枚飛彈、搭載一百三十枚彈頭打擊美國本土的能力。88 預估到二〇二五年，中國可威脅美國本土的陸基洲際彈道飛彈彈頭數量將增加至約二百枚。89 中國近期在預警系統與高超音速武器上的投資，亦加深外界疑慮——這些武器具有射程遠、飛行高度低、機動性強、可變軌飛行等特點，對飛彈防禦系統構成特殊挑戰，令人擔心中國可能正轉向更具侵略性的戰略。90

目前尚難以斷定中國的核武戰略最終將朝哪個方向發展，但「竄起者策略」仍然可以提供一些指引。首先，在核武戰略上採取創新策略的誘因仍然存在。這意味著如果中國試圖模仿美國，追求在核武數量、投射系統種類和核武戰略理論上與美國並駕齊驅，將會付

新竄起者　218

出犧牲競爭力的代價。這不僅會影響北京在投入大量資源後所能達成的目標，也會引發其他強權的回應。其次，「竄起者策略」的優勢之一，是能夠根據競爭性質的變化調整策略方向。中國近期核武現代化的變革，即使其輪廓有所調整，似乎仍與過去以創新思維為主的核武戰略方針保持一致。

這種戰略延續性的具體體現在於：中國至今仍未追求與美國的核武均勢。即便在最極端情境下：假設中國建造的約三百六十座飛彈發射井全部部署可攜帶三枚彈頭的東風四十一型洲際彈道飛彈，那麼中國的核彈頭總數仍僅約八百七十五枚。[91] 中國在一九九〇年代初期對在核武領域直接與美國競爭的迴避更加明顯，當時美國擁有的核武數量是中國的四十七倍。[92] 但即便根據最悲觀的預測，中國擁有一千枚核武，其核彈頭總數量仍僅為美國目前總量（五千二百四十四枚）的四分之一。[93]

有人或主張核武總數並非最關鍵指標，戰略家更應關注「現役部署」與「庫存儲備」的區別。根據《新削減戰略武器條約》，美國現役部署核武達一千七百七十件（條約上限為一千五百五十件，但每架可搭載多枚核彈頭的轟炸機僅計為「一件」）。換言之，比較核武庫規模時，部分觀點主張採用現役部署量（一千七百七十件）而非總持有量

（五千二百四十四件）作為基準。[94] 但即使採用此標準，中國尋求核武均勢的證據仍顯薄弱：二〇一五年前，中國完全沒有符合《新削減戰略武器條約》「現役部署」定義的核武——即處於戰備狀態的洲際飛彈、執行巡邏的戰略核潛艇或轟炸機部隊。[95] 截至二〇二三年，解放軍雖可能已運用六艘配備十二個核子飛彈發射管的「晉」級潛艇實施常態化海上威懾巡邏，但絕大多數核武仍不符合該標準。[96]

中國預計在二〇五〇年前擴充並完善其核武庫，這一發展仍與中國傳統的核武政策一致，即維持最低限度報復能力，並堅守「不首先使用」的承諾。中國目前正在研發一套「陸基中段反導系統」，可攔截短程與中程洲際彈道飛彈，主要用途是保護特定的固定指揮與控制設施。[97] 此舉可能代表中國正在修正「遭攻擊後發射」的戰略思維，但同時也符合維持二次打擊能力所需的必要措施。中國在早期預警雷達與衛星能力上的進展，可用於加強對來襲威脅的偵測與追蹤，但這些能力並不一定代表中國意圖先發制人發動攻擊。[98]

中國的戰略是發展足夠的核武器，以便在遭受首波打擊後仍能對敵方造成其無法接受的損害。在中國飛彈部隊的戰略理論中，戰略核武力量的核心是「有效且有限的核反擊」。其重點在於保存核武力量以作為實施「重點打擊」的前提，並強調「科學運用核火

新竄起者　220

力、精心設計打擊計劃」,以「用相對較小的代價達成最大的政治與軍事利益」。[99] 這種戰略理念在核武數量上保留一定的靈活性。可以說,當前戰略環境的變化可能已促使中國即使在遵循既定核武政策下,也需要一個規模更大、存活力更強的核武庫。其中最重要的變因之一是美國飛彈防禦系統的進步,中國戰略界普遍認為這對中國核反擊能力的可靠性與效能構成嚴重威脅。[100]

對海外利益的保護

隨著中國經濟的崛起,海外利益也迅速擴張。二○○○年,也就是中國加入世界貿易組織的前一年,中國與世界其他地區的貿易總額約為四千七百五十億美元(低於加拿大);而當年美國以接近二兆美元的規模領先全球。[101] 僅僅八年後,中國就成為全球最大出口國,如今更躍居世界第一大貿易國。二○二一年,中國的全球雙向貿易總額突破六兆美元,美國則為四點七兆美元。[102] 在此期間,中國對於石油與糧食等關鍵資源的進口依賴度也大為提升。一九七五至二○一八年間,中國的糧食消耗量成長三倍,達到四點二億

221　第五章　中國軍事戰略中的創新作為

噸，同時中國每年的糧食進口逆差達五百億美元。103 中國對石油的依賴程度也非常高：二〇二一年，國內消費的石油中約有百分之七十二仰賴進口。104 某些關鍵技術上中國也極度依賴進口，如半導體：僅二〇二一年就進口了超過四千億美元的半導體產品；還有某些關鍵礦產，這些資源是中國成為新能源產品領導者的必要條件。105

一九九〇年至二〇〇〇年間，中國企業開始向海外偏遠地區進行投資，通常還會同時派遣中國勞工隨行。二〇〇〇年代中期，中國公民開始大量出國，不僅是作為勞工，也包括觀光客。一九九〇年時約有六萬名中國公民在海外工作，但這個數字持續增長，到二〇一八年已接近一百萬人。目前有超過三萬家中國企業在海外營運。旅遊業也同樣蓬勃發展：二〇一九年中國出境旅客達到一點五五億人次，在本世紀初時僅有約一千萬人次。106 中國海外利益的快速增長，與習近平推動的重要經濟倡議——「一帶一路」密切相關。截至二〇二〇年，超過十萬名中國人移居非洲，尋求在一帶一路沿線的機會，使非洲大陸上的中國移民總數突破一百萬人。僅在非洲地區，就有一萬家中國企業。107 中國社會科學院在二〇二〇年《中國對外投資國別風險評級報告》中指出，百分之八十四的一帶一路投資集中在中高風險國家。108 這些報告也一貫地將參與一帶一路的國家描述為「發展

新竊起者　222

中國家，通常經濟脆弱、缺乏多元化且不穩定」，並且「由於複雜的地緣政治與政權更替頻繁，具有高度政治風險」。109 根據中華人民共和國商務部的數據，在二〇一〇年至二〇一五年間，全球共發生至少三百四十五起涉及中國公民的安全事件。110

隨著越來越多中國公民走向海外，中國政府面臨日益增長的壓力，需保護其公民免受因政治不穩、工作環境危險與自然災害引發的「風險事件」影響。111 正如中國外交部領事司副司長翟雷鳴於二〇一五年所感嘆的：「從來沒有一個國家面對過這樣龐大的任務，保護海外中國公民是國家的「首要任務」，並強調「安全應該伴隨著我們同胞的腳步」。113 二〇二一年，外交部長王毅訪問非洲時再次強調「採取有效行動全面保護中國公民的安全與權益」的重要性。114 中國國內的調查也顯示，中國民眾強烈支持撤僑行動，並將保護海外中國公民視為政府的核心職能之一。中國影史上票房第二高的電影《戰狼二》，正是一部講述特種部隊成員前往非洲某未具名國家營救中國人質的故事。

中國並不是第一個在戰略與國內政治層面上都迫切需要保護海外利益的國家。美國在第二次世界大戰後崛起為世界領導強權時，也曾面臨類似的兩難。當時，美國選擇了創新

223 第五章 中國軍事戰略中的創新作為

策略路線,不同於歐洲列強與日本帝國的方式:「征服他國、建立殖民地,以確保對關鍵資源與市場的取得」。[115]華盛頓運用設在盟國的基地進行間歇性力量投射來解決問題。自此之後,全球軍事力量投射可以說已成為美國武裝部隊的核心任務(僅次於本土防衛)。[116]《國防戰略》及其前身《四年期國防評估報告》(Quadrennial Defense Review)自一九九七年首次發布以來,每一版都討論了全球力量投射與保護議題。[117]作戰層面,這種全球性早已被整合進各軍種的特定任務之中。[118]例如,美國空軍的五大核心任務為:制空權、全球打擊、快速全球機動、情報、監視與偵察、指揮與控制;其中有兩項任務明確標示為「全球性的」,而其餘三項在實際運作上也都屬於全球性任務。[119]

美國的軍事力量建設過程中,海外領土、基地及非毗鄰屬地一直具有不可或缺的作用。[120]截至二〇二二年九月,美國約有百分之十三的現役軍人部署在海外(已較二〇〇八年時的百分之二十六降低不少)。[121]二〇二二年,美國在四十五個國家擁有約一百二十個基地與大型設施。[122]自一九五〇年代以來,海外軍事人員的數量與基地設施的位置大致保持穩定,僅根據戰略優先層級的變動進行部分調整。[123]二〇一九至二〇二一年間,美國每年維持這些海外駐軍的平均成本為二百三十三點七億美元,這個數字並不包括海外應急行

新竊起者　　224

動的成本,該項支出在同一期間內平均每年約為六百二十四點三億美元。

自二戰結束以來,美國持續運用其全球軍事力量進行海外干預。一九四六至二〇一六年間,美國共實施一百零五次軍事干預行動,範圍涵蓋除澳洲與南極洲外的所有大陸,其中百分之七十五涉及地面部隊作戰。[125]最近的反恐戰爭估計讓美國支出了六點四兆美元,另有一兆美元用於退伍軍人與傷殘補助相關支出。[126]總支出是中國自一九九五至二〇二〇年間累計國防支出約二點九兆美元的兩倍以上。[127]

在評估了美國保護海外利益的戰略之後,中國有許多理由選擇不加以仿效。首先,全球性軍事存在並不符合中國的競爭優勢。美國及其盟友在裝備與基地方面擁有壓倒性的力量投射能力。美國的海外基地網路多是透過戰爭獲得的:最初是透過征服(例如從西班牙手中取得),其次是第二次世界大戰與韓戰的結果,再來則是冷戰競爭時期基於對盟邦的承諾而設立的基地。這類全球性的軍事架構難以僅透過和平時期的談判與協議來建立。

其次,全球軍事存在對中國而言,歷來都不具備戰略必要性。美國面臨的威脅多數發生在遠離其本土之處——包括冷戰時期與蘇聯在歐洲的軍事對抗,以及近年主要源自西南亞地區的非傳統威脅(如內戰、海盜活動與恐怖主義)。相較之下,中國領導層認為該國最迫切的安全威脅主要來自東亞周邊地區。[128] 前中國外交官甄炳禧二〇一五年撰文指出，美國的鄰國加拿大與墨西哥在綜合國力上相對薄弱，使得華府享有比北京「更簡單且可控的地緣政治環境」。[129] 據中國一名高級官員表示，這些安全優先事項正因華府「亞太再平衡」戰略的干預而受到威脅。[130] 因此，中國具有強烈動機將海外軍事部署的規模最小化，並降低海外軍事承諾的開支。[131]

第三，中國戰略家認為，美國透過對外戰爭來保護其利益的做法，既昂貴又無效。這種信念正是鄧小平「韜光養晦」戰略的核心，該戰略主張避免衝突，因為「中國還不夠強，打不起仗」，而且「打仗對中國沒有好處」。[132] 中國領導人與分析人士認為，從越南戰爭的昂貴泥淖到英國、蘇聯與美國在阿富汗的經驗，都指出了力量投射所帶來的風險。[133] 曾擔任胡錦濤顧問的王緝思曾警告說，中國在崛起的過程中應該避免軍事冒險行為。[134]

其四，除效率不彰與相對低效外，模仿美國模式還可能引發他國強烈的威脅觀感。中國共產黨始終謹慎經營其國際形象，並持續向國際社會傳達：無論變得多麼強大繁榮，中國都將尊重各國主權。[135] 儘管外界對此和平形象並非全盤接受，但中國通過明確反對「冷戰思維」，刻意與美國形成區隔。中國學者尤其嚴厲批判美軍干預行動對發展中國家的負

新篡起者　226

面影響——這正是多數美國軍事干預的發生地。[136]

最後，與美國劃清界線對中共的國內形象塑造至關重要。正如學者孔適海（Isaac Kardon）所分析：

「若僅考量作戰需求，解放軍理應早已建立龐大海外後勤網絡，包括專屬軍事基地……（但）解放軍的規劃必須服從黨中央更宏觀的地緣政治目標——這決定了中國在海外軍事力量投射上採取低調漸進模式……中國在發展中國家建立的『反殖民、反霸權』形象，基於一項基本事實：中華人民共和國從未在海外進行軍事冒險行動。」[137]

事實上，當中國在吉布地建立首座（也是目前唯一一座）海外基地時，北京特別強調「永遠不尋求霸權，永遠不搞軍事擴張和軍備競賽。這些承諾不會因為建設海外保障基地而改變」。[138]

由於有限的戰略效益、企圖降低威脅觀感，以及對中國競爭優勢的評估，這些因素共

227　第五章　中國軍事戰略中的創新作為

同促使中國採取一種創新的方式來維護海外利益。中國顯然沒有追隨老牌強權的腳步。一九九〇年代末，中國沒有在海外駐留軍事人員，過去三十年來情況幾乎沒有改變。如今，美國派駐海外的軍事人員數量仍是中國的三十九倍（這種差距主要是由於美國縮減駐軍，而非中國增加部署）。總體而言，中國每年平均在海外維持約四千名軍事人員：海軍一千六百人中，八百人執行亞丁灣任務，七十名海軍特種部隊參與反海盜行動，其餘人員則為臨時部署或參與演習。另有約二千五百名陸軍人員參與聯合國維和任務；約二十名空軍人員負責人道主義救援與災難應對任務，並視需求操作兩架運輸機。[139] 中國僅有一處海外基地，即二〇一七年在吉布地設立的保障基地，該基地駐有一支小型特遣隊，包括二艘飛彈護衛艦和一艘補給艦。[140]

中國的遠征作戰能力至今仍相當有限。首款大型軍用運輸機運二十直到二〇一六年六月才正式服役，目前僅配備約三十架，而美軍C-17「全球霸王III」運輸機數量達二百二十三架。[141] 首架空中加油機轟油六更遲至二〇一五年才列裝部隊。[142] 若中國希望在全球進行傳統武力投射，尚需建立藍水海軍——即具備持續遠洋作戰能力的海軍力量。此類海軍必須擁有航行中補給能力，包括燃料、食品、零部件、彈藥的補給，以及人員輪換

新竄起者　228

等。中國首艘綜合補給艦直到二○一五年才加入海軍序列，更先進的九○一型補給艦目前仍在進行海試。事實上，在二○一一年利比亞撤僑行動中，中國不得不租用商用船隻與民航機來撤離三萬五千名公民。換言之，過去二十五年間中國利益已邁向全球化，但軍事投射範圍卻未同步擴展。除太空、網路和洲際彈道飛彈領域外，中國仍無法在亞太區域外投射進攻性武力。

相反地，自二○一○年代出現需求以來，中國採取了一種明確的「混合策略」來保護其海外利益。中國高度依賴駐在國的安全部隊、海外警力部署、私人保安公司與聯合國維和行動，以補足本國軍隊有限的貢獻。143 這種做法考量到北京在軍事上的限制（缺乏盟友、遠征能力有限），同時也強化了政治靈活性與樽節國防支出的優勢。

中國更傾向於依賴當地安全與執法力量，以及本國警務人員來保護其在各國的利益。透過深化安全交流、國防外交、經濟誘因，以及區域和多邊安全合作，中國成功爭取周邊夥伴的支持，共同保護中方利益並處理恐怖主義與人口販運等跨國議題。中國經常直接資助駐在國的安全部隊，或至少提供經濟誘因、武器或訓練，以協助駐在國提升對中國資產與人員聚集地區的安全維護能力。如本書第三章所述，中方對這些部隊提供的培訓，進一

229　第五章　中國軍事戰略中的創新作為

步完善了此戰略體系。

中國更善於運用經濟影響力，將保護責任明確納入與駐在國的協議條款中。典型案例是二〇一六年巴基斯坦宣布組建萬人規模的「特別安全部隊」，專門保護參與「中巴經濟走廊」及瓜達爾港（Gwadar Port）建設的中國人員。這項協議的簽訂，直接源自北京承諾為該經濟走廊投入數十億美元基礎建設資金。巴基斯坦也透過多個單位保護中國在瓜達爾港的利益與工人，包括：「第八十八特遣隊」，負責港口與航線的海上安全；沿海安全與港口防衛部隊；以及由巴基斯坦海軍陸戰隊組成的「部隊保護營」。144 值得注意的是，這些安保力量，以及一萬五千名巴基斯坦「特別安全師」地面部隊，其運作經費全數來自中巴經濟走廊。145

巴基斯坦並非唯一動用國內安全部隊以協助中國的國家。在緬甸，當地警方多次介入鎮壓因中國萬寶礦業公司開發萊比塘銅礦而失去土地與生計的村民抗爭。146 衣索比亞是另一個中資與當地安保力量合作的有力例證，光是中國在該國的建築與製造業項目總值就超過四十億美元。二〇二一年，中國與衣索比亞（中國稱為埃塞俄比亞）簽署諒解備忘錄，建立「一帶一路重大項目安全保障機制」。147 此前數月，衣索比亞警方曾護送數百名捲入

新竄起者　230

暴力衝突的中國公民安全撤離，隨後中國大使館捐贈了安保設備與武器給衣索比亞警察總署。[148]類似案例還包括：奈及利亞（中國稱為尼日利亞）政府為打擊博科聖地組織，從中國獲取輕型武器與無人機，這些裝備很可能用於保護當地中國企業與公民的安全。[149]中國還承諾提供六千萬美元支持非洲聯盟待命部隊，其目的明確指出是為了保障該區域的經濟穩定，進而間接保障中國經濟利益。[150]

關於內部安全培訓的詳細討論請參見第三章，但一些數據顯示這是中國海外利益保護政策的重要組成部分。在我研究的一百九十六個國家中，超過半數接受過來自中國機構的某種形式的內部（警察、鑑識、網路安全、軍事、準軍事、抗議活動管理等）培訓。在一百一十個接受中國培訓的國家中，約三分之一接受過被歸類為警察相關的培訓。作為經濟利益的指標，近九成接受中國培訓的國家也與中國簽署了「一帶一路」諒解備忘錄。三分之二簽署「一帶一路」備忘錄的國家接受過某種形式的中國培訓；而在未簽署「一帶一路」備忘錄的國家中，只有約五分之一接受過中國培訓。

二○一七年二月，中國公安部透過高層工作會議，啟動新一輪協調中國執法機構國際合作的措施。[151]當時公安部已與一百一十三個國家和地區建立合作關係，構建了

231　第五章　中國軍事戰略中的創新作為

一百二十九個雙邊與多邊合作機制、九十六條通報熱線，並與七十個國家的警察部門簽署超過四百份合作文件。[152]同年稍晚，公安部與國際刑警組織（連結一百九十五個成員國刑事警察的政府間組織）簽署協議，承諾在「貿易安全、打擊非法市場與金融犯罪及網路犯罪、保障『一帶一路』沿線關鍵基礎設施安全」等領域展開合作。[153]此後，公安部代表持續與外國夥伴保持對話，包括參與二〇一九年「世界警察高峰會」等國際會議，該高峰會聚集了一百零三國的警察首長討論「偵查協作、警察培訓與能力建設」等議題。[154]

中國的警務活動也已延伸到國境之外。中國已與義大利、塞爾維亞與克羅埃西亞達成協議，允許中國警察與當地警察在熱門旅遊景點共同巡邏，以更好地保護中國遊客，特別是防止搶劫事件。[155]但在其他情況下，中國則出於更具爭議性的目的擴展其警務行動，且未經駐在國批准。二〇二二年九月，一個非政府人權組織發表了一份報告，調查中國在世界各地大使館內設立的「警務服務站」，指出至少有五十四個這類機構；二〇二三年四月，美國聯邦調查局逮捕了兩名在紐約經營此類機構的人士。[156]中國聲稱這些設施主要提供行政服務，例如為海外中國公民更新駕照，但實際上，它們也被用來執行中國的「勸返行動」，中國當局透過社交媒體騷擾海外異議人士，試圖說服其返回中國。根據中國公安

新竊起者　232

部的數據，光是在二〇二一年，中國就「勸返」了二十一萬人回國。中國還透過部署自身安全力量（主要是武警或私營保安公司，而非傳統軍事力量）在安全領域扮演更直接的角色。武警作為準軍事組織，被北京賦予維護國內穩定以及在必要時為解放軍提供後方支援的職責。該組織負責中國駐外使領館的保安工作，二〇一五年公布的《反恐怖主義法》為其參與海外行動提供了法律依據。158 武警的海外行動主要集中於邊境地區，旨在預防當地動盪並鞏固對少數民族人口的控制。

在這樣的框架下，中國於塔吉克設立了武警哨所，並與當地警方一同在中國、塔吉克、阿富汗之間的邊境地區進行聯合反恐巡邏，目的是阻止恐怖分子流入新疆地區，同時避免「軍事」介入的指控。159 二〇一六年，中國、阿富汗、巴基斯坦與塔吉克共同成立了四方合作與協調機制，此機制促使中國武警部隊赴阿富汗參與聯合國任務，並與阿富汗、塔吉克部隊展開聯合巡邏行動。160 其他合作架構還包括：中國與阿富汗、巴基斯坦的三邊論壇、亞洲相互協作與信任措施會議、伊斯坦堡進程、與美國、阿富汗、巴基斯坦組成的四方協調小組。另外中國武警部隊每三到四年會與上海合作組織其他成員國進行聯合演習，包括哈薩克、塔吉克與烏茲別克等國，但這些演習多為基礎訓練，如徒手格鬥，而非

233　第五章　中國軍事戰略中的創新作為

高階戰術演練。161

中國政府還藉由私營保安公司來投射影響力，同時保持可推諉性（deniability），特別是在「一帶一路」沿線地區、海上領域，以及為發展中國家員警和安全部隊提供培訓方面。162 二〇〇九年，中國以公安部對私營保安行業實施嚴格的法律、行政和政治控制，使其合法化。163 二〇一三年時，在中國註冊的數千家保安公司已雇傭約四百萬保安人員。到二〇一六年已有約三千二百名專業保安人員被派駐到海外。164 目前已有三十個國家駐有中國的私人保安公司，主要集中在非洲和亞洲，但遠及阿根廷和土耳其也有。165 其中一家主要的業者是德威國際安保集團，該公司為眾多中國國企提供保安服務。根據其官方網站：自二〇一八年六月以來，該公司已在當地為合作夥伴執行超過三千場培訓，訓練超過七萬名中國承包商，並與當地安全部門合作，成功處理超過一千起涉及中國目標的事件。二〇一六年，德威還曾受命協助撤離受困於南蘇丹內戰的中國工人。166

另有證據顯示，中國正透過聯合國維和行動來保障其在動盪國家的投資安全。二〇一二至二〇一八年間，中國派遣維和部隊駐紮的國家中，約七成在中國維和人員抵達當年或三年內，曾收受中國大量投資。167 北京具備優勢地位，能在中國經濟利益集中的區域推

新竄起者　234

動維和行動授權。[168]在南蘇丹，中國以基礎建設貸款換取該國六分之一石油產量，成功遊說將石油設施納入聯合國南蘇丹特派團的保護範圍（儘管遭當地反對勢力抗議）。在剛果民主共和國，中國擁有全球最大銅鈷礦場之一的八成股權。而中國是黎巴嫩最大的貿易夥伴，中國企業積極參與該國電力、電信、交通、水利等大型基礎建設項目。值得注意的是，二〇一九年九月，中國威脅將否決聯合國阿富汗維和任務的授權延期案，除非決議文中明確提及「一帶一路」倡議（最終中國撤銷此項要求）。

儘管中國顯然沒有模仿美國建立海外駐軍以保護其全球利益的作法，但在過去五年中，中國「建造基地」的企圖仍成為西方安全分析人士擔憂的焦點之一。二〇一九年，中國與柬埔寨簽署一項秘密協議，允許解放軍在柬埔寨西哈努克省的雲壤海軍基地使用一塊六十二英畝的區域，期限長達三十年。二〇二一年，中國可能在阿拉伯聯合大公國與赤道幾內亞建設軍事基地的傳聞，震驚了美國國安界。最令人不安的發展發生於二〇二二年，中國與索羅門群島簽署了一項協議，保證中國海軍可進入該國港口，並且（更具爭議性地）允許中國派遣軍隊進入索羅門群島以保護中國公民與利益，但協議的具體細節並未公開。二〇二三年，媒體報導（後由美國政府證實）指出，中國與古巴達成協議，在古巴設立一處情報基地,該基地將使中國得以竊聽來自美國軍事基地的電子通訊。根據《華盛頓郵報》取得的文件,美國情報機構評估,中國的目標是在二〇三〇年前在海外建立五個基地與十個後勤設施,分布於東南亞、中東與非洲地區。

美國對中國建立海外基地的焦慮是可以預期的,因為在這一領域的模仿行為將直接威脅到美國既有的戰略利益。儘管本書的結論部分會進一步推測中國未來的基地戰略,但此處的重點是:儘管外界有諸多擔憂,且自從約二十年前外界首次對中國建立「珍珠鏈」(在印度洋沿線建立基地網路)的企圖發出警訊以來,解放軍至今仍僅有一個永久性的海外據點,位於吉布地。至於與索羅門群島的協議並不涉及具體設施,而是賦予中國在該國的法律權利,特別是訪問港口與派遣部隊的權利,但並未明確說明是否會建設相關的基礎設施。而對於在阿拉伯聯合大公國的設施、與柬埔寨以及赤道幾內亞的協議,目前仍難以判斷其在中國對外控制範圍的哪個位置上,因為在阿拉伯聯合大公國的建設已被取消,與柬埔寨的協議內容並未公開,而與赤道幾內亞的協議狀態也不明朗。

然而變化似乎正在發生。中國國內論述已形成共識:解放軍至少需要具備一定的遠征能力,以支援人道主義救援和災難救助任務、撤僑行動,並威懾美國以「離岸控制戰略」

封鎖關鍵水道、切斷中國與世界聯繫的企圖。[171] 二〇一五年，中國海軍戰略正式從「近海防禦」調整為「近海防禦與遠海護衛相結合」，這一轉變既源於保護海外經濟利益的新需求，也保留了控制第一島鏈內制海權的原始任務。[172] 中國已明確表達要「彌補海外行動與支援方面弱點」的意圖，具體方式包括：建設遠海力量、發展海外後勤設施以及提升執行多樣化軍事任務的能力。[173]

中國確實似乎正在建立某種形式的支援系統，但其輪廓與美國的系統截然不同。一種創新型的基地建設模式正在成形，這種模式高度依賴商業型戰略據點，用以支援遠海行動，特別是非傳統軍事行動與情報收集。事實上，中國企業目前在全球五十三個國家的九十六個港口擁有或經營碼頭設施，其中超過一半位於主要戰略水道附近。[174] 這些行動引起全球關注，始於中國招商局因斯里蘭卡政府債務違約後接管了斯里蘭卡的漢班托塔港（Hambantota Port）。中國遠洋運輸公司旗下港口業務也在該公司收購希臘比雷埃夫斯港（Piraeus Port）碼頭經營權後，引發中國是否企圖「買下整個歐洲」的關注。而作為一帶一路領頭項目的巴基斯坦瓜達爾港也被視為具有潛在軍事用途的港口，該港不僅具備停泊大型船艦的能力，還鄰近戰略要道荷姆茲海峽。[176]

237　第五章　中國軍事戰略中的創新作為

效率、效能，以及降低威脅觀感等竄起者策略的要素，正在促使中國採取這種新的基地建設方式。從中國的官方論述與行為中也可以明確看出，過去三十年來，中國刻意避免模仿美國的戰略模式。在中國內部的大多數討論中，他國的海外基地被視為對中國的戰略難題，而非值得學習的榜樣。[177] 相對地，中國戰略家認為商業型後勤樞紐具有效率優勢：它們的成本較低、能穩定供應所需的基本物資、在外交與行政層面上更容易取得准入權，而且越來越多此類設施達到了軍民兩用設施，不僅能避免中國在追求海外基地過程中耗盡資源的陷阱，還能創造收益。[178] [179] 聚焦於建設軍民兩用設施，不僅能

主張中國海軍在海上絲綢之路沿線採取更積極戰略的中國軍事評論人士，也普遍主張應採取創新方式來建構海外基地，以減少國際反彈。他們認為，透過「精心選點、低調布局、合作優先、緩慢滲透」的方式，[180] [181] 特別是借助民用設施進行這一過程，中國將能擺脫擴張主義者的指控，同時降低美國對中國海軍正成為全球性威脅的觀感。[182] 許多分析人士也已意識到這些基地在情報蒐集方面的潛在效用，由於中國遍佈全球的港口網路提供了一個廣泛蒐集資料的平台，這些數據對軍事情報（尤其是海軍）具有極高價值。[183]

雖然事實顯示，中國在其崛起過程中並未如同美國般追求全球軍事力量投射，但對於

新竄起者　238

「竄起者策略」的主要反對論點是：中國其實一直希望模仿美國，也就是建立遠征能力與海外基地，以便能夠投射進攻性軍事力量，只是尚未成功而已。二〇一〇年，米爾斯海默主張：當區域霸權實力增長時，它們「必然會受到誘惑，去模仿美國」，因為成為全球軍事霸權所帶來的利益實在是「巨大無比」。[184] 同樣地，杜如松在他二〇一〇年的著作中也預測：中國將會追求更強的力量投射能力，儘管他原則上也承認中國不太可能複製美國那種「複雜且代價高昂」的全球基地體系。但他仍然認為，一旦條件允許，中國將轉而依賴傳統軍事力量來保護其海外利益。[185]

這種「資源驅動論」——認為中國一旦有能力就會仿效美國——很難與中國實際的資源狀況相應。中國的經濟規模大約是法國的六倍，印度的五倍多。然而法國比中國早七十一年擁有航空母艦（航母被視為終極的力量投射平台），印度比中國早五十一年；法國有十二個海外基地，印度有十個。俄羅斯在五個國家設有軍事基地（包括烏克蘭、喬治亞和摩爾多瓦等有領土爭議的地區），另外在三個國家設有小型設施和駐軍。[186] 甚至泰國也比中國早十五年服役其第一艘（也是唯一一艘）航空母艦。美國和俄羅斯的運輸機數量都超過中國，印度則幾乎與中國持平。[187] 換句話說，中國早就具備與其他強權相當的能力

239　第五章　中國軍事戰略中的創新作為

（即規模可能較小）來複製美國保護海外利益的力量投射模式。這些證據支持我的論點：中國沒有選擇模仿美國並非因為能力不足，而是出於戰略選擇。

另一種對中國缺乏全球力量投射能力的另一種解釋是，中國在安全保障上搭美國的便車，也就是依賴由美國提供的安全保障。這一觀點的主要依據在於：中國依賴中東地區的石油運輸，但卻未曾主動承擔海上航道的保護責任。此外，在與塔利班合作之前，中國也曾依賴美國來保護其在阿富汗及其他中東地區的利益。188 然而，美國的安全存在雖然廣泛，但其部署範圍與中國的戰略利益分布並不完全重疊，尤其是在發展中國家地區。例如，中國透過一帶一路，在非洲，特別是東非地區有龐大的經濟投資，涵蓋海上與陸上路線，但美國與其盟國在這些區域的安全基礎建設則極為有限。再如，美國自二〇一四年起便已基本撤出中亞地區，而該地區正是一帶一路的典型代表區域，即便在那之前，美國在中亞的駐軍也非常有限。曾有觀點認為中國在中亞地區可能搭俄羅斯的便車。然而，中國通過部署武警及與中亞國家的聯合反恐巡邏，顯示了自身在該地區的安全存在，這表明北京並不願意完全依賴其他國家來保障自身安全。

儘管資源有限且能力有所不足，中國在過去三十年間，於安全與軍事領域展現強權能

新竄起者　240

力，已取得顯著進展。雖然軍事力量是中國崛起為強權的關鍵要素，但中國領導層始終刻意避免過度追求軍事實力。189 中國成功鞏固了對爭議領土的控制，並且有效且高效的保護了日益擴張的海外利益，同時沒有引發重大戰爭，也未對中共體制造成不穩定。中國之所以能達成這一切，是因為它選擇了與眾不同的作法──無論是在區域還是全球層面，在傳統軍事還是核武領域，中國都採取了符合自身競爭優勢的方式來行動。

第六章

中國在經濟政策上的模仿與利用策略

從許多方面來看，中國崛起的歷程本質上是一個經濟故事。一九七八年，中國有百分之七十一的人口從事農業，人均GDP僅為一百五十六美元，相比之下，當時美國的人均GDP為一萬零五百美元。1但隨後，中國開始推動一項經濟市場化與自由化的政策，名為「改革開放」。鄧小平開始推動農業去集體化，並向外資開放中國市場。他還設立了幾個經濟特區，如深圳、珠海與廈門，這些城市免受官僚體系的限制管制，並成為中國全國經濟增長的引擎。後續在一九八〇年代與一九九〇年代的改革中，中國開始對國有企業部門進行改革，並放鬆政府對企業的控制。

在過去三十年間，中國的經濟實力大幅躍升。到了二〇〇五年，中國的人均GDP已上升了約十倍，並且近半的人口居住於城市地區（相比之下，一九七八年時僅有百分之二十）。五年後，中國超越日本，成為世界第二大經濟體。中國也成為世界最大出口國；如今，中國每年向其他國家出口的商品總額約為三點四兆美元，而一九九五年僅為一千五百億美元。2中國的出口產品也從低價塑膠玩具等低附加價值商品，升級為高端電子產品。如今，中國在全球供應鏈中扮演關鍵角色，涵蓋領域從製藥到新能源技術不等。

新竄起者　244

全球目前在與中國的經濟關係上，處於一個前所未有的特殊局面。雖然歷史上並非首次出現由經濟競爭引發更廣泛戰略競爭的情況，但中國在國際經濟體系中的發展軌跡，與過去的新興強權相比，具有一些獨特之處。首先，中國經濟的全球地位極為廣泛；中國與美國幾乎年年輪流成為全球最大外國投資目的地。中國自稱是全球一百二十個國家的最大貿易夥伴，約占全世界國家總數的五分之三，其中甚至包括美國在印太地區的關鍵盟友，如日本與南韓。3 事實上，許多美國盟友在經濟方面對中國的依賴程度超過對美國的依賴，這使得華盛頓在與北京競爭時更為複雜。

第二個獨特的情況是，歷史上從未有一個新興強權與既有霸權在經濟上如此緊密交織。中國持有至少八千六百億美元的美國國債，佔外國持有美國國債總額的百分之十二。4 二〇二二年，美中雙邊貿易總額達到約六千九百億美元（相當於波蘭一整年的國內生產毛額）。5 若從歷史角度來看，如今美國與中國僅十天的貿易總額，就相當於第一次世界大戰爆發前一年德國與英國全年的貿易總額（以現今美元計算），而當時德國與英國就已經被視為在經濟上高度相互依賴。6 儘管美國國內普遍呼籲降低經濟上對中國的依賴，二〇二二年美國仍是中國對外投資的最大目的地。7

245　第六章　中國在經濟政策上的模仿與利用策略

中美之間的經濟相互依賴，在各合作國家內部催生出新的利益集團，這些集團使得對中國的戰略競爭變得更加複雜。隨著各國在貿易、投資或援助上越來越依賴中國市場，出現了一批有影響力的經濟利益團體，他們主張與中國維持穩定合作的關係，以保護自身利益，即使這樣做會犧牲其國家更廣泛的戰略目標。[8] 例如二○二一年，避險基金橋水公司（Bridgewater Associates）的創辦人，億萬富豪雷伊·達里歐（Ray Dalio）公開將中國的人權侵害行為與美國的種族問題相提並論。在上海擁有一家超級工廠的特斯拉創辦人伊隆·馬斯克（Elon Musk），在聲稱台灣「幾乎肯定」將被「整合」進中華人民共和國後引發爭議，此番言論既贏得北京讚賞，也招致台灣譴責。

第三，美國從未面對過一個擁有如此龐大經濟資源的競爭對手。在一九八○年代初期，蘇聯的國內生產毛額不到美國的一半；而到了二○二一年，中國的國內生產毛額已相當於美國的約百分之七十六。[9] 中國的經濟實力顯而易見，根據蓋洛普（Gallup）於二○二○年夏季在十四個主要國家所做的民調，除美國、南韓與日本以外的其他國家，多數受訪者皆認為中國是世界第一大經濟強國。[10] 從客觀數據來看，美國仍是全球經濟超級強權，且很可能會持續保持這一地位，尤其是隨著中國經濟在新冠疫情之後出現疲軟跡

新竄起者　246

象。[11]但中國仍舊擁有龐大的經濟影響力，其他國家對這種影響力深有感觸。

那麼，中國究竟是如何運用經濟工具，在國際體系中建立實力、影響力與槓桿手段的呢？答案是當條件成熟時，中國便「模仿」美國的做法，同時也積極「利用」現行體制的缺口。以自由貿易為例，這是一個適合模仿的領域，因為它不僅被視為一種有效的實力建構策略，同時也是一種能夠讓美國放心、並有助於鞏固中共在國內統治地位的政策選擇。中國還透過尋求優惠貿易，積極利用制度上的空白與漏洞，不但在國際經濟機構中取得有利地位，還擴展了其在發展中國家的市場佔有率。

中國同樣採取了美式的經濟制裁手段來影響他國政策，不過是透過具有中國特色的方式，利用體系中的漏洞與弱點來實施。中國領導人認為，比起使用軍事力量，這種手法既能更有效地達成目標，又不會造成他國的威脅觀感。在這種情況下，中共維護國內統治合法性的需求雖未削弱該策略的效力，卻限制了其適用範圍：中國主要採取單邊經濟制裁手段，迫使交易夥伴接受其國內政策。具體而言，中國憑藉其龐大市場規模作為威懾，阻止他國從事其認定有損中共統治穩定的行為。

中國在試圖挑戰美國主導的全球金融體系、並促進國內經濟成長的過程中，採取了模

247　第六章　中國在經濟政策上的模仿與利用策略

仿與利用並行的策略。一開始，北京試圖直接與美國競爭，藉由模仿美國現有的一些金融做法來推動其戰略目標。例如，中國曾努力推動將人民幣納入特別提款權，並鼓勵國際實體以人民幣進行交易。然而，這種模仿策略也面臨內在限制，但由於共產黨必須維持對金融工具的控制，因此限制了人民幣國際化的推進與成效。在此情況下，中國稍微調整了其戰略方向，轉而試圖根據自身競爭優勢，利用體制空隙：一方面鼓勵一帶一路國家以人民幣進行結算，另一方面則在數位貨幣等新興領域展開競爭，以推廣人民幣的使用。

中國對「自由貿易」的追求

美國在國際秩序中的領導地位，奠基於龐大的經濟體量。以美國為首的自由主義國際秩序之所以能長期維繫，部分歸功於促進全球繁榮的自由貿易原則。12 中國戰略學者已認識到美國這套模式的價值，中國商務部將世界貿易組織與自由貿易協定視為推動經濟全球化的兩大「車輪」。13 中國經濟學家也認為，自由貿易能促進外資直接投資：根據東協秘書處估算，中國—東協自由貿易區的建立將使東協對中投資增長百分之四十八。14 中國領

新竄起者　248

導人更深刻意識到，與他國建立自由貿易關係，既能避免美國主導的孤立圍堵，又能擴張中國在全球經濟秩序中的影響力。[15]當貿易量持續增長，各國將把對中經濟聯繫置於戰略考量之上，進而弱化其配合美國政策的動機。例如隨著中國經濟體量擴大，多邊經濟機構必須納入中國參與才能有效運作，這使得各國更加靠攏中國，並降低對其政治議題的批判意願。[16]中國還通過戰略性投資他國企業與簽訂高額商業協議，緩解他國對其經濟實力的戒心，進而換取更有利的政策立場。[17]

中國領導人同時也認為，融入全球市場是一個能讓國際社會安心的舉動。在六四事件之後，北京成功利用經濟合作的前景作為籌碼，逐步改善與他國的外交關係，先是與日本，再來是歐洲各國與加拿大，最後才是美國。[18]一九九八年，一位參與中國加入世界貿易組織談判的中國官員擔心，認為若是中國延遲或未能成功加入世界貿易組織，將會助長「中國威脅論」的蔓延。[19]中國加入世界貿易組織談判的首席代表龍永圖則主張，中國的加入可以緩解中美兩國之間的摩擦。[20]換言之，中國之所以擁抱自由貿易，背後的邏輯不僅是為了藉此壯大國力，更是一種對外釋放善意、維護對外關係穩定的策略。正如中國國務院總理朱鎔基所說：中國即使不加入世界貿易組織也能實現經濟增長，但加入是「為了

249　第六章　中國在經濟政策上的模仿與利用策略

維護中美友好合作與建立建設性戰略夥伴關係而做出的重大讓步」。[21]這項策略在相當長的一段時間內是成功的,因為「中國參與自由貿易能確保其和平崛起」這一觀點,持續流傳了近三十年。[22]

自由貿易對中國而言,既是促進經濟成長的國內策略,也是鞏固黨內控制的有效手段。中國刻意推動對外貿易以帶動國內經濟發展,這對中共維持統治正當性至關重要。以朱鎔基為代表的改革派領導人,在面對既得利益的官僚體系與黨內保守勢力阻撓時,成功將國企改革與加入世貿組織掛鉤,從而突破改革困境。[24]中國得以運用其龐大市場規模、低價製造品出口優勢,以及對數種關鍵原物料的近乎壟斷地位,來影響國際市場供需。[25]自由貿易協定更為中國企業對海外的投資鋪路,這不僅是維持經濟持續成長、邁向高收入國家的關鍵,也幫助北京獲取外國技術與專業知識。[26]這些因素使中共得以在冷戰結束後至二○一九年間,始終保持百分之六以上的經濟成長率。[27]

中國之所以選擇模仿自由貿易模式,關鍵在於其戰略效益、穩定國際關係的作用,以及符合國內需求:包括發揮競爭優勢與維護黨的領導等考量。基於這些考量,中國在崛起過程中逐步加入重要的國際金融機構:一九八六年加入亞洲開發銀行、一九九一年加入亞

新竄起者　250

太平洋經合組織、二〇〇一年加入世界貿易組織,並於二〇〇七年成為世界銀行捐助國。28 進入二十一世紀後,中國開始透過簽署雙邊自由貿易協定與美國競爭經濟影響力:二〇〇六年率先與巴基斯坦簽署,二〇〇八年相繼與紐西蘭、新加坡達成協議。29 另外早在二〇〇二年,中國就與東協簽署了自由貿易協定,比起美國同類型的協議還早了四年,藉此創建了當時全球人口最多、規模僅次於北美自由貿易區的第三大市場。

為進一步推動自由貿易,中國以《區域全面經濟夥伴協定》取代部分雙邊自由貿易協定。該協定最初由印尼於二〇一一年提出,並於二〇二〇年十一月正式簽署。《區域全面經濟夥伴協定》旨在整合東協與中國、日本、韓國、澳洲、紐西蘭及印度(後來退出該協定)之間的多項雙邊貿易協議。簽署國同意在二十年內削減百分之九十二的關稅。《區域全面經濟夥伴協定》涵蓋範圍極為廣泛,其十五個成員國約占全球人口及國內生產毛額總量的三成。也是第一個中國、日本與韓國首次同時參與的貿易協定。30 正如一位參與《區域全面經濟夥伴協定》談判的中國學者所言,此協定將重塑東亞生產網路,加速區域經濟整合,並抗衡美國的「單邊主義」政策。31

251　第六章　中國在經濟政策上的模仿與利用策略

中國在深化貿易關係的過程中，也善於利用現有國際體系中的空白與漏洞。中國分析人士始終認為「西方主導的現行國際規則存在問題」，但他們也意識到中國另起爐灶建立全新體系並不現實。32 正如第二章所討論的，中國開始在這些國際機構中謀求領導職位，其擔任的重要職位數量經常超過美國，旨在引導國際經濟事務走向。33 中國持續通過參與國際體系來實現四個關鍵目標：推動世界多極化並鞏固其區域領導地位；利用發展中國家對美國霸權的不滿來推廣自身價值觀；藉亞洲金融危機後美國主導的國際體系衰弱之機，奪取區域領導權；以及強化國際對中國的主權認知與正當性。34 為此，中國在全球經濟體系的議程設置和規則制定方面表現更為強勢。35 二〇〇八年全球金融危機後，北京看到了契機，開始透過支持較小的經濟體復甦來擴展經濟影響力、為自身經濟成長創造更有利的環境。36

川普總統首任任內美國在全球領導地位上的退卻，也留下了中國希望加以利用的權力真空。37 川普總統宣佈退出《跨太平洋戰略經濟夥伴關係協定》（譯註：美國退出後，改組並更名為跨太平洋夥伴全面進步協定），該區域性自由貿易協定原本旨在將美國與環太平洋地區的主要經濟體整合起來，而中國則明顯被排除在外。原本此協定的構想，是為了促使中國採納成員國的制度與政策，進而為世界上經濟成長最快的區域建立更公平的競爭環境。38 但在二○一八年川普政府對中國商品徵收大規模關稅之際，習近平則把握時機，於二○一七年達沃斯世界經濟論壇發表支持自由貿易的演說，他在演講中呼籲國際社會：「要堅定推動全球自由貿易與投資，透過開放促進貿易與投資自由化與便利化，堅決反對保護主義。」39

中國的輿論界也全面呼應習近平的立場，主張全球經濟惡化的元兇是美國發動貿易戰與採取保護主義政策。40 這類言論在提升中國海外形象方面究竟發揮了多大作用，仍難以確定，但它很可能對中國在發展中國家的形象有所助益。截至二○二二年，約有百分之六三的發展中國家受訪者對中國持正面看法，顯示北京在這些國家的受歡迎程度創下新高。41

目前中國已簽署十八項雙邊自由貿易協定，其中包括與東協十國簽訂的協定，這些協定共覆蓋全球GDP的百分之九。相較之下，美國僅簽署二十項雙邊自由貿易協定，卻涵蓋了全球GDP的百分之十五。42 這意味著中國參與的協定雖涉及更多國家，但美國簽署的自由貿易協定的經濟總量佔比更高。中國同時也是《區域全面經濟夥伴關係協定》的

第六章　中國在經濟政策上的模仿與利用策略

成員國，該協定首次將日本納入（在二〇二〇年簽署之前，中國與日本並沒有簽訂自由貿易協定）。《區域全面經濟夥伴關係協定》雖然覆蓋全球國內生產毛額的三成，但其中主要來自中國（佔全球百分之十八）與日本（佔全球百分之六）。[43] 透過自由貿易體系，中國不僅擴展了全球經濟影響力，更藉由經濟成長來鞏固中國共產黨的統治合法性，同時也累積更多資源以實現其國際戰略目標。

利用單邊制裁建立經濟依賴

冷戰結束後，美國日益頻繁地運用經濟制裁，作為懲罰對手或改變其行為的工具。這些制裁措施主要採取三種形式：凍結對手菁英階層的海外資產、禁止美國企業及個人與特定對象進行商業往來，以及限制美國企業對特定海外產業的投資。[44]

美國對越來越多的國家與個體實施種類繁多、規模龐大的經濟制裁。根據「新美國安全中心」的「制裁數據庫」統計：在二〇〇九年，美國共實施了四百四十四項單邊制裁行動；到了二〇二一年，這個數字暴增至一千五百五十二項。[45] 在俄羅斯入侵烏克蘭之後，

新竄起者　254

拜登政府更進一步祭出一千五百項報復性制裁。這些制裁的對象可以是外國公司，也可以是個人。美國實施制裁的目的是為了懲罰特定國家（同時也對潛在模仿者發出嚇阻訊號），以及削弱對手實現其戰略目標的能力。例如，一名美國財政部官員就曾指出，目前對俄羅斯的制裁目標是：「限制俄羅斯的軍事能力及其獲取戰場物資的途徑，以及其整體經濟基礎」。46

中國借鑑美國經驗，創造出一套具有中國特色的經濟脅迫策略，以發揮自身競爭優勢並針對他國弱點。在二〇一〇年之前，囿於國際形象考量與自身經濟實力的限制，中國鮮少動用單邊經濟制裁手段；但自二〇一一年起，北京開始頻繁運用經濟制裁手段達成外交目標，且使用頻率呈現快速增長趨勢。47

經濟制裁為中國提供了一種相較於動用武力更為有效的替代手段，來解決外交與安全問題。面對諸如美國對台軍售、南韓部署「薩德」反飛彈系統等安全壓力，以及其他國家支持新疆、西藏人權或台灣民主的政治壓力，北京雖然難以動用直接的軍事手段作為回應，但卻可以透過經濟制裁來表達其立場與決心，並迫使目標國家改變行為。

中國的制裁手段在本質上屬於「利用」體制內的漏洞：北京雖然仿效美國實施經濟制

裁，卻開創全新領域以達成不同的政治目標。其國內政治考量形成獨特的制裁動機與操作模式。正如專研中國經濟戰略的研究員詹姆斯・瑞利（James Reilly）分析的：

「與美國通常透過國內法律或總統命令將制裁明文化不同，中國極少公開宣佈經濟制裁。北京更傾向使用模糊威脅、調節領導人互訪頻率、選擇性採購（或抵制採購）等非正式手段。這類非正式措施既能保持政策靈活性（避免政策逆轉的尷尬），又為領導層提供可推諉的空間，從而最小化外交衝擊。」[48]

兩國實施制裁的動機亦存在根本差異：美國通常針對他國不良行為（如國內人權侵害、對外侵略）實施制裁；中國則公開反對這類制裁（如對緬甸、辛巴威、敘利亞及近期對俄羅斯的制裁），並常動用聯合國安理會常任理事國否決權來阻撓制裁。表6.1詳列一九九二至二〇二三年間中國主要經濟制裁行動的數據及案例。

與美國不同的是，中國的經濟制裁主要針對與中國有密切貿易往來的國家，且多數情況下是回應中國認定的「干涉內政」及損害「核心利益」的行為。例如在法國、日本及美

新竄起者　　256

表 6.1　中國的經濟制裁行動記錄

年度	制裁對象國家	制裁理由
1992-1994	法國	法國對台軍售
2002	蒙古	達賴喇嘛訪問蒙古
2009	法國	達賴喇嘛訪問法國並會晤總統薩科齊
2010	美國	美國對台軍售
2010-2016	挪威	挪威將諾貝爾和平獎頒給中國異議人士劉曉波
2010	日本、美國	釣魚台撞船事件
2012-2016	菲律賓	黃岩島事件與南海仲裁案
2015	美國	美國對台軍售
2016-2017	南韓	南韓決定部署薩德反飛彈系統
2016	蒙古	達賴喇嘛再度訪問蒙古
2016	台灣	民進黨總統候選人蔡英文當選
2006-2016	伊朗	伊朗核武計畫（伊朗同時亦受到聯合國制裁）
2017	澳洲	澳洲領導人批評中國與南太平洋島國的關係
2006-至今	北韓	北韓核武計畫（北韓同時亦受到聯合國制裁）
2019-至今	加拿大	加拿大拘留華為高層孟晚舟
2019-至今	美國（七月）	美國七月對台軍售
2019-至今	美國（八月）	美國八月對台軍售
2019-至今	美國（十二月）	美國通過《香港人權與民主法案》
2020	澳洲	澳洲政府對新冠肺炎起源展開國際調查
2021	台灣	試圖干擾蔡英文總統連任選舉
2021	立陶宛	立陶宛在首都維爾紐斯設立「台灣代表處」
2023-至今	美國、歐盟、日本	回應美國及其盟國對中國取得半導體及相關材料的限制措施

國領導人會見達賴喇嘛後，中國隨即減少從這些國家的進口。再如二○一○年九月日本扣押一名中國漁船船長後，中國實際上對日本實施了稀土出口禁令。中國外交部對此明確表態：「以中國市場的規模，我們不需要脅迫任何人。但有一點是確定的：中國人民不會允許外國一方面在中國獲利，另一方面又詆毀中國。」49

中國將這種經濟依存關係武器化的程度，也遠超過美國。50 整體而言，北京對企業主要採取行政歧視（administrative discrimination）和群眾性抵制（popular boycotts）這兩種經濟脅迫手段。所謂行政歧視，是指藉由法規與行政手段來阻礙特定企業在中國境內的經營活動。51 舉例來說，在南韓決定部署薩德反飛彈系統之後，樂天集團因提供用地給韓國政府部署薩德系統遭到中國報復，樂天在中國開設的九十九家門市中，有七十五家因被指控違反消防法規等理由而被勒令關閉。52 又如，二○一六年蔡英文當選台灣總統後，並非北京所偏好的候選人，中國即對台灣實施旅遊限制措施，到二○一九年，中國赴台灣的旅客人數較二○一五年下降逾百分之五十。53 北京也會針對在中國境內擁有高知名度與高市場依賴度的國際組織或品牌下手，使它們特別容易受到中國施壓的影響。例如，二○一九年時，NBA休士頓火箭隊總經理在推特發文「為自由而戰，與香港同在」聲援香港

新竊起者　258

抗爭運動。中國迅速做出反應：中央電視台體育頻道全面停止轉播NBA比賽十八個月，導致NBA損失數億美元的營收。54

大多數的群眾性抵制行動，都是由中國官方媒體主導發起，針對那些在中國領土議題（如台灣與香港）或人權問題上發表評論或批評的外國企業。55 例如，二〇一九年八月，精品品牌Coach與Givenchy因銷售印有將香港與台灣列為「國家」的T恤，在中國社群媒體上遭到網民發起抵制行動；Versace也因為類似情況而被抵制。二〇二一年，當多家服裝品牌關切新疆棉花產業中的強制勞動問題後，中國進行了強烈反擊，對服飾品牌H&M的聲討尤其激烈。56 在過去十年中，已有數十位國際名人與跨國企業因為被認為冒犯了中國（無論是事實還是被誤解），而選擇公開向中國道歉，以避免遭到官方或市場的懲罰。57 二〇二一年，美國演員與摔角明星約翰·希南（John Cena）在一次宣傳中稱台灣為「國家」，事後竟以中文發表道歉影片，對中國表示歉意。58

進來一種較新的發展趨勢顯示，中國似乎正從過去專注於貿易與觀光，逐漸轉而利用各國在供應鏈上的脆弱性。在二〇二〇年四月的一場內部講話中，習近平強調，提升全球供應鏈對中國的依賴性，可以作為對抗「外國人為切斷供應」的重要威懾手段，他提到的

259　第六章　中國在經濟政策上的模仿與利用策略

「人為切斷」即是指美國基於戰略目的，限制與中國貿易的各種作法。[59] 儘管中國領導人對外否認使用此種戰略手段，但這顯然是高層極為重視的議題：僅僅在兩個月內，習近平就在國內外的公開講話中提及「供應鏈安全」與相關外交事務達二十次之多。[60] 因此，中國對於其他國家試圖降低對中國依賴度的行為極為敏感，不斷重申維持現有全球供應鏈格局的必要性，並強烈反對如「脫鉤」（decoupling）與「去風險化」（de-risking）等政策主張，以避免中國失去在供應鏈中的戰略優勢。[61]

中國透過市場影響力，已迫使部分國家屈從其要求。例如韓國便承諾不再部署新的薩德系統、不加入美國導彈防禦體系，以及不尋求建立美日韓三邊軍事同盟。有證據顯示，外國政府會應中國方代表要求，或為避免與重要捐助國及交易夥伴關係緊張，而採取行動阻止或懲罰發表批評北京的內容。[62] 然而與美國的單邊經濟制裁類似，中國的施壓也不一定總是有效。例如歐盟仍持續發聲譴責中國侵犯人權行為。二○二一年中國因立陶宛允許台灣設立代表處而實施制裁，但截至二○二四年一月，台灣駐維爾紐斯辦事處仍正常運作。

從韓國「薩德」事件、越南海事爭端到美中貿易戰，中國已認知到經濟槓桿未必能轉化為政治影響力。要使制裁改變他國政策，必須滿足兩項條件：該國相關利益集團確實

新竄起者　260

受經濟政策衝擊，且該集團具備影響政府決策的能力——然而這些條件往往並不存在。[63]更關鍵的是，安全與領土議題通常優先於經濟考量，這意味著經濟手段在這些領域的影響力較為有限。[64]但這並非否定該策略的效用：經濟懲罰的威脅往往能事先阻止各國採取北京眼中的「問題行為」。[65]換言之，雖然經濟制裁未必能成功迫使各國轉向北京偏好的政策，但此類措施的威脅性，往往能預先遏止各國做出中國視為損害其核心利益的舉動。

人民幣的國際化

第二次世界大戰結束後，全球經濟幾乎處於崩潰狀態。歐洲與東亞大部分地區滿目瘡痍，戰爭所造成的損失高達一兆美元以上，這一數字相當於當時美國年度國內生產毛額的四倍以上。美國在戰後的債務水準攀升至GDP的一百二十％以上；而英國的情況更為嚴重，在戰後不久，債務甚至高達GDP的二百五十％以上。[66]為了避免再度爆發全球性災難，世界領導人開始檢視戰爭爆發的深層原因。當時有觀點認為，競爭性貨幣集團體系（currency blocs）是導致衝突的因素之一，因此，美國總統杜魯門下定結論：推動共同儲

261　第六章　中國在經濟政策上的模仿與利用策略

備貨幣將有助於促進世界和平。

其他國家也認同這一理念，於是在一九四四年，四十四個國家齊聚布雷頓森林會議（Bretton Woods Conference），共同建立戰後的國際金融秩序。會議中決定創設國際貨幣基金組織以及國際復興開發銀行（即後來的世界銀行）。為了避免他們認為導致大蕭條惡化乃至戰爭爆發的競爭性貨幣貶值，這些國家同意建立固定匯率制度。作為此制度的基石，美國承諾將美元與黃金掛鉤，每盎司黃金定價三十五美元；其他國家則依固定匯率將本國貨幣與美元掛鉤。如此一來，跨國企業便能使用美元作為共同貨幣，來購買或出售商品與服務，而各國中央銀行也會持有美元儲備以促進這類交易的順利進行。

無論好壞，美國是當時唯一能夠提供這項「公共財」的國家。戰爭期間對美國製造品的龐大需求，使得大量黃金流入美國國庫，使美國成為唯一具備足夠實力支撐全球儲備貨幣制度的國家。且若美元並非儲備貨幣，那麼美國商品在國際市場上的價格將會更低廉。價格優勢再加上美國龐大的經濟規模，將會使其他國家幾乎無法在市場上與美國競爭，這反而會阻礙自由貿易體系的建立與發展。

時至今日，美元仍是最主要的儲備貨幣。儘管二〇二〇年美國僅占全球貿易總量的百分之十三點五，但約半數國際貿易仍以美元結算。[68]事實上，二○二二年美元在全球央行外匯儲備中的占比仍高達百分之五十九。[69]美元的主導地位還得益於美國國債市場的深度與流動性——由於投資者認為即便遭遇重大經濟衝擊，國債交易仍將持續運作，這使得危機時期市場對美債需求依然強勁。

中國學者深知美元作為主導儲備貨幣的地位，為美國帶來重大的經濟與地緣政治優勢。這種現象被稱為「過度特權」（exorbitant privilege），由法國前總統季斯卡（Valéry Giscard d'Estaing）提出。此特權體現在兩方面：使美國政府得以在支付較低債務利息的同時維持預算赤字，並讓美國民眾透過廉價進口商品維持高消費水準。中國經濟學家具體指出，儲備貨幣發行國享有以下五項戰略優勢：①獲取巨額鑄幣稅收益（即貨幣面額與實際生產成本之間的利潤差）。②將外債違約與貨幣貶值的風險轉嫁予非發行國。③能夠更靈活地調節本國經濟，即便是以國際收支長期失衡為代價。④運用金融定價權從利差中獲益（透過設定利率以創造金融資產與負債的收益差）。⑤掌握多邊談判優勢（藉由影響發展中國家經濟金融政策來推進自身戰略）。[70]

美元的主導地位同時也讓美國擁有強大的經濟脅迫工具。由於大多數國際貿易皆使用

263　第六章　中國在經濟政策上的模仿與利用策略

美元作為結算貨幣，因此各國企業與政府必須取得對美國金融體系的存取權。在這樣的架構下，美國財政部得以對特定國家施加金融制裁，以迫使其改變行為。更進一步，美國可以威脅與被制裁方進行貿易的第三國或公司，切斷其美元流動管道，即使這些實體並非設立在美國境內，也可能面臨「交易對手風險」（counterparty risk）。美國還能對全球銀行金融電信協會（SWIFT）施壓，要求其將目標國家的銀行排除在其資訊系統之外，這將大幅提高該國金融交易的成本與難度。71 美國也可以透過提供或剝奪美元流動性來施壓或拉攏盟友，在美元變得稀缺昂貴時供應現金與融資援助，同時拒絕給予對手。事實上，中國分析家指出，美國將美元「武器化」的行為（如近期因俄羅斯入侵烏克蘭對俄國實施的制裁），可能會對中國的金融安全構成重大威脅。72

因此，主導國際金融體系並擁有廣受歡迎的儲備貨幣，被視為值得仿效的有效策略。事實上，如下文所述，許多發達國家如同貿易領域，更深地融入該體系將帶來穩定效應——中國將能在全球宏觀經濟政策對話與合作中扮演更重要的角色。73 此舉對中國國內也有多項好處，人民幣國際化將「有助於建立更平衡、公平的國際貨幣體系，同時降低中國舉借外債的成本和管理匯率波動風家都支持中國將人民幣國際化。若人民幣成為關鍵貨幣，中國將能在全球宏觀經濟政策對

新竄起者　264

險的壓力」。[74] 作為全球最大的貿易國，中國理論上也具備鼓勵他國採用人民幣的競爭優勢。[75] 除推動經濟現代化和發展內需市場之外，中國決策者也意識到需藉由戰略性配置來優化外匯儲備，可以幫助中國金融機構擴大海外投資。[76] 為中國企業創造了投資獲利機會並多元化其投資標的，既促進中國經濟發展，也提升其全球競爭力。

儘管存在上述優勢，中國在崛起初期（冷戰結束後的十年間）受國內因素影響而未模仿這種模式。當時的中國領導人致力於推行支持出口導向型增長的金融政策。美元在外匯市場的高匯率存在一項弊端：會提高從美國進口的成本，從而削弱美國出口商與製造業的競爭力。因此，中國將人民幣匯率與美元掛鉤，並保持較低的匯率，此舉既壓低出口價格，也幫助中國龐大的基礎製造業發展。[77] 美元的長期主導地位也讓中國對於直接挑戰它的地位興趣缺缺，尤其是在一九九〇年代與二〇〇〇年代初期，當時中國在全球貿易體系中的地位尚不顯著。（二〇〇一年時，中國僅佔全球貿易總額的約百分之四）[78]

二〇〇八年爆發的金融危機，帶來了一個難得的契機。中國戰略家認為，這場危機削弱了全球對美元的信心，使主要經濟體更可能接受使用人民幣。[79] 金融危機同時推動人民幣國際化進程，隨著中國在二〇一〇年成為全球第二大經濟體，其國際影響力也隨之提

265　第六章　中國在經濟政策上的模仿與利用策略

升。⁸⁰全球對中國日益加深的依賴，反映美國經濟出現「結構性弱化」，這種趨勢將導致美國控制全球經濟的能力正逐步衰退。⁸¹

中國領導層為爭取戰略優勢，開始仿效美國的金融主導策略，積極推動人民幣國際化進程。二〇一一年起，中國官方展開遊說行動，爭取將人民幣納入國際貨幣基金組織的特別提款權（Special Drawing Rights, SDR），特別提款權是一種由國際貨幣基金組織成員國持有的人工儲備貨幣，成員國可以將其兌換為擁有特別提款權的貨幣。當時僅有美元、歐元、日圓與英鎊四種儲備貨幣。⁸²為此，中國領導人透過密集外交訪問，先後與美國、英國、法國、德國、俄羅斯及印度等主要經濟體進行磋商，爭取支持。⁸³中方主張其經濟規模與金融改革成果，已使人民幣符合納入特別提款權的資格。⁸⁴中國官員更進一步倡議以特別提款權為基礎建構新的國際貨幣體系，取代美元的結算地位（此構想最終未獲實質進展）。⁸⁵在英、法、德、美等國相繼表態支持後，雖然人民幣並未完全符合「可自由使用」貨幣的客觀標準（該標準要求貨幣需在國際支付與主要外匯市場被廣泛使用），國際貨幣組織仍於二〇一六年十月一日正式將人民幣納入特別提款權。⁸⁶人民幣納入特別提款權的背後，是中國一場長期且艱苦的外交遊說行動，但國際貨幣組織本身也有出於自身利益的考量,人民幣的加入可擴大該組織對國際貨幣體系的影響力。

中國也仿效美國的策略,透過擴展貨幣互換協議(swap lines)來推廣人民幣。這種貨幣互換協議是指:雙方央行同意以當時市場匯率互換各自的貨幣,並在一定期間後,由最初借入貨幣的一方以原先的匯率回購本幣,無論這段期間匯率如何變動。雖然借入方央行需要支付一些利息,但由於匯率在協議中被鎖定,因此能有效避免匯率風險,對借入方而言是極具吸引力的安排。在協議期間,借入外幣的央行可以將該貨幣借給其國內的商業銀行,這麼做可確保國內銀行取得所需的外幣,以便進行跨境交易,或是償還外幣債務。

中國學者指出,美國聯邦準備理事會建立的貨幣互換網路,在全球美元融資體系中發揮著關鍵的風險緩解作用,其存在本身就是一種信號,能提振國際市場信心,同時舒緩新興經濟體外匯市場的壓力。88 簡單來說,當投資人看到聯準會願意、也有能力在危機時持續提供流動資金時,他們對於新興市場是否能取得急需的外匯的擔憂就會減輕。中國雖然擁有足夠的外匯儲備,在金融危機中扮演領導者角色,但由於人民幣的國際地位仍相對較低,這限制了中國在短期內舒緩他國金融機構流動性壓力的能力。中國學者主張,建立以人民幣計價的貨幣互換協議有助於解決這一問題,並且可透過降低交易中使用人民幣的風

267　第六章　中國在經濟政策上的模仿與利用策略

險與成本，刺激雙邊貿易成長。這將使中國產品在雙邊市場中更具競爭力，同時也增進相關國家的金融市場穩定性。[89]

中國自二〇一〇年起開始推動自身的貨幣互換協議。透過鑽現有體系的空隙，中國選擇與許多尚未與美國建立互換機制的國家合作。[90] 目前，中國已與除墨西哥外所有與美國簽署貨幣互換協議的國家簽署了類似協定，此外還與額外三十三個國家建立了人民幣互換機制。[91] 這些國家中，有許多是中國出口的重要對象國，當美元（作為主要交易貨幣）的匯率突然出現劇烈上漲時，使他國與人民幣連結的管道會變得特別重要。儘管中國簽署的貨幣互換協議規模較小，但到了二〇二一年，人民幣已成為全球貨幣互換協議中最常被使用的貨幣，互換總額達人民幣三點四七兆元。

中國經濟學家樂觀地認為，這將提升中國在全球金融市場的影響力。[92] 這些貨幣互換協議將有助於提高人民幣在國際貿易與各國外匯儲備中的使用比例，中國學者認為，這將促進國際貨幣體系的多元化，並挑戰美國在全球金融體系中的壟斷地位。[93] 隨著人民幣地位的上升，西方已開發國家將被迫更加重視新興經濟體的訴求，並在相關制度與政策上做出更多讓步與調整。[94]

許多觀察家認為，人民幣被納入特別提款權，將會鼓勵全球各國央行將人民幣納入其外匯儲備，進而提升人民幣作為儲備貨幣的地位，也將擴大中國的金融影響力。95 中國人民銀行在人民幣被納入特別提款權之後總結道：「人民幣作為國際貨幣的地位初步確立，資本項目可兌換程度提高，金融市場開放取得顯著成效。」儘管當時中國仍不願完全開放人民幣的自由兌換。96 後續研究顯示，人民幣國際化還將產生雙重效應：一方面優化中國金融機構體質，另一方面激勵企業拓展海外業務。這不僅加速中國經濟融入全球體系，更為「一帶一路」等重大經濟倡議提供金融支援。97

然而，這些發展對人民幣國際化的推動效果遠低於中國國內的預期。98 二○二二年，人民幣在全球外匯儲備中僅占百分之二點七六，遠低於美元的百分之五十九點七九和歐元的百分之十九點六六。99 同樣地，儘管中國在全球貿易中占比頗高（中國製造的商品規模是其跨境人民幣結算量的十倍），但僅有百分之三點二的國際貿易以人民幣結算。100 值得注意的是，使用人民幣的國際交易中，百分之四十八點六發生在香港，其次是新加坡（百分之十一點三）和英國（百分之五點四）。101

儘管成功將人民幣國際化會為中國帶來諸多收益，但額外的國內政治因素阻礙了中國

269　第六章　中國在經濟政策上的模仿與利用策略

進行有效競爭。一種貨幣在國際金融中的作用具有三個重要面向：資本帳戶開放度（對金融資本流入和流出的限制程度）、國際化程度（在交易中作為交換媒介的使用範圍）以及儲備地位（外國央行是否持有該貨幣資產）。歷史表明，要使本國貨幣成為國際儲備貨幣，一個國家需要具備：與同類國家相比非常龐大的經濟體量、相對更具流動性的金融市場、開放的資本帳戶，並且承諾維持通貨膨脹的穩定性與可預測性。

中國雖然具備了成為國際儲備貨幣的第一與第四項條件，也就是龐大的經濟體量，以及對通貨膨脹的控制與穩定承諾，但中國共產黨卻刻意迴避了另外兩項必要條件。首先，中國政府對銀行體系仍具有高度主導權，而且長期以來推出的多項政策傾向保障銀行部門利益，這種政策傾斜壓抑了金融市場的其他部分發展，進而阻礙了中國整體金融市場的成熟與流動性提升。102 其次，由於中國政府長期對資本外流心懷警惕（特別是在新冠疫情期間更甚），因此持續維持資本帳戶的封閉狀態，使得外國投資者在資金進出中國時面臨諸多限制與困難。

北京之所以對資本外流保持高度警惕，背後有幾個重要原因。首先，若允許資本自由流出中國，中國的經濟決策機構將喪失對宏觀經濟的高度控制權。這會削弱中國政府在調

新竄起者　270

控制經濟成長、通膨與匯率等方面的能力。其次,若發生大規模資本外逃,中國在房地產等領域所累積的龐大債務泡沫可能會破裂,因為持續支撐這些產業的投資資金將會減少。一旦泡沫破裂,導致經濟下滑,將會嚴重損害中國共產黨的統治正當性與民眾信任。[103]為了因應這些風險並彌補人民幣國際化所面臨的劣勢,中國目前正採取漸進式的改革路線,例如謹慎放寬部分資本項目的限制。自二○一○年起,中國開始逐步開放其總值約十三兆美元的債券市場,該市場約占所有新興市場債券發行量的百分之五十一,目的是吸引外國投資者進入中國金融市場。然而,這些改革的效果仍然有限,尚不足以實現讓人民幣全面國際化的目標。[104]

中國目前並不具備足以與美元正面競爭的相對優勢。一種貨幣能否成為全球儲備貨幣,與其本國金融市場的成熟程度密切相關,這也是為什麼即使瑞士的國內生產毛額僅占全球不到百分之一,瑞士法郎仍能成為全球主要儲備貨幣之一的原因。中國的金融市場在廣度(可用的金融工具範圍,包括避險工具)、深度(特定市場中金融工具的交易量)、以及流動性(市場的周轉率、成交量)方面,都遠不及美國成熟金融市場的水準。[105]這些限制部分源自於中國企業本身的結構性問題,正如經濟學家埃斯瓦爾．普拉薩德(Eswar

271　第六章　中國在經濟政策上的模仿與利用策略

Prasad）所指出的：「中國企業普遍存在公司治理薄弱、資訊透明度低、審計標準不健全以及會計實務粗糙等問題。」106

儘管面臨這些挑戰，中國仍持續推動人民幣國際化。多位中國貨幣政策領域的重要人物主張：人民幣仍能取得顯著地位，納入特別提款權只是第一步，非中國的實體很快將有足夠信心持有人民幣資產，而非僅用於支付結算。107 許多觀察家認為，中國經濟的吸引力終將促使外國政府與商業機構採用人民幣，這只是時間問題。108 二〇二二年十月中共二十大開幕會議上提交的關鍵報告，明確要求「有序推進人民幣國際化」，作為推動高水平對外開放的重要環節。109 截至二〇二三年，中國的戰略包含三大方向：第一是鼓勵國際貿易中更多使用人民幣支付結算；第二為擴大金融開放以提供更多人民幣計價資產予海外投資者；最後則是在「一帶一路」框架下加強與其他國家的合作。110

儘管在習近平領導下的中國對人民幣國際化問題日益趨於保守，強調「金融安全」並對人民幣國際化的深度更加謹慎，但這種樂觀態度依然持續存在。111 在中國最高領導層的眼中，中國金融體系的首要任務是維持審慎的貨幣政策，並推動支持實體經濟的金融活動，至於人民幣的國際化，則是次要目標。112 北京當局對於資本管控的立場堅定且具有長遠規劃。他們認為，缺乏嚴格的金融監管以及過度的資本逐利行為，正是導致一連串金融危機的根本原因。[113]因此，中國金融體系的對外開放將會持續採取漸進且有限的方式進行，以降低可能出現的金融風險。[114]

由於中國無法直接與美元競爭（部分原因在於中共需要保持對金融體系的控制），其策略似乎正轉向「利用」體制漏洞——即在競爭力較弱的領域推動人民幣國際化。中國認為新興經濟體及其他具有政治動機擺脫美元依賴的國家中存在一些機會。中國著名學者、前外交官張宇燕指出，川普政府的關稅政策及華盛頓利用美元主導的ＳＷＩＦＴ系統管控國際經濟活動的行為，強化了許多經濟體結束對美元依賴的決心。[115]

隨後，中國試圖利用其在全球貿易上的影響力來提升人民幣的地位，尤其是說服加入「一帶一路」倡議的國家，至少在與中國的貿易中使用人民幣進行結算。[116]二〇一九年，中國與巴基斯坦達成協議，人民幣將取代美元來資助「未來所有在中巴經濟走廊下的能源與交通項目」。[117]二〇二二年十一月，中國人民銀行與巴基斯坦國家銀行簽署協議，在巴基斯坦建立人民幣清算機制。[118]在過去一年中，中國也與寮國、哈薩克、巴西等國達成類似的協議。沙烏地阿拉伯方面，在二〇一八年《華盛頓郵報》專欄作家賈邁勒・卡舒吉

（Jamal Khashoggi）遇害後，沙國與美國的關係日益緊張。據報導，截至二〇二二年沙國已與中國討論以人民幣結算石油交易的可能性。[119] 在二〇二二年十二月的中國—海灣阿拉伯國家合作委員會高峰會上，習近平主席表示，中國將鼓勵在與海灣國家的石油與天然氣貿易中使用人民幣。最後，在過去五年間，中國也增加了與俄羅斯、伊朗與緬甸的人民幣貿易結算比例。[120]

中國也正試圖利用香港作為繞過其金融控制問題的管道。二〇二二年，香港交易所（HKEX）宣佈，將推出雙櫃台模式（Dual Counter Model）以及雙櫃台造市計劃（Dual Counter Market Making Program），使投資者可以「在以港元與人民幣計價的櫃台間互換證券」，而雙櫃台造市計劃則將協助最小化兩個櫃台之間的價格差異。[121] 這項「雙櫃台系統」的部分設計初衷，是為了減緩美國可能下市（delisting）中國企業所帶來的衝擊，尤其是那些同時在美國與香港交易所上市的中國公司。換句話說，香港交易所將讓香港本地的投資人有更多機會交易以人民幣計價的股票，從而進一步推動人民幣在國際資本市場上的使用。

這項「利用策略」確實讓人民幣取得了一些進展。例如，從二〇二〇年一月到二〇二二年一月,人民幣在全球結算中的占比從百分之一點六七躍升至百分之三點二,排名也從第六位上升至第四位。[122] 二〇二〇年,中國有百分之十五的對外貿易是以人民幣結算,較二〇一五年的百分之十一有所提升。[123] 二〇二二年,人民幣跨境收支總額達到四十二兆元人民幣,比二〇一七年成長了百分之三百四十。[124]

為了在競爭相對較弱的領域中另闢蹊徑,中國也建立了自己的「人民幣跨境支付系統」(CIPS),用以跟SWIFT系統競爭。[125] 截至二〇二二年,人民幣跨境支付系統已有七十六個直接參與者(即在系統中開設帳戶的機構),其中包括匯豐銀行、渣打銀行、花旗銀行和法國巴黎銀行等國際大型銀行。還有一千二百二十八個間接參與者(透過直接參與者進行互動的機構)。[126] 不過,SWIFT系統目前仍具壓倒性優勢,它連結了超過二百個國家的一萬一千多家金融機構,規模約是人民幣跨境支付系統的十倍。[127] 儘管如此,全球處理人民幣支付的銀行數量仍持續上升,從二〇一七年的一千五百家成長至二〇二〇年的二千二百一十四家,成長幅度約為百分之五十,其中大多數新增銀行來自亞洲、中東與非洲地區。[128] 由中國社會科學院金融研究所副所長整理的**表6.2**則總結了中國人民幣國際化戰略的演變,顯示中國一貫優先推動人民幣在國際交易中的使用,且所採取的方式

表 6.2　人民幣國際化戰略的演變

階段	舊三位一體 （2009-2017）	新三位一體 （2018-2022）	新新三位一體 （2022 年以後）
(1)	推動人民幣在跨境貿易與直接投資中的結算	推動人民幣計價在原油期貨交易中的使用	進一步鼓勵人民幣在跨境大宗商品交易中的計價與結算
(2)	推動離岸人民幣市場的發展	推動國內金融市場對外國機構投資者的開放	加強向境內與境外的外國機構投資者提供高品質的人民幣計價金融資產
(3)	推動雙邊貨幣互換協議的簽署	推動人民幣在周邊國家（如 RCEP 成員國）及「一帶一路」沿線國家的計價與結算	加快建設跨境人民幣支付與清算體系

資料來源：Zhang Ming（张 明），"Strategic Expansion of RMB Internationalization Against the Background of New Global Changes 全球新变局背景下人民币国际化的策略扩展 — 从新'三位一体'到新新'三位一体'," National Institution for Finance and Development 国家金融与发展实验室, December 20, 2022, http://www.nifd.cn/Uploads/Paper/19d3ea6b-6dd0-422d-8631-a002cc65eca9.pdf.

愈來愈多元與全面。

中國的解決方案或許是一種創新的路徑：打造數位人民幣（digital RMB）。這種中央銀行數位貨幣（CBDC）的功能，等同於現金的數位版本——有點像是直接在聯準會開設帳戶。中央銀行數位貨幣的特性與比特幣等數位支付方式有些相似，但其最大區別在於具備「官方監

新竄起者　　276

管」，因為是由國家中央銀行所背書與管理的。二〇一六年，中國人民銀行成立數位貨幣研究所（DCRI），為成為首個發行法定數位貨幣的主要央行奠定基礎。129 自二〇二〇年五月起，中國央行開始試行數位人民幣系統：公民可通過手機下載數位錢包應用程式使用數位人民幣進行支付。130 該體系不僅降低交易清算成本，更有助於中共重新掌控經濟中的資金與資訊流——這種控制權過去因支付寶、微信支付等平臺造成「超出黨和國家直接監管範圍」的大規模資金資料流動而削弱。131 與實體現金相比，數位人民幣的設計能讓中國央行對資金流向獲得更強的監控能力。132 中國分析人士也希望，透過使用數位人民幣進行跨境支付，中國企業與海外客戶能避開美國制裁帶來的風險，無須依賴美元交易。133

雖然現在斷言中國這些「利用」與「創新」型策略的最終成果如何還太早，但如果中國共產黨持續維持其嚴格的金融管控政策，那麼很難想像人民幣能與美元正面競爭的未來。即便數位貨幣在未來可能興起，美元仍將繼續扮演「最主要的價值儲存工具」的角色。因為以美元計價的金融資產，例如美國政府債券，仍是全球投資人最偏好的資金停泊地。134 至於中國推行的數位人民幣，則很可能面臨投資人與企業的保守對待，原因在於人民幣的數位支付系統，最終仍是由中國人民銀行運作，該銀行又受中國黨國體制控制，而

277　第六章　中國在經濟政策上的模仿與利用策略

該體制一向對私人財務權利持懷疑與干預態度。

中國經濟實力：一段模仿與利用的故事？

一九七八年在鄧小平領導下所啟動的國內經濟改革，是中國崛起的必要條件。國家對經濟的管制逐漸鬆動，中國的企業家精神得以蓬勃發展，轉向與美國爭奪影響力，其經濟互動開始帶有戰略性。中國加入世界貿易組織以促進自身崛起，同時也用以安撫其他國家，宣稱中國崛起是和平的。中國模仿美國，口頭上宣稱奉行自由貿易原則，實際上在國內仍實行優惠性政策。北京談判簽署了創紀錄數量的雙邊自由貿易協定，目前也在推動屬於自己的區域貿易協定，相對之下，美國則無法在該地區達成新的貿易協定。

中國這場驚人的崛起並非理所當然。事實上，過去三十年間，外界多次預測中國經濟將走向衰退。從一九九〇年代到二〇〇〇年代初，「中國崩潰論」一度甚囂塵上：經濟學家指出，低效的國有企業和加入世界貿易組織後加劇的競爭，將導致國企破產，進而引發

新竄起者　　278

整體銀行體系的問題。[135]到了二〇一〇年代，貪腐、缺乏法治、工資上升與龐大的政府債務，讓許多人擔憂中國的經濟崛起已經告一段落。[136]另一些經濟學家則認為，中國的經濟未必會崩潰，因為政府對經濟政策、不動產市場與銀行體系的掌控仍然強大，但一場嚴重的經濟放緩已不可避免。[137]

儘管面臨種種國內問題，中國的「竄起者策略」仍為其帶來了巨大的經濟實力。許多國家、企業與個人如今都仰賴中國市場來維持自身的繁榮。中國已運用這項優勢來取得經濟利益，試圖在國際金融體系中挑戰美元的地位，同時也藉此實現戰略勝利，對那些反對中國政治利益的國家施以經濟制裁。

中國試圖「模仿」與「利用」制度空隙的作法並非故事的全貌。在第七章中，我將舉出「竄起者策略」的第三個組成部分——中國如何以創新的方式運用經濟工具，另闢蹊徑爭奪權力。主要案例包括像「中國製造二〇二五」這類產業政策，以及透過「一帶一路」政策實施的金融發展援助，這些明確反映中國試圖取得不對稱優勢，並取得全球經濟主導地位。儘管如此，正如我們將看到的，國際社會對此類威脅的認知十分遲緩，回應也不足，這在很大程度上是因為這些政策本質上具有「創新」特徵。

第七章

中國經濟政策中的創新作為

中國在追求成為世界強國之前，其全球經濟目標相對單純——旨在建立能夠支撐國內高速經濟增長的國際經濟關係。然而進入二十一世紀後，北京開始思考如何運用經濟工具來實現更廣泛的戰略目標。1 對中國共產黨而言，建設「小康社會」具有雙重目的：既維持國內統治基礎，又為成為「現代化大國」構建全球權力基礎。2 至此，中國的經濟戰略轉變為「以大國的雄心為指引、以大國的實力為基礎、以獲取或維持大國地位為根本目標」。3

如第六章所述，中國的一些作法仿效了美國的做法，這為中國塑造出一個合作且負責任的形象。的確，有一位著名的美國學者在二〇一九年曾經得出結論認為，多數指標顯示中國正緩慢但確實地將其經濟進一步整合進全球秩序中。4 在某些領域，依然存在著認為中國是當前國際體系的主要受益者，因此不會冒險去破壞這個體系的觀點。5

但「竄起者策略」的一大好處是，中國能夠兩面討好——既可以模仿從而由體系中受益，又可以利用制度漏洞取得先機，同時還能另闢蹊徑，打造一個不依賴美國的實力基礎，而且能夠將反彈風險降到最低。本章將說明，在某些經濟政策案例中，創新性的策略確實是有其必要性的。中國領導人意識到，創新是持續經濟成長的引擎，但美國那種自由

新竄起者　282

放任的作法可能會威脅到中共的既得利益。因此，中國領導人轉而擁抱產業政策，其中包括成為科技強權的目標。這種作法充分發揮了中國作為一個「資本主義式威權國家」的競爭優勢，使其能動員龐大的經濟資源來實現戰略目標。鑑於中國並不太適合效法美國的對外援助模式，它便選擇採用「發展金融援助」的方式，並聚焦於基礎建設，這種策略更符合中國的競爭優勢。

打造國家冠軍：中國的產業政策

科技的進步與創新是美國成功故事的核心。第二次世界大戰結束後，美國憑藉科技產業的優勢，進入了一段「美國在經濟與商業科技領域無可匹敵」的時期。6 聯邦政府在二戰期間對研發空前投入，成立「科學研究與開發辦公室」，使得科學研究支出比戰前時期成長了兩倍以上。這次的戰時投資直接造就美國戰後數十年的科技霸權，截至一九七〇年，美國在科學研究與開發辦公室支持領域的專利申請數比英國與法國高出百分之五十以上。7

這些聯邦投資催生出核武器、飛彈技術、精準彈藥、電腦與網際網路、以及匿蹤技術等領域的突破性創新，這些技術支撐了美國在整個冷戰期間的硬實力。8 美國的科技產業同樣是其主導地位的核心，因為據估計，「二戰後高達一半的經濟成長可歸因於研發驅動的科技進步」。9 在全球前五十大科技公司中，美國公司按市值占總額的百分之八十五（約十七兆美元中的十五兆美元）。相比之下，中國公司排名第二，但僅占百分之五點三六。10

美國能達成上述成就，是在一個相對放任自由市場的模式下完成的。美國從未成立國家發展銀行、大型國營股權投資基金、全國性的產業指導計畫，或設立工業部。這部分是因為美國從來沒有建立「發展型國家」的需求，但也因為讓政府選擇產業贏家並賦予不公平優勢的做法，與美國文化格格不入。當然，美國政府並非完全不介入經濟；它會採取某些措施來促進經濟成長並確保美國的競爭力。主要的方式是提供稅收優惠，鼓勵企業投入研發，並直接投資具潛力的技術，特別是在國防領域（大約五至六成的聯邦研發支出流向該領域）。然而，政府的投入仍遠低於民間部門；例如，在二〇一九年，聯邦研發支出為一千三百四十億美元（其中約一半分配給企業、高等教育機構與非營利機構），而私部門的投資金額則為約為四千八百億美元。[11]

中國領導人了解，若中國要崛起成為強權，創新是不可或缺的。[12] 官方媒體開始分析缺乏技術創新是如何限制了中國的經濟成長。有些文章指出，中國在國內生產毛額、對外貿易額及主要工業產品產量等指標上雖然名列前茅，但在技術創新方面卻遠遠落後於西方國家。[13] 習近平本人則認為，創新是將一個十多億人口、資源與環境壓力俱增的國家現代化的必要手段。[14] 不論是在全球市場還是在戰場上，中國都必須在設計、適應與運用新技術方面處於前沿，方能對抗對手。[15] 正如習近平所說：「科技強則國家強。」[16] 他希望中國能變得更具「競爭力」與「抗壓力」，[17] 但他也曾於二〇一五年在中共中央會議上強調其擔憂：

「我國創新能力不強，科技發展水準總體不高，科技對經濟社會發展的支撐能力不足，科技對經濟增長的貢獻率遠低於發達國家水準，這是我國這個經濟大個頭的『阿喀琉斯之踵』」（譯註：即「阿奇里斯之腱」，此處保留引述原文），新一輪科技革命帶來的是更加激烈的科技競爭，如果科技創新搞不上去，發展動力就不

285　第七章　中國經濟政策中的創新作為

可能實現轉換，我們在全球經濟競爭中就會處於下風。」[18]

在另一次與中共中央黨員召開的全體會議上，習近平更進一步闡述了創新與大國地位之間的關聯：

「顛覆性技術不斷湧現，正在重塑世界競爭格局、改變國家力量對比⋯⋯我國既面臨趕超跨越的難得歷史機遇，也面臨差距拉大的嚴峻挑戰。惟有勇立世界科技創新潮頭，才能贏得發展主動權，為人類文明進步作出更大貢獻。」[19]

帶著這些目標，習近平為中國的創新發展設定了三個里程碑：二〇二〇年成為「創新型國家」；二〇三〇年，躋身全球創新型國家前列；二〇五〇年，成為「世界科技創新強國」。[20]

但國內政治考量，特別是中國獨特的競爭優勢以及維護黨的需要，使得仿效美國放任自由的做法變得不具吸引力。共產黨希望對經濟發展與人民行為保持牢固的掌控。21 那些憑藉個人之力而非黨或國家的認可成功崛起的企業家階層，可能會對黨構成威脅。習近平近期對這類企業家階層展開了整頓：當馬雲公開批評政府監管機構妨礙創新時，他旗下阿里巴巴集團的關聯企業「螞蟻集團」首次的公開募股即遭取消，馬雲本人也被迫離開中國。22 在自由市場競爭中，中國亦處於劣勢：美國的民主體制以及其崇尚個人主義的文化，能夠在某種程度上自然激發創新；而中國的共產主義和由上而下主導的國家體制，則無法達成同樣的效果。23

然而，中國領導人也清楚，透過差異化的創新策略，中國能發揮其獨特的優勢。中國的體制結構非常適合推動由國家主導的經濟計畫。例如，由於政府擁有全國土地的所有權，它可以以優惠價格出售土地給那些屬於重點扶植產業的企業。中國最具創新的產業政策工具之一是政府引導基金，這些是市場導向的公私合營股權基金，截至二〇二〇年底總規模已達八千二百億美元。24 雖然這些基金由專業團隊進行管理，但仍由中國政府掌控。這些基金自二〇〇二年首次啟動以來，會購買具有前景企業的股份，並藉由其股東身分引導企業按照政府的政策方向發展。25 中央計劃也是共產體制中的核心元素。自中華人民共和國成立以來，中共就一直發布五年計畫，藉此引導國家朝著符合領導階層戰略願景的方向邁進。

為善用這些優勢並在推動創新同時維護黨的掌控，中國決定採取產業政策（industrial policy）作為戰略方向。產業政策可定義為「任何具有選擇性、針對性的政府干預行為，旨在將生產部門結構轉向比無干預的市場均衡狀態下更具增長潛力的領域」。26 中國最初並未擁有完整的產業政策，僅以輕微的干預方式鼓勵如核能與民用航空等產業的發展。27 但是於二〇〇〇年代初期溫家寶擔任總理期間，中國開始系統性地選定並扶持視為未來關鍵的產業。28 二〇〇六年發佈的《國家中長期科學和技術發展規劃綱要》堪稱現行產業政策體系的源頭，其目標是通過科技進步實現生產品質的飛躍與經濟的可持續成長。29 該綱要採取「上下結合」策略。政府既制定高層目標，又為具體專案提供資金（最終形成二〇〇七至二〇〇八年啟動的十六個重大專項，其中十三項已經公開）。

二〇〇八年的金融危機為中國領導人帶來了一個在國內外推進其產業政策的獨特契機。在胡錦濤與溫家寶的領導下，一批產業政策的支持與倡導者逐漸掌控了最高層級的經濟決策權。30 金融危機對中國經濟造成衝擊，黨的領導層因此決定實施一項大規模的刺激方案以挽救中國經濟。危機過後，政府並未收回對產業的支持，反而加碼投入，促成了二

新竊起者　288

〇九年《戰略性新興產業》計畫的新一波產業政策浪潮。透過該計畫，中國政府致力於推動位於科技創新前沿的關鍵產業，包括生物科技、資訊科技與新能源車等領域。31 當習近平於二〇一二年上台時，人們普遍認為中國在技術上仍然落後。中國處於附加價值鏈的低端，先進技術產業與美國、日本和歐洲相比，仍然欠缺發展。二〇一二年，經濟合作與發展組織的一份報告評估了中國在全球價值鏈中的地位，指出中國在很大程度上依賴進口中間產品，將其組裝成高品質產品後再出口。32 中國在全球高科技價值鏈中的主要角色基本上就是一個「組裝工廠」。

為了應對上述劣勢，中國在二〇一五年啟動了新一波的產業政策。這波政策聚焦於新興科技，並高度重視創新導向的成長，這些要素使其有別於過往的產業政策。33 包括了數項習近平主導的新倡議，其中最廣為人知的是《中國製造二〇二五》。《中國製造二〇二五》提出了一項三步驟戰略，目標是在二〇四九年之前將中國打造為「製造業強國」，透過改善或升級中國在十個關鍵領域的產業基礎，以「提升其創新能力並掌握這些尖端技術」。34 二〇一六年，中國領導人推出了《創新驅動發展戰略》，這是一項總體願景，旨在整合中國的產業政策以促進國家的創新能力。自該戰略提出以來，中國領導人持續強

289　第七章　中國經濟政策中的創新作為

調創新在國家發展中的核心地位。習近平讚揚創新是國家發展的「第一驅動力」,並誓言要實現科技的自主自強。李克強在二○二三年的政府工作報告中一共提了三十四次「創新」,宣示中國應依靠創新來推動實體經濟發展、增強經濟成長動能,並應對外部的壓制與圍堵(此處顯然是指來自美國的壓力)。35 表7.1彙整了中國政府於各項倡議下所著重發展的產業領域。

這些規劃揭示了中國推動創新背後的地緣政治本質。除了推動國內經濟增長外,北京還希望終結中國在某些技術上對外國勢力的依賴。欠缺這些所謂的「卡脖子」技術,將會阻礙中國的發展,而外國勢力在這些領域的主導地位則可能成為限制中國成長的手段。36 在第十四個「五年規劃」(二○二一~二○二五年)中,中國的國家規劃者提出了「雙循環」的發展目標,根據此策略,中國應依賴其龐大的國內市場來維持經濟的基本運作,同時透過國際貿易與投資保持與國際市場的聯繫。該戰略要求中國的「國內大循環」必須能夠抵禦外部波動與衝擊,而「國際循環」則應用來使中國對外部世界變得不可或缺。正如習近平於二○二○年在中共中央財經委員會的一次講話中所言,中國「必須加強國際產業鏈對中國的依賴,形成對外方人為斷供的強有力反制和威懾能力」。37 其核心觀點是:世

新竄起者　290

表 7.1　中國主要產業政策推動項目一覽表

重大科技專案	戰略性新興產業	中國製造 2025
1. 水污染與治理	節能環保： A. 高效節能設備 B. 環境保護 C. 資源回收再利用	1. 新一代資訊技術
2. 超大規模積體電路製造	新一代資訊技術： D. 新一代互聯網 E. 核心電子元件 F. 高端軟體、資訊服務	2. 高端數控機床與機器人
3. 次世代寬頻無線通訊	生物科技： G. 生物製藥 H. 生物醫學工程 I. 生物農業 J. 生物製造產業	3. 航太裝備
4. 核心電子與高端軟體	精密與高端機械製造： K. 民用飛機 L. 衛星及應用 M. 鐵路與運輸裝備 N. 海洋工程裝備	4. 海洋工程裝備與高端船舶
5. 重大新藥開發	智慧製造設備	5. 高端軌道交通設備
6. 重大傳染病防治	新能源： O. 風能 P. 太陽能 Q. 生質能	6. 節能與新能源汽車
7. 基因改造與作物育種	新材料： R. 新材料	7. 電力設備

重大科技專案	戰略性新興產業	中國製造 2025
8. 大型客機研發	新能源汽車： S. 電動車、插電式混合動力車	8. 農業機械裝備
9. 高解析度地球觀測系統		9. 新材料，如聚合物等
10. 載人航天與登月		10. 生物醫藥與高端醫療設備
11. 高端數控機床		
12. 大型油氣與煤氣化裝備		
13. 高壓大型核反應爐		

資料來源：Barry Naughton, The Rise of China's Industrial Policy: 1978 to 2020 (Mexico City: Catedra Mexico-China, 2021), 54-57; State Council of the People's Republic of China 中华人民共和国国务院, "Made in China 2025 中国制造 2025," May 8, 2015, http://www.gov.cn/zhengce/cont ent/2015-05/19/content_9784.htm; "The 13th FYP National Strategic Emerging Industry Development Plan '十三五'国家战略性新兴产业发展规划," State Council of the People's Republic of China 中华人民共和国国务院, November 29, 2016, http://www.gov.cn/zhengce/content/2016-12/19/content_5150090.htm.

[a] Naughton, The Rise of China's Industrial Policy,54-57.

[b] The 13th FYP National Strategic Emerging Industry Development Plan "十三五"国家战略性新兴产业发展规划, The State Council of the People's Republic of China 中华人民共和国国务院, November 29, 2016, http://www.gov.cn/zhengce/content/2016-12/19/content_5150090.htm.

[c] The State Council of the People's Republic of China 中华人民共和国国务院, Made in China 2025, 中国制造 2025 May 8, 2015, http://www.gov.cn/zhengce/content/2015-05/19/content_9784.htm

界對中國的依賴程度越高,各國加入反中聯盟的可能性就越低。[38]

為了發展主要產業政策所規劃的戰略性產業,中國主要運用了兩項工具:對企業的直接補貼,以及國企優惠貸款。雖然提供直接補貼並非創新的做法,但中國在這方面的投入規模堪稱空前(二〇一九年,中國的補貼金額高達五百三十億美元,而美國僅為二十八點九五億美元)。軟體業、科技硬體業、汽車產業、運輸業以及半導體產業是最大的受益群體。然而,中美兩國做法之間的主要差異在於優惠貸款。二〇一九年,美國在這方面的投入約為四億美元,而中國則高達七百四十億美元。[39]

中國政府的干預也有助於壓低關鍵商品與原料的價格,這使得中國企業比外國競爭者更具競爭力。例如,中國鋼鐵價格較低(該產業由國有企業主導),幫助中國風力發電機製造商以全球平均價格的一半出售發電機。這一點,再加上中國可利用龐大的國內需求(自二〇一一年以來一直是陸上風電的最大消費國),使中國自二〇二一年起主導全球風電市場。[40]

儘管中國的作法並未仿效美國,但其中某些方面與亞洲經濟奇蹟締造者的「追趕策略」(catch-up strategies)有相似之處,這些策略涉及在成熟領域與技術中發展專業能力。

293　第七章　中國經濟政策中的創新作為

經典例子包括亞洲四小龍：香港、新加坡、南韓與台灣。儘管中國官方媒體與政策文件鮮少提及仿效這些國家，但有跡象顯示中國的戰略家曾經深入研究過這些案例。41 然而，中國干預的強度與廣度遠遠超過這些先例。例如，二〇一九年，中國政府花費了一點七一兆人民幣，相當於其國內生產毛額的百分之一點七三，以支持產業。42 排名第二的是韓國，該國對產業的支持僅占國內生產毛額的百分之零點六七，還不到中國的一半。而以實際金額來看，中國的二千四百八十億美元也遠超過排名第二的美國，美國僅支出八百三十億美元。

中國的產業政策中還有兩項非正式但同樣重要、且具有中國特色的工具：強制技術轉讓與透過網路進行的商業間諜活動。外國企業若想在中國經營，往往必須與中國夥伴組成合資企業，且通常不得持有絕對控股權。中國政府也經常施壓，要求外企將敏感技術移轉給中方的合作夥伴。43 中國會依據企業願意與中方分享多少技術，來決定是否讓其進入龐大的中國市場。44 根據美國國防創新單位（Defense Innovation Unit）的資料顯示，二〇一五至二〇一七年間，中國實體資助了約百分之十至十六的風險投資案，且許多交易附帶董事會席位與潛在的技術轉讓協議。45

中國還有一些動作，例如「千人計畫」，不僅鼓勵具備關鍵專業知識的中國國民返國發展，也積極鎖定在其研究領域中享有盛名的國際學者與科學專家。為了吸引這些人才，中方提供優渥的薪資、研究經費及其他誘因，並期望受邀人士能公開或秘密地為增強中國的研發實力作出貢獻。接受這些資助往往伴隨與中國政府簽訂的合約義務，這些義務可能要求受資助者配合特定指示，包括參與非法行為，如竊取智慧財產權或將技術轉移至中國。46

數十年來，中國政府及其支持的個體，持續對全球各地的企業發動駭客攻擊，以竊取敏感技術資訊。47 根據美國貿易代表辦公室的說法，這些駭客行動讓中國取得了「廣泛的機密商業資訊，包括商業機密、技術資料、談判立場，以及敏感且專屬的內部通訊內容」。48 儘管中國曾多次承諾停止技術轉移與網路竊密等行為，但這些活動仍然持續發生。49 根據二○一三年的一項研究，智慧財產權盜竊每年對美國經濟造成超過三千億美元的損失，而中國可能占其中的五成至八成。50 在二○二二年的一項調查中，美國企業仍將「網路竊密」列為其在中國營運面臨的五大挑戰之一，僅次於美中緊張局勢、法規與執法不一致、勞動成本上升，以及法規遵循風險。51

不可否認，中國在創新方面已取得令人印象深刻的成就，這在一定程度上得益於其產業政策。根據美國智庫資訊技術與創新基金會的分析顯示，中國在「創新與先進產業能力」方面，從二〇一〇年相當於美國的百分之五十八，提升至二〇二〇年的近百分之七十五。[52] 雖然中國仍落後於美國，排名第十一，但這已較二〇〇七年的第二十九名大幅進步。[53] 儘管美國仍是全球最主要的外國直接投資目的地，中國的地位也有所提升，從一九九〇年僅為美國總額的百分之七成長至二〇二二年的百分之五十八。[54] 中國每年發表的科學論文數量、專利申請數量，以及培養的科學家數量，均已超過美國。雖然這些數字並非衡量創新實力的完美指標，但與一九九〇年代末相比已是巨大的進步。[55] 當時中國僅占全球科學論文的百分之三點二，高引用度論文的占比更只有百分之一點八。[56] 根據榮鼎集團（Rhodium Group）的年度評估《Pathfinder Report》，中國的創新表現已優於加拿大、義大利與西班牙等國。[57] 世界智慧財產權組織所編製的《全球創新指數》（Global Innovation Index）亦將中國列為二〇二二年全球第十一大創新國家，超越日本與加拿大。[58]

中國的產業政策也讓中國企業在關鍵產業中取得主導地位。以太陽能板為例，中國將

新竄起者　296

其視為關鍵技術領域，自二〇〇〇年以來，政府已頒布超過一百項支持光電產業的政策，包括提供出口信貸、增加研發投資、並在多家領先企業設立國家資助的實驗室。59 中國在新的光電產業上投資超過五百億美元，為歐洲的十倍，並對美國進行所謂的「傾銷」行為，也就是中國企業以低於市場價格出售太陽能板，藉此打擊並排除美國競爭對手。60 結果就是中國在這個產業位居領導地位：全球前十大太陽能光電製造設備供應商全都位於中國，中國也掌握了太陽能板製造鏈上的所有環節。61

中國在電動車產業方面也取得了顯著成功。儘管中國在二〇〇〇年代初期已經有強大的汽車工業，但由於「產品品質低劣，且未能達到安全與排放標準」，中國企業缺乏國際競爭力。62 然而，透過政府的支持、技術創新以及龐大的製造基礎，中國從二〇一四年生產全球百分之三十三的純電動車，迅速成長至二〇二一年占全球產量的百分之五十九。中國的產量是歐洲的兩倍以上，接近美國的五倍。63 **圖7.1** 顯示了中國如何從與美國和歐洲相同的起點迅速超越，取得領先地位。

中國也鎖定潔淨能源供應鏈中的關鍵產業在海外進行投資。以鎳為例，中國已經主導了用於電動車電池生產的鎳礦加工（估計全球有三分之一到四分之三的鎳加工是在中國進

297　第七章　中國經濟政策中的創新作為

單位：百萬台

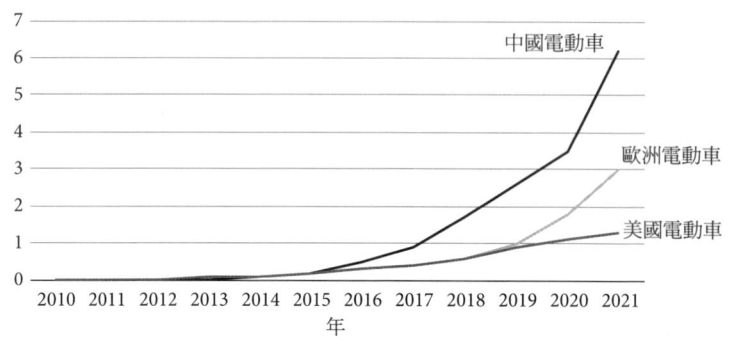

圖 7.1　二〇一〇～二〇二一年電動車生產量

資料來源："Global Electric Car Stock, 2010-2021," International Energy Agency, May 23, 2022, https://www.iea.org/data-and-statistics/charts/global-electric-car-stock-2010-2021.

行）。[64] 在中國以外地區進行的鎳加工大多也由中國企業主導。[65] 因此，隨著未來幾十年電動車需求的急遽成長，中國已經為自身在這一關鍵產業中的領先地位奠定了穩固基礎。

中國也透過創新的企業型策略在5G電信技術領域對美國企業形成強力挑戰。中國政府在這個產業的發展上採取了非常有計畫性的做法，事實上，自二〇〇六年以來，每一份主要的產業政策文件中都包含了電信業的發展內容。[66] 中國所有主要的電信公司都是國有企業，並且已奉令對電信技術進行大量投資：從二〇一三到二〇一八年，投入了一千億美元於4G技術；而預計在二〇二五年之前將針對5G技術投入一千五百億美元。中國建設的5G基地台數量是美國的十倍，且中國用戶的平均5G網速接近美國用戶的四倍。67 正如美國五角大廈的一份報告指出，中國在5G領域的先行優勢以及積極推動全球5G領導地位的舉動，「將使中國得以推動其偏好的5G網路標準與規範，並將對全球5G產品市場的發展方向產生深遠影響。」68

儘管中國的產業政策取得了顯著成就，但這種由國家主導的模式並未能保證在所有領域都實現創新。中國在生產先進半導體方面仍面臨挑戰——半導體是全球第四大貿易商品，而中國正是最大的消費國。69 這並非因為中國不曾努力發展。中國領導層充分意識到半導體對未來創新的關鍵性，例如行動裝置、電動與自駕車、5G網路與人工智慧等。70 資訊技術正是《中國製造二〇二五》所列出的十大關鍵技術領域之首，中國也計劃在二〇三〇年前在這一領域成為世界領導者。71 第十三個五年計劃（二〇一六—二〇二〇）明確提出需聚焦於記憶體模組與半導體，因這些正是中國最依賴美國的技術。72 而習近平更於二〇二〇年將這一產業推上國家戰略層級，呼籲加強中國的「創新引擎」。73 而美國對華為的制裁（二〇二〇年禁止其採購美國關鍵技術）以及二〇二二年通過的《晶片與科學法

299　第七章　中國經濟政策中的創新作為

案》（禁止接受聯邦資金的企業在中國大陸生產先進半導體）進一步加劇了中國追求在先進半導體上自給自足的緊迫性。74

中國為扶植本國半導體產業，採取了多項措施，包括稅收減免、低價出售土地以及由政府資助的債務融資。75 全球在政府資助債務融資方面受益最多的三家企業皆來自中國，分別為清華紫光集團、中芯國際與江蘇長電科技；三家公司於二〇一四至二〇一八年間合計獲得近五十億美元的資金支持。二〇一四年九月，中國政府啟動了「國家集成電路產業投資基金」（譯註：集成電路，台灣稱為積體電路），這是中國最重要、規模最大的政府引導基金之一，起始資本達二百一十億美元。該基金的目標包括投資及收購海外的積體電路公司，亦透過龐大資金吸引外資進入中國，並推動與外國企業建立合資夥伴關係。76 二〇二二年十二月，《路透社》報導中國計劃推出高達一千四百三十億美元的超大規模扶持計畫，用以支持其晶片製造產業。77 中國企業亦試圖收購外國公司以獲取專有技術，甚至曾派遣間諜竊取商業機密。78

儘管中國投入了大量資金，但迄今在這一關鍵產業仍未能真正取得競爭優勢。二〇二一年，中國在全球半導體銷售市場的占比為百分之七點六，相比於基金啟動初期的約百

新竊起者　300

分之五有所成長，但中國企業在高端晶片領域仍「明顯缺席」。[79] 中國目前在該領域最成功的企業中芯國際，在製造先進晶片方面仍落後於台積電等競爭對手。雖然美國本身在晶片製造上也不如亞洲的競爭者，但美國企業在晶片設計方面擁有全球領先的技術，並主導晶片製造所需的軟體、設備與零組件市場。[80] 儘管中國仍處於落後地位，但在政府支持與「軍民融合」政策的推動下，中國企業已在超級電腦領域取得進展，並發展出可用於雷達與衛星應用的軍用等級圖形處理器（GPU）設計。[81]

中國還在人工智慧這一相關產業取得了較大的成功，但最終結果可能憂喜參半。[82] 中國政府認為，人工智慧是各主要國家發展戰略的核心。人工智慧被描述為「新一輪產業變革的引擎」，將根本性地決定一個國家的國際競爭力。[83] 習近平則將人工智慧視為當今科學革命的戰略性技術，並認為它是帶動多個產業產生外溢效益的強大創新動力。[84] 中國的軍事專家也認為，人工智慧不僅在軍事領域的應用日益廣泛，更將改變未來戰爭的形態。[85] 二〇一七年七月，中國國務院發佈《新一代人工智能發展規劃》，此文件與《中國製造二〇二五》一樣，是中國人工智慧戰略的核心，目標是讓中國成為全球人工智慧技術的領導者，並降低對外國進口的依賴。[86]

第七章　中國經濟政策中的創新作為

中國在人工智慧領域具備若干優勢，而這些優勢主要建立在「運算能力、數據量、演算法」這三大支柱之上。人工智慧工程師必須設計出能在極其強大電腦上運行的演算法，來處理海量數據。儘管中國在製造支撐這些演算法的晶片方面仍面臨挑戰，但其研究人員在演算法設計和利用龐大資料庫訓練出高效模型方面，已取得顯著成就。二○一七年三月，百度成立了「國家深度學習技術工程實驗室」。阿里雲專注在智慧城市建設，騰訊則聚焦於醫療影像，科大訊飛則致力於智慧語音技術的開發。值得注意的是，這些開放共享的技術資源，也可能被利用於軍事用途。[87]

總而言之，由於中國封閉的政治體制，美國所採用的自由市場創新推動模式，對北京而言並不可行。中國因此選擇了另一條道路，透過國家主導的產業政策，在其政治限制下，仍相對成功地建立了技術與經濟實力。中國未來仍將延續這種模式，繼續推進產業政策，以期成為全球經濟與科技強國。在接下來的十年間，中國的目標是降低對外國技術的依賴，透過發展本土製造來取而代之，最終以中國自主開發的技術主導國際市場。為了實現這一目標，中國持續大力投資於電腦、通訊及其他電子設備的製造，電機機械、汽車、通用與專用機械的生產，致力於在高品質與高科技製造領域成為全球領導者。[88]然而，中

新竊起者　302

國共產黨並未因此放棄對科技發展的控制。二〇二三年三月，中共中央成立了「中央科技委員會」，專責指導中國的創新發展與軍民兩用科技戰略。[89]

當然，如果中國採用了美國的自由市場路線，有可能（甚至是很有可能）其表現會更加出色。儘管中國在許多產業中取得了主導地位，但在某些領域的表現仍不如預期。目前，中國仍在三十多個關鍵領域仰賴進口技術，例如重型燃氣發動機、核心工業軟體與光刻機等。[90]然而，從共產黨的角度來看，創新方面的邊際收益，似乎無法彌補控制力流失所帶來的風險。中共堅持在每一家擁有超過五十名員工的企業中設立黨支部。這種自上而下的監管文化，加上中共對於顛覆性變革的深層恐懼，可能會扼殺某些創意的誕生。黨的獎勵機制更偏向於漸進式的成就，而非鼓勵顛覆性的創新，這可能限制了中國創造出能改變世界的發明上的可能性。[91]嚴格控制的動機並不完全是出於政治考量。中國領導人也希望穩定經濟，而科技巨頭的壟斷行為可能帶來金融風險。黨同時也試圖重新導引中國企業的投資與努力方向，使之更契合黨所設定的戰略目標與國家利益。[92]

303　第七章　中國經濟政策中的創新作為

中國的「對外援助與發展援助」

當人們走訪世界各地時,特別是在亞洲與非洲,中國的經濟影響力展現得淋漓盡致。在衣索比亞,各種建築物上都可見中國建設公司的招牌。在波斯灣沿岸的產油國,中國出資修建的輸油管將原油輸送至同樣由中國資助的港口,接著裝載上油輪運往寧波與青島等地。中國企業還在具有戰略意義的兩個相鄰非洲國家:吉布地與衣索比亞,興建了全新的電氣化鐵路。

表面上看來,中國似乎是仿效了美國的做法。數十年來,對外發展援助一直是美國外交政策的重要工具。從冷戰初期開始,美國便利用經濟援助來塑造世界秩序。馬歇爾計畫(Marshall Plan)就是一例,該計畫以今日價值接近一千五百億美元的資金援助了十六個歐洲國家,其核心理念是歐洲需要額外的大量經濟協助,以建立「自由制度得以存在的政治與社會條件」。[93] 美國延續了這種以地緣政治動機推動經濟發展的傳統;事實上,擔任聯合國安全理事會非常任理事國的國家在其兩年任期內,獲得的美國援助通常會顯著增加。[94]

美國的發展援助主要由美國國際開發署（USAID）負責，該機構是依據一九六一年《對外援助法》設立的。95 此援助涵蓋範圍廣泛，約三分之一用於健康相關計畫，四分之一用於治理相關計畫，剩餘部分則分配至行政、農業、教育及其他類型的計畫。儘管這些資金遍布全球各地，但援助的重點區域為撒哈拉以南非洲（占比百分之三十一點四）以及歐洲與歐亞地區（占比百分之二十六點三）。96 儘管國際開發署將民主治理與人權視為持續發展的關鍵因素，但民主化或良好的人權紀錄並非獲得援助的必要條件。97

有數個因素使中國不願仿效美國透過發展援助來建立國際影響力。首先，中國的經濟資源遠不如美國。一九九四年中國成立第一家政策性銀行：中國進出口銀行時，其經濟規模不到美國的十分之一，且當時近三分之二的中國人口仍生活在世界銀行所定義的貧窮線（每天二點一五美元）以下。98 由於中國在經濟上處於競爭劣勢，若仿效美國的援助模式，無論在戰略效果方面，都可能難以奏效。

國內情勢使中國更難仿效美國的援助模式。鑑於中國當時仍是一個發展中國家，「對外援助」這一概念在國內引發爭議。批評者認為，對外援助將外國人的福祉置於中國公民

305　第七章　中國經濟政策中的創新作為

之上。即便在媒體高度管控的環境下，中國公民仍時常對中國政府免除外債或提供無償援助的行為表示不滿。[99]的確，在二〇一〇年以前，中國政府對其他國家的援助金額屬於國家機密。直到二〇一一年，中國才開始公布《對外援助白皮書》（後續於二〇一四年與二〇二一年再次發布類似報告），但北京至今仍對援助計畫的具體細節嚴格保密。[100]

仿效美國的援助方式是否能對美國起到「安撫」作用，也並不明朗。蘇聯與後來的日本就提供了先例，顯示即便是在發展援助領域的直接競爭，也可能被視為一種威脅。蘇聯的對外援助始於赫魯雪夫時期，他認為透過向剛獨立的新興國家（例如印度）提供經濟援助，蘇聯便可控制這些國家的對外貿易，進而促使它們採納社會主義體制。[101]美國分析人士對蘇聯涉足對外援助深感威脅，因為他們擔心，蘇聯在南亞、東南亞或中東等地區並無殖民歷史，這反而讓其在打入這些發展中國家時，比西方更具優勢。[102]同樣地，一九八〇年代當日本成為二十五個發展中國家的最大援助國時，許多美國人對日本的援助計畫也抱持著懷疑與戒心。[103]

事實上，當中國在二〇一六年成立亞洲基礎設施投資銀行（簡稱亞投行，ＡＩＩＢ），仿效美國對外援助策略中的監管機制時，美國視此舉為對其全球地位的直接挑戰。[104] 雖然與國際貨幣基金和世界銀行相比，亞投行在透明度與治理標準方面有所不足，但支持設立亞投行也是合理的：亞洲國家對基礎建設的投資有著龐大需求，若中國願意透過多邊機構投入資金，總比單邊行動更好。[105] 然而美國拒絕加入，認為亞投行將削弱其主導的亞洲開發銀行與世界銀行的影響力，並威脅到美國在「以規則為基礎的國際秩序」中的主導地位。[106] 中國財政部長樓繼偉曾試圖向美國釋疑，聲稱亞投行並非競爭者，而是補充性機構，因為其重點在於基礎設施建設，而非社會項目或一般性貸款。[107] 但他未能說服美國，雖然美國的多數盟友最終都加入了亞投行（該行目前擁有一百零六個成員國），但美國至今仍未加入。[108]

鑑於仿效美國在發展援助上的作法，在成效上存疑，且不太可能讓美國感到放心，中國領導人自二〇〇〇年代起開始思考與美國不同的對外援助與發展協助政策。[109] 畢竟，這方面的策略是有必要的，因為援助他國被視為有助於直接改善與其他國家的關係、鼓勵受援國在外交爭議中支持中國，並提升中國在全球的形象。[110]

幾項因素共同塑造了中國最終採取的對外援助策略。首先，中國希望任何政策路線都能支持國內的經濟發展（藉此爭取民意支持）。當時，中國企業生產的供給已遠超過市場

307　第七章　中國經濟政策中的創新作為

需求。中國政府在二〇〇八年金融危機後實施的大規模經濟刺激方案，更加劇了這個問題。中國在鋼鐵、水泥等重工業領域，面臨嚴重的產能過剩問題（即市場無法吸收過量的產品）。但若要改革這些以國有企業為主的產業，將帶來極大的政治代價，因為這會涉及大規模裁員。將資金借給他國，以便其購買中國基礎建設產品，雖然不是長久之計，但卻能創造緩衝時間，延緩這些艱難的改革。111而多年來對美國的貿易順差使中國積累了龐大的外匯儲備，卻苦無出口，而這資金正好可以用來資助海外專案，由中國本國企業承包執行。112同時，對鐵路、公路、機場與海運走廊等關鍵基礎設施的投資，將強化區域連結性，進一步刺激中國經濟的發展。113

中國共產黨亦有必要善加利用中國政治與經濟體制所帶來的一些競爭優勢。首先，國家主導的作法符合中國這種高度集中與由國家主導的經濟體系特性，使其能夠協調規模龐大的投資案。114其次，中國企業具備快速且低成本建設基礎設施的生產能力與經驗。根據麥肯錫公司（McKinsey & Company）的一項分析顯示，一九九二至二〇一一年間，中國將國內生產毛額的百分之八點五投入基礎建設，明顯高於工業化國家平均約百分之五的投入。115支撐這些基礎建設投資的是龐大的國有企業，其涉足鋼鐵、水泥、鐵路等領域，結

新崛起者　308

合了國家提供的龐大資金與長年來累積的專業知識與經驗，正是在全球規模最大、最密集的基礎設施建設中所培養出來的。[116]

最後，中國領導人認為他們能為發展中國家提供獨特價值。在中國看來，在中國國內實踐過的脫貧模式成效顯著。[117]相較之下，西方援助基於現代化理論，而中國分析人士認為該理論與發展中國家的實際經驗和國情不符。[118]

中國思想家相信，中國在提供此類專業知識上擁有特殊優勢，且不過分強調政治結構與自由化的做法更適合發展中國家。[119]他們還指出，中國近期通過基建、投資與重工業擺脫貧困的經驗，使其相比西方（如今以服務業與知識經濟為主導）更具優勢。[120]

最終形成的是一種創新型的影響力拓展路徑——它充分利用前述競爭優勢，同時降低國內政治風險。主要透過「一帶一路」倡議提供基礎建設發展融資援助，既能為中國商品開拓新市場，又有助於緩解國內產能過剩問題。[121]

中國的發展融資援助與美國的官方發展援助（official development assistance, ODA）明顯不同。美國與其他西方國家所定義的發展援助，是指由政府提供、明確針對發展中國家的經濟發展與福祉的援助資金。[122]在西方語境中，「援助」通常是指附帶高度優惠

第七章　中國經濟政策中的創新作為

條件的資金,例如零利率或低利率的發展性貸款。但中國的「援助」更準確地說是「債務」,因為其貸款利率普遍高於西方同類型援助,而且中國資助的許多項目並不明確以「發展」為目的。例如,在二○○○年至二○一七年間,中國官方支持的貸款平均「贈與成分」(即衡量貸款優惠程度的指標)僅為百分之二十八,而經濟合作暨發展組織成員國的平均值則為百分之六十四。中國學者也承認,與美國主要以傳統發展援助的形式不同,中國的援助結構是以少量傳統發展援助為基礎,輔以大量的「其他官方金流」(Other Official Flows, OOF)。[124] 自從推動一帶一路倡議以來,中國援助中的貸款與補助金比例高達三十一比一,而其他官方金流與發展援助的比例也達到九比一。[125] 根據資料顯示,二○○○至二○一七年間,中國的發展援助支出總額僅為一千零一十億美元,但「其他官方金流」則超過六千八百億美元。[126]

第二,與西方援助相比,中國貸款更常附帶「抵押條款」,也就是說,如果借款國無法償還債務,則需提供某種形式的資產作為抵押。例如,中國可以直接以自然資源收益作為還款方式,像是安哥拉就以石油收入抵債;又如斯里蘭卡則將港口權益作為抵押。[127] 事實上,中國的援助計畫是以「投資回報」為導向,而非像美國援助計畫那樣強調民主、人權與良善治理等非經濟目標。中國的對外貸款並不以利他主義為前提，而是期待獲利。舉例來說，二○一六年一名中國官員匿名表示：「中國需要投資於能產生利潤的項目。」這顯然與傳統援助的無償性質大相逕庭。128 中國對外貸款的主要提供者之一為中國進出口銀行，其成立的主要目的之一就是幫助中國企業向海外拓展出口與投資。

第三，中國資助的項目和類型與美國截然不同。中國的發展融資大多集中於非洲與亞洲的最不發達國家，且重點在於基礎設施建設，這正是中國具備競爭優勢的領域。例如，在二○○五至二○一九年間，中國與非洲國家簽訂了五百四十四項建設合約，總價值達二千六百七十七億美元，占中國全球建設項目總價值的三分之一。129 中美兩國在援助資金的用途方面也截然不同。根據美國國務院資料，二○一三至二○一七年間，美國對外援助的著重領域包括：緊急援助、愛滋病防治，以及政府與公民社會發展。131 而美國國際開發總署約三百億美元的預算中，前三大優先項目為：打擊貪腐、強化民主與人權，以及提供工具以對抗威權體制政權的數位壓迫與虛假資訊。132 這些領域顯然不是中國所關心或願意投入的方向。**圖 7.2** 顯示中國對各地區的發展融資歷年波動情況。

第四，中國的發展融資支出在方式上也與西方國家大不相同，因為它表面上是「不附

單位：十億美元（按照2017年的美元計價）

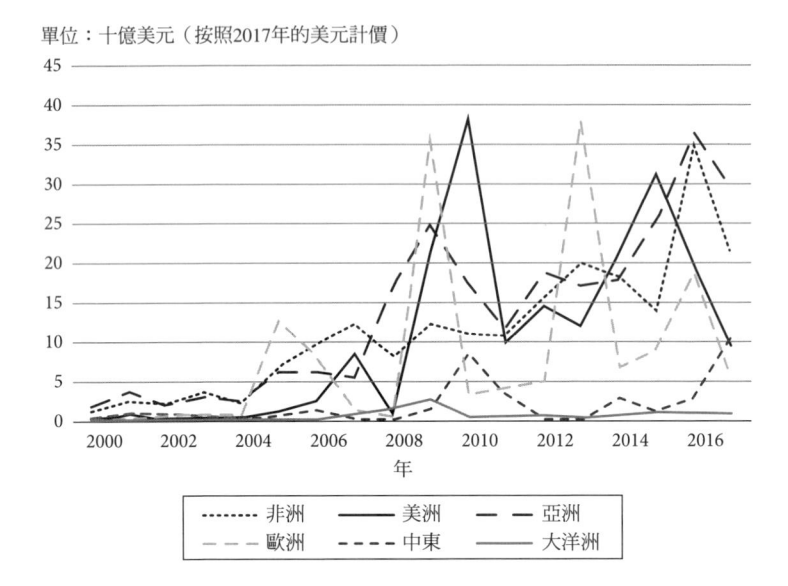

```
非洲 ........
美洲 ———
亞洲 — —
歐洲 — — —
中東 - - - -
大洋洲 ———
```

圖 7.2 二〇〇〇～二〇一七年中國政府對外國政府的融資

資料來源：Samantha Custer et al., "Tracking Development Finance: An Application of AidData's TUFF 2.0 Methodology," AidData, 2021, https://www.aiddata.org/data/aiddatas-global-chinese-development-finance-dataset-version-2-0.

帶政治條件」的（或至少附帶的政治條件較少）。西方主導的發展計畫通常會要求受援國履行問責、透明度查核、並要求更嚴格的借貸標準（包括減債與債務豁免等）等條件。相較之下，北京對受援國的國內治理問題則甚少著墨。中國學者普遍聲稱，這種做法反映的是對發展中國家人民「經濟生計」的尊重。[133]中國高層領導的公開演講與官方文件也

新竄起者　312

持續強調，中國所推動的方式是一種「獨特、非意識形態」的全球經濟合作方式，並且強調其有助於推動多邊主義與促進經濟全球化。

第五，中國在發展援助融資的規模之大，使其獨樹一幟。中國的對外發展融資始於一九九九年的「走出去政策」，該政策明確要求動用高達三兆美元的資金，鼓勵中國企業進行海外投資，藉此擴大中國的全球經濟影響力。自二○○九年起，中國已成為全球最大的雙邊發展融資提供者。[134] 在二○○五年以前，美國的發展融資總額（包括官方發展援助與其他官方金流）仍遠高於中國。但到了二○○九年，中國超車，該年中國的對外貸款金額突破一千億美元，而美國僅約三百五十億美元。二○一三至二○一七年間，中國的國家主導型融資（包括官方發展援助與其他官方金流）平均每年達八百五十億美元，是美國及其他主要國家的兩倍以上。[135] 二○○○至二○一八年間，中國向低收入國家提供了一千零四十億美元的貸款，幾乎與世界銀行的一千零六十億美元持平。[136] 在撒哈拉以南非洲地區，中國的累積貸款總額為六百六十億美元，略高於世界銀行提供的六百二十億美元。其中，安哥拉作為中國主要的石油供應國，是中國發展融資的最大受益者之一。[137]

中國在發展援助上的「創新式策略」可從四個核心元素明顯看出來，而這些元素正全

313　第七章　中國經濟政策中的創新作為

面體現在習近平於二○一三年推出的「一帶一路」倡議之中。一帶一路倡議是中國首次有系統的運用其新獲得的經濟實力，來擴展影響力與實力的重大舉措，特別針對周邊國家與開發中國家。它的最終目標是實現「中華民族偉大復興」的中國夢。一帶一路的兩個主要組成部分是絲綢之路經濟帶（Silk Road Economic Belt），其橫跨中亞內陸，最終延伸至歐洲的已開發市場；以及海上絲綢之路（Maritime Silk Road），經由海路將中國與東南亞、中東和歐洲的重要市場連結起來。138 除了這兩個主要組成部分外，還包含數位絲綢之路（Digital Silk Road）等計畫，該計畫涵蓋中國推動合作國家的電信、運算及其他高科技的努力，以及綠色絲綢之路（Green Silk Road），這是一個旨在將一帶一路與環保事業相結合的口號。

中國專注於基礎建設的援助發展策略，是否有助於其躍升為強權？許多經濟學者認為，一帶一路倡議在很大程度上是一場失敗，原因與浪費性支出與資本外逃密切相關。過去五年來，由於中國國內經濟放緩以及國外的反彈聲浪（源自貪污醜聞與借貸國家的財政困境），該計畫的規模已大幅縮減。

然而，許多對中國這種做法的批評，著重的並非其對中國本身的影響，而是對其他國

新竄起者　314

家的影響。例如，經濟學者指出，中國的放貸做法助長了斯里蘭卡與尚比亞等地的債務危機，目前已知有四十二個國家對中國的公共債務超過其國民生產毛額的百分之十。139 一帶一路倡議中的基礎建設項目似乎問題最多：其中百分之三十五的專案遭遇重大執行問題，例如貪污醜聞、勞工違規、環境危害與民眾抗議，相較之下，中國政府在不屬於一帶一路倡議中的基建項目則僅有百分之二十一出現類似問題。140 部分地區已對中國出現反彈，在許多民主國家，人民已表達出反對意見，將較不熱衷於中國援助的候選人推上台。141

即便中國的援助導致更多貪污與債務問題，目前仍不清楚這樣的情況是否會削弱中國的影響力。中國已成功將自己打造為許多中低收入國家的「首選融資者」。這些項目同時也支持了中國企業在海外的發展，並有助於其推動人民幣國際化。142 儘管外界有不少批評，中國顯然找到了真正的需求，且有許多國家願意加入其中。一項分析指出，若一帶一路能全面落實，將可使運輸時間與貿易成本各減少一成，並可使全球貿易總量成長超過百分之六。143 世界銀行的一份報告也有類似結論，估計該倡議可在二○三○年以前讓全球所得增加百分之零點七，並「協助七百六十萬人脫離極端貧困，三千二百萬人擺脫中度貧困」。144 不論風險為何，各國仍對參與中國倡議抱持興趣。二○二二年，全球將近八成

315　第七章　中國經濟政策中的創新作為

的國家接受了中國的資金援助（不論是補助還是貸款），而中國在其五十個最大借貸國的「外部債務總額」中，平均佔比已超過百分之四十。[145]

中國提供援助的目的，或許與幫助其他國家經濟成長的初衷有所不同。中國計畫通過經濟援助獲得政治支持，以此替代美國基於軍事或意識形態標準建立聯盟的模式。不可否認，隨著發展融資規模的擴大，中國的影響力也隨之成長。[146]接受中國援助的夥伴國必須支持北京的「一個中國政策」，並反對台灣獨立；它們也傾向於在聯合國大會上與北京保持一致立場。研究表明，當中國希望獲得地緣政治回報時，會提供較優惠的援助條件；而對於預計能帶來經濟回報的專案，則使用優惠程度較低的貸款來融資。[147]中國來源的說法亦常指出，一帶一路倡議與亞洲基礎設施投資銀行共同旨在推動全球權力再平衡，以及改革國際金融秩序。[148]事實上，西方國家之所以對加入一帶一路顯得猶豫，正是因為此倡議顯然是推廣中國外交影響力的工具。[149]透過區域整合，一帶一路也協助中國推動其西部地區的發展，藉此緩解該地區的不穩定與叛亂問題。中國所指定納入一帶一路規劃的十四個省份中，有九個屬於西部地區。[150]

中國也利用其對一帶一路國家的影響力，以及本身經濟的吸引力，來影響全球產業標

新竄起者　316

準的制定方式，藉此提升中國企業的全球競爭力。二〇一八年，中國啟動「中國標準二〇三五計畫」，目的是為中國政府與領先科技企業擬定藍圖，以在新興科技領域（如5G、物聯網、人工智慧）中主導全球標準的制定。二〇二一年與二〇二二年的後續計畫則針對特定產業提出明確方向，鼓勵中國企業推動「中外標準互認」，並指派具體的政府部門負責各項工作。[151]與此同時，美國基本上將標準制定交由商業部門自行運作，但中國政府則確保自身利益能在國際電信聯盟（International Telecommunications Union）等產業組織會議中獲得代表。[152]華為尤其積極推廣其技術標準，透過在歐亞與非洲地區大規模投資5G基礎設施、資料中心與智慧城市等建設，推廣中國技術標準。

中國也透過發展金融援助策略，在取得經濟持續成長所需的天然資源方面有所進展。這並不令人意外，因為俄羅斯、委內瑞拉與安哥拉是中國非優惠貸款的前三大接受國，同時也是中國主要的石油供應國。[153]中國以約百分之六的相對高利率向資源豐富的國家提供貸款，並以商品出口收入作為抵押──如果借款國無力償還，中國將通過資源出口收益獲得補償。[154]「海上絲綢之路」及中國在海外建設的商業港口，旨在確保中國能夠自由進出對能源（特別是石油）進口至關重要的海運通道。[155]值得注意的是，中國一帶一路倡議下的首筆海外港口投資便是來自珠海港控股公司對巴基斯坦瓜達爾港（Gwadar Port）所做的十六億美元投資。156

在中國成為全球國家主導型融資的首要提供者十年之後，美國及其盟國開始試圖尋求一種能與之抗衡的方式。美國的首次嘗試是在二〇一九年推出的「藍點網路」（Blue Dot Network，簡稱BDN），該倡議結合了公部門、私部門與公民社會，目的是確保基礎建設項目符合國際間對透明度、永續性與可行性的標準，藉此吸引私人投資，以對抗中國的國家主導型融資。157 拜登政府所推動的「重建更好世界」（Build Back Better World，簡稱B3W）在公共資金的運用上更具野心，但無論是BDN還是B3W，在規模上皆未能達到與中國相當的水準。另外，儘管強調透明度與永續性的作法，確實吸引了一些國家，但對某些國家而言，正是因為中國不設這些條件，它們才選擇與中國合作。

二〇二二年六月，七大工業國推出「全球基礎設施與投資夥伴關係」，這是對先前倡議的重新包裝。參與國期望透過該計畫動員六千億美元資金。然而，儘管官方聲明預期這項協議將促成超過二千億美元的投資，目前所列出的具體專案卻規模有限。其中規模最大的項目，是印尼與美國之間的一項合作協議，但美方實際承諾的資金僅有六點五億美元。

新竄起者　318

二○二二年九月，美國又成立了「美國—太平洋夥伴關係」（US-Pacific Partnership），其中包括一項承諾投入八點一億美元的計畫，內容涵蓋氣候適應能力建設、教育、太平洋地區領導人培訓以及執法能力建構等領域。158

中國似乎正因應外界批評以及美國新的重點策略，來調整自身策略。在二○二一年十一月舉行的第三屆「一帶一路」建設座談會上，習近平強調未來一帶一路項目應優先推動「高品質」、「小而美」的項目。159 中國高層也強調將以人民民生為核心，推動疫情後的經濟復甦，聚焦於貧困、失業、健康與教育等議題。160 為了回應外界對環境影響的批評，中國亦推出「綠色絲綢之路」倡議，承諾推動關於氣候變遷、清潔能源及生態保護的援助項目。161 中國還試圖回應「債務陷阱」的指控，例如在二○二二年宣布免除十七個非洲國家的二十三筆貸款。

然而，儘管北京正在調整其發展援助的方式，但顯然並未放棄其整體的創新策略。二○一七年，「一帶一路」被寫入中國共產黨黨章，作為其對外承諾之一。到了二○二一年，習近平又推出了「全球發展倡議」（Global Development Initiative，簡稱GDI），作為與「一帶一路」相關的新舉措。162 如果說「一帶一路」起初是為了將中國的過剩產能向外轉移，那麼全球發展倡議則代表著中國企圖從更宏觀的層面重新定義「發展」的話語權。[163] 中國將其譽為「應對全球挑戰的中國方案」，尤其是在新冠肺炎疫情帶來重大衝擊之後。這一倡議標誌著中國在國際發展事務上的重大轉變，明確顯示出北京已經在全球舞台上更加自信，並有意在這一領域扮演領導角色。[164]

中國在創新發展，以及與發展中國家的經濟聯繫方面，已形成與美國自由企業模式和對外發展援助截然不同的路徑。中國選擇發揮其資源體量龐大和國家機器強大的競爭優勢——這種體制能戰略性調配資源。由此產生的結果是：中國對世界的依賴度降低，而世界對中國的依賴度上升。這種不對稱依賴為北京創造了西方難以複製的獨特影響力。即便美國對中國這種創新式經濟手段的某些做法持保留甚至批評態度，但與軍事領域相比，中國在經濟領域的「創新」策略並未引發同等程度的強烈反彈。中國也相當謹慎地避免造成威脅的印象，即便其影響力不斷擴張，卻始終未將拉丁美洲納入「一帶一路」倡議就是一個明顯的例子。[165]（編註：後來二〇二五年仍然加入了哥倫比亞）因此，中國透過擴展其經濟力量，得以有效且高效率地與美國在全球的存在相抗衡。

新竄起者　320

結論

強權競爭的啟示

中國的崛起，數十年來一直讓外界著迷。關於中國經濟奇蹟的書籍更是汗牛充棟。[1]

然而，經濟實力既不是成為強權的前提（蘇聯的經驗便是證明），也不是充分條件（如一九八〇年代的日本）。成為強權需要一套有意識的策略，來縮小與既有霸主國在政治、經濟與軍事力量上的差距。追求霸權是一種選擇，並非所有新興強權都會做出這個選擇：有些國家滿足於在特定領域內稱霸。但中國顯然不是這樣的國家。過去三十年間，中國採取了一套「竊起者」策略，以實現其成為世界霸權的目標。

透過解釋中國如何建立實力，以及哪些因素影響其決策，我提供了對中國未來十年希望達成之目標的深入理解，也讓人們得以判斷北京是否有可能實現這些目標，並探討美國及其盟友如何最有效的捍衛自身利益。在本書最終章中，我將根據研究成果提出對政策制定的啟示，向美國政策制定者提出具體且可執行的建議。「竊起者」邏輯提示了哪些因素可能促使北京在其策略的不同構面之間轉換。我也將說明這一策略對國際關係理論的貢獻，提供一套框架以辨識美國的競爭優勢所在，以及如何將競爭推向這些具優勢的領域。

新竊起者　322

中國未來二十年的戰略

「竄起者」理論提供了一個框架，用以理解中國過去三十年如何成功大幅縮小與美國的差距。然而，無論對學者或政策制定者而言，關鍵問題在於未來三十年將如何發展。該框架可作為分析師的指南，用以解讀中國政府的具體決策，並理解中國戰略可能發生變化的條件。以下將探討這些條件。

北京在選擇「竄起者」策略的具體方針時，關鍵考量因素之一在於判斷「美國將如何解讀特定戰略」。這種判斷導致中國採取以下策略：當模仿行為能緩解美國疑慮時，便選擇模仿；而當模仿可能過度直接挑戰美國利益時，則轉為創新突破。此種策略選擇的核心動機，始終是避免引發美國的強烈反制。

在避開霸主國核心利益並累積足夠實力以威懾──必要時甚至能成功對抗霸主國後，新興強權可能會轉向更直接挑戰霸主國的實力構築方式。隨著中美實力差距縮小，對北京而言，「無法直接競爭」的顧慮可能逐漸降低。換言之，在某些情況下，實力的增強可能使「模仿戰略」變得更具策略效益與效率，甚至使其收益超過負面反應所帶來的成本。

323　結論　強權競爭的啟示

對中國而言，許多戰略選擇取決於領導人對國家相對實力的認知。一方面，中國在討論其大國地位時，仍帶有一種理想抱負的色彩——這與「建成社會主義現代化強國」這一目標密切相關但又有所區別，該目標作為習近平「中國夢」的重要組成部分，承載著民族復興與建設強大國家的願景。這一願景包括要成為「品質製造強國」、「科技強國」、「太空強國」、「交通強國」、「海洋強國」、「高品質貿易國」、「體育強國」、「文化先進國」、「教育領先國」以及「人才強國」。如習近平所言，這一切尚未完成。中國需要保持經濟的持續繁榮，提高軍事能力，穩定推行「一國兩制」政策，促進「國家統一」，以及增強創新能力。[2]

中國領導階層清楚認知到，中國的綜合實力尚未能與美國全面匹敵。具體而言：中國人均對外直接投資額仍遠低於其他強權國家；國內市場體系與高附加值產品製造能力尚在發展階段；[3]人民幣國際化程度不足，無法成為定價貨幣或儲備貨幣，目前僅佔全球跨境支付總額的百分之二，且尚未實現自由兌換（其國際化進程取決於未來金融改革成效）；在國際貿易規則制定方面，中國尚未成為主導性力量。[4]另有觀點指出，中國在基礎研究、科學理論創新及新興領域探索方面的能力，仍遜於其他主要強權國家。[5]

新竄起者　324

另一方面，中國無疑已在總體實力上縮小了與美國之間的差距。因此，相較於過去「竄起者策略」中所強調的因素，中國對於「美國是將某項戰略視為安全或威脅」的判斷，未來對中國決策的影響可能會減弱。考量到中國目前的軍事與經濟實力，中國軍事戰略家已普遍認為，對美國而言，發動預防性戰爭如今將會帶來災難性的後果。西方普遍已形成一項共識，認為過去對中國的認知存在謬誤；與中國接觸的政策從未能使中國變成美國期望的模樣。更重要的是，如今幾乎不可能再營造出「中國崛起無害」的印象。西方普遍已形成一項共識，認為過去對中國的認知存在謬誤；與中國接觸的政策從未能使中國變成美國期望的模樣。更重要的是，如今幾乎不可能再營造出「中國崛起無害」的印象。中國普遍認為，在川普總統任內，美中關係進入新階段，其核心目標就是圍堵中國並「在競爭中獲勝」，防止中國實力與美國匹敵。習近平經常引用的「百年未有之大變局」一詞，反映出中國認為，全球秩序正面臨一次深刻的地緣政治重塑，權力正在東移。與過去官方講話避免直接批評美國不同，習近平在二○二三年三月的演講中公開指出：「以美國為首的西方國家，對我國進行了全方位的遏制、圍堵和打壓，給我國發展帶來前所未有的嚴峻挑戰。」9

但即便中國對自身實力的信心日增，且對能否安撫西方的信心減弱，美國對中國戰略的回應仍可能持續影響「竄起者策略」各組成部分的成本與效益，從而影響中國的戰略選

325　結論　強權競爭的啟示

擇。大多數觀察家已接受現實，即美國對中國的政策將日趨強硬，對中國崛起各方面的反制措施也會愈發頻繁。10 然而，中國仍會試圖降低與美國及其他發達國家的摩擦，而這一傾向值得鼓勵。美國還可以在「是否存在可利用的戰略縫隙」、以及「某些路徑的戰略效果與效率」方面發揮關鍵影響。例如，若華盛頓努力彌補在某些領域中競爭力不足的缺陷，或開始對中國特定策略加以施壓（例如威脅因中國對某些國家出售武器而施加制裁），那麼「利用」戰略空隙這種做法的吸引力就會下降。又如，隨著俄羅斯因入侵烏克蘭而與美國與北約關係持續惡化，中國或許會認為策略性地強化中俄夥伴關係或在國際事務中扮演調停角色是更具吸引力的做法。換言之，本書的一個重要啟示是：若要預測中國未來的戰略走向，首先必須對未來三十年美國的整體戰略方針有清晰的理解。

「模仿」策略的擁護者可能會認為，一旦具備了足夠的能力，中國就會開始追隨美國的腳步。然而，「竊起者策略」提供了有力的證據，反駁了這種對中國未來過於簡化的看法。能力的提升是否會影響中國的戰略，取決於決策背後的邏輯。如果中國在過去三十年中拒絕效法美國，是因為其領導人認為某些戰略對美國自身都未必奏效，那麼即使中國日後具備執行這些戰略的能力，北京也不太可能會選擇效法美國。換句話說，中國不太可能

新竊起者　　326

追求與美國的核武平衡、不太可能建立傳統的軍事聯盟、也不太可能建立一個能促進海外軍事干預的基地網路。如果中國的決策者拋棄了「竄起者策略」的智慧，轉而一味仿效，例如發展航空母艦，中國很可能會在投入大量資源之後，卻僅收穫極小的競爭優勢。即便未來中美之間的實力差距持續縮小，中國也仍可能堅持進行一些具創新性的策略，如政權中立、產業政策、以及數位貨幣，因為這些策略的替代方案會對中共的控制構成威脅。

最有可能出現變化的領域，是中國在採用相同策略的情況下，轉向不同的競爭領域，也就是「竄起者策略」中的「利用」。在這些領域，中國認為自己尚不具備直接競爭的優勢，但仍判斷該策略具有價值。像是：高層外交訪問、軍售、強調反介入／區域拒止，而非遠距投射能力、運用灰色地帶手段而非直接軍事行動、爭取對國際金融體系的話語權等。然而，一旦中國認為自己獲得了新的力量優勢，就可能開始與美國直接競爭。商業世界中也有類似的現象。企業常常先從利基市場起步，等到資源足夠時，才向主流市場發起挑戰。例如，沃爾瑪（Walmart）最初只在小型鄉村市場立足，但當其資源累積到一定程度後，便開始向大城市中的百貨公司發動全面競爭。

如果中國在未來三十年間變得更加虛弱，會發生什麼情況？有些專家認為中國作為新

327　結論　強權競爭的啟示

興強權的高峰已過，正面臨即將到來的衰退，這種情勢會提高北京在機會之窗關閉前變得更加具侵略性的危險與風險。[11] 然而，美國學者過去多年來早就一直指出中國的弱點，有些甚至預測中國即將崩潰，因此中國經濟前景黯淡的說法並非定論。[12] 從竄起者策略的角度來看，「中國正在走下坡」這種說法的框架本身就存在問題。這種邏輯預設了中國若要達成美國所達成的事，就必須擁有與美國相同的資源，以及以相同的方式建立並行使實力。但事實上，中國未必需要相同的力量形式或相同規模的資源，也可能對美國構成挑戰，甚至取而代之。過去三十年間，中國正是憑藉著這種竄起者策略，從一個資源相對較弱的位置與美國競爭。沒有任何理由認為它未來不能繼續如此行事。即使中國經濟成長停滯，北京在未來二十五年可運用的總體資源數量（無論是政治、軍事還是經濟）也仍將多於過去三十年。因此，它完全有可能延續甚至深化其競爭力。

然而，中國的競爭方式可能會隨之演變。若中國經濟面臨嚴峻挑戰，例如人口結構疲弱與債務問題日益嚴重，而中國領導層又認為自己在競爭所需的資源上處於劣勢，那麼「戰略效能」與「確保黨的控制」這兩項因素將更強烈地影響其選擇何種竄起者策略的構成部分。具體來說，這些情勢將使中國更傾向於依賴「創新型策略」與「利用型策略」，

新竄起者　328

而非「模仿型策略」。

當前美國關於如何應對中國崛起的政策辯論，給了我們哪些具體啟示呢？肯尼斯・沃爾茲曾經指出，強權往往可以不必汲取教訓，因為能對其造成嚴重損害的威脅極少，且只有當這些威脅真的付諸實行時才會造成傷害。[13] 中國的崛起正是這種少見的重大威脅之一，因此，美國是時候必須進行調整與應變了。儘管美國可以從歷史中獲取經驗，但目前所面對的情況實屬前所未見：它正與一個正在新興的強權對手競爭，這個對手目前主要是在累積並運用政治與經濟力量（至少目前是如此）；雙方所在的國際體系是前所未有地制度化與一體化；霸主國（即美國）本身所受到的約束也比以往更加明顯；而此競爭又發生在整體正在崛起中的亞洲地區。換言之，美國面對的不再是一個孤立、對抗性的威脅（如冷戰時期的蘇聯），而是一個深度嵌入全球體系、且正在靈活運用該體系漏洞與自身制度優勢的對手——中國。這種複雜的挑戰要求美國進行新的思考，並採取有別於過往單純遏制或改造對手的戰略。

美國必須採取針對性的策略，建立並維持自身的競爭優勢，發展出屬於自己的「窺起者策略」。具體而言，美國與其盟友應該：①避免全面仿效中國的成功經驗；②鼓勵中國模仿美國仍具有競爭優勢的領域；③堵住可供中國利用的漏洞；④發展自身的創新策略。整體目標是：將競爭場域導向美國具有優勢的領域，同時削弱中國在其優勢領域中的戰略成效。[14]

一、**不要全面仿效中國的做法**。正如中國不一定會從模仿美國的成功經驗中獲益，美國仿效中國的成功模式也未必是最佳選擇。美國若盲目模仿，將面臨商業理論中所說的「定位困境」（position stranding）風險。這種情況指的是，市場領導者為了應對其他競爭對手的挑戰，在試圖維持自身長期戰略的同時，也模仿了對方的創新做法（例如：蘋果企圖保持原有品牌定位，卻模仿三星推出大螢幕手機）。[15]然而，這類「兩面討好」的策略往往適得其反。就像企業一樣，國家若試圖同時保有自身的獨特優勢、又想複製他國策略，最後常常落得投入更多、收效更小的局面。競爭策略專家麥可・波特（Michael Porter）便曾警告：企業不應該單純模仿其他公司的策略或技術，而應該思考如何將對方的做法調整並融入自身的獨特定位，藉此擴大自身價值與優勢。[16]

問題在於，美國並不具備與中國相同的競爭優勢，因此透過模仿來進行直接競爭可能會適得其反。美國無法在全球基礎建設領域和中國競爭、也不可能擁抱國家主導的產業政策，或參與灰色地帶活動來維持其地位。中國的體制更適合這些類型的控制與協調。中國也可能正在從事與美國價值觀不一致的行為——例如庇護威權統治者，或對關鍵經濟領域施加國家控制。美國必須避免陷入一場「逐底競爭」的賽局。

這段討論並不是為了支持當前那種「中國體制在某種程度上更穩定、更靈活、更有效，且總體而言在競爭上更優越」的說法。17 無庸置疑的是，中共為了維持黨的控制，已經減少了自身的戰略選項，經常導致次佳的結果（例如在塑造軟實力和人民幣國際化方面的嘗試），也被迫耗費了本可用於更有價值之處的大量資源。但同樣不能否認的是：中國領導人經常能夠成功地調整其手法，以發揮其體制的優勢。不論是政體中立、訓練外國執法人員、國家主導的產業政策，還是針對在政治或經濟上具有問題的基礎建設項目提供發展融資——這些策略都最適合一個列寧式威權政體。

換句話說，冷戰後普遍認為的：「封閉的共產主義社會無法在軍事或經濟上與自由國家競爭」，這種傳統觀點其實並不完全正確。18 美國的政治與經濟體制確實可以在強權競逐中成為一項重要，甚至是決定性的優勢，但這是一種策略選擇，並非理所當然的結果。美國不能只是坐等中國失敗，而是需要主動地取得成功。以創新為例，一項北京做不出來

331　結論　強權競爭的啟示

的選擇就是更開放的移民政策,吸引技術勞工在美國落地生根。然而,移民是否能成為一項優勢,端看美國是否願意積極採取行動,例如取消目前針對大學畢業移民工作簽證的數量上限,並為STEM(科學、技術、工程、數學)領域的博士畢業生設立快速取得永久居留權的途徑。[19]

二、**在有利領域鼓勵中國模仿**。我的研究主要發現之一是:當中國選擇透過模仿來直接競爭時,美國通常能享有優勢。中國似乎也可能因為對國際聲望的渴求,或因為這麼做能顯著降低與美國以及其他已開發國家之間的摩擦,而選擇模仿之路。因此,美國應該鼓勵中國進一步模仿,或許可以透過傳遞一些訊息來達成這個目的,例如強調中國若未具備某些能力或未從事特定類型的活動,便無法被視為一個真正的「強權」。事實上,假設中國參與國際機構會導致其價值觀與利益發生轉變,因此呼籲中國成為「負責任的利害關係人」顯得過於樂觀,但這種說法的確對中國的資源分配產生了一些影響。舉例來說,若中國更多地將援助資源投入到災難救援領域,或因為想要主導國際金融體系而被迫讓人民幣匯率浮動、並開放資本自由流動,那對美國來說將是有利的。

這項關於鼓勵模仿的建議,同樣適用於「設立海外軍事基地」這種高度敏感領域。中國的軍事優勢僅限於其沿海附近的地區。而建立一個全球性的軍事部署體系，代價高昂，並可能分散原本投入於其他常規軍事能力的資源。正因如此，中國一直避免採用美國保護其海外利益的軍事模式。然而，如果中國感到有必要在這方面直接與美國競爭，反而會讓美國在整體的軍事競爭中更容易佔到上風。

最後，在某些領域中國的模仿行為確實會增強其影響力與實力，但美國仍應予以鼓勵，因為這能為美國其他方面的利益帶來正面外部效應。例如：朝鮮半島發生突發事件時，若中國能參與其中，將降低使用核武的可能性。20 中國也處於獨特地位，能鼓勵俄羅斯回到談判桌以結束烏克蘭戰爭。若要任何談判有望達成和解協議，就必須對中國（可能還包括俄羅斯）做出讓步。中國也必須向烏克蘭證明其價值——這可能意味著北京在戰後重建中將可獲得更大的經濟利益。儘管問題重重，但中國積極參與，仍然可能是實現烏克蘭和平的最佳選擇。

三、**填補漏洞**。中國建立實力的一種方式，就是利用美國戰略與國際秩序中的空隙。無論是銷售無人機、對開發中國家展開外交行動、發展反介入／區域拒止能力以針對美軍基地，或是竊取外國技術來支撐其產業政策，中國都在發現機會後予以利用。對美國而

333　結論　強權競爭的啟示

言，最好的應對方式就是填補這些漏洞。

有一個領域特別值得關注，那就是以規則為基礎的國際秩序。學者們普遍自信地認為由美國主導的世界秩序是全方位且穩固的。[21]然而，中國發現世界上某些地區基本上處於該體系之外，因此未能從中受益。這些地區包括美國鮮少往來的不受歡迎的政權，以及美國忽視的一些區域。中國的戰略家還主張，中國應加強國際事務發言權，尤其是在西方（特別是川普政府時期）所忽略的國際機構中提升影響力。[22]美國必須在外交和經濟上加強存在感，並善用自身的競爭優勢。例如，拜登政府提出的「印太經濟框架」若能提供簽署國進入美國市場的優惠待遇，將會大大提升其吸引力。[23]

世界貿易組織（WTO）就是一個值得重新檢視的國際機構。世貿組織的根源可追溯至第二次世界大戰及其戰後時期，那時美國占全球經濟產出的半數，而自由世界大多仰賴華盛頓的援助。最近一次的談判——杜哈回合談判已經是十多年前的事了，且最終以失敗告終。該組織最後一次真正的成功達成共識是在一九九四年的烏拉圭回合談判，而那還是在中國成為成員國之前。中國利用世貿組織缺乏共識這點來逃避對其違反入會協議的處罰，並藉此實現其四大貿易優先事項：「推動自主創新、促進自給自足、強化國家安全，推進市場改革與開放」。[24] 值得注意的是，一九九四年烏拉圭回合談判所達成的框架中完全沒有被提及「國有企業」這個術語，這實際上使得中國經濟中極為龐大的部分得以免於遵守世貿組織關於關稅、智慧財產權以及其他關鍵貿易問題的規範。[25]

為了對抗這種情況，美國應對中國加更大壓力，要求其履行加入世貿組織時所承諾的義務，理想情況下還應與其他七大工業國合作，鼓勵受到中國經濟脅迫的國家向世貿組織提出申訴。[26] 至少這樣可以降低中國「利用」漏洞戰略的效益與效率。但若要實現這點，美國必須強化，而不是削弱該組織的功能。川普總統當初拒絕任命世貿組織上訴機構（最高法院）的新法官，導致該機構實質停擺，這反而加強了中國利用此種不確定性的空間。

在軍事領域中，彌補漏洞的方式是透過「韌性嚇阻」來降低自身的脆弱性。與「懲罰性嚇阻」類似，「韌性嚇阻」同樣注重塑造對手對嚇阻方能力的認知。但與懲罰性嚇阻不同，其目標不是讓對手害怕報復，而是讓對手認為發動破壞性行動的效果有限。當對手認為製造麻煩帶來的收益有限時，就較不可能採取行動。這個概念也和「拒止性嚇阻」相關，但兩者不同之處在於，拒止性嚇阻旨在防止對手成功執行軍事行動，而韌性嚇阻則承認戰術或作戰層級的行動可能會成功，但戰術成功無法像對手預期的轉化為戰略成功。

此處說的「韌性」（resiliency）指的是一個國家在面對一定程度的暴力行為時，能夠承受並轉移成本的能力。因此，韌性的重點在於向中國傳遞一個訊號：某項軍事行動所能帶來的好處，實際上將比中國所預期的要少。這可能是因為相關國家擁有可行的替代方案、多重備援系統，或是防禦效能的提升。舉例來說，在太空資產的問題上，很難透過傳統手段來嚇阻中國進行攻擊，因為中國可能認為攻擊太空資產的作戰效益極高，而付出的代價卻很低。在這種情況下，提升防禦能力或許不切實際，但美國可以採取多種行動，來顯示這類攻擊實際上無法對美軍行動造成重大影響。或許美國已具備比以往更快速地重新發射衛星的能力，或是已部署多個衛星來強化備援系統，甚至與其他國家簽訂協議，可在必要時迅速以他國的衛星取代本國衛星。27 美國在亞洲的軍事基地佈署方面同樣適用這個原則。美國能運作的據點越多，部隊的應變能力就越強，對中國來說，對這些基地發動飛彈攻擊的吸引力就越低。

美國也應該在那些缺乏明確、強烈國際共識的領域投入時間與資源，例如網路空間、人工智慧與反太空武器等。在這些領域建立明確的限制，將有利於美國建立優勢。美中網

新竄起者　336

路關係已惡化，中國在聯合國「政府專家小組」中阻撓由美國主導制定規範，並自二〇一四年起，在浙江烏鎮舉辦年度「世界互聯網大會」，作為對抗。28 儘管在歐巴馬政府時期，美中曾成功建立「對於網路間諜活動的共同理解」，並達成一項協議，即不會「從事或蓄意支持以網路為手段竊取智慧財產權的行為」，但中國的網路間諜行為與各類惡意網路活動日益成為雙邊緊張的主要因素，而雙方至今尚未達成全面協議。29 雖然聯合國「政府專家小組」於二〇一五年制定了一套網路空間規範，並在二〇二一年由所有聯合國會員國透過「開放式工作小組」正式同意並採納，但這些規範基本上仍屬自願性質，缺乏強制力，也尚未落實執行。30

在制訂反太空武器規範，包括直升式反衛星飛彈系統方面，中美雙方展現出較多合作的可能性，這是因為中國長期反對太空軍事化，包括中國在二〇〇八年提出的〈防止在外空放置武器、對外空物體使用或威脅使用武力條約草案〉（編按：外空指外太空），以及美國在二〇二二年宣布暫停反衛星武器測試。31 人工智慧領域也似乎具有合作潛力。儘管現在下定論還為時過早，但本研究指出，中國對人工智慧規範的態度將取決於它認為哪些人工智慧的應用會限制美國，哪些則能為中國帶來軍事優勢。總體而言，中國對於將人工

337　結論　強權競爭的啟示

智慧應用於軍事領域抱有極大期待。中國國務院於二○一七年發布的一份文件聲稱，中國必須「把握人工智能發展的重大戰略機遇，建立我國在人工智能發展上的先發優勢」，以在二○三○年之前成為人工智能領域的世界領導者。32 這反過來將使中國人民解放軍在資訊應用能力較弱的對手面前取得重大優勢。33

四、採取創新策略。 美國必須重新思考建構與運用實力的方式，才能在二十一世紀保持競爭力。在商業領域中，「領導者確立競爭現狀」，但若「不主動打破現狀」，通常會走向衰退。34 然而，即使面臨來自追趕者的實力挑戰，既有霸主國往往仍難以採取新策略。正如產業領導者一樣，霸主國會因為主導地位而較缺乏創新動機。35 與其一味堅守那些最初讓他們變得強大的策略、最終走向衰落，國際體系中的領導者必須認識到：「他們必須近乎無情地在現有產品與流程最具利潤之際，就將其淘汰，並展開新一輪的探索」。36

美國若要維持相對於中國的優勢地位，唯一的方法就是採取自身的創新行動。這意味著必須有意識地思考是否該改變美國的既有做法。例如，美國是否應該重新考慮與問題國家增強接觸，而不是中斷外交關係？美國是否應該對南海的領土爭議表態？美國國防工業該如何重組，以因應未來在亞洲可能發生的突發狀況，並能大量生產所需彈藥？是否是時

新竄起者　338

候與盟友共享技術或能力，例如最近的澳英美三方安全夥伴（AUKUS）協議？若要成功，就必須採取嶄新的方法，而不僅僅是對舊策略的小修小補。這也包括推動新政策，以削弱中國創新型策略的有效性與效能。舉例來說，美國可以推動建立一個新的國際機制，以監管和規範各國之間的內部安全合作。

在核武領域中，本研究顯示中國並不追求與美國的核武平衡——中國的邏輯認為，只要達成核報復能力的門檻，之後核武數量的邊際增加便不再具有戰略意義。無論美國核武的數量是中國的十八倍還是六倍，對於衝動動態的影響是相同的。真正的問題在於美國在印太地區的常規武力嚇阻能力正在衰退，這使北京可能動用武力來奪取台灣的控制權。正如第四與第五章所指出的，這些常規武力的挑戰是真實存在的，且難以解決。因此，美國或許應該採取更具創新性的軍備控制方式。具體來說，我建議美國考慮「不對稱性軍武控制協議」，例如，美國可以在削減其戰區飛彈防禦能力或甚至核彈頭數量方面作出讓步，以換取中國放棄部署特定類型與數量的常規飛彈。這種方式能降低中國對美軍的反介入／區域拒止威脅，且對核武實力平衡幾乎沒有戰略影響——但由於中國也擔憂其核武二次打擊能力的生存性，或許會同意此方案。

339　結論　強權競爭的啟示

在南海問題上，美國目前的應對策略不足以遏制中國鞏固對這些水域的控制。美國應考慮擴大行動範圍，包括為盟友與夥伴國家護航其漁船與石油勘探船，尤其是那些缺乏足夠海軍或海巡力量的國家。美國還可以明確表示，對區域國家的防衛承諾將延伸至保護這些國家在其專屬經濟區內的權益。同樣地，美國也應對外釋出訊號：若中國在該區域採取侵略性行動，美國將重新考慮對爭議島嶼主權所採取的外交中立立場。

與此同時，美國應主導一項大規模外交行動，促使東南亞地區對南海島嶼聲稱主權的各國，就主權以及這些島嶼所賦予的權利達成協議，並承諾不會單方面改變現狀。一旦這些國家達成共同的理解與共識，他們便應請求國際社會協助執行該協議，以對抗中國。此時，華盛頓可以設置多項經濟與外交領域的施壓手段，以懲罰中國的不合作行為。這些政策可以包括：將中國逐出國際組織、對中國實施經濟制裁、以及進一步限制對中國的科技出口。

在經濟嚇阻戰方面，美國需要重新構思其同盟關係。對亞洲的許多參與者而言，來自中國最可能的威脅並非入侵與佔領，而是透過經濟、政治與軍事手段的結合，來限制他國的行動自由，也就是讓盟友無法按照自身利益行事。中國已多次表現出將經濟作為外交工

新竄起者　340

具的意願與能力。美國與其盟友也應採取同樣的作法。中國對小型經濟體（如立陶宛與澳洲等）的打壓行為應予以不可容忍，當中國以抵制或關稅手段傷害這些國家時，美國與其他七大工業國組織成員應予以支援與彌補。有些分析人士建議，美國應該買下中國抵制的所有產品──例如在中國對澳洲葡萄酒加徵關稅後，建立所謂的「戰略葡萄酒儲備」。37 雖然這個說法帶有些許玩笑意味，但其核心概念其實相當正確。不過，更有力的做法，或許是建立一種集體回應的威脅機制，目標不限於軍事攻擊，也包括經濟攻擊。例如當中國限制某國的觀光業以施壓，美國與其盟友也應對中國採取相同的觀光限制。美國應進行模擬與「兵棋推演」，來判斷如何跨領域、跨國家協調行動，從而達到嚇阻中國動用經濟懲罰的效果。

我在其他著作中，已廣泛論述過如何強化對台灣海峽的威懾力，但在此議題上，比以往任何時候都更需要採取創新型的策略。38 關鍵的戰略目標應是摧毀中國入侵部隊的運輸、登陸以及維持在台行動的能力。基於這一點，盟國應該投資反艦飛彈、潛艦以及水雷等戰力。美國也需加強轟炸機編隊，以便向台海投射更強大的火力；美國國務院與國防部也應加倍努力，在區域內爭取更多的駐軍基地與飛越權。近期美國與菲律賓達成的協議，允許美軍以輪調方式進駐更多基地,便是一項值得期待的發展。[39]

改革預算撥款制度對於加速武器彈藥的生產與交付至美軍部隊,以及像台灣這樣的夥伴而言至關重要;若今日亞太地區爆發戰爭,美國在短短數日內便會耗盡彈藥。為了解決這個迫在眉睫的彈藥短缺問題,專家建議應從單年度的國防預算撥款模式轉向批准多年期合約。[40]但也許需要更激進的改革,例如重新思考國防承包商與美國政府之間的公私合作關係。其中一項主要問題是技術勞工不足;在失業率低與勞動參與率已高的情況下,招募與留住工人變得更加困難。美國可以考慮設立一支新的技術勞工後備部隊,當有需要時,能迅速投入與國防承包商合作,支援生產。

「韌性」的概念也延伸至經濟政策層面。美國一直在積極思考如何防止中國取得美國技術。正如美國國家安全顧問傑克・蘇利文(Jake Sullivan)所言:

「在出口管制方面,我們必須重新審視長期以來對某些關鍵技術僅維持『相對』優勢的前提。我們過去採取的是一種『滑動尺度』的做法,認為只要領先競爭對手幾個世代就足夠。但今天的戰略環境已非如此。鑑於某些技術的基礎性質,例如先進邏輯與記憶體晶片，我們必須維持儘可能大的領先幅度。」

二○二二年十月，美國商務部產業與安全局通過新規定，以防止關鍵技術流向中國，尤其針對人工智慧發展。同年，美國國會通過《晶片與科學法案》（CHIPS and Science Act），不僅大幅增加聯邦對科學研發的資助，還撥款五百二十億美元支持半導體產業，並包含其他針對與中國競爭的條款。該法案也提供數十億美元給五角大廈資助半導體研究，以及數百萬美元給國務院，用在與供應鏈中扮演關鍵角色的盟友協調合作。該法案還透過稅收優惠措施，強化對私營先進製造業的投資誘因。在二○二三年初，拜登政府再度取得一項重要的外交勝利：成功說服在全球半導體供應鏈中擔任關鍵角色的日本和荷蘭，採取類似的出口管制措施，進一步加強了全球對中國獲取高端晶片的限制。

美國還需要一套與世界其他地區互動的策略──培養並重視理解每個特定情勢及其所需對應行動的專業知識。這一點對於美國長期忽視的發展中國家尤其重要。如今，僅僅作為外部安全合作夥伴已不再足夠。有一點是確定的：美國必須在與發展中國家的關係上，投入比中國更多的資金，並聚焦於自身具有競爭優勢的領域。美國可以擴大在醫療領域的援助，也可以拓展至教育與技術訓練領域，提供給有興趣的國家。華盛頓也應該借鑑中國的做法，不應該再將發展援助與政治改革捆綁，可想而知，許多國家將會轉而接受中國所提供的「無附帶條件」投資。這並不是說美國應該放棄推廣良善治理與民主規範的政策，而是應該採取長期策略，與這些國家建立關係，在更長時間範圍內逐步推動更好的治理實踐。

同樣地，美國應該加強與那些「令人反感」的威權政體互動。當美國與某個國家出現問題時，應該加強其在該國的存在與接觸，而不是關閉大使館或中斷外交關係。42 將對話視為一種獎勵的作法，只會削弱美國在這些國家的影響力，並導致美國在解決全球最重要議題時反而需要依賴北京的協助。更根本的，美國需要重新評估那些過去曾讓美國得益的做法，是否仍然是維護美國安全與利益的最佳途徑。政府官僚體系也必須做出調整，獎勵那些勇於嘗試、提出靈活政策建議的人，而不是繼續偏好維持現狀、固步自封的行事方式。

雖然冒著顯而易見的風險，但競爭——即使是零和競爭——也能促使所有國家發揮出最好的自己。對科技創新的追求、全球經濟發展、制度的成長與改革，甚至軍事擴張，都

新竄起者　344

有可能促成一個更加和平、繁榮與可持續的世界。這樣的競爭可以讓中小型國家擁有更大的自由，去推行最適合其人民的政策，也能迫使美中兩國的領導人為全人類打造一個更好的未來。43 中國的領導人永遠都會想讓中國成為最強大的國家──試圖說服他們放棄這一點無異於痴人說夢。但美國可以確保，在這個不再由自己單獨主導的新世界中的策略，能讓它在國內與國際上成為一個更好的國家。儘管中國不太可能全面仿效美國的模式，但美國可以讓某些追求權力的路徑比其他方式更具吸引力。即便中國如今身居高位、實力日增，美國與其所倡導的「以規則為基礎的國際秩序」不僅能存續，還能在未來三十年中蓬勃發展。我們只需要找到屬於自己的「竄起者策略」，並創造出恰當的「模仿、利用與創新」的組合。

理解中國及其崛起所帶來的挑戰

本書對中國如何建構實力的深入剖析，也提供了一些關於實力與國際體系的更宏觀見解。首先，為何有些新興強權能夠成功爭取霸權地位，而其他國家卻未能如願？本書提供一個初步的答案,並提出未來研究的方向。我認為關鍵在於「模仿、創新與利用」這三者的組合。若一個國家在條件不成熟時採取模仿策略,不僅投入資源所換得的成果有限,還可能引來既有霸權的反制與壓力,付出更高昂的代價。正確的組合模式可能會因國家與時代而異,國內政治則會影響這三種崛起策略的成本與效益。當一個新興強權擁有與既有霸權類似的制度時,模仿可能更有效且更具安撫性;但若雙方制度差異甚大,則結果往往相反。也許,日本在十九世紀末與二十世紀初崛起時所犯下的最大錯誤,就是「有意地仿效了西方的政治制度、社會習俗、經濟活動與軍事技術」。44 相較於模仿策略,中國透過創新與利用策略——例如灰色地帶活動、反介入/區域拒止、產業政策、發展融資,以及政權中立立場,所累積的實力則顯得更加可觀。

模仿、利用與創新三者之間的最佳平衡,也很可能會因國家而異,並隨著歷史變遷,權力的本質與國際秩序的演化而改變。對學者而言,這帶來一個明確的啟示:研究過去如英國、法國、蘇聯與美國等國如何成功爭取強權地位的歷史經驗,對於理解未來強權的崛起,其實具有相當的侷限性。「竄起者理論」表明,從理論與實證的角度來看,我們有充分理由預期中國的案例將與以往截然不同。45

新竄起者　346

國際體系本身的性質，也可能是決定國家能否成功崛起的關鍵因素之一。換句話說，某些世界秩序可能更有利於新興強權的崛起。例如，當代的自由主義秩序（liberal order）或許就是一個促進國家崛起、同時延緩對手反制行動的理想系統，原因有二。首先，這個體系強調全球化與多邊主義，創造了前所未有的機會，讓國家得以用和平的方式（也就是令人放心的方式）累積實力。而這些好處是所有國家皆可享有的。因此，中國得以在未引發美國高度威脅感知的情況下累積實力——試想如果中國成立的是一個「中國版北約」而非「一帶一路」，美國的反應會有多麼不同。第二，過去一個衰退中的霸主國，仍可能選擇對挑戰者發動先發制人的戰爭，但現今的國際規範與制度性約束，使得這種選項已不再可行。正如約翰・艾肯伯里（John Ikenberry）所指出的，美國所建立的是一個以制度為基礎的國際秩序，美國的權力受到約束，以換取較弱國家對此體系的共識。[46] 這些觀點表明，我們有必要進一步研究國際體系如何影響大國競爭中，各種策略手段的成本與效益。

為什麼霸主國經常無法在實力差距被縮小之前反制挑戰？大多數國際關係的學術著作，會傾向由霸主國的戰略和決策來解釋，新興國家是如何成功累積實力到某種程度。[47]

具體而言，有三種主要的解釋：霸主國可能會做出不明智的選擇、可能會接受自身的衰

347　結論　強權競爭的啟示

退、或可能需要與新興國家合作來對抗另一個更具威脅性的國家。

本書提供了一種不同的解釋，這種解釋更能說明新興強權在塑造既有霸主國反應時所扮演的主動角色。正如我所展示的，中國領導人明確考量了美國對特定戰略可能做出的感知與反應，並優先採取那些能夠抑制或至少延遲美國反制的做法，因為美國的反制可能會阻礙、削弱或拖延中國的崛起。「竄起者策略」在某種程度上就是為了安撫既有霸主國，並避免構成直接威脅。換句話說，霸主國未能作出反應並非孤立現象，而是新興強權可能設計好戰略，使既有霸主國對其實力累積產生延遲反應。

本研究同樣鼓勵學者重新思考「修正主義」這個概念。許多學者與戰略家一直關注該如何界定中國的意圖。[48] 本書翻轉將「意圖」視為可被解讀的客觀事實的傳統觀點，提出一種可能不受歡迎的詮釋：對「意圖」的認知是主觀的。武力的使用可以是為了維護現狀，也可以是為了改變現狀；改變國際秩序既可能促進和平（就如同二戰後美國建立一套國際機構網路），也可能破壞和平。美國可能會將模仿視為威脅，也就是修正主義（意圖修改現狀）行為，例如中國如果仿效美國建立全球軍事基地網路；但模仿也可能令人放心，被視為維持現狀的行為，例如中國對人道援助與災害救援或聯合國維和行動的貢獻。

新竄起者　　348

中國了解,在某種程度上,是由美國來定義何為「威脅」或「令人放心」的行為。為了成功崛起,中國在選擇特定領域中累積實力的最佳方式時,必須將這個因素納入考量。換句話說,並不只是中國的行為會形塑外界對其意圖的看法,對其意圖的看法本身也會反過來影響中國的行為。

我同時也清楚說明了美國戰略以多種方式影響中國戰略的具體情況。其他研究中國的專家也已經認識到其中某些部分。[49] 當中國領導人做出決策時,他們會考慮美國的觀感、體制中的漏洞,以及國內政治因素。但若認為僅靠其中單一因素就能決定中國的外交、經濟或軍事戰略,那將是一種過度簡化,且與實證不符的說法。「窺起者策略」放大了視角,呈現這些因素如何與中國對美國戰略有效性的認知互動,進而形塑中國領導人選擇獲取實力之路的方式。

這樣的結果呈現出一幅更動態的中國大戰略圖像──中國領導人不斷地進行調整與重新校準。雖然具體的「窺起者策略」會隨著情勢變化而改變,但中國對於成為強權的渴望始終如一。依照中國語彙的說法,在過去三十年間,中國已經取得了大量的「戰略空間」,也就是足以嚇阻外部干預的綜合國力,特別是針對美國阻撓中國崛起軌跡的企

349　結論　強權競爭的啟示

圖。50 在所有的評估與調整中，中國的行為、論述與能力表現出一個明確的訊號：美國的戰略是決定中國策略的最主要因素。換言之，在過去三十年間，美國並非中國的「敵人」，而是中國衡量標準的對象──透過美國的實踐與戰略來定義什麼是值得仿效的、什麼是可以加以利用的盲點、以及什麼是值得以創新手段來對應的挑戰。正是因為美國處於這樣獨特的位置上，它有機會影響中國的未來，進而確保整個世界擁有一個更加光明的未來。

致謝

在撰寫本書的過程中，我非常幸運地獲得了大量的支持與鼓勵。丹尼爾・柯茲―費蘭（Dan Kurtz-Phelan）是第一位鼓勵我將關於中國崛起的獨特想法寫出來的人，該想法後來以〈隱形的超級強權〉（The Stealth Superpower）為題，刊登於《外交事務》（Foreign Affairs）二〇一九年一～二月號。我也有幸獲得史密斯理查森基金會（Smith Richardson Foundation）戰略與政策獎助學人計畫，以及加拿大亞太基金會（Asia Pacific Foundation of Canada）約翰・麥克阿瑟（John H. McArthur）傑出獎助金的支持，使我能擴展並深化這項構想，最終發展成為本書。

美國企業研究院（American Enterprise Institute, AEI）為我提供了一個近七年的政策研究基地，並給予我極大的支持。發展團隊協助我處理各項補助申請，媒體團隊則負責本書所見圖像的製作。如果說沒有美國企業研究院研究助理艾蜜莉・卡爾（Emily Carr）與湯瑪斯・柯西（Thomas Causey）的辛勞，就不可能完成本書。湯瑪斯有效率地協調所有研究助理，確保我能獲得所需資料，而且他在處理這些任務時從未顯露出絲毫壓力或倉促（這點我非常感激，畢竟我是個很容易感到壓力與不知所措的人）。美國企業研究院也在我動筆初期為我舉辦了一場專書工作坊――來自外部評論者湯瑪斯・曼肯（Thomas

新竄起者　352

我在史丹佛的同事：史考特・薩根（Scott Sagan）、肯・舒茲（Ken Schultz）、賴瑞・戴蒙特（Tyler Jost）與柯慶生（Tom Christensen）不辭千里前來，提供關鍵意見；同時也感謝年五月在史丹佛舉辦的專書工作坊。我非常感謝珍妮・林德（Jenny Lind）、泰勒・約斯提供了旅費、研究用品與各項研究支援，使本書得以順利完成。部分資金也用於二〇二三國基金（China Fund）與舒思深亞太研究中心（Shorenstein APARC）教師研究獎助計畫則全與合作中心（Center for International Security and Cooperation）與史丹頓基金會（Stanton for International Studies, FSI）資深研究員的第一年開始撰寫本書的。史丹佛大學的國際安Foundation）慷慨提供支持，資助我針對本書中核子相關議題的研究與撰寫。FSI的中我是在擔任史丹佛大學傅里曼・斯伯格里國際問題研究所（Freeman Spogli Institute

（Al Song）等人的意見，幫助我在這關鍵階段釐清思路。

艾哈德（Thomas Ehrhard）、林碧瑩（Bonny Lin）、法蘭克・米勒（Frank Miller）與宋安Beckley）、丹・布魯門撒爾（Dan Blumenthal）、札克・庫柏（Zack Cooper）、湯瑪斯・馬利（Mark Montgomery）、內森・博尚（Nathan Beauchamp）、麥克・貝克利（Michael Mahnken）、白潔曦（Jessica Chen Weiss），以及葛來儀（Bonnie Glaser）、馬克・蒙哥

我衷心感謝我的編輯團隊：牛津大學出版社的大衛・麥克布萊德（David McBride），自本專案伊始便全力支持，協助提升本書的可讀性；菲比・奧德里奇—特納（Phoebe Aldridge-Turner）則專業地引導本書完成整個出版流程。我的經紀人，三叉媒體公司（Trident Media）的唐・費爾（Don Fehr），協助我撰寫出版提案，並在我尚屬無名之輩時就願意接下此出版計畫。摩根・卡普蘭（Morgan Kaplan），你的見解總是一針見血。羅傑・海頓（Roger Haydon）曾指導我完成第一本書的出版過程，也十分慷慨地多次通

（Larry Diamond）、麥克・布朗（Mike Brown）、馮稼時（Thomas Fingar）、戴慕珍（Jean Oi）、麥克・麥克福爾（Mike McFaul）與石露蕊（Laura Stone）──正因為有你們，這本書才變得更加完整、更加出色。最後，同樣重要的是沒有我在史丹佛的夢幻研究團隊，本書絕無可能誕生：主要研究助理包括 Janpal LaChapelle、Vivian Zhu、Jerome He、Chengyang Zhang；其他成員還有 Linda Liu、Zhenwei Gao、Kasha Tyranski、George San Miguel、Hannah Kohatsu、Joshua Goodwin、Kevia McComb、Jaden Morgan、JB Lim、Shirley Cheng、Jaden Kaplan、Tianyi Chen、Yifan Xu、Isabel Cai、Khushmita Dhabhai 與 Nicholas Welch。

讀這本書的草稿，協助我提升可讀性。艾莉森・范・德文特（Allison Van Deventer）展現出極為專業的文字編修技巧，確保本書盡可能簡潔明瞭；比吉特・奈瑟薩里（Birgitte Necessary）則挺身而出，協助編製索引。

我非常幸運能夠獲得這麼多機構的支持。但事實上，就如同本書的撰寫過程，我的致謝也必須稍具非傳統性。當疫情爆發時，我剛迎來一個新生兒，還有一個二十個月大的孩子。隨著老大需要待在家中，我必須安排他的學前課程，確保他不會落後，同時還要照顧一個從不肯用奶瓶的嬰兒（也就是我得隨時準備餵奶）——在那樣的情況下，能夠完成這樣一本書幾乎令人難以置信。

若不是因為一些人與機構的幫助，我大概真的無法完成這本書。因此，以下是一段非傳統的致謝。首先，要感謝澳洲政府。當我們需要一個可以逃離的地方時，是你們接納了我們。經歷在華府封城四個月、還要照顧兩個免疫系統脆弱的孩子之後，能夠來到一個對我孩子來說安全的地方，讓我感到無比寬慰。這也讓我們能找到育兒協助（謝謝你，Alba！），而我則可以到附近的咖啡館工作，離開家裡但隨時能回來哺乳。我要特別感謝 Sweet Spot 和 Clovelly Social House，總是歡迎我，為我送上固定的飲品（謝謝你，

V！），而且從不對我長時間坐在你們店內表示任何不悅。亞歷克斯・柯羅列夫（Alex Korolev）協助我在新南威爾斯大學（University of New South Wales）建立學術據點。而理查・麥葛瑞格（Richard MacGregor）及其家人則在咖啡館關門後，慷慨讓我使用他們家的書房。

人們常說「養育一個孩子需要一整個村莊」，但對我而言，要支持我與我的抱負，可能需要整整一個國家。感謝賓恩幼兒園（Bing Nursery School）與馬德拉格羅夫托育中心（Madera Grove Childcare Center）的所有托育人員——你們幾乎見不到我，但那正是因為我的孩子在你們那裡學得開心、過得充實，這就是最好的證明。感謝羅莎・赫南德茲（Rosa Hernandez）、潔德・瑞迪（Jade Reidy）與海蒂・史東斯（Haidee Storms），若沒有你們的幫助，我實在無法想像要如何打理我們的家庭。你們對我與我的家庭所展現出的無條件承諾與不加批判的支持，使我能成為一位更好的母親與妻子。感謝勞倫斯・卡普蘭醫師（Dr. Laurence Kaplan），一路以來關照我的心理健康。還要特別感謝安恩・柯卡斯（Aynne Kokas），這位真正的女戰士。如果疫情帶來了什麼好事，那便是使我們之間的友誼更加深厚。那些充滿職涯建議、自信提振，以及人生享樂秘訣的每週通話，為我提供了

新竊起者　356

完成本書所需的策略與動力。

感謝我的父母，詹姆斯（James）與克勞蒂雅（Claudia），每當我們需要幫助時，他們總是不辭辛勞地跨越整個國家而來，彌補我力有未逮之處。正是他們灌輸給我堅韌與毅力，使我得以完成這項計畫。也感謝我的夫家人，特別是艾咪·塔拉波爾（Amy Tarapore），我們在澳洲期間她對孩子們的照顧，讓我得以稍微喘口氣。還有馬托尼（Muttoni）一家，持續提醒我：人生不只是工作而已。

我真的找不到足夠的言語，來表達對那位勇敢與我一同踏上人生冒險旅程的男人──阿爾贊·塔拉波爾（Arzan Tarapore）的感激之情。深夜的起床照料、我出差時他一人獨力育兒、在兒童疫苗尚未普及前無止盡地在家照顧孩子們，以及為我們準備營養的餐點──這一切早已超乎尋常。但這不僅僅是日復一日的支持，更是我們在每一個重大人生決定中彼此信賴的知識夥伴與精神同行者。你讓我感受到：無論發生什麼，我們都可以平安度過。而正是這樣的安全感，使我能夠在工作與人生中勇於冒險，並因此收穫最豐富的成果。

強尼·凱許（Johnny Cash）說得沒錯：我們是這個世界上最棒的搭檔。

最後，獻給我的兩個兒子──這本書正是獻給你們的。你們為我的每一天帶來歡笑與喜悅,更賦予我人生的使命感。我希望這個世界能成為一個美麗、開放且安全的地方,讓你們能自由探索。我期盼這本書能為那樣的願景略盡一份心力。

註釋

導論

1. See comments quoted from Li Ruihan, former Politburo Standing Committee member and chairman of the People's Consultative Conference, in Zong Hairen [宗海仁],China's Leaders: The Fourth Generation [中国掌舵者：第四代] (New York: Mirror Books [明镜出版社], 2002), 123-124; Jiang Zemin [江泽民], The Selected Works of Jiang Zemin, Volume 3 [江泽民文选 (第三卷)] (Beijing: People's Publishing House [人民出版社], 2006), 578-585.
2. For a perspective from a high-ranking diplomat in the Hu Jintao administration on needing to avoid upsetting the United States while China developed, see Dai Bingguo [戴秉国], Strategic Dialogues: Dai Binguo's Memoirs [战略对话：戴秉国回忆录] (Beijing: People's Publishing House [人 民 出 版 社], 2016), 75. For references to national humiliation and building a stronger China in official rhetoric, see Jiang Zemin [江泽民], "Accelerating the Reform, the Opening to the Outside World and the Drive for Modernization, so as to Achieve Greater Successes in Building Socialism with Chinese Characteristics [加快改革开放和现代化建设步伐 夺取有中国特色社会主义事业的更大胜利]," 14th Party Congress Political Report, Beijing, October 12, 1992; Hu Jintao [胡锦涛], "Firmly March on the Path of Socialism with Chinese Characteristics and Strive to Complete the Building of a Moderately Prosperous Society in All Respects [坚定不移沿着中国特色社会主义道路前进 为全面建成小康社会而奋斗]," 18th Party Congress Political Report, Beijing, November 8, 2012;Xi Jinping [习近平], "Secure a Decisive Victory in Building a Moderately Prosperous Society in All Respects and Strive for the Great Success of Socialism with Chinese Characteristics for a New Era [决胜全面建成小康社会 夺取新时代中国特色社会主义伟大胜利]," 19th Party Congress Political Report, Beijing, October 18, 2017.
3. For example, this point was emphasized particularly by former premier Zhu Rongji when he was working to enable China's joining of the WTO in 2001. See Zhu Rongji [朱镕基], Zhu Rongji Meets the Press [朱镕基答记者问] (Beijing: People's Publishing House [人民出版社], 2009), 254.
4. "Asia Power Index 2021: Diplomatic Influence," Lowy Institute, https://power.lowyinstit ute. org/comp are/?countries= united-states,china.
5. Jim Garamone, "China's Capabilities Growth Shows Why U.S. Sees Nation as Pacing Challenge," Department of Defense News, October 27, 2021,https://www.defense.gov/News/ News-Stories/Article/Article/2824060/chinas-capabilities-growth-shows-whyus-sees-nation-as-pacing-challenge/.
6. Thomas J. Shattuck, "Assessing One Year of PLA Air Incursions into Taiwan's ADIZ,"Global Taiwan Brief 6, no. 20 (2021): 14-17.
7. "Full Text of the Report to the 20th National Congress of the Communist Party of China," Ministry of Foreign Affairs of the People's Republic of China [中华人民共和国外交部], October 25, 2022, https://www.fmprc.gov.cn/eng/zxxx 662 805/202210/t20221025_10791 908. html.
8. "Upstart," Oxford English Dictionary online, https://www.oed.com/view/Entry/220196, accessed May 20, 2023.
9. "Upstart," Britannica Dictionary, https://www.britannica.com/dictionary/upstart,accessed May 20, 2023.

10. Andrew Hill and Stephen Gerras, "Systems of Denial: Strategic Resistance to Military Innovation," Naval War College Review 69, no. 1 (Winter 2016): 110. See also Clayton Christensen, The Innovator's Dilemma: The Revolutionary Book That Will Change the Way You Do Business (New York: Harper Business Books, 2011).
11. Pepsi, for instance, was able to exploit Coke's blind spot in the US domestic market,as the latter had begun to concentrate primarily on foreign markets based on the mistaken belief that the US soft drink market had little room left for growth. Curtis M. Grimm, Hun Lee, and Ken G. Smith, Strategy as Action: Competitive Dynamics and Competitive Advantage (Oxford: Oxford University Press, 2006), 115-119.
12. New market entrants such as Under Armour and Wal-Mart gained market share by doing things differently. Grimm, Lee, and Smith, Strategy as Action, 113-114.
13. Grimm, Lee, and Smith, Strategy as Action, 194.
14. For example, Quibi, an app that aimed to deliver high-quality short-form content to users, failed to disrupt its competitors, such as TikTok and YouTube, and collapsed after less than a year despite raising nearly $2 billion in funding. Dade Hayes, Jill Goldsmith, Dominic Patten, "Quibi to Shut Down, Ending $2B Streaming Experiment," Deadline, October 21, 2020, https://deadline.com/2020/10/quibi-toshut-down-ending-2b-streaming-experiment-1234601356/.
15. M. Taylor Fravel, for example, splits China's strategy into the pre-and post-1993 periods in his book on Chinese military strategy. M. Taylor Fravel, Active Defense: China's Military Strategy Since 1949 (Princeton, NJ: Princeton University Press, 2019), 182-216. Avery Goldstein, in his assessment of Chinese grand strategy, puts the beginning of China's deliberate efforts to rise to great power status in 1996, when the Chinese leader Jiang Zemin began to pursue the rejuvenation of the Chinese nation. Avery Goldstein, "China's Grand Strategy Under Xi Jinping: Reassurance, Reform, and Resistance," International Security 45, no. 1 (2020): 164-201. Rush Doshi argues that China's grand strategy to displace the United States has consisted of three stages, the first of which started in 1989 with the goal of "quietly blunting" American power over China. Rush Doshi, The Long Game: China's Grand Strategy and the Displacement of American Order (New York: Oxford University Press, 2021).
16. Wang Lisheng [王 立 胜],"Deng Xiaoping's Grasping of the'Important Period of Strategic Opportunity' and His Thought [邓小平对 ' 重要战略机遇期 ' 的把握及其思想]," Literature of Chinese Communist Party [党的文献], no. 4 (2006): 41-42.
17. " 'China's Rise' Has Become a Buzzword in the World Again, Foreign Media Comment at Great Length [' 中国崛起 ' 再成世界流行语 境外媒体评论连篇累牍]," China Daily [中国日报], February 26, 2008, http://www.chi nada ily.com.cn/hqzg/2008-02/26/content_ 6484 556.htm.
18. Theo Farrell, "Improving in War: Military Adaptation and the British in Helmand Province, Afghanistan, 2006-2009," Journal of Strategic Studies 38, no. 4 (2015): 570.
19. These datasets can be found at www.orianaskylarmastro.com/upstart.
20. The full appendix of Chinese sources can be found at www.ori anaskylarmastro.com/upstart.
21. Robert A. Dahl, "The Concept of Power," Behavioral Science 2, no. 3 (1957): 202;Michael Beckley, Unrivaled: Why America Will Remain the World's Sole Superpower(Ithaca, NY: Cornell University Press, 2018).
22. For example, see Yuan Peng [袁 鹏], "The Coronavirus Pandemic and the Great Changes Unseen in a Century [新冠疫情与百年变局]," Contemporary International Relations [现代国际关系], no. 5 (2020): 1-6.
23. David A. Baldwin, Power and International Relations (Princeton, NJ: Princeton University Press, 2016), 174.
24. Kenneth Waltz, "The Emerging Structure of International Politics," International Security 18,

no. 2 (Autumn 1993): 50; Hans Morgenthau, Politics Among Nations: The Struggle for Power and Peace (New York: McGraw-Hill, 1993), 72.

25. Yan Xuetong [阎学通] et al., "A Conversation by Writing on the 'Rise of Powers and China's Choices' [' 大国崛起与中国的选择 ' 笔谈]," Social Sciences in China [中国社会科学], no. 5 (2005): 58. To be considered "rising," a country has to have the ambition to influence the world. Men Honghua [门洪华], "The Rise of China and Changes in the Global Order [中国崛起与国际秩序变革]," Quarterly Journal of International Politics [国际政治科学], no. 1 (2016): 73.

26. "Military and Security Developments Involving the People's Republic of China 2020," US Department of Defense, 2020, i, https://media.defense.gov/2020/Sep/01/2002488689/-1/-1/1/2020-DOD-CHINA-MILIT ARY-POWER-REP ORT-FINAL.PDF.

27. Paul Kennedy, The Rise and Fall of the Great Powers: Economic Change and Military Conflict from 1500 to 2000 (New York: Random House, 1987), 539; Jack S. Levy, War in the Modern Great Power System: 1495-1975 (Lexington: University Press of Kentucky, 1983), 15-16; Baldwin, Power and International Relations, 175; John Mearsheimer, The Tragedy of Great Power Politics (New York: W. W. Norton, 2001), 5.

28. "Military and Security Developments Involving the People's Republic of China 2020," ii.

29. Robert Gilpin, War and Change in World Politics (Cambridge: Cambridge University Press, 1981), 215-216; Daniel Deudney, "Hegemony, Nuclear Weapons, and Liberal Hegemony," in Power, Order, and Change in World Politics, ed. G. John Ikenberry (Cambridge: Cambridge University Press, 2014), 203.

30. Hans M. Kristensen and Matt Korda, "Status of World Nuclear Forces," Federation of American Scientists, May 2021, https://fas.org/issues/nuclear-weapons/statusworld-nuclear-forces/.

31. A. F. K. Organski and Jacek Kugler, The War Ledger (Chicago: University of Chicago Press, 1980); Therese Anders, Christopher J. Fariss, and Jonathan N. Markowitz, "Bread Before Guns or Butter: Introducing Surplus Domestic Product (SDP)," International Studies Quarterly 64, no. 2 (2020): 392-405; Jacek Kugler and William Domke, "Comparing the Strength of Nations," Comparative Political Studies 19, no. 1 (1986): 39-69.

32. "Are Patents Indicative of Chinese Innovation?," ChinaPower, February 15, 2016, https://chi napower.csis.org/patents/; Central Intelligence Agency, "China," The World Factbook (Washington, DC: Government Printing Office, 2021); "Literacy Rate, Adult Total (% of People Ages 15 and Above)— China," World Bank, https://data.worldbank.org/indicator/SE.ADT.LITR.ZS?locations= CN, accessed January 19, 2024.

33. "Thucydides's Trap Case File: 16. 1990s-Present—United Kingdom and France vs. Germany—NO WAR," Harvard Kennedy School Belfer Center for Science and International Affairs, March 17, 2017, https://www.belfercenter.org/thucydides-trap/case-file.

34. "Can India Become a Great Power?," The Economist, March 30, 2013, https://www.econom ist.com/leaders/2013/03/30/can-india-become-a-great-power.

35. Gian Luca Gardini, "Brazil: What Rise of What Power?," Bulletin of Latin American Research 35, no. 1 (2016): 5.

36. Manjari Chatterjee Miller, Why Nations Rise: Narratives and the Path to Great Power (New York: Oxford University Press, 2021), 10.

37. Hu Angang [胡鞍钢] et al., "The Rise and Decline of Great Power and China's Opportunity: Assessment of Comprehensive National Power [大国兴衰与中国机遇：国家综合国力评估]," Economic Heralds [经济导刊], no. 3 (2017): 14-25. See also Hu Angang [胡鞍钢] et al., "Assessment of China's and the US's Comprehensive National Power (1990-2013) [对

中美综合国力的评估 (1990-2013)]," Journal of Tsinghua University [清华大学学报], no. 1 (2015): 26-39. For other early studies of CNP, see Zhao Xuebo [赵雪波], "Analysis of the Components of Comprehensive National Power [综合国力构成要素辨析]," World Economy and Politics [世界经济与政治], no. 5 (2001); Wang Ling [王玲], "Measuring Comprehensive National Power [关于综合国力的测度]," World Economy and Politics [世界经济与政治], no. 6 (2006): 45-51. This last assessment by Wang Ling cites 2003 results from the Chinese Academy of Sciences Sustainable Development Strategy Study Group that ranked the United States as number one in power and China as number seven.

38. Wang Jisi [王缉思], "Is China the Second Greatest Power in the World? [中国是世界第二强国吗 ?]," China.com.cn [中国网], April 14, 2011, http://opinion.china.com.cn/opinion_94_14694.html; Fu Ying [傅莹], "Is China a Great Power? [中国是强国吗 ?]," Ministry of Foreign Affairs of the People's Republic of China [中华人民共和国外交部], May 7, 2009, https://www.fmprc.gov.cn/web/gjhdq676201/gj676 203/oz_678 770/1206 679 906/ywfc679928/200 905/t20090 507_ 9355 291.shtml.

39. Yan Xuetong, "The Rise of China and Its Power Status," Chinese Journal of International Politics 1, no. 1 (2006): 21, 30; Wang Yi [王毅],"Write a Marvelous Chapter on Great Power Diplomacy with Chinese Characteristics [谱写中国特色大国外交的时代华章]," State Council of the People's Republic of China [中华人民共和国中央人民政府], September 23, 2019, http://www.gov.cn/guowuyuan/2019-09/23/content_ 5432243.htm; "What Should a Great Power Look like? President Xi Will Tell You [大国应该是什么样子?习近平主席告诉你]," CCTV.com [央视网], April 20, 2021, https://news.cctv.com/2021/04/20/ARTIzqlZxTBV8rJrva0YxANX210420.shtml;"2018, These Great Power Projects Make Me Proud [2018, 这些大国重器让我骄傲]," People's Daily [人民日报], December 26, 2018, https://baijia hao.baidu.com/s?id= 1620 8780 3638 5131 751&wfr= spider&for= pc.

40. "Yang Jiechi Elucidates China's Stances in the Opening Remark of the China-US High-Level Strategic Talks [杨洁篪在中美高层战略对话开场白中阐明中方有关立场]," Xinhua.com [新华网], March 19, 2021, http://www.xinhua net.com/world/2023/19/c_112 7230 729.htm.

41. For a broader discussion about how to best conceptualize revisionism, see Oriana Skylar Mastro, "Understanding the Challenge of China's Rise: Fixing Conceptual Confusion About Intentions," Journal of Chinese Political Science 27, no. 3 (2022): 585-600.

第一章

1. Statistic calculated from Graham Allison, Destined for War: Can America and China Escape Thucydides's Trap? (Melbourne: Scribe Publications, 2018).

2. Allison, Destined for War.

3. Michael Beckley and Hal Brands, Danger Zone: The Coming Conflict with China (New York: W. W. Norton, 2022).

4. Kenneth N. Waltz, Theory of International Politics (Reading, MA: Addison-Wesley, 1979), 127-128.

5. Niccolò Machiavelli, The Prince, trans. Tim Parks (New York: Penguin, 2009), 59.

6. Barry R. Posen, "Nationalism, the Mass Army and Military Power," International Security 18, no. 2 (Fall 1993): 80-124; Scott Sagan, "Why Do States Build Nuclear Weapons? Three Models in Search of a Bomb," International Security 21, no. 3 (Winter 1996): 54-86.

7. Aidan Powers-Riggs, "Covid-19 Is Proving a Boon for Digital Authoritarianism," Center for Strategic and International Studies, August 17, 2020, https://www.csis.org/blogs/new-perspectives-asia/covid-19-proving-boon-digital-authoritarian ism.

8. Steve Wood, "Prestige in World Politics: History, Theory, Expression," International Politics 50, no. 3 (May 2013): 388; Rohan Mukherjee, "Rising Powers and the Quest for Status in International Security Regimes" (PhD dissertation, Princeton University, 2016), 140.

9. Nick Smith, "Grand Delusions: The Psychology of Aircraft Carriers," Harvard International Review 24, no. 3 (Fall 2002): 7-8; Lilach Gilady, The Price of Prestige: Conspicuous Consumption in International Relations (Chicago: University of Chicago Press, 2018); Michelle Murray, "Identity, Insecurity, and Great Power Politics: The Tragedy of German Naval Ambition Before the First World War," Security Studies 19, no. 4 (2010): 675; Joslyn N. Barnhart, "Prestige, Humiliation and International Politics" (PhD dissertation, UCLA, 2013).

10. William C. Wohlforth et al., "Moral Authority and Status in International Relations: Good States and the Social Dimension of Status Seeking," Review of International Studies 44, no. 3 (2017): 527, 532.

11. Raymond Kuo, Following the Leader: International Order, Alliance Strategies, and Emulation (Stanford, CA: Stanford University Press, 2021), 33.

12. Alastair Iain Johnston, Social States: China in International Institutions, 1980-2000 (Princeton, NJ: Princeton University Press, 2007), 23.

13. Heather Berry, Mauro Guillen, and Arun Hendi, "Is There Convergence Across Countries? A Spatial Approach," Journal of International Business Studies (2014): 387-404, https://www.ncbi.nlm.nih.gov/pmc/artic les/PMC 4286 895/#R6.

14. Clark Kerr, Frederick Harbison, John Dunlop, and Charles Myers, "Industrialism and Industrial Man," International Labour Review 71, no. 3 (1955): 236-251; Frank Dobbin, Beth Simmons, and Geoffrey Garrett, "The Global Diffusion of Public Policies: Social Construction, Coercion, Competition, or Learning?," Annual Review of Sociology 33 (2007): 449-472; Simone Polillo and Mauro F. Guillén, "Globalization Pressures and the State: The Worldwide Spread of Central Bank Independence," American Journal of Sociology 110, no. 6 (2005): 1764-1802; Klaus Weber, Gerald F. Davis, and Michael Lounsbury, "Policy as Myth and Ceremony? The Global Spread of Stock Exchanges, 1980-2005," Academy of Management Journal 52, no. 6 (2009): 1319-1347.

15. David Strang and Stephen Meyer, "Institutional Conditions for Diffusion," Theory and Society 22, no. 4 (August 1993): 487-511.

16. Paul J. DiMaggio and Walter W. Powell, "The Iron Cage Revisited: Institutional Isomorphism and Collective Rationality in Organizational Fields," American Sociological Review 48, no. 2 (April 1983): 147-160.

17. Johnston, Social States, 45-46.

18. Amitav Acharya, "How Ideas Spread: Whose Norms Matter? Norm Localization and Institutional Change in Asian Regionalism," International Organization 58, no. 2 (2004): 239-275.

19. "Roman Aqueducts," National Geographic, September 29, 2022, https://education.nationalgeographic.org/resource/roman-aqueducts/.

20. Manousos E. Kambouri, The Rise of Persia and the First Greco-Persian Wars: The Expansion of the Achaemenid Empire and the Battle of Marathon (Yorkshire, UK: Pen and Sword Military, 2022).

21. Nicola Di Cosmo, Ancient China and Its Enemies: The Rise of Nomadic Power in East Asian History (Cambridge: Cambridge University Press, 2002), https://doi.org/10.1017/CBO97 8051 1511 967.

22. Alexander Anievas and Kerem Nişancıoğlu, "How Did the West Usurp the Rest? Origins of the Great Divergence over the 'Longue Durée,'" Comparative Studies in Society and History 59,

no. 1 (2017): 34-67, http://www.jstor.org/stable/26293 559.

23. "Part I: Expansion and Conflict," in The Cambridge History of Communism, ed. N. Naimark, S. Pons, and S. Quinn-Judge (Cambridge: Cambridge University Press, 2017), 13-314.

24. To be sure, some may maintain that the United States protects its interests via perma¬nent occupation— consider, for instance, Puerto Rico or the Philippines (hence the American Anti-Imperialist League). Indeed, the extent to which the United States' foreign behavior constitutes imperialism is a hotly contested matter, one that falls well outside the scope of this writing. Michael Gerson and Alison Lawler Russell, "American Grand Strategy and Seapower," CNA Analysis and Solutions, November 2011, https://www.cna.org/arch ive/CNA_ Fi les/pdf/d0025 988.a2.pdf.

25. Geoffrey L. Herrera and Thomas G. Mahnken, "Military Diffusion in Nineteenth Century Europe: The Napoleonic and Prussian Military Systems," in The Diffusion of Military Technology and Ideas, ed. Emily Goldman and Leslie Eliason (Stanford, CA: Stanford University Press, 2003), 205-242.

26. "The Naval Race Between Britain and Germany before the First World War," Imperial War Museums, n.d., https://www.iwm.org.uk/hist ory/the-naval-race-betw een-brit ain-and-germ any-bef ore-the-first-world-war, accessed June 2, 2023; John D. Maurer, "The Anglo-German Naval Rivalry and Informal Arms Control, 1912-1914," Journal of Conflict Resolution 36, no. 2 (1992): 284-285.

27. Deborah Welch Larson and Alexei Shevchenko, "Status Seekers: Chinese and Russian Responses to U.S. Primacy," International Security 34, no. 4 (2010): 78.

28. Larson and Shevchenko, "Status Seekers," 82.

29. The "international order" is best understood as "the emergent property of the interactions of multiple state and nonstate actors" across different domains (miliitary, human rights, trade, environment, information, etc.). Alastair Iain Johnston, "China in a World of Orders: Rethinking Compliance and Challenge in Beijing's International Relations," International Security 44, no. 2 (2019): 12.

30. In addition to the actions of competitors, Porter argues that there are five forces that impact the degree of competitiveness within an industry, and thus the prospects for profitability: the bargaining power of buyers, the bargaining power of suppliers, the threat of new entrants, the threat of substitute products or services, and rivalry among existing competitors. Michael E. Porter, Competitive Strategy: Techniques for Analyzing Industries and Competitors (New York: Free Press, 1980).

31. Stacie E. Goddard, "Brokering Change: Networks and Entrepreneurs in International Politics," International Theory 1, no. 2 (2009): 250.

32. In contrast, Yu-Ming Liou, Paul Musgrave, and J. Furman Daniel argue that rising states will typically choose to imitate the hegemonic state's military innovations and strategies rather than investing heavily in their own military innovations because of the lower risk of destabilization. Yu-Ming Liou, Paul Musgrave, and J. Furman Daniel III, "The Imitation Game: Why Don't Rising Powers Innovate Their Militaries More?," Washington Quarterly 38, no. 3 (Fall 2015): 157-174.

33. Curtis M. Grimm, Hun Lee, and Ken G. Smith, Strategy as Action: Competitive Dynamics and Competitive Advantage (Oxford: Oxford University Press, 2006), 103. In political science, the concept has mainly been used in political analysis to under¬stand the motivations of non-state actors that serve as norm entrepreneurs, political entrepreneurs, and brokers. For a thorough review of the concept of entrepreneurship across disciplines, see Goddard, "Brokering Change."

34. The causal relationship between entrepreneurship and innovation is still a matter of debate. See, for example, Alexander Brem, "Linking Innovation and Entrepreneurship: Literature Overview and Introduction of a Process-Oriented Framework," International Journal of Entrepreneurship and Innovation Management 14, no. 1 (June 2011): 6-35.
35. Definition inspired by Goddard, "Brokering Change," 251.
36. G. John Ikenberry, After Victory: Institutions, Strategic Restraint, and the Rebuilding of Order After Major Wars (Princeton, NJ: Princeton University Press, 2001).
37. Margaret MacMillan, The War That Ended Peace: How Europe Abandoned Peace for the First World War (London: Profile Books, 2013), 38.
38. For more on China's emulation of other countries, see William H. Overholt, China's Crisis of Success (Cambridge: Cambridge University Press, 2017), 7-45.
39. Yan Xuetong [阎学通], "Yan Xuetong: The Overall 'Periphery' Is More Important than the United States [阎学通：整体的'周边'比美国更重要]," Carnegie Endowment for International Peace, January 13, 2015, https://carnegieendowment.org/2015/01/13/zh-pub-57696.
40. Sun Xuefeng [孙学峰], "Strategic Choice and the Success or Failure of Great Power Rise [战略选择与大国崛起成败]," in The Rise of China and Its Strategy [中国崛起及其战略], ed. Yan Xuetong [阎学通] and Sun Xuefeng [孙学峰] (Beijing: Peking University Press [北京大学出版社], 2015), 43-45; Sun Xuefeng [孙学峰], "Strategic Choices for Solving the Rising Dilemma [缓解崛起困境的战略选择]," in The Dilemma of China's Rise: Theoretical Reflections and Strategic Choices [中国崛起困境：理论思考与战略选择], ed. Sun Xuefeng [孙学峰] (Beijing: Social Sciences Academic Press [社会科学文献出版社], 2011), 24.
41. Sun, "Strategic Choices for Solving the Rising Dilemma," 33-34.
42. Liu Zhongmin [刘中民], "Thoughts on Sea Power and the Rise of a Great Power [关于海权与大国崛起问题的若干思考]," World Economics and Politics [世界经济与政治], no. 12 (2007): 10-13.
43. Li Qiang [李强], "Peaceful Rise and the Choice of China's Developmental Strategy [和平崛起与中国发展战略的选择]," Social Sciences in China [中国社会科学]," Aisixiang.com [爱思想], November 29, 2011, https://www.aisixiang.com/data/6547.html.
44. Ren Tianyou [任天佑], Road to Reform Strengthening the Military [问道改革强军] (Beijing: National Defense University Press [国防大学出版社], 2015), 32.
45. Fu Ying [傅莹], "Sino-American Relations After the Coronavirus [新冠疫情后的中美关系]," China-US Focus [中美聚焦], June 26, 2020, http://cn.chinausfocus.com/foreignpolicy/20200629/41939.html.
46. Sun, "Strategic Choice and the Success or Failure of Great Power Rise," 43-45; Yan, "Yan Xuetong: The Overall 'Periphery' Is More Important than the United States."
47. Hu Jintao [胡锦涛], "Coordinate Both Domestic and International Situations and Improve the Level of Diplomatic Work [统筹国内国际两个大局，提高外交工作能力水平]," in Selected Writings of Hu Jintao, Volume III [胡锦涛文选（第三卷）], ed. CPC Editorial Committee [中共中央文献编辑委员会] (Beijing: People's Publishing House [人民出版社], 2016), 236; Jiang Zemin [江泽民], "Jiang Zemin: The International Situation and Military Strategic Policy [江泽民：国际形势和军事战略方针]," Reform Data [中国改革信息库], January 13, 1993, http://www.reformdata.org/1993/0113/5616.shtml.
48. Jiang Zemin [江泽民], Jiang Zemin on Socialism with Chinese Characteristics (Special Excerpts) [江泽民论有中国特色社会主义（专题摘编）] (Beijing: Central Party Literature Press [中央文献出版社], 2002), 527-528; Yan, "Yan Xuetong: The Overall 'Periphery' Is More Important than the United States."

49. Hu Jintao [胡锦涛], "Integrating Both the Domestic and International Imperatives, Improving the Capability of Diplomatic Work [统筹国内国际两个大局，提高外交工作能力水平]," in Selected Writings of Hu Jintao, Volume III [胡锦涛文选（第三卷）], ed. CPC Editorial Committee [中共中央文献编辑委员会] (Beijing: People's Publishing House [人民出版社], 2016), 236.

50. Jiang Zemin [江泽民], The Selected Works of Jiang Zemin, Volume III [江泽民文选（第三卷）] (Beijing: People's Publishing House [人民出版社], 2006), 542; Tao Chun [陶春], "Seize the Important Period of Strategic Opportunity of Our Nation's Development with Determination [牢牢把握国家发展重要战略机遇期]," Study Times [学习时报], December 4, 2012, http://theory.people.com.cn/n/2012/1204/c49150-19785409.html; Zhu Feng [朱锋], "The Period of Strategic Opportunity in China's Next Ten Years: Must We Make New Choices? [中国未来十年的战略机遇期：我们必须做出新的选择吗？]," Journal of International Studies [国际政治研究], no.2 (2014): 10.

51. Evan S. Medeiros, China's International Behavior: Activism, Opportunism, and Diversification (Santa Monica, CA: RAND, 2009), 57.

52. Joseph A. Schumpeter, Capitalism, Socialism and Democracy (New York: HarperCollins, 1962), 105.

53. Robert Jervis, "Hypotheses on Misperception," World Politics 20, no. 3 (April 1968): 454-479.

54. Grimm, Lee, and Smith, Strategy as Action, 194.

55. Grimm, Lee, and Smith, Strategy as Action, 119.

56. Jack S. Levy, "Prospect Theory and International Relations: Theoretical Applications and Analytical Problems," Political Psychology 13, no. 2 (June 1992): 283-310.

57. Randall Schweller, Unanswered Threats: Political Constraints on the Balance of Power (Princeton, NJ: Princeton University Press, 2008), 21.

58. Medeiros, China's International Behavior, 56.

59. Efficiency is the "balance between economy in terms of resources such as time, money, space, or materials, and the achievement of an organization's goals and objectives." "Efficiency," in QFinance: The Ultimate Resource, 5th ed., ed. Qatar Financial Center (London: A. & C. Black, 2014).

60. Andy Marshall argues that efficiency and effectiveness are key if the United States is to prevail against another country with commensurate resources. Andy W. Marshall, Long-Term Competition with the Soviets: A Framework for Strategic Analysis (Santa Monica, CA: RAND Corporation, 1972), viii-x.

61. Aaron L. Friedberg, In the Shadow of the Garrison State: America's Anti-Statism and Its Cold War Grand Strategy (Princeton, NJ: Princeton University Press, 2000), 333.

62. Michael Beckley, Unrivaled: Why America Will Remain the World's Sole Superpower(Ithaca, NY: Cornell University Press, 2018).

63. Stephen G. Brooks and William C. Wohlforth, "Power, Globalization, and the End of the Cold War: Reevaluating a Landmark Case for Ideas," International Security 25, no. 3 (Winter 2000): 22.

64. Richard N. Foster, Innovation: The Attacker's Advantage (New York: Summit Books, 1986); Michael Porter, Competitive Advantage: Creating and Sustaining Superior Performance (Berkeley: University of California Press, 1985).

65. A clear illustration is the rise of Microsoft as a personal computing hegemon in the 1980s despite the earlier dominance of IBM. Grimm, Lee, and Smith, Strategy as Action, 83-84. See also Stephen Young, Chun-Hua Huang, and Michael McDermott, "Internationalization and

Competitive Catch-up Processes: Case Study Evidence on Chinese Multinational Enterprises," Management International Review 36, no. 4 (1996): 295-314.

66. Philippe Aghion, Stefan Bechtold, Lea Cassar, and Holger Herz, "The Causal Effects of Competition on Innovation: Experimental Evidence," Journal of Law, Economics, and Organization 34, no. 2 (May 2018): 163.

67. Grimm, Lee, and Smith, Strategy as Action, 103.

68. Peter Liberman, "The Spoils of Conquest," International Security 18, no. 2 (1993): 126; Stephen G. Brooks, "The Globalization of Production and the Changing Benefits of Conquest," Journal of Conflict Resolution 43, no. 5 (October 1999): 646-670.

69. Eric Lipton, "Faced with Evolving Threats, U.S. Navy Struggles to Change," New York Times, September 4, 2023, https://www.nytimes.com/2023/09/04/us/politics/us-navy-ships.html.

70. For example, Mancur Olson, in The Rise and Decline of Nations: Economic Growth, Stagflation, and Social Rigidities (New Haven, CT: Yale University Press, 1985), argues that the accumulation of interest groups and the rent-seeking behavior they engage in will, over time, lead to economic stagnation and decline. Likewise, Douglass North, in Institutions, Institutional Change and Economic Performance (Cambridge: Cambridge University Press, 1990), emphasizes the role of institutions in shaping economic development and suggests that institutional rigidity can contribute to a country's decline.

71. Zhang Ruizhuang [張 睿 壯], "Where Is the City upon the Hill Today? [山 巔 之 城 今 安 在]," People.cn [人 民 网], October 16, 2016, http://opinion.people.cn/n1/2016/1016/c1003-28781314.html; Liang Yabin [梁亚滨], "The Cost of Hegemony— An Analysis of the Cause of the Financial Crisis from the Perspective of US Decline [霸权的代价—从美国霸权衰落分析美国金融危机的起因]," Pacific Journal [太平洋学报], no. 5 (2010): 30-40; Liang Yabin [梁亚滨], "From Stakeholder to Strategic Assurance: The Sino-US Relationship during the Decline of the US [从利益攸关方到战略再保证：霸权衰落下的中美关系]," Contemporary Asia-Pacific [当代亚太], no. 3 (2010): 22-40.

72. Liu Jianfei [刘建飞], "Meddling with Everything, Leave a Mess Everywhere: The Mismatch Between Ends and Means [四处插手反而留下烂摊子，目标与现实之间存在差距]," People.cn [人 民 网], October 16, 2016, http://opinion.people.com.cn/n1/2016/1016/c1003-28781317.html.

73. Liu, "Meddling with Everything, Leave a Mess Everywhere"; Lin Ziheng [林子恒], "Xi Jinping: World Political Parties Should Coordinate to Address Challenges [习近平：全球各政党应开展协作应对挑战]," Zaobao [联合早报], December 2, 2017, http://www.zaobao.com.sg/special/report/politic/cnpol/story20171202-815500.

74. Hal Brands, "Democracy vs. Authoritarianism: How Ideology Shapes Great-Power Conflict," Survival 60, no. 5 (2018): 63.

75. Rebecca Friedman Lissner and Mira Rapp-Hooper, "The Day After Trump: American Strategy for a New International Order," Washington Quarterly 41, no. 1 (2018): 7-25.

76. Dan Reiter and Allan C. Stam, Democracies at War (Princeton, NJ: Princeton University Press, 2002), https://press.princeton.edu/books/paperback/9780691089 492/democracies-at-war.

77. Stephen G. Brooks and William C. Wohlforth, "The Rise and Fall of the Great Powers in the Twenty-First Century: China's Rise and the Fate of America's Global Position," International Security 40, no. 3 (2016): 7-53.

78. Erik Gartzke and Kristian Skrede Gleditsch, "Why Democracies May Actually Be Less Reliable Allies," American Journal of Political Science 48, no. 4 (2004): 775-795; Stephen M. Walt, "America's Polarization Is a Foreign Policy Problem, Too," Foreign Policy, March 11, 2019, http://foreignpolicy.com/2019/03/11/americas-polarizat ion-is-a-foreign-policy-problem-

too/; Brands, "Democracy vs. Authoritarianism"; Rachel Kleinfeld, "Do Authoritarian or Democratic Countries Handle Pandemics Better?," Carnegie Endowment for International Peace, March 31, 2020, https://carnegieendowment.org/2020/03/31/do-authoritarian-or-democratic-countries-handle-pandemics-better-pub-81404.

79. Ian Bremmer, "How China's Economy Is Poised to Win the Future," Time, November 2, 2017, https://time.com/5006971/how-chinas-economy-is-poised-to-win-the-future/.
80. Michael J. Mazarr et al., "Understanding the Emerging Era of International Competition," RAND Corporation, 2018, 12, https://www.rand.org/pubs/resea rch_reports/RR2726.html.
81. Porter, Competitive Advantage. Unlike competitive advantage, comparative advan-tage does not necessarily signify differentiation; it refers to a relative measure of effi-ciency in production. David Ricardo, On Principles of Political Economy and Taxation (London: John Murray, 1817).
82. Deborah Avant, Political Institutions and Military Change: Lessons from Peripheral Wars (Ithaca, NY: Cornell University Press, 1994).
83. Strang and Meyer, "Institutional Conditions for Diffusion"; David Strang and Sarah A. Soule, "Diffusion in Organizations and Social Movements: From Hybrid Corn to Poison Pills," Annual Review of Sociology 24 (1998): 265-290.
84. "Party, Government, Military, Civilians, Academia; East, West, South, North, Center, Party Is the Leader of All [党政军民学，东西南北中，党是领导一切的]," People. cn [人民网], February 14, 2022, http://dangjian.people.com.cn/n1/2022/0214/c117 092-32351226.html.
85. Gao Yu [高瑜], "Xi Jinping the Man [男儿习近平]," Deutsche Welle Chinese Website [德国之声中文网], January 26, 2013, https://www.dw.com/zh/ 男儿习近平 /a-16549520.
86. CPC History and Literature Research Institute [中共中央党史和文献研究院] ed., Excerpts from Xi Jinping's Statements on the Concept of Comprehensive National Security [习近平关于总体国家安全观论述摘编] (Beijing: Central Party Literature Press [中央文献出版社], 2018), 33-34.
87. Ikenberry, After Victory, 23.
88. Goddard argues that if a rising power's claims are inconsistent with prevailing norms and rules, then great powers are more likely to see its actions as threatening. Stacie E. Goddard, When Right Makes Might (Ithaca, NY: Cornell University Press, 2018), 2.
89. Mazarr et al., "Understanding the Emerging Era of International Competition," 16.
90. Porter, Competitive Strategy, 59.
91. The fixed costs of a particular strategy are those that do not change in relation to the "output" of the activity, whereas variable costs are those that "vary with the quantity of output produced." N. Greg Mankiw, Principles of Economics (Mason, OH: South-Western, 2007), 275-277.
92. Johnston's chart on the number of reports on China's Cooperative Actions shows how the 70 percent of cooperative reports can be thought to overshadow the 30 per-cent of non-cooperative reports. Johnston, "China in a World of Orders," 15.
93. James G. March and Johan P. Olsen, "The Institutional Dynamics of International Political Orders," International Organization 52, no. 4 (Autumn 1998): 943-944.
94. Johnston, "China in a World of Orders," 12.
95. This argument is inspired by a critique of modernization theory: Suzanne Berger and Ronald Dore, National Diversity and Global Capitalism (Ithaca, NY: Cornell University Press, 1996).
96. Wang Yizhou [王逸舟] et al., eds., Report on Global Politics and Security (2010) [全球政治

与安全报告(2010)] (Beijing: Social Sciences Literature Press [社会科学文献出版社], 2009), 274-275.

97. He Fang [何方], "Is It Multipolarity or 'One Superpower, Several Great Powers' [是多极化还是"一超多强"]," World Affairs [国际政治], no. 17 (1998): 20-22; Du Xiaoqiang [杜小强], "New Investigations into the Multipolarization of the International Strategic Landscape [国际战略格局多极化新探]," World Economy and Politics [世界经济与政治], no. 4 (1987): 1-7; Wu Guifu [武桂馥], "The Competition Between the US, Japan, and Western Europe and the Multipolar Trends of the Global Landscape [美、日、西欧竞争与世界格局的多极化趋势]," Future and Development [未来与发展], no. 6 (1990): 16-19.

98. Avery Goldstein, Rising to the Challenge: China's Grand Strategy and International Security (Stanford, CA: Stanford University Press, 2005), 133.

99. Liu Huaqing [刘华清], Memoirs of Liu Huaqing [刘华清回忆录] (Beijing: PLA Publishing House [解放军出版社], 2004), 637.

100. Social identity theory posits three ways in which individuals, groups, or states seek to join higher-status groups: social mobility, wherein status-seekers "emulate a higher status group"; social competition, wherein status-seekers "compete with [the higher status group] for preeminence"; and social creativity, wherein the status-seeker "establish[es] excellence in a different area." Deborah Welch Larson and Alexei Shevchenko, "Russia Says No: Power, Status, and Emotions in Foreign Policy," Communist and Post-Communist Studies 47, no. 3-4 (2014): 269-279. My argument is similar, but there are two key differences. First, my theory focuses on how rising powers build power, not status for its own sake. Second, rising power strategies will have all three of these components, though in a unique combination. Specifically, all rising powers are competing with the incumbent great power, and they will do so partly through emulation, but most critically through creative approaches. The entrepreneurial approach, however, is also about how they build power, in that they may seek excellence in the same areas as the great power, but in different ways.

101. For example, see Li Zhaolong [李朝龙] et al., eds., A Review of Major Military Reforms in the Major Powers Since the 20th Century [二十世纪以来世界主要国家重大军事改革述评] (Beijing: National Defense University Press [国防大学出版社], 2015).

102. John Lewis Gaddis, Strategies of Containment: A Critical Appraisal of American National Security Policy During the Cold War (Oxford: Oxford University Press, 2005), 60.

103. Gaddis, Strategies of Containment, 94-95.

104. Gaddis, Strategies of Containment, 60, 145, 159.

105. There is a nascent literature that evaluates rising power strategies as well. For ex-ample, David M. Edelstein, Over the Horizon: Time, Uncertainty, and the Rise of Great Powers (Ithaca, NY: Cornell University Press, 2017); Joshua R. Itzkowitz Shifrinson, Rising Titans, Falling Giants (Ithaca, NY: Cornell University Press, 2018).

106. This is the dominant policy narrative. See Kurt M. Campbell and Ely Ratner, "The China Reckoning: How Beijing Defied American Expectations," Foreign Affairs, March-April 2018; "How the West Got China Wrong," The Economist, March 1, 2018, https://www.economist.com/leaders/2018/03/01/how-the-west-got-china-wrong?gclid=CjwKCAjwrdmhBhBBEiwA4Hx5gz0uYyzm5oNCLtqUmF7loJt7oF 2FdwW3wnabdGcpqw7lklhYFVnXnxoC-0IQAvD_BwE&gclsrc=aw.ds.

第二章

1. In 1989, China participated in 37 intergovernmental organizations and 677 in-ternational non-governmental organizations. In 2022, the numbers were 743 and 4,803, respectively. Union of

International Associations, Yearbook of International Organizations (1990/1991); Union of International Associations, Yearbook of International Organizations (2021/2022).
2. Niu Jun [牛 军], "Cycle: China-US Relations and the Evolution of the Asia-Pacific Order (1978-2018)] [轮回：中美关系与亚太秩序演变 (1978-2018)]," Chinese Journal of American Studies [美国研究], no. 6 (2018): 9-25.
3. "Asia Power Index 2021: Diplomatic Influence," Lowy Institute, https://power.lowyinstitute.org/explore/diplomatic-influence/.
4. Jim Richardson, "To Win Friends and Influence People, America Should Learn from the CCP," Foreign Policy, July 22, 2021; Nahal Toosi, "'Frustrated and Powerless': In Fight with China for Global Influence, Diplomacy Is America's Biggest Weakness," Politico, October 23, 2022, https://www.politico.com/news/2022/10/23/china-diplomacy-panama-00062828.
5. Peter Wallensteen and Isak Svensson, "Talking Peace: International Mediation in Armed Conflicts," Journal of Peace Research 51, no. 2 (2014): 315-237; Kyle Beardsley, "Agreement Without Peace? International Mediation and Time Inconsistency Problems," American Journal of Political Science 52, no. 4 (2008): 723-740.
6. Patrick M. Regan et al., "Diplomatic Interventions and Civil War: A New Dataset," Journal of Peace Research 46, no. 1 (2009): 135-146.
7. "George Mitchell: Building Peace in Northern Ireland," United States Institute of Peace, 2011, https://www.usip.org/public-education-new/george-mitchell-building-peace-northern-ireland; "Camp David Accords and the Arab-Israeli Peace Process," Office of the Historian, Foreign Service Institute, United States Department of State, https://history.state.gov/milestones/1977-1980/campdavid#:~:text=In%20the%20end%2C%20while%20the,Gaza%20and%20the%20West%20Bank.
8. Fu Yuhong [富育红], "The Major Opportunities and Challenges China Faces After the US Withdrawal from Afghanistan [美国撤离阿富汗后中国面临的机遇与挑战]," International Relations Studies [国际关系研究], no. 5 (2014): 81-92.
9. Yan Xuetong [阎学通], "From Keeping a Low Profile to Striving for Achievement [从韬光养晦到奋发有为]," Chinese Journal of International Politics [国际政治科学], no. 4 (2014): 1-35; Men Honghua [门洪华] and Zhong Feiteng [钟飞腾], "Studies on China's Overseas Interests: Past, Present and Prospects [中国海外利益研究的历程、现状与前瞻]," Foreign Affairs Review [外交评论], no. 5 (2009): 58.
10. Edward Wong, "U.S. Officials Repeatedly Urged China to Help Avert War in Ukraine," New York Times, February 25, 2022, https://www.nytimes.com/2022/02/25/us/polit ics/us-china-russia-ukraine.html.
11. Dai Bingguo [戴秉国], Strategic Dialogues: Dai Bingguo's Memoirs [战略对话：戴秉国回忆录] (Beijing: People's Publishing House [人民出版社], 2016), 217.
12. Cheng Xin [成欣] and Wang Huihui [王慧慧], "Promoting the Resumption of Diplomatic Relations Between Saudi Arabia and Iran Shows China's Leadership as a Major Power [促成沙特、伊朗复交展现中国大国担当]," People's Daily [人民日报], March 14, 2023, http://paper.people.com.cn/rmrbhwb/html/2023-03/14/conte nt_25970291.htm. Zhang Zhiyong [张智勇], "China's Efforts to Mediate Ukraine Crisis in the Spotlight [中国斡旋乌克兰危机的努力备受瞩目]," Guangming Daily [光明日报], March 20, 2022, https://epaper.gmw.cn/gmrb/html/2022-03/20/nw.D11 0000gmrb_20220320_1-08.htm.
13. "China Will Set Up a Preparatory Office for the International Organization for Mediation in the Hong Kong Special Administrative Region [中方将在香港特区设立国际调解院筹备办公室]," Ministry of Foreign Affairs of the People's Republic of China [中华人民共和国外交部], November 1, 2022, https://www.mfa.gov.cn/web/wjbxw_673019/202211/

t20221101_10795358.shtml.
14. For the appendix on Chinese mediation activities, please go to www.orianaskylarmas tro.com/upstart.
15. Zha Daojiong [查道炯],"China's Oil Interests in Africa: A Topic of International Politics [中国在非洲的石油利益：国际政治课题]," International Politics Quarterly [国际政治研究], no. 4 (July 2006): 53-67.
16. For the appendix on Chinese mediation activities, please go to www.orianaskylarmas tro.com/upstart.
17. Yee Nee Lee, "Trump Says China Has Been 'a Big Help' in US Dealings with North Korea," CNBC, February 28, 2019, www.cnbc.com/2019/02/28/trump-says-china-has-been-a-big-help-in-us-dealings-with-north-korea.html.
18. I-wei Jennifer Chang, "China and Yemen's Forgotten War," United States Institute of Peace, January 16, 2018, https://www.usip.org/publications/2018/01/china-and-yem ens-forgotten-war.
19. Li Zhaoxing [李肇星], Untold Stories of My Diplomatic Life [说不尽的外交] (Beijing: CITIC Publishing House [中信出版社], 2014), 113.
20. Li, Untold Stories of My Diplomatic Life, 113.
21. Shi Jiangtao, "Israel-Gaza Crisis an Opportunity for China to Position Itself as Peace Broker," South China Morning Post, May 22, 2021, https://www.scmp.com/news/china/diplomacy/article/3134478/israel-gaza-crisis-opportunity-china-position-its elf-peace; "The Latest: China Calls for UN Council Action, Slams US," Associated Press, May 15, 2021, https://apnews.com/article/middle-east-a240cfbb37bc3662a 98d20e92bd38069.
22. Oriana Skylar Mastro, "Noninterference in Contemporary Chinese Foreign Policy: Fact or Fiction?," in China and International Security: History, Strategy, and 21st Century Policy, ed. Donovan Chau and Thomas Kane (Santa Barbara, CA: Praeger, 2014), 2:95-114; Wang Meng [王猛], "Darfur Crisis: The Challenge to and Juncture of Changes in China's Foreign Policy [达尔富尔危机：中国外交转型的挑战与契机]," World Economy and Politics [世界经济与政治], no. 6 (2005): 38; An Huihou [安惠侯], "Non-Interference Must Be Insisted Upon [坚持不干涉内政原则不动摇]," Jiefang Daily [解放日报], December 10, 2013.
23. Cheng Qian, "The Culture of China's Mediation in Regional and International Affairs," Conflict Resolution Quarterly 28, no. 1 (2010): 53-65; Wang Yizhou [王逸舟], A Wise and Benevolent Power: Creative Involvement in a Nutshell [仁志大国：创造性介入概说] (Beijing: Peking University Press [北京大学出版社], 2018).
24. Wang Jisi [王缉思], "Wang Jisi: 'Marching Westward': The Rebalancing of China's Geostrategy [王缉思：'西进',中国地缘战略再平衡]," Aisixiang.com [爱思想], October 19, 2012, https://www.aisixiang.com/data/58232.html.
25. Robert O. Keohane, "The Demand for International Regimes," International Organization 36, no. 2 (Spring 1982): 325-355.
26. G. John Ikenberry, "Institutions, Strategic Restraint, and the Persistence of American Postwar Order," International Security 23, no. 3 (Winter 1998-1999): 43-78.
27. "National Security Strategy," White House, March 1990, https://nssarchive.us/wp-content/uploads/2020/04/1990.pdf.
28. "Assessment of Member States' Advances to the Working Capital Fund for 2022 and Contributions to the United Nations Regular Budget for 2022," United Nations Secretariat, January 4, 2022, http://undocs.org/en/ST/ADM/SER.B/1038; "How We Are Funded," United Nations Peacekeeping, https://peacekeeping.un.org/en/how-we-are-funded, accessed

November 15, 2022.
29. Dai, Strategic Dialogues, 121-122.
30. "Revenue by Government Donor," United Nations Chief Executive Board, https://uns ceb.org/fs-revenue-government-donor, accessed September 14, 2022.
31. Ann Kent, "China's Participation in International Organisations," in Power and Responsibility in Chinese Foreign Policy, ed. Yongjin Zhang and Greg Austin (Canberra: Australia National University Press, 2013), 132-166.
32. Wang Yizhou [王逸舟], Global Politics and Chinese Diplomacy [全球政治和中国外交] (Beijing: World Affairs Press [世界知识出版社], 2003), 143.
33. Tang Yongsheng [唐永胜], ed., On National Competitive Strategy [国家竞争战略论] (Beijing: Current Affairs Press [时事出版社], 2018), 241.
34. Wang, Global Politics and Chinese Diplomacy, 51-52.
35. Dataset constructed in conjunction with Texas A&M University's Economic Statecraft Program. It can be found at www.orianaskylarmastro.com/upstart.
36. "What Are UN Specialized Agencies, and How Many Are There?," United Nations, accessed January 19, 2024, https://ask.un.org/faq/140935.
37. Lily Kuo, "China Is Set to Dominate the Deep Sea and Its Wealth of Rare Metals," Washington Post, October 19, 2023, https://www.washingtonpost.com/world/inte ractive/2023/china-deep-sea-mining-military-renewable-energy/.
38. Colum Lynch and Robbie Gramer, "Outfoxed and Outgunned: How China Routed the U.S. in a U.N. Agency," Foreign Policy, October 23, 2019, https://foreignpolicy. com/2019/10/23/china-united-states-fao-kevin-moley/.
39. "China's Meng Hongwei Elected President of INTERPOL," INTERPOL, November 10, 2016, https://www.interpol.int/en/News-and-Events/News/2016/China-s-Meng-Hongwei-elected-President-of-INTERPOL.
40. Mikko Huotari et al., "China's Emergence as a Global Security Actor: Strategies for Europe," MERICS, July 2017, 39.
41. While China was reelected in 2020, the number of countries that voted for it decreased by forty-one. See Sophie Richardson, "China Grudgingly Gets UN Rights Body Seat," Human Rights Watch, October 13, 2020, https://www.hrw.org/news/2020/10/13/china-grudgingly-gets-un-rights-body-seat#.
42. Li, Untold Stories of My Diplomatic Life, 237-238.
43. Andréa Worden, "China at the UN Human Rights Council: Conjuring a 'Community of Shared Future for Humankind'?," in An Emerging China-Centric World Order: China's Vision for a New World Order in Practice, ed. Nadège Rolland (Seattle: National Bureau of Asian Research, 2020), 33-48.
44. "A/HRC/51/L.6 Vote Item 2—40th Meeting, 51st Regular Session Human Rights Council," United Nations Human Rights Council, October 6, 2022, https://media. un.org/en/asset/k1w/k1w9tube8v.
45. Kelley E. Currie, "How to Stop China Killing Human Rights at the U.N.," Foreign Policy, November 9, 2022, https://foreignpolicy.com/2022/11/09/china-human-rig hts-un-xinjiang-resolution-international-system/.
46. Rana Siu Inboden, "China and the International Human Rights Regime: 1982-2011" (PhD dissertation, Oxford University, 2014), 9, https://ethos.bl.uk/OrderDetails. do;jsessionid=3AC660B99F42571C5775F3F23B4AB665?uin=uk.bl.ethos.686939, quoted in Ted Piccone, "China's

Long Game on Human Rights at the United Nations," Brookings Institution, September 2018, 2, https://www.brookings.edu/wp-content/uploads/2018/09/FP_20181009_china_human_rights.pdf.

47. Culture (in places that find it appealing), political values (when the country lives up to them at home and abroad), and foreign policies (when they are seen as legitimate and having moral authority) are the main sources of soft power. Joseph S. Nye Jr., "The Limits of Chinese Soft Power," Project Syndicate, July 10, 2015, https://www.proj ect-syndicate.org/commentary/china-civil-society-nationalism-soft-power-by-jos eph-s--nye-2015-07.

48. Joseph S. Nye Jr., "Soft Power," Foreign Policy, no. 80 (1990): 153-171.

49. Justina Crabtree, "'China Is Everywhere' in Africa's Rising Technology Industry," CNBC, July 28, 2017, https://www.cnbc.com/2017/07/28/china-is-everywhere-in-africas-rising-technology-industry.html.

50. Samantha Custer et al., Influencing the Narrative: How the Chinese Government Mobilizes Students and Media to Burnish Its Image (Williamsburg, VA: AidData at William & Mary, 2019), 27.

51. "The Interpretation of the 17th National Congress of China's Communist Party: Improve the Nation's Cultural Soft Power [党的十七大报告解读：提高国家的文化软实力]," Xinhua.com [新华网], December 28, 2007, http://www.gov.cn/jrzg/2007-12/28/content_845741.htm.

52. "The Interpretation of the 17th National Congress of China's Communist Party: Improve the Nation's Cultural Soft Power." Many leadership statements also focused on the cultural aspect. See Liu Yunshan [刘云山], "Cultural Practitioners Should Spread Positive Energy and Build Soft Power [文化工作者要传播正能量，建设软实力]," People.cn [人民网], February 1, 2013, http://politics.people.com.cn/n/2013/0201/c70731-20407850.html.

53. "Bo Xilai: Advanced Culture Is the Backbone of Social Progress [薄熙来：先进文化是社会进步的主心骨]," Federation of Literary and Art Circles of the Hong Kong SAR [香港特别行政区文学艺术界联合会], http://www.xgwl.hk/hk/?action-viewn ews-itemid-275.

54. "China Lacks Initiative in the Global Community, There Is a Need to Strengthen Soft Power [中国缺乏国际话语权 需增强软实力]," China Gate [热点论坛], December 24, 2009, https://m.wenxuecity.com/bbs/military/623477.html.

55. Guo Linxia [国林霞], "Analysis of China's Current Soft Power [中国软实力现状分析]," The Contemporary World [当代世界], no. 3 (March 5, 2007): 37-39; Chen Yugang [陈玉刚], "An Attempt to Illustrate China's Soft Power Construction in Globalization [试论全球化背景下中国软实力的构建]," International Review [国际观察], no. 2 (March 5, 2007): 40; Yan Xuetong [阎学通], "The Core of Soft Power Is Political Capability [软实力的核心是政治实力]," Century Journal [世纪行], no. 6 (June 15, 2007): 42-43.

56. Joseph S. Nye Jr., Elizabeth Economy, and David Shambaugh, "Is China's Soft Power Strategy Working?," ChinaPower, February 27, 2016, http://chinapower.csis.org/is-chinas-soft-power-strategy-working/.

57. Rachelle Peterson, "Outsourced to China: Confucius Institutes and Soft Power in American Higher Education," National Association of Scholars, April 5, 2017, https://www.nas.org/reports/outsourced-to-china/full-report#ConfuciusInstitutesWo rldwide.

58. "China Is Spending Billions to Make the World Love It," The Economist, March 23, 2017, https://www.economist.com/china/2017/03/23/china-is-spending-billions-to-make-the-world-love-it; CNN Press Room, "CNN Worldwide Fact Sheet," February 2023, https://cnnpressroom.blogs.cnn.com/cnn-fact-sheet/; "Overseas Branches [派驻国外分支机构]," Xinhua News Agency [新华社], http://www.xinhuanet.com/xhsld/2021/02/09/c_1211019859.htm.

59. Paul Mozur, "Live from America's Capital, a TV Station Run by China's Communist Party," New York Times, February 28, 2019, https://www.nytimes.com/2019/02/28/business/cctv-china-usa-propaganda.html; James Griffiths, "Trump Is Right That China Uses Its Media to Influence Foreign Opinion, but So Does Washington," CNN, September 30, 2018, https://www.cnn.com/2018/09/29/politics/china-media-influe nce-intl/index.html; Samantha Custer et al., "Ties That Bind: Quantifying China's Public Diplomacy and Its 'Good Neighbor' Effect," AidData at William & Mary, July 27, 2018, https://www.aiddata.org/publications/ties-that-bind.
60. "Xi Jinping Attends the Central Conference on Work Relating to Foreign Affairs and Makes Important Remarks [习近平出席中央外事工作会议并发表重要讲话]," Xinhuanet.com [新 华 网], November 29, 2014, http://www.xinhuanet.com/politics/2014-11/29/c_1113457723.htm. Such rhetoric continued through Xi's tenure. See "General Secretary Xi Jinping Speaks About International Communication [习近平总书记这样谈国际传播]," Wenming.cn [中国文明网], August 16, 2021, http://www.wenming.cn/ll_pd/ll_xgzt/202108/t20210816_6143596.shtml.
61. "General Secretary Xi Jinping Speaks About International Communication."
62. "World Soft Power Index 2023," Indian Strategic Studies Forum, 2023, https://issf. org.in/.
63. Laura Silver, Kat Devlin, and Christine Huang, "Unfavorable Views of China Reach Historic Highs in Many Countries," Pew Research Center, October 6, 2020, https://www.pewresearch.org/global/2020/10/06/unfavorable-views-of-china-reach-histo ric-highs-in-many-countries/.
64. Megan Brennan, "Record-Low 15% of Americans View China Favorably," Gallup, March 7, 2023, https://news.gallup.com/poll/471551/record-low-americans-view-china-favorably.aspx.
65. Laura Silver, Christine Huang, and Laura Clancy, "How Global Public Opinion of China Has Shifted in the Xi Era," Pew Research Center, September 28, 2022, https://www.pewresearch.org/global/2022/09/28/how-global-public-opinion-of-china-has-shifted-in-the-xi-era/.
66. Sharon Seah et al., The State of Southeast Asia: 2021 (Singapore: ISEAS-Yusof Ishak Institute, 2021).
67. Around a quarter of the entries at Cannes in 2018 were from China, but China had only nine winners. "China Brands Go Global," R3, October 21, 2019, https://rthree. com/insights/china-brands-go-global/.
68. "At Home with External Propaganda," China Media Project, December 8, 2021, https://chinamediaproject.org/2021/12/08/at-home-with-external-propaganda/.
69. Nicole Talmacs, "Africa and Africans in Wolf Warrior 2: Narratives of Trust, Patriotism and Rationalized Racism Among Chinese University Students," Journal of Asian and African Studies 55, no. 8 (2020): 1230-1245.
70. Marty Swant, "The 2020 World's Most Valuable Brands," Forbes, July 24, 2020, https://www.forbes.com/the-worlds-most-valuable-brands/.
71. Kathryn Virzi and Carol Parrington, "Identifying Factors That Hinder the Acceptance of Chinese Brands Among US Consumers," OALib, no. 6 (July 2019): 1-12.
72. Caroline Gray et al., "Caught in the Middle: Views of US-China Competition Across Asia," Eurasia Group Foundation, June 2023, https://egfound.org/wp-content/uplo ads/2023/06/Caught-in-the-Middle.pdf.
73. Joshua Kurlantzick, Charm Offensive: How China's Soft Power Is Transforming the World (New Haven, CT: Yale University Press, 2007), 11.
74. Lee Edwards, "Confucius Institutes: China's Trojan Horse," Heritage Foundation, March 27, 2021, https://www.heritage.org/homeland-security/commentary/confuc ius-institutes-chinas-

trojan-horse.
75. "How Many Confucius Institutes Are in the United States?," National Association of Scholars, June 22, 2023, https://www.nas.org/blogs/article/how_many_confucius_institutes_are_in_the_united_states; Sarah Cook, "Beijing's Global Megaphone," Freedom House, January 11, 2020, https://freedomhouse.org/report/special-report/2020/beijings-global-megaphone.
76. "China's Confucius Institutes: An Inquiry by the Conservative Party Human Rights Commission," Conservative Party Human Rights Commission, February 2019, https://web.archive.org/web/20191016144832/http://www.conservativehumanrig hts.com/news/2019/CPHRC_Confucius_Institutes_report_FEBRUARY_2019.pdf.
77. Dov S. Zakheim, "Time to Shut Down All Confucius Institutes—Whatever They Might Be Called," The Hill, November 11, 2022, https://thehill.com/opinion/natio nal-security/3729453-time-to-shut-down-all-confucius-institutes-whatever-they-might-be-called/.
78. Li Mingjiang, "China Debates Soft Power," in Chinese Scholars and Foreign Policy, ed. Huiyin Feng, Kai He, and Yan Xuetong (New York: Routledge, 2020), 45.
79. Fu Ying [傅 莹], "Sino-American Relations After COVID-19 [新 冠 疫 情 后 的 中 美 关 系]," China-US Focus [中 美 聚 焦], June 26, 2020, http://cn.chinausfocus.com/foreignpolicy/20200629/41939.html.
80. Data generated using People's Daily's Graphic and Textual Database [人民日报图文数据库], available via http://data.people.com.cn/rmrb, accessed December 16, 2022.
81. "China's Economy and the Beijing Olympics," Congressional Research Service, August 6, 2008, https://www.everycrsreport.com/reports/RS22936.html; Nye, Economy, and Shambaugh, "Is China's Soft Power Strategy Working?"
82. For Xi's views on soft power, see "Xi Jinping Talks About the Nation's Cultural Soft Power: Strengthens Chinese People's Confidence and Integrity [习近平谈国家文化软实力 : 增强做中国人的骨气和底气]," People.com.cn [中国共产党新闻网], June 25, 2015, http://cpc.people.com.cn/xuexi/n/2015/0625/c385474-27204268.html; Bai Guolong [白 国 龙] et al., "Whether It Is Hard or Soft Power, Both Rely on Talents' Abilities—Xi Jinping's Important Speech at the Meeting of the Chinese Academy of Sciences and the Chinese Academy of Engineering Attracted Huge Resonation [实力、软实力，归根到底要靠人才实力—习近平总书记在两院院士大会上的重要讲话引起热烈反响之四]," Youth.cn [中国青年网], June 1, 2018, http://news.youth.cn/sz/201806/t20180601_11634058. htm; Fan Zhou [范 周] and Zhou Jie [周 洁], "Study on China's Cultural Soft Power Construction Under the 'One Belt, One Road' Strategic Background [' 一带一路 ' 战略背景下的中国文化软实力建设研究]," Tongji University Journal Social Science Section [同济大学学报社会科学版] 27, no. 5 (November 14, 2016): 45; Hu Jian [胡 键], "'One Belt, One Road' and China's Rise in Soft Power [' 一带一路 ' 与中国软实力的提升]," Journal of Social Sciences [社会科学], no. 1 (January 10, 2020): 18.
83. Custer et al., Influencing the Narrative, 23.
84. Erich Schwartzel, "How China Captured Hollywood," The Atlantic, February 8, 2022, https://www.theatlantic.com/international/archive/2022/02/china-captured-hollywood/621618/.
85. Yao Wen, "Branding and Legitimation: China's Party Diplomacy amid the COVID-19 Pandemic," China Review 21, no. 1 (February 2021): 55-89.
86. Timothy D. Hoyt, Military Industry and Regional Defense Policy: India, Iraq and Israel (New York: Routledge, 2011), 56; Keith Krause, "Military Statecraft: Power and Influence in Soviet and American Arms Transfer Relationships," International Studies Quarterly 35, no. 3 (1991): 313-336.
87. "U.S. Arms Sales and Defense Trade," US Department of State, January 20, 2021, https://www.

state.gov/u-s-arms-sales-and-defense-trade/.
88. Aaron Mehta, "US Increases Dominance of Global Arms Exports," Defense News, March 15, 2021, https://www.defensenews.com/global/2021/03/15/us-increases-dominance-of-global-arms-exports/.
89. "U.S. Arms Transfers Increased by 2.8 Percent in FY 2020 to $175.08 Billion," US Department of State, January 20, 2020, https://www.state.gov/u-s-arms-transfers-increased-by-2-8-percent-in-fy-2020-to-175-08-billion/.
90. "Fiscal Year 2021 U.S. Arms Transfers and Defense Trade," US Department of State, December 22, 2021, https://www.state.gov/fiscal-year-2021-u-s-arms-transfers-and-defense-trade/.
91. William D. Hartung, Christina Arabia, and Elias Yousif, "The Trump Effect: Trends in Major U.S. Arms Sales 2019," Center for International Policy, May 2020, https://securityassistance.org/publications/the-trump-effect-trends-in-major-arms-sales-in-2019/; William D. Young and Elias Yousif, "US Arms Sales Trends: 2020 and Beyond from Trump to Biden," Security Assistance Monitor, April 2021, https://sec urityassistance.org/publications/u-s-arms-sales-trends-2020-and-beyond-from-trump-to-buden/.
92. "US Arms Sales to Taiwan," Forum on the Arms Trade, https://www.forumarmstr ade.org/ustaiwan.html.
93. Andrew J. Pierre, "Arms Sales: The New Diplomacy," Foreign Affairs 60, no. 2 (Winter, 1981): 267.
94. Zhang Qingmin [张清敏], "The Formation and Evolution of American Policy on Transfer of Conventional Weapons (1947-1992) [美国常规武器转让政策的形成与转变 (1947-1992)]," Chinese Journal of American Studies [美国研究] 23, no. 3 (2009): 73-91.
95. Zhang, "The Formation and Evolution of American Policy on Transfer of Conventional Weapons," 88; Li Chen [李 晨], "The US Sold Arms to Saudi Arabia, Where Did the 100 Billion Protection Fee Go? [美国向沙特出售千亿武器 ' 保护费 ' 花哪了 ?]," 81.cn [中国军网], May 22, 2017, http://www.81.cn/gjzx/2017-05/22/content_7612637.htm.
96. These sources point out that most recently the United States is pursuing such a strategy to deal with competition in the South China Sea. See Zhao Yi [赵 毅], "The Current Military Presence of USA in Southeast Asia [当前美国在东南亚的军事存在探析]," Southeast Asian Studies [东南亚研究], no. 5 (2014): 64; Zhai Kun [翟崑] and Song Qirun [宋清润], "The Development of US-Thailand Maritime Security Cooperation and Its Motivation [美泰海洋安全合作的演变及动因]," Pacific Journal [太平洋学报] 27, no. 1 (2019): 16-17.
97. But it is also pointed out that this strategy entails the downsides of possibly fu-eling regional conflicts and equipping potential future enemies. For some rep-resentative Chinese sources on the United States' arms sales, see Qi Haixia [漆海霞] and Zhou Jiaren [周建仁], "Arms Sales and US Strategic Deployment in the Asia-Pacific [军售与美国亚太地区战略布局]," Chinese Social Science [中国社会科学], no. 5 (2015): 161-162; Jiao Shixin [焦世新], "The Asia-Pacific Rebalancing and the Adjustment of US Policy Towards the South China Sea [' 亚太再平衡 ' 与美国对南海政策的调整]," American Studies [美国研究] 30, no. 6 (2016): 83-86; Zhang Shirong [张 仕 荣], "The US's Asia-Pacific Rebalance Strategy and Its Impact on China-US Relations [美国 ' 亚太再平衡战略 ' 及对中美关系的影响],"Contemporary World and Socialism [当代世界与社会主义], no. 4 (2012): 30-32.
98. Sidhant Sibal, "Several Countries Concerned over Faulty Chinese Military Equipment," WION, November 7, 2020, https://www.wionews.com/world/several-countries-concerned-over-faulty-chinese-military-equipment-341382.
99. Sixty-six percent of offers in 2019 were of aircraft. Hartung, Arabia, and Yousif, "The Trump Effect," 6.

100. Zhou Jiaren [周 建 仁], "Coping with America's Alliance Strategy Within the Context of the Rebalancing to Asia and the Pacific [同盟理论与美国 ' 重返亚太 ' 同盟战略应对]," Contemporary Asia-Pacific [当代亚太], no. 4 (2015): 34; Qi Haixia [漆海霞], "View Partial Feature of the US's Strategic Shift to the East from Arms Sales [从军售看美国战略重心东易的局部特征]," Journal of University of International Relations [国际关系学院学报], no. 4 (2012); Qi and Zhou, "Arms Sales and US Strategic Deployment in the Asia-Pacific"; Jiao, "The Asia-Pacific Rebalancing and the Adjustment of US Policy Towards the South China Sea."

101. Data generated using Stockholm International Peace Research Institute's Arms Transfers Database, available via https://www.sipri.org/databases/armstransfers. The United States recorded 14.515 billion trend-indicator value (TIV) in 2022, while China recorded a total of 2.017 billion TIV.

102. A. Trevor Thrall and Jordan Cohen, "Explaining U.S. Arms Sales," Cato Institute, June 18, 2020, https://www.cato.org/blog/explaining-us-arms-sales; "SIPRI Arms Transfers Database," Stockholm International Peace Research Institute, https://www.sipri.org/databases/armstransfers.

103. "Congressional Research Service Reports on Conventional Weapons Systems," Congressional Research Service, https://sgp.fas.org/crs/weapons/index.html. The values of the arms transfers are adjusted to the USD values in 2022 for comparison.

104. "Comparison: China-US, Global Arms Trade Data," Lowy Institute Asia Power Index, 2023, https://power.lowyinstitute.org/data/defence-networks/global-arms-transfers/arms-export-partnerships/.

105. "China Spreads Its Tentacles with Arms Exports," ANI News, February 25, 2021, https://www.aninews.in/news/world/asia/china-spreads-its-tentacles-with-arms-exports20210225132552.

106. "Why China's Submarine Deal with Bangladesh Matters," The Diplomat, January 20, 2017, https://thediplomat.com/2017/01/why-chinas-submarine-deal-with-banglad esh-matters/.

107. "World Development Indicators—GDP Per Capita (Current US$)," World Bank, https://data.worldbank.org/indicator/NY.GDP.PCAP.CD, accessed June 9, 2023.

108. Nilotpal Bhattacharjee, "China's Warning to Bangladesh on the Quad," The Diplomat, May 18, 2021, https://thediplomat.com/2021/05/chinas-warning-to-ban gladesh-on-the-quad/.

109. "Embargoed and Sanctioned Countries," University of Pittsburgh Office of Trade Compliance, https://www.tradecompliance.pitt.edu/embargoed-and-sanctioned-countries, accessed June 7, 2023.

110. Marwaan Macan-Markar, "Myanmar Embraces Russian Arms to Offset China's Influence," Nikkei Asia, February 9, 2021, https://asia.nikkei.com/Spotlight/Myan mar-Coup/Myanmar-embraces-Russian-arms-to-offset-China-s-influence.

111. ChinaPower Team, "How Dominant Is China in the Global Arms Trade?," ChinaPower, April 26, 2018, http://chinapower.csis.org/china-global-arms-trade/.

112. In 1991, the George H. W. Bush administration enacted sanctions against China, accusing Beijing of transferring missile technology to Pakistan. After Beijing pledged to abide by the MTCR, the administration lifted those sanctions. However, the US government has since accused Beijing of violating that pledge— China maintains at best what could be called a "spotty" record when it comes to the MTCR pledge. Paula A. DeSutter, "China's Record of Proliferation Activities," US State Department, July 24, 2003, https://2001-2009.state.gov/t/vci/rls/rm/24518.htm.

113. Daryl G. Kimball, "U.S. Aims to Expand Drone Sales," Arms Control Association, July/August 2020, https://www.armscontrol.org/act/2020-07/news/us-aims-exp and-drone-sales.

114. ChinaPower Team, "How Dominant Is China in the Global Arms Trade?"; Ergen Hu [胡尔根],

"China's CASC Rainbow Exports to More than a Dozen Countries with More than 200 Orders in a Year [中国彩虹无人机出口十多国家 年交付 200 余架]," Huanqiu.com [环球网], January 13, 2017, https://mil.huanqiu.com/article/9CaKrnJZIdj.

115. ChinaPower Team, "Drone Transfers Data," ChinaPower, https://chinapower.csis.org/data/sipri-drones-transfer-data/, accessed December 6, 2022.

116. ChinaPower Team, "Is China at the Forefront of Drone Technology," ChinaPower, May 29, 2018, https://chinapower.csis.org/china-drones-unmanned-technology/.

117. "SIPRI Arms Transfers Database," Stockholm International Peace Research Institute, https://www.sipri.org/databases/armstransfers.

118. Oil data from "Customs Statistics Online Query Platform [海关统计数据在线查询平台]," General Administration of Customs of the People's Republic of China [中华人民共和国海关总署], http://stats.customs.gov.cn/, accessed June 7, 2023. Data on arms transfers from "SIPRI Arms Transfers Database."

119. Shi Lei [石 磊], "Military Partnership Between the United States and South America After the Cold War [冷战后美国与南美洲国家的军事合作]," Latin American Studies [拉丁美洲研究] 38, no. 3 (2016); ChinaPower Team, "How Dominant Is China in the Global Arms Trade?"

120. Zhao Jiandong [赵建东], "US Media: China's Arms Exports Have Unique Advantages [美媒：中国武器出口具有独特优势]," Huanqiu.com [环球网], October 12, 2022, https://oversea.huanqiu.com/article/4A22gvyepsX.

121. Guo Xiaobin [郭晓兵], "US Arms Sales: The 'Political Scheme' Behind the 'Business Plan' [美国军售：' 生意经 ' 背后的 ' 政治账 ']," PLA Daily [解放军报], December 17, 2020.

122. "The Fear of No War: US Arms Sales Grow Against the Odds, Who is a Better War Dealer Than the US [唯恐天下无战!美国军售逆势增长 战争贩子舍美其谁?]," CCTV News [央视新闻], March 17, 2022, https://news.cctv.com/2022/03/17/ARTIoIchOyZfAbMyTDpdDYH9220317.shtml; Sun Ding [孙 丁], "US Arms Sales Grow Against the Odds, Exporting Unrest and Harming the World [美国军售逆势增长输出动乱危害世界]," Xinhua News Agency [新华社], March 15, 2022, http://www.news.cn/world/2022-03/15/c_1128473330.htm.

123. 22 CFR § 126.1, "Prohibited Exports, Imports, and Sales to or from Certain Countries."

124. "Arms Embargoes," SIPRI, https://www.sipri.org/databases/embargoes.

125. "EU Arms Embargo on China," SIPRI, November 20, 2012, https://www.sipri.org/databases/embargoes/eu_arms_embargoes/china.

126. Ni Ligang [倪利刚], "China Squeezed Out Russia and Suddenly Second in the World in Arms Sales? [中国挤掉俄罗斯 突然 ' 军售世界第二 ' 了 ?]," iFeng [凤凰网], December 12, 2020, https://news.ifeng.com/c/829COcWfjZC; Tang Yihong [唐宜红] and Qi Xianguo [齐先国], "Changes in Global Arms Trade Policy and Its Lesson to China [全球军品贸易政策变迁及对我国的启示]," International Trade [国际贸易], no. 2 (2015): 30.

127. Hans J. Morgenthau, "Diplomacy," Yale Law Journal 55, no. 5 (August 1946): 1067.

128. "1996, Bringing-In and Going-Out Strategy [1996, ' 引进来 ' 和 ' 走出去 ' 战略]," Xinhua News Agency [新华社], December 8, 2021, http://www.news.cn/politics/2021-12/08/c_1211478976.htm.

129. ChinaPower Team, "What Do Overseas Visits Reveal About China's Foreign Policy Priorities?," ChinaPower, March 29, 2021, https://chinapower.csis.org/diplomatic-visits/.

130. China has 27 regional embassies, 179 global embassies, and 48 second-tier regional consulates, while the United States has 26, 178, and 28, respectively. "Lowy Institute Asia Power Index

2023 Edition," Lowy Institute, 2023, https://power.lowyinstitute. org/data/diplomatic-influence/diplomatic-network/.
131. Yan Xuetong [阎 学 通], "Yan Xuetong: The Overall 'Periphery' Is More Important than the United States [阎学通：整体的 ' 周边 ' 比美国更重要]," Global Times [环球时报], January 13, 2015, http://opinion.huanqiu.com/1152/2015-01/5392 162.html.
132. Abdi Latif Dahir, "The Reason American Presidents Keep Visiting the Same African Countries," Quartz, October 9, 2018, https://qz.com/africa/1417273/the-reason-american-presidents-keep-visiting-the-same-few-african-countries/.
133. Kemi Lijadu, "Chinese Leaders Visit Africa More Often than You Think and Not Always the Places You Expect," Quartz, July 26, 2018, https://qz.com/africa/1335 418/chinese-leaders-visit-africa-more-often-than-you-think-and-not-always-the-places-you-expect/.
134. "Travels of Barack Obama," Office of the Historian, US Department of State, https://history. state.gov/departmenthistory/travels/president/obama-barack; "Travels of Donald J. Trump," Office of the Historian, US Department of State, https://history. state.gov/departmenthistory/travels/president/trump-donald-j.
135. China Power Team, "What Do Overseas Visits Reveal About China's Foreign Policy Priorities?"
136. Wilder Alejandro Sanchez, "No US President Has Ever Visited Central Asia. Biden Can Change That," World Politics Review, April 9, 2021, https://www.worldpolitic sreview. com/articles/29559/no-u-s-president-has-ever-visited-central-asia-biden-can-change-that; ChinaPower Team, "What Do Overseas Visits Reveal About China's Foreign Policy Priorities?"
137. ChinaPower Team, "What Do Overseas Visits Reveal About China's Foreign Policy Priorities?"; Diplomatic Agenda, Ministry of Foreign Affairs of the People's Republic of China [中华人民共和国外交部], https://www.fmprc.gov.cn/mfa_eng/wjdt_665 385/wsrc_665395/.
138. ChinaPower Team, "What Do Overseas Visits Reveal About China's Foreign Policy Priorities?"
139. Richard R. Verma, "Remarks to the Foreign Policy for America 2023 Leadership Summit," US Department of State, June 12, 2023, https://www.state.gov/remarks-to-the-foreign-policy-for-america-2023-leadership-summit/.
140. Neil Thomas, "Far More World Leaders Visit China than America," The Interpreter, July 28, 2021, https://www.lowyinstitute.org/the-interpreter/far-more-world-lead ers-visit-china-america.
141. ChinaPower Team, "What Do Overseas Visits Reveal About China's Foreign Policy Priorities?"
142. Yang Jiechi [杨 洁 篪], "Continue to Create New Prospects for Foreign Work Under the Guidance of General Secretary Xi Jinping's Diplomatic Thoughts [在习近平总书记外交思想指导下不断开创对外工作新局面]," Ministry of Foreign Affairs of the People's Republic of China [中 华 人 民 共 和 国 外 交 部], January 14, 2017, https://www.mfa.gov.cn/web/gjhdq_676201/gjhdqzz_681964/sgwyh_682446/zyjh_682456/201701/t20170114_9385067. shtml.
143. Wang Jisi [王 缉 思], "Wang Jisi: 'Marching Westward': The Rebalancing of China's Geostrategy [王缉思：' 西进',' 中国地缘战略再平衡]," Huanqiu.com [环球网], October 17, 2012, http://opinion.huanqiu.com/opinion_world/2012-10/3193760.html.
144. China's list of peripheral countries includes Russia, Japan, North Korea, South Korea, Mongolia, ASEAN nations, India, Pakistan, and Central Asian countries. See "China's Relations with Peripheral Countries [中国与周边国家的关系]," Gov.cn [中国政府网], June 30, 2005, https://www.gov.cn/test/2005-06/30/content_11177. htm. See also Yan, "Yan Xuetong: The Overall 'Periphery' Is More Important than the United States."
145. Li, Untold Stories of My Diplomatic Life, 185.

146. Roderick Kefferpütz, "Big Fish in Small Ponds: China's Subnational Diplomacy in Europe," MERICS, November 18, 2021, https://merics.org/en/report/big-fish-small-ponds-chinas-subnational-diplomacy-europe.

147. Sun Cheng [孙承], "China 'Surrounds Cities with Rural Areas' and Uses Local Governments in Western Countries to Oppose Countries' Policies Toward China [中国'以农村包围城市'，利用西方国家地方政府对抗各国对华政策]," Voice of America, December 8, 2021, https://www.voachinese.com/a/china-subnatio nal-diplomacy-20211207/6343105.html; Chen Xiang [陈翔] and Wei Hong [韦红], "China's Local Diplomacy Under the Perspective of 'One Belt, One Road' ['一带一路'建设视野下的中国地方外交]," International Review [国际观察] 6, no. 35.

148. Emily de La Bruyère and Nathan Picarsic, "All Over the Map," Foundation for the Defense of Democracies, November 15, 2021, https://www.fdd.org/analysis/2021/11/15/all-over-the-map/.

149. Salvatore Babones, "A House Divided: The AFRB and China's Subnational Diplomacy in Australia," Analysis Paper 17, Centre for Independent Studies, November 2020, 3, https://www.cis.org.au/publications/analysis-papers/a-house-divided-the-afrb-and-chinas-subnational-diplomacy-in-australia/.

150. Reuters Staff, "U.S. Designates Chinese Body a Foreign Mission, Quits Local Cooperation Agreement," Reuters, October 28, 2020, https://www.reuters.com/arti cle/us-usa-china-pompeo/u-s-designates-chinese-body-a-foreign-mission-quits-local-cooperation-agreement-idUSKBN27D305.

151. "Safeguarding Our Future: Protecting Government and Business Leaders at the U.S. State and Local Level from People's Republic of China (PRC) Influence Operations," National Counterintelligence and Security Center, July 2022, https://www.dni.gov/files/NCSC/documents/SafeguardingOurFuture/PRC_Subnational_Influence-06-July-2022.pdf.

152. Custer et al., Ties That Bind, 23.

153. ChinaPower Team, "How Is China Bolstering Its Military Diplomatic Relations?," ChinaPower, October 27, 2017, https://chinapower.csis.org/china-military-diplomacy/.

154. Larry Hanauer and Lyle J. Morris, "China in Africa: Implications of a Deepening Relationship," RAND Corporation, 2014, 3, https://www.rand.org/pubs/research_ briefs/RB9760.html.

155. Dai Bingguo [戴秉国], "Remarks by Dai Bingguo at Center for Strategic and International Studies," Embassy of the People's Republic of China in Georgia [中华人民共和国驻鲁吉亚大使馆], July 6, 2016, http://ge.china-embassy.gov.cn/eng/xwdt/201607/t20160706_1056446.htm.

第三章

1. "Deng Xiaoping's Speech at the Sixth Special Session of the UN General Assembly [邓小平在联大第六届特别会议上的发言]," Communist Party Network [共产党员网], delivered April 11, 1974, https://news.12371.cn/2015/09/28/ARTI144338487 4163974.shtml?ticket=.

2. Yang Jiemian [杨洁勉], "70 Years of Chinese Diplomacy: Innovative Practices and Theory Building [中国外交 70 年：实践创新和理论建设]," China International Studies [中国国际问题研究], no. 5 (2019): 6-19.

3. Secretariat of the Center for the Study of Xi Jinping's Diplomatic Thought [习近平外交思想研究中心秘书处], "Constructing a Unique Style of Chinese Diplomacy: Meaning and Paths to Realization [塑造中国外交独特风范：内涵与实践路径]," International Studies [国际问题研究], no. 6 (2021): 10.

4. Secretariat of the Center for the Study of Xi Jinping's Diplomatic Thought, "Constructing a Unique Style of Chinese Diplomacy," 10.
5. Derek Scissors, "China's Overseas Investment Starts the Long Climb Back," American Enterprise Institute, 2021, https://www.aei.org/research-products/rep ort/chinas-overseas-investment-starts-the-long-climb-back/.
6. Lindsey W. Ford and James Goldgeier, "Retooling America's Alliances to Manage the China Challenge," Brookings Institution, 2021, https://www.brookings.edu/research/retooling-americas-alliances-to-manage-the-china-challenge/.
7. Harry Bliss and Bruce Russett, "Democratic Trading Partners: The Liberal Connection, 1962-1989," Journal of Politics 60, no. 4 (1998): 1126-1147; Mira Rapp-Hooper, Shields of the Republic (Cambridge, MA: Harvard University Press, 2020); G. John Ikenberry, "Liberalism and Empire: Logics of Order in the American Unipolar Age," Review of International Studies 30, no. 4 (2004): 609-630. For a review of all US alliance commitments, see Brett Leeds et al., "Alliance Treaty Obligations and Provisions, 1815-1944," International Interactions 28, no. 3 (2002): 237-260.
8. Rapp-Hooper, Shields of the Republic; Fareed Zakaria, The Post-American World (New York: W. W. Norton, 2007), 178.
9. For some representative sources, see Xu Jin [徐 进], "The Cause of Contemporary China's Aversion to Alliances [当代中国拒斥同盟心理的由来]," International Economic Review [国际经济评论], no. 5 (2015): 143-154; Su Xiaohui [苏晓晖], "Chinese Diplomacy 'Finds Partners Not Allies' [中国外交 ' 结伴而不结盟 ']," People's Daily Global Edition [人民日报海外版], January 2, 2015; Ling Shengli [凌胜利], "Why Doesn't China Set Up Alliances? [中国为什么不结盟 ?]," Foreign Affairs Review [外交评论], no. 3 (2013): 20-33.
10. Sun Degang [孙 德 刚], "On 'Quasi-Alliance' Strategy [论 ' 准 联 盟 ' 战 略]," World Economics and Politics [世界经济与政治], no. 2 (2011): 55-79.
11. Adam P. Liff, "China and the US Alliance System," China Quarterly, no. 233 (2018): 156-157.
12. Ling Shengli [凌胜利], "Can China Form Alliances? [中国可以结盟吗 ?]," Friends of the Leader [领导之友], no. 1 (2012): 52-53.
13. Zhang Bowen [张博文], "Will China Abandon the 'Non-Alliance' Policy? [中国会放弃 ' 不结盟 ' 政策吗 ?]," Global Prospect [国际展望], no. 10 (2000): 17-18; Yan Xuetong [阎学通], "Is Russia Reliable [俄罗斯可靠吗 ?]," International Economic Review [国际经济评论], no. 3 (2012): 21-25.
14. "Why Is the Sino-Russian Relationship So Good but Still Not Allied [中俄关系这么好，为啥不结盟]," Xinhua News Agency [新 华 社], March 22, 2023, http://www. news.cn/world/2023-03/22/c_1211740381.htm.
15. Sun Ru [孙茹], "Building Partnership Network: An Upgrade of China's Non-Alliance Policies [构建伙伴关系网：中国不结盟政策的升级版]," World Affairs [世界知识], no. 6 (2015): 58-60. For an assessment of the debate among Chinese scholars, see Liu Ruonan and Liu Feng, "Contending Ideas on China's Non-Alliance Strategy," Chinese Journal of International Politics 10, no. 2 (2017): 151-171.
16. Dai Weilai [戴维来], "Initial Discussion on Medium-Power Nations' Global Leadership [中等强国的国际领导权问题初探]," Forum of World Economics and Politics [世界经济与政治论坛], no. 2 (2016): 58; Guo Shuyong [郭树勇], "The Leadership in Global Governance and China's Role [全球治理领导权问题与中国的角色定位]," People's Forum [人民论坛], no. 14 (2017): 25-36; Zhou Jianren [周 建 仁], "Theories of Alliance Formation: A Review and Considerations for Chinese Policy [联盟形成理论：评估及对中国的 政策启示]," Contemporary Asia-Pacific [当代亚太], no. 3 (2012): 61.

17. The United States leads the world in nominal GDP, and seven of the other top ten countries are US allies.
18. Sun Ru [孙 茹], "Building a Partnership Network: An Upgrade of China's Non-Alliance Policies [构建伙伴关系网：中国不结盟政策的升级版]," World Affairs [世界知识], no. 6 (2015): 58-60; Li Ziguo, "An Evolving Partnership," Beijing Review, October 16, 2014, http://www.bjreview.com.cn/world/txt/2014-10/13/content_644116_2.htm.
19. Sheng Ping [盛平] and Wang Zaixin [王再兴], Chronology of Hu Yaobang's Thought 1975-1989 [胡耀邦思想年谱，1975-1989] (Hong Kong: Taide Times Publishing House [泰德时代出版社], 2007); Song Yimin [宋以敏], "Hu Yaobang Made Corrections on China's Foreign Relations [胡耀邦在对外关系上的拨乱反正]," Yanhuang Chunqiu [炎黄春秋], no. 5 (2013); Sun Degang [孙德刚], "On 'Quasi-Alliance' Strategy [论 ' 准联盟 ' 战略]," World Economics and Politics [世界经济与政治], no. 2 (2011): 55-79.
20. Hu Jintao [胡锦涛], Hu Jintao's Selected Work (Volume I) [胡锦涛文选 (第一卷)] (Beijing: Military Science Publishing House [人民出版社], 2016), 188; Yu Ruidong [余瑞冬], "Full Text of Hu Jintao's Speech at SCO Moscow Summit [胡锦涛在上海合作组织莫斯科峰会上讲话全文]," Xinhua.com [新华网], May 30, 2003, https://www.chinanews.com/n/2003-05-30/26/308504.html; Nie Lubin, "Hu Jintao Illustrates the Five Big Achievements of the SCO [胡锦涛阐述上合组织五大成就]," Huanqiu.com [环球网], June 6, 2012, https://m.huanqiu.com/article/9CaK rnJvHYC.
21. Zhang Hongliang [张宏良], "How to View Qin Gang and Wang Yi's 'Three-Noes' [如何看待秦刚的 ' 三不原则 ' 和王毅的 ' 三无原则 ']," Fuxing Net [复兴网], January 14, 2023, https://www.mzfxw.com/e/action/ShowInfo.php?classid=12&id=171317.
22. Ling, "Why Doesn't China Set Up Alliances?"; Wang Fan [王 帆], "Alliance Management Theory and Dilemma [联盟管理理论与联盟管理困境]," Chinese Journal of European Studies [欧洲研究], no. 4 (2006): 111-125; Zhang Yunling [张 蕴 岭], "Overestimate One's Own Power, Abducted by Extremist Opinions—Two Risks in the Process of a Great Power's Rise [高估自己的力量，被极端舆论绑架 大国崛起过程中的两大风险]," People's Forum [人民论坛], no. 4 (2013): 50-51.
23. Lei Yu, "China's Strategic Partnership with Latin America: A Fulcrum in China's Rise," International Affairs 91, no. 5 (2015): 1054.
24. Lucyna Czechowska et al., States, International Organizations and Strategic Partnerships (Cheltenham, UK: Edward Elgar, 2019), 19; Thomas S. Wilkins, "Russo-Chinese Strategic Partnership: A New Form of Security Cooperation?," Contemporary Security Policy 29, no. 2 (2008): 358-383, https://doi.org/10.1080/13523260802284365.
25. Georg Strüver, "China's Partnership Diplomacy: International Alignment Based on Interests or Ideology," Chinese Journal of International Politics 10, no. 1 (2017): 31-65; Dai Zheng [戴正] and Zheng Xianwu [郑 先 武], "The Evolution of Alliance Theory—Its Mirroring Effect on the Chinese Thinking of International Relations [同盟理论的演进过程—兼论其对中国国际关系理念的镜鉴作用]," Guangxi Social Sciences [广西社会科学], no. 12 (2019): 73-79.
26. "Speech by H. E. Wen Jiabao, Premier of the State Council of the People's Republic of China," Mission of the People's Republic of China to the European Union, May 12, 2004, http://www.chinamission.be/eng/zt/t101949.htm.
27. Deng Yong, "Remolding Great Power Politics: China's Strategic Partnerships with Russia, the European Union, and India," Journal of Strategic Studies 30, no. 4-5 (2007): 863.
28. Wang Yi [王 毅], "Insist on Correct View of Righteousness and Benefits, Actively Play the Role of Responsible Great Powers: Deeply Comprehend the Spirit of Comrade Xi Jinping's Important Speech on Diplomatic Work [人民日报：坚持正确义利观 积极发挥负责任大国作用：深刻领会习近平同志关于外交工作的重要讲话精神]," People.cn [人民网],

September 10, 2013; "China's Peripheral Diplomacy: Advancing Grand Strategy [中国周边外交：推进大战略]," Xinhua. com [新华网], October 26, 2013, http://news.sina.com.cn/o/2013-10-26/201028540 080.shtml; "Yang Jiechi: Promote the Construction of a Community of Shared Future for Mankind [杨洁篪：推动构建人类命运共同体]," CPC News [中国共产党新闻网], November 19, 2017, http://cpc.people.com.cn/n1/2017/1119/c64094-29654 801.html.

29. Han Zhen and Mihaela Papa, "Alliances in Chinese International Relations: Are They Ending or Rejuvenating?," Asian Security 17, no. 2 (2020): 7.

30. Evan S. Medeiros, China's International Behavior: Activism, Opportunism, and Diversification (Santa Monica, CA: RAND, 2009), 82; see online appendix at www.orianaskylarmastro.com/upstart.

31. Full dataset can be found at www.orianaskylarmastro.com/upstart.

32. Han and Papa, "Alliances in Chinese International Relations."

33. Yan Xuetong [阎学通], "Yan Xuetong: The Overall 'Periphery' Is More Important than the United States [阎学通：整体的'周边'比美国更重要]," Global Times [环球时报], January 13, 2015, http://opinion.huanqiu.com/1152/2015-01/5392 162.html.

34. China has formed bilateral strategic partnerships with forty developing nations. Of all covered in these deals, eighty-nine are developing. Full appendix available online at www.orianaskylarmastro.com/upstart.

35. Hua Yisheng [华益声], "'One Belt, One Road' Is a Blessing for World Peace [一带一路是世界和平稳定之福]," People's Daily [人民日报], May 18, 2017; Su Xiaohui [苏晓晖], "A New Model of International Relations Is Needed Under the New Historical Conditions [新的历史条件下需要新型国际关系]," People's Daily Global Edition [人民日报海外版], April 29, 2015; "Yang Jiechi: Promote the Construction of a Community of Shared Future for Mankind."

36. Lei Yu, "China's Strategic Partnership with Latin America: A Fulcrum in China's Rise," International Affairs 91, no. 5 (2015): 1047-1048; Sun Ru [孙茹], "Building Partnership Network: An Upgrade of China's Non-Alliance Policies [构建伙伴关系网：中国不结盟政策的升级版]," World Affairs [世界知识], no. 6 (2015): 58-60.

37. Sun Degang, "China's Partnership Diplomacy in the Middle East," The Asia Dialogue, March 24, 2020, https://theasiadialogue.com/2020/03/24/chinas-partnership-diplomacy-in-the-middle-east/.

38. Strüver, "China's Partnership Diplomacy," 55.

39. Ling, "Why Doesn't China Set Up Alliances?," 24, 28, 32-33.

40. The goal is to "seek common ground on major issues while shelving differences on the minor ones" [求同存异]. Zhou Hong [周弘] and Jin Ling [金玲], "Seventy Years of China-Europe Relations: The Formation of Multi-Facet Partnership [中欧关系70年：多领域伙伴关系的发展]," Chinese Journal of European Studies [欧洲研究] 37, no. 5 (2019): 1-15.

41. Twenty-six of the 64 countries with which China has signed bilateral strategic partnerships scored as "free" on Freedom House's Freedom in the World index. Of all the countries covered, 48 of 128 scored as "free" or up. See appendix on China's stra-tegic partnerships online at www.orianaskylarmastro.com/upstart.

42. Jin Canrong [金灿荣] et al., "The Rise of Middle Powers and the New Focus of Chinese Diplomacy [中等强国崛起与中国外交的新着力点]," Contemporary International Relations [现代国际关系], no. 8 (2010): 1-6.

43. Cheng Xin [成欣] and Wang Huihui [王慧慧], "Promoting the Resumption of Diplomatic Relations Between Saudi Arabia and Iran Shows China's Leadership as a Major Power [促成

沙特、伊朗复交展现中国大国担当]," People's Daily [人民日报], March 14, 2023, http://paper.people.com.cn/rmrbhwb/html/2023-03/14/conte nt_25970291.htm.

44. Wang Jianwei, "China: A Challenge or Opportunity for the United States?," Journal of East Asian Studies 3, no. 2 (2003): 293-333; "President Jiang Zemin and U.S. President Bush Met with Press," Embassy of the People's Republic of China in the Independent State of Papua New Guinea, October 19, 2001, http://pg.china-embassy.gov.cn/eng/zt/fh/200110/t20011019_980230.htm.

45. "Remarks by President Obama and President Xi Jinping of the People's Republic of China," White House, June 7, 2013, https://sunnylands.org/article/remarks-by-presid ent-obama-and-president-xi-jinping-of-the-peoples-republic-of-china/.

46. Stephen M. Walt, "The Sunnylands Summit Won't Stop Sino-American Rivalry," Foreign Policy, June 5, 2013, https://foreignpolicy.com/2013/06/05/the-sunnylands-summit-wont-stop-sino-american-rivalry/.

47. Michael J. Green, By More than Providence: Grand Strategy and American Power in the Asia Pacific Since 1783 (New York: Columbia University Press, 2017), 526-527.

48. Adam P. Liff, "China and the US Alliance System," China Quarterly, no. 233 (March 2018): 156-157.

49. Shen Zhihua [沈志华], "From Xibaipo to Moscow: Mao Zedong's Announcement of 'Leaning to One Side'—Rediscussions on the Background and Basis of Sino-Soviet Alliance [从西柏坡到莫斯科：毛泽东宣布向苏联'一边倒'—关于中苏同盟建立之背景和基础的再讨论]," CCP Party History [中共党史研究], no. 4 (2009): 14-33; Wu Juan [武娟], "China's Diplomatic Policy Is Independent and Sovereign, an Actual Non-Alliance [中国的对外政策是独立自主的，是真正的不结盟]," People.cn [人民网], September 12, 2017, http://cpc.people.com.cn/n1/2017/0912/c69113-29529 025.html; John Garver, China's Quest: A History of the Foreign Relations of the People's Republic of China (Oxford: Oxford University Press, 2016), 114-116.

50. R. Clarke Cooper, "America as the Security Partner of Choice: Highlights of 2019 and a Look Ahead to 2020," US Department of State, January 15, 2020, https://2017-202.state.gov/america-as-the-security-partner-of-choice-highlights-of-2019-and-a-look-ahead-to-2020/; Donald J. Trump, "National Security Strategy of the United States 2017," White House, December 2017, https://trumpwhitehouse.archives.gov/wp-content/uploads/2017/12/NSS-Final-12-18-2017-0905.pdf; Carla Babb, "US Wants to Remain 'Partner of Choice' in South America," Voice of America, August 13, 2018, https://www.voanews.com/americas/us-wants-remain-partner-choice-south-america.

51. Charles Hooper, "Defense Security Cooperation Agency Chief on the Value of Partnerships," Defense News, December 4, 2019, https://www.defensenews.com/outl ook/2019/12/02/defense-security-cooperation-agency-chief-on-the-value-of-partn erships/.

52. Susan B. Epstein and Liana W. Rosen, "U.S. Security Assistance and Security Cooperation Programs: Overview of Funding Trends," Congressional Research Service, February 1, 2018, https://crsreports.congress.gov/product/pdf/R/R45 091/3.

53. Epstein and Rosen, "U.S. Security Assistance and Security Cooperation Programs."

54. "International Military Training and Education Programs," Defense Security Cooperation Agency, https://www.dsca.mil/50th-anniversary/international-milit ary-and-education-programs, accessed June 14, 2023.

55. Alexandra Gheciu, "Security Institutions as Agents of Socialization? NATO and the 'New Europe,'" International Organization 59, no. 4 (2005): 973-1012.

56. "China's National Defense in the New Era," State Council Information Office of the People's

Republic of China, July 2019, https://www.andrewerickson.com/2019/07/full-text-of-defense-white-paper-chinas-national-defense-in-the-new-era-english-chinese-versions/; "Key NATO and Allied Exercises in 2019," North Atlantic Treaty Organization, February 2019, https://www.nato.int/nato_static_fl2014/assets/pdf/pdf_2019_02/1902-factsheet_exercises_en.pdf.

57. ChinaPower Team, "How Is China Bolstering Its Military Diplomatic Relations?," ChinaPower, October 27, 2017, https://chinapower.csis.org/china-military-diplomacy/.

58. Jonah Victor, "China's Security Assistance in Global Competition," in The PLA Beyond Borders: Chinese Military Operations in Regional and Global Context, ed. Joel Wuthnow et al. (Washington, DC: National Defense University Press, 2021), 281.

59. Most of these are non-combat, often multilateral international exercises. ChinaPower Team, "How Is China Bolstering Its Military Diplomatic Relations?"

60. Kyuri Park, "Ripe for Cooperation or Rivalry? Commerce, Realpolitik, and War Memory in Contemporary Sino-Japanese Relations," Asian Security 4, no. 2 (2008): 18.

61. "From 2003 to 2017, China loaned $2.53 billion to eight African countries explic-itly for military and national defense purposes" compared to the United States' "$753 million in foreign military financing to African countries, with only $15.4 mil-lion for military construction projects." Victor, "China's Security Assistance in Global Competition," 285.

62. Jessica Chen Weiss, "A World Safe for Autocracy? China's Rise and the Future of Global Politics," Foreign Affairs 98, no. 4 (2019); Adrian Zenz, "China's Domestic Security Spending: An Analysis of Available Data," China Brief 18, no. 4 (2018); Josh Chin, "China Spends More on Domestic Security as Xi's Powers Grow," Wall Street Journal, March 6, 2018, https://www.wsj.com/articles/china-spends-more-on-domes tic-security-as-xis-powers-grow-1520358522.

63. "The New Big Brother—China and Digital Authoritarianism," United States Senate Foreign Relations Committee Staff Report, July 21, 2020, 7.

64. Amy Qin, "Chinese City Uses Facial Recognition to Shame Pajama Wearers," New York Times, January 21, 2020, https://www.nytimes.com/2020/01/21/business/china-pajamas-facial-recognition.html.

65. Lin Chunyin [林春茵] and Peng Lifang [彭莉芳], "Learning Kungfu, Studying the Goose Step, and Speak in Chinese—Many Foreign Police Now Have Their 'Chinese Shifu' [学功夫踢正步说中文，好多外国警察有了' 中国师傅 ']," China News Service [中国新闻社], February 27, 2019, https://www.chinanews.com.cn/m/sh/2019/02-27/8766233.shtml; Sun Wenyu, "PLA's Goose-Stepping Highlight of Qatari National Day Military Parade," People.cn, December 20, 2017, http://en.people.cn/n3/2017/1220/c90000-9306770.html.

66. The complete dataset can be found at www.orianaskylarmastro.com/upstart. Exact numbers are not reported. Data is gleaned from technical studies such as the fol-lowing: Zhong Sheng [钟 声], Liu Jianchang [刘 建 昌], and Zhang Ling [张 玲], "On the Experiences and Inspirations from the Overseas Police Training in China: A Case Study of Overseas Police Training Practice in Guangxi Police Academy [外警培训的经验和启示：以广西警察学院外警培训实践为例]," Journal of Guangxi Police Higher Occupation School [广西警官高等专科学校学报], no. 6 (December 1, 2016): 100; Yin Bo [尹波], "The Current Needs, Problems and Perfection of the Foreign Police Training Work in China [当前我国外警培训工作的需求，问题与完善]," Journal of Liaoning Police Academy [辽宁警察学院学报], no. 5 (2020): 81-85.

67. "China to Build Asia's Largest UN Police Training Center," People's Daily Online, August 20, 2002, http://en.people.cn/200208/20/eng20020820_101732.shtml.

68. "About the Center [中心概况]," China Peacekeeping Police Training Center [中国维和警察培训中心], http://39.100.105.116/pages/overview/about.html.

69. "The 2019 Foreign Police Training Working Session Was Held in Our School [我校召开 2019 年外警培训工作会议]," People's Public Security University of China [中国人民公安大学], May 16, 2019, http://www.ppsuc.edu.cn/info/1016/7469.htm.

70. Ge Tailiang [戈 太 亮] and Wang Lu [王 露], "Zhenjiang Police Hosted Foreign Training Program for the First Time [镇江警方首次承接公安部外警培训项目]," Jschina.com.cn [中国江苏网], October 25, 2018, https://baijiahao.baidu.com/s?id= 1615260178350728242&wfr=spider&for=pc; Zhang Weihua [张 卫 华], "Experts from the International Cooperation Bureau of the Ministry of Public Security Came to Our School and Led the Foreign Police Training [公安部国际合作局专家到我院指导外警培训工作]," Henan Police College [河南警察学院], October 18, 2017, https://pxb.hnp.edu.cn/info/1056/1352.htm; "Vice President Hu Chuanping and Others Participated in the National Public Security Forum on Foreign Police Training [胡传平副院长一行参加全国公安机关外警培训工作座谈会]," Railway Police College [铁道警察学院], April 17, 2018, http://www.rpc.edu.cn/info/1020/2841.htm.

71. "Friendship on the Sea: Coast Guard Law Opened up a New Chapter for Law Enforcement Cooperation [宗海谊：《海警法》开启海上执法合作新篇章]," Huanqiu.com [环球网], April 29, 2020, https://baijiahao.baidu.com/s?id=16983230 21814705096&wfr=spider&for=pc.

72. "Chinese, Philippine Coast Guards Hold Joint Exercise to Achieve Interoperability at Sea," China Military [中国军网], January 16, 2020, http://eng.chinamil.com.cn/view/2020-01/16/content_9718789.htm.

73. "CCG 'Haijing 3306' Debuts at International Multilateral Exercise and Returns Triumphantly ['中国海警 3306 船'首秀国际多方演习后凯旋]," Chinanews.com [中国新闻网], June 25, 2015, https://www.chinanews.com/gn/2015/06-25/7366312. shtml.

74. Zhao Lei [赵 磊] and Su Hongfeng [苏 红 锋], "China Coast Guard Visits South Korea for the First Time and Conducts Joint Maritime Exercise [中国海警首次访韩并与韩海警开展海上联演]," China Daily [中国日报], June 18, 2016, https://china.chi nadaily.com.cn/2016-06/18/content_25757883.htm.

75. Liu Xiaolin [刘晓林] and Zhang Yiqi [张一琪], "Four Days and Three Nights, Experience Mekong River Patrol [四天三夜，亲历湄公河巡航]," People's Daily [人民日报], May 5, 2018, http://world.people.com.cn/GB/n1/2018/0505/c1002-29966381. html; "China-Laos-Myanmar-Thailand Mekong River Joint Patrol Command Center Established in Yunnan [中老缅泰湄公河联合巡逻执法联合指挥部在云南成立]," Xinhua News Agency [新华社], December 9, 2011, http://www.gov.cn/jrzg/2011-12/09/content_2016216.htm.

76. Deng Yanyan [邓 彦 妍], Jin Jijian [金 继 坚], and Dong Guiying [董 桂 英],"The 100th China-Laos-Myanmar-Thailand Joint Patrol on the Mekong River Was Officially Launched [第 100 次中老缅泰湄公河联合巡逻执法行动正式启动]," Yunnan TV [云 南 电 视 台], December 10, 2020, https://baijiahao.baidu.com/s?id=1685665147650095474&wfr=spider&for=pc.

77. Alina Polyakova and Chris Meserole, "Exporting Digital Authoritarianism," Brookings Institution, August 2019, 6.

78. Margaret Roberts, Censored: Distraction and Diversion Inside China's Great Firewall (Princeton, NJ: Princeton University Press, 2018).

79. Connor Fiddler, "The 3 Pillars of Chinese Foreign Policy: The State, the Party, the People," The Diplomat, February 3, 2021, https://thediplomat.com/2021/02/the-3-pill ars-of-chinese-foreign-policy-the-state-the-party-the-people/.

80. Polyakova and Meserole, "Exporting Digital Authoritarianism." We do not have details about the content of the training, but we know that many officials return home to implement cybersecurity laws similar to those of China. "The New Big Brother," 31.

81. Adrian Shahbaz, Allie Funk, and Kian Vesteinsson, "Freedom on the Net 2022: Countering an Authoritarian Overhaul of the Internet," Freedom House, 2022.
82. Aidan Powers-Riggs, "Covid-19 Is Proving a Boon for Digital Authoritarianism," Center for Strategic and International Studies, August 17, 2020, https://www.csis.org/blogs/new-perspectives-asia/covid-19-proving-boon-digital-authoritarianism.
83. Katherine Atha et al., "China's Smart Cities Development," SOSi International, January 2020, https://www.uscc.gov/sites/default/files/China_Smart_Cities_Deve lopment.pdf.
84. Sheena Chestnut Greitens, "Dealing with Demand for China's Global Surveillance Exports," Brookings Institution, April 2020, 2; Steven Feldstein, "The Global Expansion of AI Surveillance," Carnegie Endowment for International Peace, 2019.
85. Feldstein, "The Global Expansion of AI Surveillance," 1.
86. Feldstein, "The Global Expansion of AI Surveillance," 2.
87. Greitens, "Dealing with Demand for China's Global Surveillance Exports," 6.
88. Elly Cosgrove, "One Billion Surveillance Cameras Will Be Watching Around the World in 2021, a New Study Says," CNBC, December 6, 2019, https://www.cnbc. com/2019/12/06/one-billion-surveillance-cameras-will-be-watching-globally-in-2021.html..
89. Ross Andersen, "The Panopticon Is Already Here: China's Artificial Intelligence Surveillance State Goes Global," The Atlantic, September 2020; Feldstein, "The Global Expansion of AI Surveillance," 2.
90. "The New Big Brother," 27.
91. Cheng Jie [程結] and Ouyang Xu [欧阳旭], "Research on Cross-Cultural Communication of Foreign Police Training Under the Perspective of 'One Belt, One Road' [' 一带一路 ' 視閾下外警培训跨文化交流研究]," Journal of Liaoning Public Security and Judiciary Officials [辽宁公安司法管理干部学院学报], no. 2 (2019): 36.
92. "US Report Accuses China of Digital Authoritarianism," BBC News, July 21, 2020, https://www.bbc.com/news/technology-53490042.
93. Marian L. Lawson and Susan B. Epstein, "Democracy Promotion: An Objective of U.S. Foreign Assistance," Congressional Research Service, January 4, 2017, https://www.everycrsreport.com/files/20190104_R44858_aaa79dc011a9a071c15be af4bcb8e1accefc564c.pdf; Peter M. Haas and John A. Hird, eds., Controversies in Globalization: Contending Approaches to International Relations (Los Angeles: CQ Press, 2012), 491.
94. Scholars have amplified the message. See Thomas Carothers, "Democracy Promotion Under Clinton," Washington Quarterly 18, no. 4 (1995): 13-25. Michael McFaul and Francis Fukuyama posit that every US enemy has been either an autoc-racy or a political movement built upon undemocratic ideals. Francis Fukuyama and Michael McFaul, "Should Democracy Be Promoted or Demoted?," Washington Quarterly 31, no. 1 (2007): 23-45. Americans also view democracy promotion as cultural and an inherent moral obligation; even the founding fathers view US democracy promotion abroad as part of the United States' destiny. See Tony Smith, America's Mission (Princeton, NJ: Princeton University Press, 2012). The benefits of promoting democracy are prominent in every US National Security Strategy of this period. See for example, Bill Clinton, "A National Security Strategy of Engagement and Enlargement," White House, February 1996, https://fas.org/spp/military/docops/national/1996stra.htm; Barack Obama, "National Security Strategy," White House, May 2010, https://obamawhitehouse.archives.gov/sites/default/files/rss_viewer/national_security_strategy.pdf, 37. "Free governments do not oppress their people or attack other free nations. Peace and international sta-bility are most reliably built on a foundation of freedom." George W. Bush, "National Security Strategy of the United States of America 2002," White House,

September 2002, https://2009-2017.state.gov/documents/organization/63562.pdf.

95. These include the Afghanistan Security Forces Fund (ASFF), Coalition Readiness Support Program (CRSP), DoD Regional Centers for Security Studies, Foreign Security Forces: Authority to Build Capacity—Section 333, Global Security Contingency Fund (GSCF) (Section 1207), Humanitarian Assistance, Indo-Pacific Maritime Security Initiative (MSI), Mine Action (MA) Programs, Regional Defense Combating Terrorism and Irregular Warfare Fellowship Program (CTFP), Service-Sponsored Activities, and "Miscellaneous, DoD/DOS Non-Security Assistance" and "Non-Security Assistance, Unified Command." See "Fiscal Year (FY) 2021 President's Budget: Justification for Security Cooperation Program and Activity Funding," Office of the Secretary of Defense, April 2020.

96. Dov H. Levin, "Partisan Electoral Interventions by the Great Powers: Introducing the PEIG Dataset," Conflict Management and Peace Science 36, no. 1 (2019): 88-106.

97. Monica Duffy Toft, "Why Is America Addicted to Foreign Interventions?," National Interest, December 10, 2017, https://nationalinterest.org/feature/why-america-addicted-foreign-interventions-23582; James Meernik, "United States Military Intervention and the Promotion of Democracy," Journal of Peace Research 33, no. 4 (1996): 391-402.

98. Steven Finkel, Anibal Perez-Linan, and Mitchell Seligson, "The Effects of U.S. Foreign Assistance on Democracy Building, 1990-2003," World Politics 59, no. 3 (2007): 404-438.

99. Lawson and Epstein, "Democracy Promotion."

100. In 2017, seventy-one countries incurred net declines compared to thirty-five that made gains. This marked the twelfth consecutive year in which declines outnumbered improvements. See Michael J. Abramowitz, "Freedom in the World, 2018," Freedom House, February 5, 2018, https://freedomhouse.org/report/free dom-world/2018/democracy-crisis; "Democracy in Retreat," Freedom House, 2019, https://freedomhouse.org/report/freedom-world/2019/democracy-retreat.

101. Larry Diamond, "Facing Up to the Democratic Recession," Journal of Democracy 26, no. 1 (2015): 142.

102. Chen Ling and Barry Naughton, "A Dynamic China Model: The Co-Evolution of Economics and Politics in China," Journal of Contemporary China 26, no. 103 (2017): 18-34. See this source for an extensive history and analysis of how it has adapted since 1992.

103. Zhao Suisheng, "The China Model: Can It Replace the Western Model of Modernization?," Journal of Contemporary China 19, no. 65 (2010): 1; Joseph Fewsmith, "Debating 'the China Model,'" China Leadership Monitor, no. 35 (2011): 7.

104. For one of the earliest views of the term "China model," see Rowan Callick, "How Long Can Economic Freedom and Political Repression Coexist? Rowan Callick Examines Beijing's Sinister Policy Formulation," The American, November 13, 2007, http://www.american.com/archive/2007/november-december-magazinecontents/the-china-model.

105. Gary S. Becker, "Democracy or Autocracy: Which Is Better for Economic Growth?," Hoover Institution, October 10, 2010, https://www.hoover.org/research/democr acy-or-autocracy-which-better-economic-growth.

106. The European Union is counted as one partner. The two non-democracies are Hong Kong and Vietnam. "Democracy Index 2020," Economist Intelligence Unit, https://www.eiu.com/n/campaigns/democracy-index-2020/; Feng Zhongping and Huang Jing, "China's Strategic Partnership Diplomacy: Engaging with a Changing World," European Strategic Partnerships Observatory, Working Paper, June 2014, https://www.files.ethz.ch/isn/181324/China%E2%80%99s%20strategic%20partners hip%20diplomacy_%20engaging%20with%20a%20changing%20world%20.pdf.

107. Andrew J. Nathan, "China's Challenge," Journal of Democracy 26, no. 1 (2015): 157.
108. Luo Yanhua [罗 艳 华], "The Strategic Means and Realistic Dilemma of U.S. Democratic Export [美国民主输出的战略手段与现实困境]," People's Forum [人民论坛], no. 35 (2021): 40-43.
109. Zhao Qizheng [赵启正], "How to Approach the China Model of Development? [如何看待中国发展模式?]," State Council Information Office [国务院新闻办公室], March 2, 2010, http://www.scio.gov.cn/ztk/xwfb/jjfyr/21/mtbd/Document/558 321/558321.htm; Zhang Yesui [张 业 遂], "Zhang Yesui Responds to the Question of Whether China Exports Its Model Because It Wants to Change the World Order [中国向外输出中国模式是要改变国际秩序?张业遂回应]," China News [中国新闻网], March 4, 2018, http://www.chinanews.com/gn/2018/03-04/8459318.shtml.
110. Su Changhe [苏长和], "China Will Not Export Its Model, the China Model Is Also Not Easy for Others to Follow [中国模式不会出口，别人也不易学]," Aisixiang. com [爱思想], January 31, 2021, https://www.aisixiang.com/data/89824.html.
111. Barry Naughton, "China's Distinctive System: Can It Be a Model for Others?," Journal of Contemporary China 19, no. 65 (2010): 437-460; Wade Shepard, "Why China's Development Model Won't Work in Africa," Forbes, October 31, 2019, https://www.forbes.com/sites/wadeshepard/2019/10/31/why-chinas-development-model-wont-work-in-africa/?sh=5e1e6a8257af; Yuen Yuen Ang, "The Real China Model: It's Not What You Think It Is," Foreign Affairs, June 29, 2018, https://www.for eignaffairs.com/articles/asia/2018-06-29/real-china-model.
112. Seva Gunitsky, "Democracy's Future: Riding the Hegemonic Wave," Washington Quarterly 41, no. 2 (2018): 115-135.
113. Ya Mei, "Full Text of President Xi's Speech at Opening of Belt and Road Forum," Xinhua.com, May 14, 2017, http://www.xinhuanet.com/english/2017-05/14/c_13 6282982.htm.
114. Wang Xiangping, "An Analysis of the Chinese Communist Party Leaders' Discourse on the China Model [解析中共领导人关于 ' 中国模式 ' 的论述]," CPC News [中国共产党新闻网], October 9, 2013, http://theory.people.com.cn/n/2013/1009/c83 867-23139105-8.html.
115. "Xi Jinping: 'China Does Not Import Foreign Models, and Does Not Export China Model' [习近平：'中国不输入外国模式，也不输出中国模式 ']," RFI [法国国际广播电台], January 12, 2017, https://www.rfi.fr/cn/%E4%B8%AD%E5%9B%BD/20171201%E4%B9%A0%E8%BF%91%E5%B9%B3%E4%B8%AD%E5%9B%BD%E4%B8%8D%E8%BE%93%E5%85%A5%E5%A4%96%E5%9B%BD%E6%A8%A1%E5%BC%8F%EF%BC%8C%E4%B9%9F%E4%B8%8D%E8%BE%93%E5%87%BA%E4%B8%AD%E5%9B%BD%E6%A8%A1%E5%BC%8F.
116. Cheng Cheng, "China Will Not 'Export' Chinese Model: Xi," Xinhua.com [新 华 网], December 1, 2017, http://www.xinhuanet.com/english/2017-12/01/c_136793 833.htm; Shi Zhiyu [石之瑜], "What Is the China Model That the West Has Been Opposing To? [西方反对的是什么中国模式]," Zaobao [联合早报], November 7, 2017, http://www.haozaobao.com/mon/keji/20171107/40997_2.html.
117. "Will China 'Export Its Values?' [中国会搞 ' 文化输出 ' 吗?]," People's Daily [人民日报], November 14, 2013, http://theory.people.com.cn/n/2013/1114/c371516-23543 735-2.html; Qi Peiyu [祁 培 育], "Foreign Ministry: China Has Never 'Exported' the China Mode, and Has Never Asked Other Countries to 'Replicate Its Homework' [外交部：中国从不 ' 输出 ' 中国模式，也从未要求 ' 抄中国作业 ']," State Council of the People's Republic of China [中华人民共和国中央人民政府], April 10, 2020, http://www.gov.cn/xinwen/2020-04/10/content_5500781.htm.
118. Secretariat of the Center for the Study of Xi Jinping's Diplomatic Thought [习近平外交思想研究中心秘书处], "Constructing a Unique Style of Chinese Diplomacy: Meaning and Paths

to Realization [塑造中国外交独特风范：内涵与实践路径]," International Studies [国际问题研究], no. 6 (2021): 10.
119. Joshua Cooper Ramo, The Beijing Consensus (London: Foreign Policy Centre, 2004), 4.
120. Garver, China's Quest, 380.
121. David Dollar, "Seven Years into China's Belt and Road," Brookings Institution, October 1, 2020, https://www.brookings.edu/blog/order-from-chaos/2020/10/01/seven-years-into-chinas-belt-and-road/.
122. There are a few cases in which China issued no comment, particularly in cases of very small island nations. In the case of democratic elections that have not been free and fair, China has also offered its congratulations to the winner.
123. Raymond Zhong, "China Congratulates Biden on Presidential Victory," New York Times, November 13, 2020, https://www.nytimes.com/2020/11/13/world/asia/china-congratulations-biden.html.
124. Richard Wike and Janell Fetterolf, "Global Public Opinion in an Era of Democratic Anxiety," Pew Research Center, December 7, 2021, https://www.pewresearch.org/global/2021/12/07/global-public-opinion-in-an-era-of-democratic-anxiety/.
125. Nathan, "China's Challenge," 158.
126. Garver, China's Quest, 477-480.
127. Nathan, "China's Challenge," 158.
128. Sophie Richardson, "China's Influence on the Global Human Rights System," Human Rights Watch, September 14, 2020, https://www.hrw.org/news/2020/09/14/chinas-influence-global-human-rights-system.
129. Lindsey W. Ford, "Refocusing the China Debate: American Allies and the Question of US-China 'Decoupling,'" Brookings Institution, February 7, 2020, https://www. brookings.edu/blog/order-from-chaos/2020/02/07/refocusing-the-china-debate-american-allies-and-the-question-of-us-china-decoupling/.
130. Steven Lee Myers, "An Alliance of Autocracies? China Wants to Lead a New World Order," New York Times, March 29, 2021, https://www.nytimes.com/2021/03/29/world/asia/china-us-russia.html.
131. "China's Warning to Biden," Wall Street Journal, March 21, 2021, https://www.wsj. com/articles/chinas-warning-to-biden-11616360915.
132. "Full Text: The Report on Human Rights Violations in the United States in 2020," Xinhua.com [新 华 网], March 24, 2021, http://www.xinhuanet.com/english/2021-03/24/c_139832301.htm.
133. Yuan Peng, president of the China Institutes of Contemporary International Relations, a government think tank, quoted in Myers, "An Alliance of Autocracies?"
134. "CCP Buys Media Influence by Paying Millions to US Dailies, Magazines: Report," Times of India, July 4, 2021, https://timesofindia.indiatimes.com/world/china/ccp-buys-media-influence-by-paying-millions-to-us-dailies-magazines-report/articles how/84109897.cms.
135. Matt Schrader, "Friends and Enemies: A Framework for Understanding Chinese Political Interference in Democratic Countries," German Marshall Fund Alliance for Securing Democracy, April 2020.
136. Sarah Cook, "The Globalization of China's Media Controls: Key Trends from 2018," The Diplomat, December 15, 2018, https://thediplomat.com/2018/12/the-globalizat ion-of-chinas-media-controls-key-trends-from-2018/.

137. Renée Diresta et al., "Telling China's Story: The Chinese Communist Party's Campaign to Shape Global Narratives," Stanford Internet Observatory, 12, https://purl.stanford.edu/pf306sw8941.

138. "Beijing's Global Media Influence 2022," Freedom House, https://freedomhouse.org/report/beijing-global-media-influence/2022/authoritarian-expansion-power-democratic-resilience.

139. Jonathan E. Hillman, "Corruption Flows Along China's Belt and Road," Center for Strategic and International Studies, January 18, 2019, https://www.csis.org/analysis/corruption-flows-along-chinas-belt-and-road.

140. Schrader, "Friends and Enemies."

141. Diresta et al., "Telling China's Story," 7. For a comprehensive review of Chinese in-fluence activities in a number of countries, especially key liberal democracies, see Larry Diamond and Orville Schell, eds., China's Influence and American Interests (Stanford, CA: Hoover Institution Press, 2018), 145-186; Anne-Marie Brady, "Magic Weapons: China's Political Influence Activities Under Xi Jinping," Wilson Center, September 18, 2017, https://www.wilsoncenter.org/article/magic-weapons-chinas-political-influence-activities-under-xi-jinping.

142. Schrader, "Friends and Enemies."

143. See Appendix 1, "Chinese Influence Operations Bureaucracy," in Diamond and Schell, eds., China's Influence and American Interests, 151-163.

144. "SPJ Code of Ethics, Society of Professional Journalists," revised September 6, 2014, https://www.spj.org/ethicscode.asp.

145. "China Publishes Revised Code of Ethics for Journalists," Xinhua, December 15, 2019, https://www.chinadaily.com.cn/a/201912/15/WS5df63766a310cf3e3557e 3b7.html.

146. Kurt M. Campbell and Jake Sullivan, "Competition Without Catastrophe: How America Can Both Challenge and Coexist with China," Foreign Affairs 98, no. 5 (2019).

147. Mark Hannah and Caroline Gray, "Global Views of American Democracy," Eurasia Group Foundation, March 31, 2020, https://egfound.org/2020/03/modeling-democracy/.

148. Lawson and Epstein, "Democracy Promotion," 20.

149. John Dotson, "The CCP's Renewed Focus on Ideological Indoctrination, Part 1: The 2019 Guidelines for 'Patriotic Education,'" Jamestown Foundation, December 10, 2019, https://jamestown.org/program/the-ccps-renewed-focus-on-ideological-ind octrination-part-1-the-2019-guidelines-for-patriotic-education/; John Dotson, "The CCP's Renewed Focus on Ideological Conditioning, Part 2: The New Five-Year Plan for Training Party Cadres," Jamestown Foundation, December 31, 2019, https://jamestown.org/program/the-ccps-renewed-focus-on-ideological-condition ing-part-2-the-new-five-year-plan-for-training-party-cadres/.

150. Abby Johnston and Catherine Trautwein, "What Is the China Model? Understanding the Country's State-Led Economic Model," Frontline, PBS, May 17, 2019, https://www.pbs.org/wgbh/frontline/article/china-trade-war-trump-tariff/.

151. Maya Wang, "China's Techno-Authoritarianism Has Gone Global," Foreign Affairs, April 8, 2021, https://www.foreignaffairs.com/articles/china/2021-04-08/chinas-techno-authoritarianism-has-gone-global. As of 2020, Beijing reportedly had 1.15 mil-lion closed-circuit television surveillance cameras installed to observe a population of roughly 20 million. Matthew Keegan, "The Most Surveilled Cities in the World," US News, August 14, 2020, www.usnews.com/news/cities/articles/2020-08-14/the-top-10-most-surveilled-cities-in-the-world.

152. Yang Yuan, "China Stifles Foreign Internet to Control Coronavirus Coverage," Financial Times,

February 17. 2020, https://www.ft.com/content/0aa9c0ec-517a-11ea-8841-482eed0038b1.

153. "Two Arrested and 13 Charged in Three Separate Cases for Alleged Participation in Malign Schemes in the United States on Behalf of the Government of the People's Republic of China," US Department of Justice Office of Public Affairs, October 24, 2022, https://www.justice.gov/opa/pr/two-arrested-and-13-charged-three-separ ate-cases-alleged-participation-malign-schemes-united.

154. "MEPs Refuse Any Agreement with China Whilst Sanctions Are in Place," European Parliament, May 20, 2021, https://www.europarl.europa.eu/news/en/pressroom/20210517IPR04123/meps-refuse-any-agreement-with-china-whilst-sanctions-are-in-place.

155. Liang Shengwen [梁生文], "A New Political Party System Contributes Chinese Wisdom to the Development of World Party Politics-International Online [新型政党制度为世界政党政治发展贡献中国智慧]," CRJ Online [国际在线], March 8, 2018, http://news.cri.cn/20180308/962b9850-3a41-45ac-57c0-a4afdaa2d9e4. html; "How China's Communist Party Trains Foreign Politicians," The Economist, December 10, 2020, https://www.economist.com/china/2020/12/10/how-chinas-communist-party-trains-foreign-politicians.

156. "Xi Jinping: Fully Confident to Provide a Chinese Solution for Mankind's Exploration of a Better Social System [习近平：完全有信心为人类对更好社会制度的探索提供中国方案]," The Paper [澎湃新闻], July 1, 2016, https://www. thepaper.cn/newsDetail_forward_1492012; "Full Text of Xi Jinping's Report at 19th CPC National Congress," China Daily, November 4, 2017, https://www.chinadaily.com.cn/china/19thcpcnationalcongress/201711/04/content_34115212.htm.

157. Seva Gunitsky, Aftershocks: Great Powers and Domestic Reforms in the Twentieth Century (Princeton: Princeton University Press, 2017).

158. Evan S. Medeiros and Taylor Fravel, "China's New Diplomacy," Foreign Affairs 82, no. 6 (2003): 22-35, 23.

159. "Liu Xiaoming, Ambassador to the UK: The Reason There Is 'Wolf Warrior' Is Because There Are 'Wolves' in the World [驻英大使刘晓明：之所以有'战狼'是因为这个世界有'狼']," CCTV.com [央视网], May 25, 2020, http://m.news.cctv. com/2020/05/24/ARTI8BYmADeqivsgNvMiMRF4200524.shtml.

160. Zhu Zhiqun, "Interpreting China's 'Wolf-Warrior Diplomacy,'" The Diplomat, May 15, 2020, https://thediplomat.com/2020/05/interpreting-chinas-wolf-warrior-diplomacy/.

161. "The Glorious Course of China's Cross-Century Diplomacy (Abstract) [中国跨世纪外交的光辉历程 (摘要)]," Ministry of Foreign Affairs of the People's Republic of China [中华人民共和国外交部], October 17, 2002, https://www.mfa.gov.cn/web/ziliao_674904/zt_674979/ywzt_675099/zt2002_675989/2319_676055/200210/t20021017_7965253.shtml.

162. Xi Jinping [习近平], "Xi Urges Breaking New Ground in Major Country Diplomacy with Chinese Characteristics [努力开创中国特色大国外交新局面]," Xinhua. com [新华网], June 22, 2018, http://www.xinhuanet.com/politics/2018-06/23/c_ 1123025806.htm; Wang Yi [王毅], "Speech by Minister Wang Yi at the Luncheon of the Second World Peace Forum [王毅部长在第二届世界和平论坛午餐会上的演讲]," Ministry of Foreign Affairs of the People's Republic of China [中华人民共和国外交部], June 27, 2013, https://www.mfa.gov.cn/web/wjbzhd/201306/t20130627_349225.shtml.

163. "The Enrichment and Development of the Theoretical and Practical Innovations of Major-Country Diplomacy with Chinese Characteristics (People's Opinion) [丰富发展了中国特色大国外交理论和实践创新成果(人民观点)]," People.cn [人民网], October 11, 2022, http://theory.people.com.cn/n1/2022/1011/c40531-32542 668.html.

第四章

1. Valerie Insinna, "A US Air Force War Game Shows What the Service Needs to Hold Off—or Win Against—China in 2030," Defense News, April 12, 2021, https://www.defensenews.com/training-sim/2021/04/12/a-us-air-force-war-game-shows-what-the-service-needs-to-hold-off-or-win-against-china-in-2030/.
2. "A Conversation with US Indo-Pacific Command's Adm. Philip Davidson," American Enterprise Institute event, March 4, 2021, https://www.aei.org/events/a-conversat ion-with-us-indo-pacific-commands-adm-philip-davidson/.
3. The rationale behind China's anti-ship ballistic missile program, for example, highlights the need to target US carriers, avoid the humiliation of 1996, and "reunify" with Taiwan. Liu Min [刘 敏], "Can the US Stop China's ASBMs? [美军能拦截中国反舰弹道导弹吗?]," The Paper [澎 湃 新 闻], October 27, 2020, https://www.thepa per.cn/newsDetail_forward_9745432.
4. Lu Jun [陆 军], "What Is the Real Informatized War—Reflections on the Pattern of Future Wars [什么是真正的信息化战争—对未来战争形态的思考]," PLA Daily [解放军报], January 12, 2017, http://www.xinhuanet.com//mil/2017-01/12/c_1294 43322_2.htm
5. Ren Tianyou [任 天 佑], Road to Reform Strengthening the Military [问 道 改 革 强 军] (Beijing: National Defense University Press [国防大学出版社], 2015).
6. Hu Jintao [胡锦涛], "Building a Consolidated National Defense and a Strong Military That Is Commensurate with National Security and Development Interests [建设与国家安全和发展利益相适应的巩固国防和强大军队]," in Selected Writings of Hu Jintao, Volume III [胡锦涛文选，第三卷], ed. CPC Editorial Committee [中共中央文献编辑委员会] (Beijing: People's Publishing House [人民出版社], 2016), 37.
7. Zheng Bijian, "China's 'Peaceful Rise' to Great-Power Status," Foreign Affairs, September 2005, https://www.foreignaffairs.com/articles/asia/2005-09-01/chi nas-peaceful-rise-great-power-status. The concept was later revised to peaceful development.
8. Robert B. Zoellick, "Whither China: From Membership to Responsibility?," Remarks to the National Committee on US-China Relations, September 21, 2005, https://2001-2009.state.gov/s/d/former/zoellick/rem/53682.htm.
9. David Shambaugh, China Goes Global: The Partial Power (New York: Oxford University Press, 2013), 217.
10. Hu Jintao [胡 锦 涛], "Integrating Both the Domestic and International Imperatives, Improving the Capability of Diplomatic Work [统筹国内国际两个大局，提高外交工作能力水平]," in Selected Writings of Hu Jintao, 236-238.
11. Hu Jintao [胡 锦 涛], "Integrating Both the Domestic and International Imperatives, Improving the Capability of Diplomatic Work [统筹国内国际两个大局，提高外交工作能力水平]," in Selected Writings of Hu Jintao, 236-238.
12. Luo Jianbo [罗 建 波], "What Kind of Great Power Responsibility Should China Assume [中国应该承担什么样的大国责任]," Xuexi Daily [学习时报], September 15, 2014, http://theory.people.com.cn/n/2014/0915/c40531-25660831.html. See also Xu Jin [徐 进], "How China Should Fulfill Its International Responsibilities [中 国 应 该 如 何 履 行 国 际 责 任]," China Daily, October 11, 2014, https://column.chinadaily. com.cn/a/201410/11/WS5bed2437a3101a87ca93e050.html.
13. Xiao Tianliang [肖 天 亮], ed., Science of Military Strategy [战 略 学] (Beijing: National Defense University Press [国防大学出版社], 2015), 297.
14. Hu Erjie [胡二杰], "UN Peacekeeping Operations and China's National Image Building [联

合国维和行动与中国国家形象建设]," Quarterly Journal of Public Diplomacy [公共外交季刊], no. 3 (2017): 92-99.
15. Alan J. Vick et al., Preparing the U.S. Air Force for Military Operations Other than War (Santa Monica, CA: RAND Corporation, 1972).
16. James Siebens and Ryan Lucas, Military Operations Other than War in China's Foreign Policy (Washington, DC: Stimson Center, 2022).
17. Meng Wenting [孟文婷], "Literature Review on China's Participation in UN Peacekeeping Operations [中国参与联合国维和行动的研究述评]," Journal of International Studies [国际政治研究], no. 4 (2017): 92-94.
18. Hu, "UN Peacekeeping Operations and China's National Image Building," 92-99.
19. Tang Hao [唐昊], "Strategic Considerations on China's Protection on Overseas Interests [关于中国海外利益保护的战略思考]," Contemporary International Relations [现代国际关系], no. 6 (2011): 4-5; Oriana Skylar Mastro, "China Can't Stay Home," National Interest, no. 135 (January/February 2015): 38-45.
20. Mastro, "China Can't Stay Home," 39-40.
21. Mastro, "China Can't Stay Home," 41.
22. "The Diversified Employment of China's Armed Forces," State Council Information Office, April 2013, http://english.www.gov.cn/archive/white_paper/2014/08/23/content_281474982986506.htm.
23. Tuan Vu, "The PLAN's Anti-Piracy Missions in the Gulf of Aden, Africa," Journal of Military and Strategic Studies 20, no. 1 (2019): 226-233; "United Nations Documents on Piracy," United Nations Division for Ocean Affairs and the Law of the Sea, May 24, 2012, https://www.un.org/depts/los/piracy/piracy_documents.htm.
24. "China's 41st Naval Escort Taskforce Sets Off for Gulf of Aden," Chinese Ministry of Defense, May 19, 2022, http://eng.mod.gov.cn/news/2022-05/19/content_4911 166.htm; "10 Years of China's Gulf of Aden Journey: A Global Player with More Responsibility," CGTN, December 27, 2018, https://news.cgtn.com/news/3d3d774e3 2456a4e31457a6333566d54/share_p.html.
25. Wang Hairong [王海荣], "Forging the Shield of Peace: China Accelerates Modernization of National Defense and Military Through Reforms [铸造和平之盾：中国通过改革加快国防和军队现代化建设]," Beijing Review [北京周报], August 12, 2022.
26. "Troop and Police Contributors," United Nations Peacekeeping, https://peacekeep ing.un.org/en/troop-and-police-contributors, accessed June 26, 2023.
27. Daniel M. Hartnett, "China's First Deployment of Combat Forces to a UN Peacekeeping Mission—South Sudan," US-China Economic and Security Review Commission, March 13, 2012, https://www.uscc.gov/sites/default/files/Research/MEMO-PLA-PKO_final_0.pdf.
28. State Council Information Office of the People's Republic of China [中华人民共和国国务院新闻办公室], "The Diversified Employment of China's Armed Forces [中国武装力量的多样化运用]," April 2013, https://www.gov.cn/zhengce/2013-04/16/content_2618550.htm.
29. See "Documentary of China's Evacuation of Overseas Chinese from Yemen [中国从也门撤侨纪实]," People's Daily Online [人民网], April 17, 2015, http://politics.peo ple.com.cn/n/2015/0407/c70731-26809482.html.
30. "Most of the Chinese Citizens in Sudan Have Been Evacuated in Batches, Orderly and Safely [大部分在苏丹中国公民已分批、有序、安全撤离]," Ministry of Foreign Affairs of the People's Republic of China [中华人民共和国外交部], April 26, 2023, https://www.mfa.gov.cn/wjbzwfwpt/kzx/tzgg/202304/t20230426_11066 274.html.
31. For the full dataset, see www.orianaskylarmastro.com/upstart.

32. Matthew Southerland, "The Chinese Military's Role in Overseas Humanitarian Assistance and Disaster Relief: Contributions and Concerns," US-China Economic and Security Review Commission, July 11, 2019, 2, https://www.uscc.gov/research/chinese-militarys-role-overseas-humanitarian-assistance-and-disaster-relief-contri butions.

33. Tang Yongsheng [唐永胜], "China and UN Peacekeeping Operations [中国与联合国维和行动]," World Economics and Politics [世界经济与政治], no. 9 (2002): 42.

34. Joel Wuthnow, "PLA Operation Lessons from UN Peacekeeping," in The PLA Beyond Borders: Chinese Military Operations in Regional and Global Context, ed. Joel Wuthnow et al. (Washington, DC: National Defense University Press, 2021), 236.

35. Lv You [吕 游], "Research on Building Up the Support Capability of Military Airlifting in Overseas Non-War Military Actions [涉外非战争军事行动航空运输保障能力建设研究]," Traffic Engineering and Technology for National Defense [国防交通工程与技术], no. 6 (2015): 1; Tan Wenhu [谈 文 虎], "Diversified Military Tasks Draw Innovations in Military Training [多样化军事任务牵引军事训练创新]," PLA Daily [解放军报], July 1, 2008.

36. Southerland, "The Chinese Military's Role in Overseas Humanitarian Assistance and Disaster Relief," 4-5.

37. Zhang Xin [张 鑫], "China: The PLA's Logistical Base in Djibouti Is a Decision Made by Friendly Consultation Between China and Djibouti [中方：解放军驻吉布提保障基地系中吉两国友好协商作出的决定]," Global Times [环球时报], July 12, 2017, https://world.huanqiu.com/article/9CaKrnK41VZ.

38. Tang Yongsheng [唐永胜], ed., On National Competitive Strategy [国家竞争战略论] (Beijing: Current Affairs Press [时事出版社], 2018), 241-242.

39. Liu Wanli [刘万利], "Put the People First, Diplomacy for the People [以人为本外交为民]," People's Daily Online [人民网], April 7, 2014, http://military.people.com.cn/n/2015/0407/c172467-26804330.html.

40. Ren Huai [任怀], "This Is Our Home Country That You Can Always Trust [这就是祖国，你永远可以相信她]," People's Daily [人民日报], May 7, 2023, http://world.people.com.cn/n1/2023/0507/c1002-32680345.html.

41. Data taken from IMDB's Box Office Mojo, https://www.boxofficemojo.com/release/rl4093871617/, accessed July 28, 2023.

42. In 2012, their behavior improved, with China starting to escort all merchant ships, regardless of nationality. Vu, "The PLAN's Anti-Piracy Missions in the Gulf of Aden, Africa," 230.

43. "How We Are Funded," UN Peacekeeping, https://peacekeeping.un.org/en/how-we-are-funded, accessed June 26, 2023; "UN Document A/67/224/Add. 1: Scale of Assessments for the Apportionment of the Expenses of the United Nations Peacekeeping Operations," United Nations General Assembly, December 27, 2015, https://documents-ddsny.un.org/doc/UNDOC/GEN/N12/665/78/PDF/N1266578.pdf?OpenElement.

44. "Troop and Police Contributors," United Nations Peacekeeping, downloaded June 26, 2023, https://peacekeeping.un.org/en/troop-and-police-contributors; "China Takes First Step in $1 Billion Pledge to U.N. to Fund Peace, Development," Reuters, May 6, 2016, https://www.reuters.com/article/us-china-un-idUSKCN0XX1YI/.

45. See appendix on China's HADR activities at www.orianaskylarmastro.com/upstart.

46. Southerland, "The Chinese Military's Role in Overseas Humanitarian Assistance and Disaster Relief," 6, 10; "Ebola: From Recovery to Self-Reliance," USAID, https://2017-2020.usaid.gov/ebola, accessed August 4, 2023.

47. Evan S. Medeiros, Reluctant Restraint: The Evolution of China's Nonproliferation Policies and

Practices, 1980-2004 (Stanford, CA: Stanford University Press, 2007).
48. Alastair Iain Johnston, Social States: China in International Institutions, 1980-2000, Vol. 108 (Princeton: Princeton University Press, 2008), xxi.
49. "China in the Nuclear Suppliers Group (NSG)," US Department of State Archive, May 18, 2004, https://2001-2009.state.gov/t/isn/rls/rm/32570.htm.
50. These seventeen treaties are: the Comprehensive Test Ban Treaty, the Partial Nuclear Test Ban Treaty, the Convention on Nuclear Safety, the London Convention on Nuclear Dumping, the Convention on Assistance in Case of Nuclear Accident, the Convention on Early Notification of Nuclear Accident, the Convention on the Physical Protection of Nuclear Material, the International Convention on the Suppression of Acts of Nuclear Terrorism, the Nuclear Non-Proliferation Treaty, the Biological Weapons Convention, the Chemical Weapons Convention, the Arms Trade Treaty, the Convention on Certain Conventional Weapons, the Environmental Modification Techniques Treaty, the Outer Space Treaty, the Seabed Arms Control Treaty, and the Antarctic Treaty.
51. Jeff Abramson and Greg Webb, "U.S. to Quit Arms Trade Treaty," Arms Control Association, May 2019, https://www.armscontrol.org/act/2019-05/news/us-quit-arms-trade-treaty.
52. Xu Nengwu [徐能武] and Long Kun [龙坤], "Practical Arguments, Theoretical Logic, and Engagement Strategies for Arms Control in Space [太空军备控制的现实争辩、理论逻辑和参与策略]," International Outlook [国际展望], 6 (2021): 65, 73.
53. Tang Yongsheng [唐永胜], ed., On National Competitive Strategy [国家竞争战略论] (Beijing: Current Affairs Press [时事出版社], 2018), 241-242.
54. State Council Information Office of the People's Republic of China [中华人民共和国国务院新闻办公室], "China's National Defense in 2010 [2010 年中国的国防]," March 31, 2011, http://www.gov.cn/zhengce/2011-03/31/content_2618567.htm; "Statement by H. E. Amb. Li Song on Nuclear Non-Proliferation at the Tenth NPT Review Conference," Ministry of Foreign Affairs of the People's Republic of China [中华人民共和国外交部], August 10, 2022, https://www.fmprc.gov.cn/eng/wjb_663 304/zzjg_663340/jks_665232/kjfywj_665252/202208/t20220810_10738694.html.
55. Medeiros, Reluctant Restraint.
56. Johnston, Social States, xxvi.
57. Fan Jishe [樊吉社], "China-US Arms Control: Cooperation and Divergence, Motivations and Trends [中美军控_合作与分歧、动因与走势]," International Economic Review [国际经济评论], 5 (2001): 41.
58. Xin Yi [忻怿], "From Resistance to Participation: China-US Nuclear Dialogue (1976-1992) [由抵制到参与：中美核军控对话 (1976-1992)]," Military History Studies [军事历史研究], no. 5 (2018): 55-70.
59. Gao Wanglai [高望来], "New Security Doctrine and China's Participation in the Arms Control System [新安全观与中国参与军控体系的实践]," Social Sciences [社会科学], no. 4 (2014): 29-36.
60. Yang Wenjing [杨文静], "China's Integration into International Regimes and the US Factors [中国融入国际机制与美国因素]," Contemporary International Relations [现代国际关系], no. 10 (2004): 29-35.
61. "The Hague Code of Conduct (HCOC)," Center for Arms Control and Non-Proliferation, https://armscontrolcenter.org/wp-content/uploads/2019/12/HCOC-new.pdf, accessed July 29, 2023.
62. Alastair Iain Johnston, "China in a World of Orders: Rethinking Compliance and Challenge in

Beijing's International Relations," *International Security* 44, no. 2 (2019): 9-60.

63. Shirley A. Kan, "China and Proliferation of Weapons of Mass Destruction and Missiles: Policy Issues," Congressional Research Service, January 5, 2015.

64. Yin Chengde [尹承德], "New START Treaty and the Dream of Nuclear-Weapon-Free World [美俄核裁军条约与无核世界神话]," *International Studies* [国际问题研究], no. 4 (2010): 11-18.

65. Steven Jiang and Ben Westcott, "China Says It Won't Join Nuclear Talks Until the US Reduces Its Arsenal," CNN, July 8, 2020, https://www.cnn.com/2020/07/08/asia/china-us-nuclear-treaty-intl-hnk/index.html.

66. Academy of Military Science, Military Strategy Research Center [军事科学院军事战略研究部], ed., *Science of Military Strategy* [战略学] (Beijing: Military Science Press [军事科学出版社], 2013), 177.

67. "Editorial: On China-Related Nuclear Arms Control Issues, the US Side Should Not Forcefully Lead the Rhythm [社评：关于涉华核军控问题，美方莫强带节奏]," *Global Times* [环球时报], November 18, 2021, https://opinion.huanqiu.com/article/45dYHEuRtod.

68. "The First Gulf War," Office of the Historian, US Department of State, https://history.state.gov/departmenthistory/short-history/firstgulf, accessed January 19, 2024.

69. Jiang Zemin [江泽民], "On Military Strategic Guidelines and National Defense Technology [关于军事战略方针和国防科技问题]," in *Selected Writings of Jiang Zemin, Volume I* [江泽民文选，第一卷] (Beijing: People's Publishing House [人民出版社], 2006), 142-147.

70. Zhang Wannian Writing Group [张万年写作组], *Biography of Zhang Wannian, Volume II* [张万年传（下）] (Beijing: PLA Publishing House [解放军出版社], 2011), 62; Liu Huaqing [刘华清], "Unswervingly Advance Along the Road of Building a Modern Army with Chinese Characteristics [坚定不移地沿着建设有中国特色现代化军队的道路前进]," *PLA Daily* [解放军报], August 6, 1993.

71. Zhang Wannian Writing Group, *Biography of Zhang Wannian, Volume II*, 63.

72. Liu, "Unswervingly Advance Along the Road of Building a Modern Army with Chinese Characteristics."

73. He Zhu [荷竹], *Experts Evaluate the Iraq War* [专家评说伊拉克战争](Beijing: Military Science Press [军事科学出版社], 2004), 147-148; PLA Academy of Military Sciences [军事科学院军事历史研究部], *The Complete History of the Gulf War* [海湾战争全史] (Beijing: PLA Publishing House [解放出版社], 2000), 458; Jiang Zemin [江泽民], *Selected Writings of Jiang Zemin, Volume III* [江泽民文选，第三卷] (Beijing: People's Publishing House [人民出版社], 2006), 359-360.

74. Li Chenggang [李成刚], "Local Wars After the End of the Cold War—Gulf War [冷战结束后的局部战争—海湾战争]," *Military History* [军事史林], no. 2 (2021): 17-29.

75. Zhang Zhen [张震], *Zhang Zhen's Memoir, Volume II* [张震回忆录（下）] (Beijing: PLA Publishing House [解放军出版社], 2003), 363; He, *Experts Evaluate the Iraq War*, 151.

76. Jiang, "The International Situation and Military Strategic Guidelines [国际形势和军战略方针]," in *Selected Writings of Jiang Zemin, Volume III*, 278-294; Bai Ruixue [白瑞雪], Xiong Zhengyan [熊争艳], and Li Zhihui [李志辉], "China's Active Defense Military Strategic Guidelines Have Undergone Many Adjustments [中国积极防御军事战略方针历经多次调整]," *People's Daily Online* [人民网], May 26, 2015, http://military.people.com.cn/n/2015/0526/c172467-27057937.html.

77. Bai, Xiong, and Li, "China's Active Defense Military Strategic Guidelines Have Undergone Many Adjustments"; M. Taylor Fravel, *Active Defense: China's Military Strategy since 1949*

(Princeton: Princeton University Press, 2019), 218.
78. Bai, Xiong, and Li, "China's Active Defense Military Strategic Guidelines Have Undergone Many Adjustments."
79. Jiang Zemin [江泽民], The Selected Works of Jiang Zemin, Volume III [江泽民文选 (第三卷)] (Beijing: People's Publishing House [人民出版社], 2006), 359-360.
80. "China's National Defence in 2004 [2004年中国的国防]," State Council Information Office of the People's Republic of China [中华人民共和国国务院新闻办公室], May 27, 2005, http://www.gov.cn/zhengce/2005-05/27/content_2615731.htm.
81. Tan, "Diversified Military Tasks Draw Innovations in Military Training"; Liu, "Unswervingly Advance Along the Road of Building a Modern Army with Chinese Characteristics"; Tan Wenhu [谈文虎], "Diversified Military Tasks Draw Innovations in Military Training [多样化军事任务牵引军事训练创新]," PLA Daily [解放军报], July 1, 2008.
82. For some examples of how the services worked to meet these goals, see Second Artillery Political Department [第二炮兵政治部], Glorious Era: Reflecting on the Second Artillery's Development and Advances During the Period of Reform and Opening [辉煌年代：回顾在改革开放中发展前进的第二炮兵] (Beijing: CCP Central Committee Literature Publishing House [中央文献出版社], 2008), 534-538; "Navy Commander: China's Five Major Naval Services Are Transforming to Information Technology [海军司令员：中国海军5大兵种正向信息化转型]," Xinhua News [新华社], April 15, 2009, http://mil.news.sina.com.cn/2009-04-15/1834548881.html; Li Zhihui [李志晖] et al., "Chinese Navy Launches Strategic Transformation [中国海军启动战略转型]," Xinhua News [新华社], May 26, 2015, http://www.xinhuanet.com/politics/2015-05/26/c_1115408221.htm; Zhang Li [张力], "Chinese Air Force's Strategic Transformation: From Zero to 'Integrating Aviation and Space Power, and Strike and Defense Capabilities' [中国空军战略转型历程：从零到空天一体攻防兼备]," News China [中国新闻周刊], November 12, 2014, http://news.sina.com.cn/c/2014-11-12/170731133436.shtml.
83. Xi Jinping [习近平], "Secure a Decisive Victory in Building a Moderately Prosperous Society in All Respects and Strive for the Great Success of Socialism with Chinese Characteristics for a New Era—Delivered at the 19th National Congress of the Communist Party of China [决胜全面建成小康社会夺取新时代中国特色社会主义伟大胜利—在中国共产党第十九次全国代表大会上的报告]," State Council of the People's Republic of China [中华人民共和国中央人民政府], October 18, 2017, https://www.gov.cn/zhuanti/2017-10/27/content_5234876.htm.
84. Chen Jiesheng [陈杰生] et al., Strategic Conception of Space Military Utilization [太空军事运用战略构想] (Beijing: National Defense Industry Press [国防工业出版社], 2021).
85. Li Daguang [李大光], "On Space Control [试论制天权]," Journal of the Academy of Equipment Command and Technology [装备指挥技术学院学报] 15, no. 3 (June 2004): 55-60.
86. Chang Xianqi [常显奇], "Space Strategy and National Security [空间战略与国家安全]," Chinese Military Sciences [中国军事科学], no. 1 (2002): 12.
87. Chang Xianqi [常显奇], "Space Strength and the New Revolution in Military Affairs [空间力量与新军事变革]," Chinese Military Sciences [中国军事科学], no. 3 (2003): 59.
88. Zhu Tingchang [朱听昌] and Liu Jing [刘菁], "Vying for Space Supremacy: The Development and Influence of America's 'High Frontier' Strategy [争夺制天权：美国'高边疆'战略的发展历程及其影响]," Military History Studies [军事历史研究], no. 3 (2004): 115-126.
89. "Aerospace Science and Technology Group Released the 'Blue Book on China's Aerospace

Science and Technology Activities (2021)' [航天集团发布 ' 中国航天科技活动蓝皮书(2021年)]," China Aerospace Science and Technology Corporation [中国航天科技集团有限公司], February 11, 2022; China Power Team, "How Is China Advancing Its Space Launch Capabilities?," ChinaPower, November 5, 2019, https://chinapower.csis.org/china-space-launch/.

90. ChinaPower Team, "How Is China Advancing Its Space Launch Capabilities?"

91. William J. Broad, "How Space Became the Next 'Great Power' Contest Between the U.S. and China," New York Times, January 24, 2021, https://www.nytimes.com/2021/01/24/us/politics/trump-biden-pentagon-space-missiles-satellite.html; Peter Wood, Alex Stone, and Taylor E. Lee, China's Ground Segment: Building the Pillars of a Great Space Power (Montgomery, AL: China Aerospace Studies Institute, 2021).

92. "Two Chinese Missiles Failed to Launch in 1996 GPS Suspected to Be Tampered with by the US Military [96 年 我 2 枚导弹发射失败 GPS 疑被美军做手脚]," Global Times [环球时报], December 30, 2012, https://mil.huanqiu.com/article/9CaKrnJy pD4; Liu Jingfeng [刘景丰], "A Brief History of Beidou: Understanding the 26-Year Growth Path of the Domestic Navigation System [北斗简史：一文读懂国产导航的 26 年成长路]," The Paper [澎湃], June 24, 2020, https://m.thepaper.cn/baijia hao_7979721.

93. "UCS Satellite Database," Union of Concerned Scientists, January 1, 2023, https://www.ucsusa.org/resources/satellite-database.

94. ChinaPower Team, "How Is China Advancing Its Space Launch Capabilities?"

95. Jia Huajie [贾华杰] et al., "Network-centric Warfare and Its New Technologies [网络中心战及其新技术]," Defense Science and Technology [国防科技] 32.04 (2011): 44.

96. Ashley Townshend, Brendan Thomas-Noone, and Matilda Steward, "Averting Crisis: American Strategy, Military Spending and Collective Defence in the Indo-Pacific," United States Study Centre, August 19, 2019, https://www.ussc.edu.au/analysis/averting-crisis-american-strategy-military-spending-and-collective-defe nce-in-the-indo-pacific.

97. "World Fleet Statistics 1999," Lloyd's Register Foundation, 2000.

98. Ronald O'Rourke, "China Naval Modernization: Implications for U.S. Navy Capabilities—Background and Issues for Congress," Congressional Research Service, May 25, 2023, https://crsreports.congress.gov/product/pdf/RL/RL33 153/267.

99. James R. Holmes and Toshi Yoshihara, Red Star over the Pacific, 2nd ed. (Annapolis: US Naval Institute Press, 2018), 156-157.

100. Jiang, The Selected Works of Jiang Zemin, Volume III, 542.

101. Zhu Feng [朱 锋], "The Period of Strategic Opportunity in China's Next Ten Years: Do We Have to Make Different Choices? [中国未来十年的战略机遇期：我们必须做出新的选择吗 ?]," Journal of International Studies [国际政治研究], no. 2 (2014).

102. Han Weifeng [韩卫锋] et al., Practical Military Reform [实战化的军事改革] (Beijing: PLA Press [解放军出版社], 2015).

103. "General Secretary Xi Jinping Discusses How to Understand and Take Advantage of the Important Period of Strategic Opportunity [习近平总书记谈如何认识和把握重要战略机遇期]," Qiushi [求 是 网], September 5, 2022,http://www.qstheory.cn/zhuanqu/202209/05/c_1128976641.htm.

104. "The Maritime Strategy, 1984," in John B. Hattendorf and Peter M. Swartz, U.S. Naval Strategy in the 1980s: Selected Documents (Newport, RI: Naval War College Press, 2008).

105. "US Aircraft Carrier Commander Asserts Freedom to Navigate the South China Sea," Radio Free Asia, September 13, 2021, https://www.rfa.org/english/news/china/usa-

southchinasea-09132021185504.html.

106. For a discussion of the role that carriers play in US strategy, see Michael E. O'Hanlon, "The Future of the Aircraft Carrier and the Carrier Air Wing," Joint Forces Quarterly 90, no. 3 (2018): 16-23.
107. For a good review of the debate over the carrier's utility, see Robert C. Rubel, "The Future of the Future of Aircraft Carriers," Naval War College Review 64, no. 4 (2011): 1-16.
108. Ronald O'Rourke, "Navy Ford (CVN-78) Class Aircraft Carrier Program: Background and Issues for Congress," Congressional Research Service, March 27, 2023, https://crsreports.congress.gov/product/pdf/RS/RS20643.
109. Liu Huaqing [刘华清], Memoirs of Liu Huaqing [刘华清回忆录] (Beijing: PLA Publishing House [解放军出版社], 2004), 478.
110. Liu, Memoirs of Liu Huaqing, 480.
111. Ye Zicheng [叶自成], "China's Sea Power Must Be Subordinate to Its Land Power [中国海权须从属于陆权]," International Herald Leader [国际先驱导报], March 2, 2007, http://news.sina.com.cn/c/2007-03-02/101312410732.shtml.
112. Cheng Gang [程刚] and Zhang Mian [张勉], "Why China Did Not Build Aircraft Carrier [中国为何不造航母]," Party Forum [党政论坛], no. 1 (2003): 24.
113. "The Significance of the Varyag Aircraft Carrier to China's National Strategy Is Something That Cannot Be Purchased with Money [瓦良格号航母对中国意义国家战略金钱买不来]," Sina.com [新浪军事], March 24, 2015, http://mil.news.sina.com.cn/2015-03-24/1058825518.html; Liu Huaqing Chronicles, Volume 3 [刘华清年谱（下卷）] (Beijing: PLA Publishing House [解放军出版社], 2016), 1195.
114. "China's First Aircraft Carrier Liaoning Formally Enters Service [中国首艘航空母舰"辽宁舰"正式交接入列]," China News [中国新闻网], September 25, 2012, https://www.chinanews.com.cn/mil/2012/09-25/4209663.shtml.; Xiong Songce [熊崧策], "The Varyag That Came All This Distance [不远万里来到中国的'瓦良格'号]," Science and Technology Review [科技导报] 30, no. 5 (2012).
115. Liu Zhaohui [刘朝晖], "What Is the Status of China's Aircraft Carrier Development [中国航母发展到什么地位了]," Xinmin Weekly [新民周刊], June 18, 2021, https://m.xinminweekly.com.cn/content/16015.html.
116. "China's 048 Aircraft Carrier Project Is Revealed: Building 10 Carriers by the Nation's 100th Anniversary [中国"048航母建造工程"曝光 建国百年将有10艘]," iFeng [凤凰网], January 17, 2017, http://imil.ifeng.com/50587137/news.shtml?src tag=pc2m&back&back.
117. For example, see Lara Seligman, "Nothing Projects Power Like an Aircraft Carrier. Does the Pentagon Think Otherwise?," Foreign Policy, March 1, 2019, https://foreig npolicy.com/2019/03/01/nothing-projects-power-like-an-aircraft-carrier-does-the-pentagon-think-otherwise-mattis-military-uss-truman/.
118. "Military and Security Developments Involving the People's Republic of China 2022," US Department of Defense, November 2022, https://media.defense.gov/2022/Nov/29/2003122279/-1/-1/1/2022-MILITARY-AND-SECURITY-DEVEL OPMENTS-INVOLVING-THE-PEOPLES-REPUBLIC-OF-CHINA.PDF.
119. Rush Doshi, The Long Game: China's Grand Strategy and the Displacement of American Order (New York: Oxford University Press, 2021), 207.
120. Robbie Gramer and Jack Detsch, "China Eyes Pacific Supremacy with New Carrier," Foreign Policy, July 15, 2021, https://foreignpolicy.com/2021/07/15/china-aircraft-carrier-pacific-security/.

121. "Nuclear Submarines and Aircraft Carriers," United States Environmental Protection Agency, updated July 14, 2022, https://www.epa.gov/radtown/nuclear-submarines-and-aircraft-carriers; ChinaPower Team, "What Do We Know (So Far) About China's Second Aircraft Carrier?," ChinaPower, April 22, 2017, https://chi napower.csis.org/china-aircraft-carrier-type-001a/. ChinaPower Team, "How Does China's First Aircraft Carrier Stack Up?," ChinaPower, December 9, 2015, https://chinapower.csis.org/aircraft-carrier/. More bullish Chinese assessments claim the Fujian is getting close to US carrier capabilities.

122. "Navy Aircraft Carriers: Cost-Effectiveness of Conventionally and Nuclear-Powered Carriers," Government Accountability Office, National Security and International Affairs Division, August 1998, https://www.govinfo.gov/content/pkg/GAOREPO RTS-NSIAD-98-1/html/GAOREPORTS-NSIAD-98-1.htm.

123. David Axe, "Why China Is Relentlessly Pursuing Nuclear Aircraft Carriers," National Interest, January 27, 2022, https://nationalinterest.org/blog/reboot/why-china-relen tlessly-pursuing-nuclear-aircraft-carriers-200024.

124. Jun Wu [军 武], "What Difficulties Does China Face in Building a Giant Nuclear-Powered Aircraft Carrier [中国要造巨型核动力航母还面临哪些难关]," Life and Disaster [生命与灾害], no. 3 (2022).

125. Jun Wu [军武], "How Will China's Aircraft Carrier Fleet Develop in the Future [中国海军航母舰队，未来会向哪方面发展]," Life and Disaster [生命与灾害], no. 12 (2021).

126. "China's Next Aircraft-Carrier Will Be Its Biggest," The Economist, July 3, 2021, https://www.economist.com/china/2021/07/03/chinas-next-aircraft-carrier-will-be-its-biggest.

127. "The Liaoning Carrier Launched and Recovered 200 Aircraft in Just 10 Days, Japan Is Anxious [辽宁舰舰载机 10 天起降超 200 次 日本很焦虑]," CCTV [央视网], May 18, 2022, https://v.cctv.com/2022/05/18/VIDENeVqD9AIz565aPRmSz1x220 518.shtml.

128. Chad Peltier, "China's Logistics Capabilities for Expeditionary Operations," US-China Economic and Security Review Commission, April 15, 2020, available at https://www.uscc.gov/research/chinas-logistics-capabilities-expeditionary-ope rations.

129. "The Significance of the Varyag Aircraft Carrier."

130. Li Gang, "China Refitting Aircraft Carrier Body for Research, Training," Xinhua News, July 27, 2011, https://web.archive.org/web/20140104005718/http://eng.mod.gov.cn/TopNews/2011-07/27/content_4284108.htm; "Beijing Says Liaoning Is Now a 'Combat Carrier,' " Asia Times, April 25, 2019, https://asiatimes.com/2019/04/beij ing-says-liaoning-is-now-a-combat-carrier/.

131. Ni Guanghui [倪 光 辉], "Domestic-Made Aircraft Carrier, Expanding China's New Blue Ocean [国产航母开拓中国新蓝海]," People.cn [人民网], April 27, 2017, http://opinion.people.com.cn/n1/2017/0427/c1003-29238768.html; Yang Zhen [杨 震] and Cai Liang [蔡亮], "On Aircraft Carriers and China's Seapower [论航空母舰与中国海权]," Contemporary World [当代世界], no. 8 (2017): 42-45.

132. Zhong Sheng [钟声], "No One Has the Rights to Judge Our Development of Aircraft Carriers [对我发展航母说三道四没资格]," Huanqiu.com [环球网], September 29, 2012, https://mil.huanqiu.com/article/9CaKrnJxfDm; "China Aircraft Carrier: Sailing from Today to the Future [中国航母：从今天驶向未来]," PLA Daily [解放军报], September 26, 2012, http://mil.news.sina.com.cn/2012-09-26/0639702133.html.

133. "Premier Zhou: I Cannot Be Resigned to the Fact I Haven't Seen the Aircraft Carrier [周总理：看不到航母我不甘心啊！]," State Administration of Science, Technology and Industry for National Defense, PRC [国家国防科技工业局], September 29, 2013, http://gfplatform.cnsa.gov.cn/n6909/n7005/c39340/cont ent.html.

134. "Chinese Aircraft Carrier Under Construction, Will Not Enter Other Countries [中国航母在建不会驶入他国]," Hong Kong Business Report [香港商报], June 7, 2011, quoted in Adam Liff, "Shadowing the Hegemon? Great Power Norms, Socialization, and the Military Trajectories of Rising Powers" (PhD dissertation, Princeton University, June 2014).
135. Liu, Memoirs of Liu Huaqing, 477-479.
136. "Stories of Aircraft Carrier Liaoning," CCTV, August 26, 2017, available at https://www.youtube.com/watch?v=vzQ_I_aVusA.
137. Liu, Memoirs of Liu Huaqing, 479.
138. "Aircraft Carrier Made in China," CCTV Voice of China, June 17, 2017, https://youtu.be/XsrdFSqOWB8; "People's Navy Pursues Its Dream for 70 Years: Reviewing the Past Life of the First Aircraft Carrier Liaoning!," CCTV National Memories, April 24, 2019, https://youtu.be/Q lvdZd3DM.
139. Li Longyi [李 龙 伊], "The First Aircraft Carrier (New China's 'Firsts' Chapter of National Defense) [第一艘航空母舰(新中国的第一'·国防篇)]," People.cn [人民网], October 7, 2019, http://politics.people.com.cn/n1/2019/1007/c1001-31385 573.html; Liu, Memoirs of Liu Huaqing, 479.
140. Wang Hongliang [王宏亮], "Toward the Deep Blue: What the Fujian Could Do in the Long Term (2/2) [走向深蓝：福建舰的远期愿景（下）]," The Paper [澎湃新闻], July 14, 2022, https://www.thepaper.cn/newsDetail_forward_18978204.
141. Jake Wilson, "China's Domestic Aircraft Carrier Program: Modernization and Challenges," Wild Blue Yonder, November 12, 2021, https://www.airuniversity. af.edu/Wild-Blue-Yonder/Article-Display/Article/2842336/chinas-domestic-aircr aft-carrier-program-modernization-and-challenges/.
142. Military Balance 2001 (London: International Institute for Strategic Studies, 2001), 333-335.
143. "Trends in World Military Expenditure, 2022," Stockholm International Peace Research Institute, April 2023, https://www.sipri.org/sites/default/files/2023-04/230 4_fs_milex_2022.pdf.
144. Xue Zhiliang [薛志亮], "Beware of Strategic Disruptive Mistakes [谨防战略性颠覆性错误]," PLA Daily [解 放 军 报], January 30, 2018, http://m.xinhuanet.com/mil/2018-01/30/c_129801390.htm.
145. Zuo Fengrong [左凤荣], "Causes and Consequences of the Soviet Union's Path to the Arms Race [苏联走上军备竞赛之路的原因与后果]," Heilongjiang Social Sciences [黑龙江社会科学], no. 5 (2001): 33-36; Han Yichen [韩奕琛], "How the Soviet Union Was Dragged Down by the United States [苏联是如何被美国拖垮的]," Lingdao Wencui [领导文萃], no. 18 (2016): 113.
146. Zuo Fengrong [左 凤 荣], "Lessons from the Soviet Union on the Issue of Civil-Military Integration [苏联在军民融合问题上的教训]," Exploration and Free Views [探索与争鸣], no. 8 (2020): 133-141.
147. "To Jointly Create the Glorious Achievement of the Complete Reunification of the Motherland and the Great Rejuvenation of the Nation [共同创造祖国完全统一、民族伟大复兴的光荣伟业]," People's Daily [人民日报], October 12, 2021, http://opinion.people.com.cn/n1/2021/1012/c1003-32250220.html.
148. Jiang Zemin [江 泽 民], "Revisiting and Summarizing the Work of the Central Military Committee in the Last Ten Years [十年来军委工作的回顾和总结]," in The Selected Works of Jiang Zemin, Volume III [江泽民文选，第二卷] (Beijing: People's Publishing House [人民出版社], 2006), 461.

149. For example, see "Missiles Expert: Develop What the Enemy Fears, Put the Target Firmly on the Achilles Heel of Our Strongest Foes [导弹专家：敌人怕啥发展啥 瞄准强敌死穴 打]," Huanqiu.com [环 球 网], February 28, 2015, https://www.gfbzb. gov.cn/zbbm/gfzs/201502/20150228/1430988518.html; Tian Yuanfa [田 元 发], "One Cannot Chart New Paths When Following Others' Footsteps [踩着别人的脚印走不出新路]," PLA Daily [解放军报], March 1, 2017, http://military.people. com.cn/n1/2017/0301/c1011-29115671.html; "Striving to Realize Higher Quality and More Efficient Sustainable Development [努力实现更高质量更高效益更可持续的发展]," State Administration for Science, Technology and Industry for National Defense [国家国防科技工业局], July 31, 2017, http://www.sastind. gov. cn/n152/n6759499/n6759501/c6793977/content.html; Zhang Wannian [张万年], Zhang Wannian Military Writings [张万年军事文选] (Beijing: PLA Publishing House [解放军出版社], 2008), 732.

150. Zhang Wannian Writing Group [张万年写作组], Biography of Zhang Wannian, Volume II [张万年传（下）] (Beijing: People's Liberation Army Publishing House [解放军出版社], 2011), 63.

151. Eric Heginbotham et al., The US-China Military Scorecard: Forces, Geography, and the Evolving Balance of Power, 1996-2017 (Santa Monica, CA: RAND, 2015).

152. ChinaPower Team, "Does China's J-20 Rival Other Stealth Fighters?," ChinaPower, February 23, 2018, https://chinapower.csis.org/china-chengdu-j-20/.

153. "Military and Security Developments Involving the People's Republic of China 2022," 81-82.

154. In a RAND simulation of an attack on Kadena, 36 Chinese missiles closed the runways for 4 days, scaling up to 43 days of closure if 274 missiles were to be used. The study also noted that the "DF-21C-class missile could carry hundreds of submunitions, blanketing hundreds of square feet so that every aircraft parked in the area would have a high probability of being damaged." With just 108 missiles, China could shut down the airfield for a week and, with a high probability of suc-cess, destroy every fighter on the base. Heginbotham et al., The US-China Military Scorecard, 60.

155. "The Five Chinese Weapons That the US Army Is Most Afraid Of: DF-21D Is the First [美军最害怕的 5 款中国武器 DF-21D 导弹居首]," China Military [中国军网], May 8, 2014, http://www.81.cn/bqtd/2014-05/08/content_5895795.htm; "The Vulnerability of America's Asia-Pacific Bases Is Revealed: 34 Chinese Missiles Can Overwhelm Kadena [美亚太基地弱点被曝光：中国 34 枚导弹可瘫痪嘉纳]," Xilu.com [西陆网], March 5, 2016, http://junshi. xilu.com/20160305/100001000 0933219.html; "US Experts Simulate Chinese Missile Surprise Attack on US Pacific Base: Warships in Port Wiped Out [美国专家模拟中国导弹奇袭美军太平洋基地：港内军舰覆灭]," iFeng [凤凰网], July 12, 2017, http://inews.ifeng.com/51419 992/news.shtml?&back; Ge Tengfei and Chen Xi, "An Analysis of the United States' Deterrence by Denial Strategy Against China," Journal of International Security Studies, September 16, 2022, available at https://interpret.csis.org/translations/an-analysis-of-the-united-states-deterrence-by-denial-strategy-against-china/.

156. "Military and Security Developments Involving the People's Republic of China 2005," US Department of Defense, 2005, 45, available at http://www.andrewerick son.com/wp-content/uploads/2015/11/DoD_China-Report_2005.pdf; "Military and Security Developments Involving the People's Republic of China 2022," 167.

157. "Military and Security Developments Involving the People's Republic of China 2010," US Department of Defense, 2010, 66, available at http://www.andrewerick son.com/wp-content/uploads/2015/11/DoD_China-Report_2010.pdf; "Military and Security Developments Involving the People's Republic of China 2022," 167.

158. David Webb, "Dong Feng-16 (CSS-11)," Missile Defense Advocacy Online, February 2017,

https://missiledefenseadvocacy.org/missile-threat-and-proliferation/todays-missile-threat/china/dong-feng-16/; "DF-15," Missile Threat, Center for Strategic and International Studies, August 5, 2021, https://missilethreat.csis.org/missile/df-15-css-6/.

159. Chen Haidong [陈海东] et al., "Study for the Guidance Scheme of Reentry Vehicles Attacking Slowly Moving Targets [再入飞行器攻击慢速活动目标的制导方案研究]," Missiles and Space Vehicles [导弹与航天运载技术], no. 6 (2000): 6-9.

160. "F-35C Combat Radius Lightning Flash Fact," Defense Visual Information Distribution Service, May 10, 2022, https://www.dvidshub.net/video/846199/f-35c-combat-radius-lightning-flash-fact#:~:text=The%20F%2D35C%20has%20a,19%2C200%20lb%20internal%20fuel%20capacity; "DF-21 (CSS-5)," MissileThreat, Center for Strategic and International Studies, updated March 28, 2022, https://missilethreat.csis.org/missile/df-21/.

161. "Military and Security Developments Involving the People's Republic of China 2022," viii; Eric Heginbotham et al., The US-China Military Scorecard, 170.

162. "A Constructive Year for Chinese Base Building," Asia Maritime Transparency Initiative, December 14, 2017, https://amti.csis.org/constructive-year-chinese-building/

163. Lonnie Henley, "PLA Operational Concepts and Centers of Gravity in a Taiwan Conflict," Testimony Before the US-China Economic and Security Review Commission Hearing on Cross-Strait Deterrence, February 18, 2021, https://www.uscc.gov/sites/default/files/2021-02/Lonnie_Henley_Testimony.pdf.

164. "Military and Security Developments Involving the People's Republic of China 2022," 61.

165. Kris Osborn, "Could the US Military Gain Air Supremacy in a War with China?," National Interest, November 8, 2021, https://nationalinterest.org/blog/buzz/could-us-military-gain-air-supremacy-war-china-195867.

166. Jin Lin [金霖], "From the United States Air Force's 'Crushing Victory' (Continued) [从美国空军 '惨胜' 说开去 (续)]," Grandview Institution [国观智库], April 26, 2021, https://www.grandviewcn.com/shishipinglun/590.html.

167. Timothy A. Walton and Bryan Clark, "Resilient Aerial Refueling: Safeguarding the US Military's Global Reach," Hudson Institute, November 2021, 29, https://s3.amazonaws.com/media.hudson.org/Walton%20Clark_Resilient%20Aerial%20Refueling.pdf.

168. Wei Chengxi [魏晨曦], "Space War and Its Operational Environment [太空战及其作战环境]," Aerospace China [中国航天], no. 10 (2001): 40; Zhang Yuliang [张玉良] et al., eds., The Science of Campaigns [战役学] (Beijing: National Defense University Press [国防大学出版社], 2006): 87.

169. Yu Jixun [于际训], The Science of Second Artillery Campaigns [第二炮兵战役学] (Beijing: PLA Publishing House [解放军出版社], 2004), 341; Huang Zhicheng [黄志澄], "Thinking and Knowledge About Space War [关于太空战的认知与思考]," Aerospace International [国际太空], no. 6 (2003): 10-15; Tan Heyi [谈何易] and Zhang Ke [张珂], Network Electronic Warfare [网电战] (Beijing: Publishing House of Electronics Industry [电子工业出版社], 2019). .

170. Zhang Yan [张岩], Theory of Strategic Deterrence [战略威慑论] (Beijing: Social Sciences Literature Press [社会科学文献出版社], 2018), 97-98.

171. David Talbot, "How Technology Failed in Iraq," MIT Technology Review, November 1, 2004, https://www.technologyreview.com/2004/11/01/232152/how-technology-failed-in-iraq/.

172. Yu, The Science of Second Artillery Campaigns, 341.

173. Long Kun [龙坤] and Zhu Qichao [朱启超], "Algorithmic Warfare: Concept, Characteristics and Implications ['算法战争' 的概念、特点与影响]," National Defense Science and

Technology [国防科技] 38, no. 6 (2017): 41.

174. Dai Yifang [戴怡芳], ed., Reflections and Prospects for Military Studies [军事学研究回顾与展望] (Beijing: Military Sciences Press [军事科学出版社], 1995), 94.

175. "Cyber Capabilities and National Power: A Net Assessment," International Institute for Strategic Studies, June 28, 2021, https://www.iiss.org/blogs/research-paper/2021/06/cyber-capabilities-national-power.

176. Omer Yoacimik and Vivek Ganti, "DDoS Attack Trends for Q4 2021," i, January 10, 2022, https://blog.cloudflare.com/ddos-attack-trends-for-2021-q4/. In its 2021 annual report, cybersecurity firm CrowdStrike found that Chinese state-affiliated hacker groups were responsible for 67 percent of intrusions in the year leading up to June 2021. "Nowhere to Hide: 2021 Threat Hunting Report," CrowdStrike, June 2021, https://go.crowdstrike.com/rs/281-OBQ-266/images/Report2021Threat Hunting.pdf.

177. "China and Russia Jointly Submitted the Draft Treaty on PPWT to the Conference on Disarmament," Ministry of Foreign Affairs of the People's Republic of China, February 2, 2008, https://www.fmprc.gov.cn/mfa_eng/wjb_663304/zzjg_663340/jks_665232/jkxw_665234/200802/t20080212_599177.html.

178. Todd Harrison, "International Perspectives on Space Weapons," Center for Strategic and International Studies, May 27, 2020, https://www.csis.org/analysis/internatio nal-perspectives-space-weapons.

179. Xi Jinping, "Remarks at the Opening Ceremony of the Second World Internet Conference," Ministry of Foreign Affairs of the People's Republic of China, December 16, 2015, https://www.fmprc.gov.cn/eng/wjdt_665385/zyjh_665391/201 512/t20151224_678467.html.

180. The predicted cost of a DF-21D is reported here as the approximate per-unit cost for the United States to produce a similar missile, because China does not pub-lish missile costs. Jacob Cohn et al., "Leveling the Playing Field: Reintroducing US Theater-Range Missiles in a Post-INF World," Center for Strategic and Budgetary Assessments, 2019, https://csbaonline.org/uploads/documents/Leveling_the_ Playing_Field_web_Final_1.pdf; Ronald O'Rourke, "Navy Ford (CVN-78) Class Aircraft Carrier Program: Background and Issues for Congress," Congressional Research Service, April 28, 2022, https://sgp.fas.org/crs/weapons/RS20643.pdf; "F-16 Fighting Falcon," United States Air Force, accessed July 6, 2022, https://www. af.mil/About-Us/Fact-Sheets/Display/Article/104505/f-16-fighting-falcon/. The av-erage anti-air missile test costs approximately $2 million, which is the benchmark used in the text.

181. James Mattis, "Summary of the 2018 National Defense Strategy of the United States of America: Sharpening the American Military's Competitive Edge," US Department of Defense, January 21, 2018, https://dod.defense.gov/Portals/1/Documents/pubs/2018-National-Defense-Strategy-Summary.pdf.

182. Graham Allison and Jonah Glick-Unterman, "The Great Military Rivalry: China vs the US," Belfer Center for Science and International Affairs, December 16, 2021, https://www.belfercenter.org/publication/great-military-rivalry-china-vs-us.

183. Liu, Memoirs of Liu Huaqing, 637.

184. Dai Yifang [戴怡芳], ed., Reflections and Prospects for Military Studies [军事学研究回顾与展望] (Beijing: Military Sciences Press [军事科学出版社], 1995), 34.

第五章

1. Daron Acemoglu et al., "A Dynamic Theory of Resource Wars," Quarterly Journal of Economics 127, no. 1 (2012): 283-331.

2. "NSC 68: United States Objectives and Programs for National Security," National Security Council, April 14, 1950, available at https://irp.fas.org/offdocs/nsc-hst/nsc-68.htm.
3. Bill Clinton, "1999 National Security Strategy," White House, December 2, 1999, https://clintonwhitehouse4.archives.gov/media/pdf/nssr-1299.pdf.
4. "National Defense Strategy of the United States of America," US Department of Defense, March 2005, 5, https://history.defense.gov/Portals/70/Documents/nds/2005_NDS.pdf?ver=tFA4Qqo94ZB0x_S6uL0QEg%3d%3d; "Sustaining US Global Leadership: Priorities for 21st Century Defense," US Department of Defense, January 2012, https://nssarchive.us/wp-content/uploads/2020/04/defense_strategic_guida nce.pdf; "Summary of the 2018 National Defense Strategy," US Department of Defense, January 2018, https://nssarchive.us/wp-content/uploads/2020/04/2018_NDS.pdf; "2022 National Defense Strategy," US Department of Defense, October 27, 2022, 1, https://media.defense.gov/2022/Oct/27/2003103845/-1/-1/1/2022-NATIONAL-DEFENSE-STRATEGY-NPR-MDR.PDF.
5. Joseph R. Biden, "2022 National Security Strategy," White House, October 12, 2022, https://www.whitehouse.gov/wp-content/uploads/2022/10/Biden-Harris-Administ rations-National-Security-Strategy-10.2022.pdf.
6. Lu Nanquan [陆南泉], "Deng Xiaoping's Theories on the Soviet Union's Socialist Model [邓小平对苏联社会主义模式的论述]," Eeo.com.cn [经济观察网], August 18, 2014, http://www.eeo.com.cn/2014/0818/265117.shtml.
7. Zhang Yunling [张蕴岭], "The Comprehensive Security Concept and Reflecting on China's Security [综合安全观及对我国安全的思考]," Contemporary Asia-Pacific [当代亚太], no. 1 (2000): 13; Liu Yong [刘勇], "The US and Japan Have Massively Increased Their Military Spending. It Is Self-Evident Who They Are Targeting. How Should China Avoid Falling into an Arms Race? [美日大举增加军费，针对谁不言而喻，中国该如何避免陷入军备竞赛]," NetEase News [网 易 新 闻], December 19, 2022, https://www.163.com/dy/article/HOVB3ABH0552UZ8P.html; Feng Yaren [冯 亚 仁] et al., "US Spurs Arms Race Around China [美在中国周边刺激军备竞赛]," Global Times [环球时报], March 13, 2023, https://world.huanqiu.com/article/4C50 rIqXCAx.
8. Jiang Zemin [江 泽 民], Jiang Zemin on Socialism with Chinese Characteristics (Special Excerpts) [江泽民论有中国特色社会主义 (专题摘编)] (Beijing: Central Party Literature Press [中央文献出版社], 2002).
9. "China Began New Military Reform [中国开始新军事变革]," State Council of the People's Republic of China [中华人民共和国中央人民政府], http://www.gov.cn/test/2005-06/28/content_10531.htm; "Deng Xiaoping's Theories on Military Construction in the New Era [邓小平新时期军队建设思想]," International College of Defense Studies, PLA National Defense University [中国人民解放军国防大学国际防务学院], December 4, 2020, http://www.cdsndu.org/index.php/zgjswha/40.html.
10. Marina Rudyak, "The CMP Dictionary: Modernization," China Media Project, May 2, 2023, https://chinamediaproject.org/the_ccp_dictionary/modernization/.
11. The PLAN had commissioned at most four Jin-class nuclear missile submarines in 2010, but the submarines suffered from reactor problems and were not yet oper-ational. See Bernard Cole, The Great Wall at Sea: China's Navy in the Twenty-First Century (Annapolis: US Naval Institute Press, 2011), 97, 109.
12. James R. Holmes and Toshi Yoshihara, Red Star over the Pacific, 2nd ed. (Annapolis: US Naval Institute Press, 2018); Ronald O'Rourke, "China Naval Modernization: Implications for U.S. Navy Capabilities—Background and Issues for Congress," Congressional Research Service, May 25, 2023, https://crsreports.congr ess.gov/product/pdf/RL/RL33153/267.
13. Andrew Salerno-Garthwaite, "J-20 Chengdu: Mighty Dragon in the Heart of China's

Military Modernisation," Airforce Technology, September 14, 2022, https://www. airforce-technology.com/features/j-20-and-chinas-military-modernisation/; "Air Force F-22 Fighter Program," Congressional Research Service, July 11, 2013, 5, https://www.everycrsreport.com/files/20130711_RL31673_c70b986e6de321f9f00cc bb5173d56d3fc781d1a.pdf.

14. Taken from J. David Singer, Stuart Bremer, and John Stuckey, "Capability Distribution, Uncertainty, and Major Power War, 1820-1965," in Bruce Russett, ed., Peace, War, and Numbers, Correlates of War National Material Capabilities, Vol. 6 (Beverly Hills, CA: Sage Publishing, 1972): 19-48.

15. Singer, Bremer, and Stuckey, "Capability Distribution, Uncertainty, and Major Power War."

16. ChinaPower Team, "What Does China Really Spend on Its Military?," ChinaPower, December 28, 2015, updated May 27, 2021; "SIPRI Military Expenditure Database," Stockholm International Peace Research Institute, https://www.sipri.org/databases/milex, accessed August 25, 2023.

17. M. Taylor Fravel, Active Defense: China's Military Strategy Since 1949 (Princeton, NJ: Princeton University Press, 2019), 205.

18. John A. Vasquez, "Why Do Neighbors Fight? Proximity, Interaction, or Territoriality," Journal of Peace Research 32, no. 3 (1995): 284.

19. Anthony J. Blinken, "Sixth Anniversary of the Philippines-China South China Sea Arbitral Tribunal Ruling," US Department of State, July 11, 2022, https://www.state. gov/sixth-anniversary-of-the-philippines-china-south-china-sea-arbitral-tribunal-ruling/.

20. "Why the South China Sea Has Once Again Become a Stage for Great Power Competition [南海緣何再度成為大國角逐的舞台]," National Institute for South China Sea Studies [中國南海研究所], February 27, 2021, http://www.nanhai.org.cn/review_c/528.html.

21. Liu Yijian [刘一建], Shi Ping [时平], and Feng Liang [冯梁], On the History of China's Sea Power [中華海权史论] (Beijing: National University of Defense Press [国防大学出版社], 2000).

22. Michael Mazarr, "Mastering the Gray Zone: Understanding a Changing of Conflict," United States Army War College, December 2015, 58, https://publications.armywar college.edu/pubs/2372.pdf.

23. ChinaPower Team, "Are Maritime Law Enforcement Forces Destabilizing Asia?," ChinaPower, August 18, 2016, https://chinapower.csis.org/maritime-forces-destab ilizing-asia/.

24. Bonny Lin et al., "Countering China's Coercion Against U.S. Allies and Partners in the Indo-Pacific," in Competition in the Gray Zone (Santa Monica, CA: RAND Corporation, 2022), https://www.rand.org/pubs/research_reports/RRA594-1.html.

25. They describe "gray zone activities" as a Western concept whose purpose is to at-tack and manipulate public opinion on China's legitimate strategic and diplomatic actions. See, for example, Chinese Academy of Social Sciences, "One Belt, One Road" Research Center [中国社会科学院"一带一路"研究中心], "Great Attention Should Be Paid to the Strategic Games and Contests Between Major Powers in the 'Gray Zone' [应高度重视大国在'灰色地带'的战略博弈与较量]," Friends of Party Members and Cadres [党员干部之友], no. 4 (2022): 40-41; Shen Zhixiong [沈志雄], "Gray Zones and China-US Strategic Competition ['灰色地带'与中美战略竞争]," World Affairs, no. 12 (2019): 17-19.

26. Huang Zongding [黃宗鼎], "China's Maritime Militia Under Xi Jinping [習近平主政之下的中國海上民兵]," Defense Security Biweekly [國防安全雙週報], June 11, 2019, https://indsr.org.tw/respublicationcon?uid=12&resid=704&pid=2564.

27. Gregory B. Poling and Harrison Pretat, "Pulling Back the Curtain on China's Maritime Militia," Center for Strategic and International Studies, November 18, 2021, https://www.csis.

org/analysis/pulling-back-curtain-chinas-maritime-militia.
28. Andrew S. Erickson, "Shining a Spotlight: Revealing China's Maritime Militia to Deter Its Use," National Interest, November 25, 2018, https://nationalinterest. org/feature/shining-spotlight-revealing-china%E2%80%99s-maritime-mili tia-deter-its-use-36842.
29. ChinaPower Team, "Are Maritime Law Enforcement Forces Destabilizing Asia?"; Military Balance 2022 (London: International Institute for Strategic Studies, 2022), 238.
30. Central Intelligence Agency, "The United Front in Communist China," May 1957, xi, 1.
31. "The 2003 Political Work Guidelines of the People's Liberation Army [中国人民解放军政治工作条例 (2003)]," Reform Data [中国改革信息库], December 5, 2003, http://www.reformdata.org/2003/1205/4925.shtml.
32. Li Mingjun [李明峻], "Legal Warfare [法律战]," New Century Think Tank Forum [新世纪智库论坛], no. 43 (2008): 51-52.
33. Fan Gaoyue [樊高月], "Public Opinion Warfare, Psychological Warfare, and Legal Warfare to Accelerate the Victory of the War [舆论战、心理战、法律战三大战法加速战争胜利]," March 8, 2005, Sina News [新浪网], http://news.sina.com.cn/o/2005-03-08/10245297499s.shtml.
34. "Mao Zedong Values the Importance of the Battlefield of Public Opinion, Emphasizing Holding Pamphlets in the Left Hand and Guns and Bullets in the Right Hand [毛泽东重视舆论战场 强调左手拿传单右手拿枪弹]," China News [中国新闻网], September 13, 2010, https://www.chinanews.com.cn/cul/2010/09-13/2528 710.shtml.
35. Peng Dunwen [彭敦文], "Contemporary Value of Mao Zedong's 'On Protracted War' [毛泽东 ' 论持久战 ' 的当代价值]," People's Forum [人民论坛], no. 28 (2020): 80-81; Wang Wen [王文], "US-China Competition in the Next Five Years [未来五年的中美博弈]," China Business Journal [中国经营网], January 19, 2021, http://www.cb.com. cn/index/show/zl/cv/cv13454491859/p/s.html. See also Deng Yuwen [邓聿文], "Guest Remarks: Protracted Warfare Between the CCP and the US [客座评论：中共对美的持久战]," Deutsche Welle Chinese website [德国之声中文网], October 25, 2020, https://www.dw.com/zh/%E5%AE%A 2%E5%BA%A7%E8%AF%84%E8%AE%BA%E4%B8%AD%E5%85%B1%E5%AF%B9%E7%BE E%8E%E7%9A%84%E6%8C%81%E4%B9%85%E6%88%98/a-55370231; and "Six Advantages of China and the US in Their Great Power Competition [中美深度博弈下，中国和美国的各六大优势]," Guancha.cn [观察者网], August 1, 2020, https://user.guancha.cn/main/content?id=358564&page=2.
36. Peter Mattis, "China's Three Warfares in Perspective," War on the Rocks, January 30, 2018, https://warontherocks.com/2018/01/chinas-three-warfares-perspective/.
37. Zhang Yuliang [张玉良] et al., ed., The Science of Campaigns [战役学] (Beijing: PLA National Defense University Press [国防大学出版社], 2006), 203, 206.
38. Clint Watts, Messing with the Enemy: Surviving in a Social Media World of Hackers, Terrorist, Russians, and Fake News (Sydney: HarperCollins, 2019), 301.
39. Fan, "Public Opinion Warfare, Psychological Warfare, and Legal Warfare to Accelerate the Victory of the War"; Xiao Tianliang [肖天亮], Science of Military Strategy [战略学] (Beijing: Military Sciences Press [军事科学出版社], 2015).
40. Oriana Skylar Mastro, "How China Is Bending the Rules in the South China Sea," The Interpreter, February 17, 2021, https://www.lowyinstitute.org/the-interpreter/how-china-bending-rules-south-china-sea.
41. "Foreign Ministry Spokesperson Lu Kang's Remarks on Statement by Spokesperson of US State Department on South China Sea Arbitration Ruling," Ministry of Foreign Affairs of the People's Republic of China, July 12, 2016, https://www.fmprc.gov.cn/mfa_eng/xwfw_665399/

s2510_665401/2535_665405/201607/t20160713_696 684.html.
42. Mazarr, "Mastering the Gray Zone," 72.
43. Kapil Bhatia, "Coercive Gradualism Through Gray Zone Statecraft in the South China Seas: China's Strategy and Potential U.S. Options," Joint Forces Quarterly 91, no. 4 (2018): 24-33.
44. Michael Green et al., "Countering Coercion in Maritime Asia: The Theory and Practice of Gray Zone Deterrence," Center for Strategic and International Studies, May 9, 2017.
45. Alastair Iain Johnston, Cultural Realism: Strategic Culture and Grand Strategy in Chinese History (Princeton, NJ: Princeton University Press, 1998), 248-250, 99-102.
46. Johnston, Cultural Realism, 103.
47. Bonny Lin et al., "Competition in the Gray Zone: Countering China's Coercion Against US Allies and Partners in the Indo-Pacific," RAND Corporation, 2022, https://www.rand.org/pubs/research_reports/RRA594-1.html.
48. Mazarr, "Mastering the Gray Zone," 88.
49. Michael Green, "The Legacy of Obama's 'Pivot' to Asia," Foreign Policy, September 3, 2016, https://foreignpolicy.com/2016/09/03/the-legacy-of-obamas-pivot-to-asia/.
50. Harry S. Truman, "The President's News Conference, November 30, 1950," in Public Papers of the Presidents of the United States: Harry S. Truman, 1950 (Washington, DC: US Government Print Office, 1965), 724-728.
51. "Memorandum of Discussion at a Special Meeting of the National Security Council on Tuesday, March 31, 1953," in Foreign Relations of the United States, 1952-1954, Korea, Volume XV, Part 1 (Washington: US Government Printing Office, 1984), 826.
52. "142. Memorandum of a Conversation Between the Secretary of State and Senator Walter George, Department of State, Washington, March 7, 1955," in Foreign Relations of the United States, 1955-1957, China, Volume II (Washington, DC: US Government Printing Office, 1986), 337.
53. Shen Zhihua [沈 志 华], "Aid and Restriction: The USSR and the Development of Atomic Weapons in China (1949-1960) [援助与限制：苏联与中国的核武器研制 (1949-1960)]," Historical Research [历史研究], no. 3 (2004): 491.
54. The Chronicles of Zhou Enlai's Life, 1949-1976 [周恩来年谱 , 1949-1976] (Beijing: Central Party Literature Press [中央文献出版社], 1997), 445.
55. The Chronicles of Mao Zedong's Life, 1949-1976, Volume II [毛泽东年谱 , 1949-1976 (第二卷)] (Beijing: Central Party Literature Press [中央文献出版社], 2013), 567.
56. The Chronicles of Mao Zedong's Life, 1949-1976, Volume IV [毛泽东年谱 , 1949-1976 (第四卷)] (Beijing: Central Party Literature Press [中央文献出版社], 2013), 386, 467.
57. The Chronicles of Deng Xiaoping's Life, 1975-1997, Volume I [邓小平年谱 (上册)] (Beijing: Central Party Literature Press [中央文献出版社], 2004), 308.
58. M. Taylor Fravel and Evan S. Medeiros, "China's Search for Assured Retaliation: The Evolution of Chinese Nuclear Strategy and Force Structure," International Security 35, no. 2 (2010): 87.
59. "Nonstrategic Nuclear Weapons," Congressional Research Service, July 15, 2021, https://fas.org/sgp/crs/nuke/RL32572.pdf.
60. For example, Jiang Zemin highlighted China's limited resources and the importance of developing conventional capabilities in Jiang Zemin [江泽民], The Selected Works of Jiang Zemin, Volume I [江泽民文选 (第三卷)] (Beijing: People's Publishing House [人民出版社], 2006), 74-79; Volume II, 269-270, 458.
61. Shou Xiaosong [寿 晓 松], The Science of Military Strategy [战 略 学] (Beijing: Military

Sciences Press [军事科学出版社], 2013); Li Tilin [李体林], "Creative Development of the Nuclear Strategic Theory of China Since the Reform and Opening-Up [改革开放以来中国核战略理论的发展]," China Military Science [中国军事科学], no. 6 (2008): 42.

62. General Office of the Central Military Commission [中央军委办公厅], ed., Selection of Deng Xiaoping's Expositions on Army Building in the New Period [邓小平关于新军队建设论述选编] (Beijing: Bayi Publishing House [八一出版社], 1993), 44-45.

63. Headquarters of the Second Artillery [第二炮兵司令部], The Science of Military Strategy of the Second Artillery [第二炮兵战略学] (Beijing: Lantian Press [蓝天出版社], 1996), 83-85.

64. "SIPRI Military Expenditure Database"; Stephen I. Schwartz, Atomic Audit: The Costs and Consequences of US Nuclear Weapons Since 1940 (Washington, DC: Brookings Institution Press, 1998).

65. "Projected Costs of U.S. Nuclear Forces, 2021 to 2030," Congressional Budget Office, May 2021, https://www.cbo.gov/publication/57240.

66. "Global Nuclear Stockpiles, 1945-1996," Brookings Institution, August 1998, https://web.archive.org/web/20160513152457/http://www.brookings.edu/about/projects/archive/nucweapons/stockpile.

67. Schwartz, "The Hidden Costs of Our Nuclear Arsenal." For the costs of different delivery systems, see "Average Unit Acquisition Costs for Strategic Nuclear Delivery Vehicles," Brookings Institution, 1998, https://www.brookings.edu/average-unit-acquisition-costs-for-strategic-nuclear-delivery-vehicles/.

68. Hans M. Kristensen, Matt Korda, and Eliana Reynolds, "Chinese Nuclear Weapons, 2023," Bulletin of the Atomic Scientists 79, no. 2 (2023): 108-133.

69. Hans M. Kristensen and Matt Korda, "Nuclear Notebook: United States Nuclear Weapons, 2023," Federation of Atomic Scientists 79, no. 1 (2023): 29.

70. Fravel and Medeiros, "China's Search for Assured Retaliation," 49-50.

71. "China's National Defense in 2006 [2006年中国的国防]," State Council Information Office of the People's Republic of China [中华人民共和国国务院新闻办公室], December 2006, http://www.gov.cn/zwgk/2006-12/29/content_486759.htm.

72. Shou Xiaosong [寿晓松], The Science of Military Strategy [战略学] (Beijing: Military Sciences Press [军事科学出版社], 2013), 173, argues that China's limited arsenal initially created the necessity for a no-first-use pledge. This commitment to a minimal deterrence with a no-first-use pledge has been communicated explicitly in its 2006, 2008, 2010, and 2013 white papers.

73. Wu Chunsi [吴莼思], "Nuclear Security Summit, Global Nuclear Order and the Role of China [核安全峰会、全球核秩序建设与中国角色]," International Security Research [国际安全研究] 33, no. 2 (2015): 56-57.

74. David J. Trachtenberg, "US Extended Deterrence: How Much Strategic Force Is Too Little?," Strategic Studies Quarterly 6, no. 2 (2012): 68.

75. "China's National Defense in 2008 [2008年中国的国防]," State Council Information Office of the People's Republic of China [中华人民共和国国务院新闻办公室], January 2009, http://www.gov.cn/zwgk/2009-01/20/content_1210224.htm.

76. "Nuclear Posture Review Report," US Department of Defense, April 2010, https://dod.defense.gov/Portals/1/features/defenseReviews/NPR/2010_Nuclear_Posture_Review_Report.pdf; "The Bush Doctrine," Carnegie Endowment for International Peace, October 7, 2002, https://carnegieendowment.org/2002/10/07/bush-doctrine-pub-1088.

77. "Nuclear Posture Review," US Department of Defense, February 2018, 21, https://media.defense.gov/2018/Feb/02/2001872886/-1/-1/1/2018-NUCLEAR-POSTURE-REVIEW-FINAL-REPORT.PDF.
78. William Burr, "The 'Launch on Warning' Nuclear Strategy and Its Insider Critics," George Washington University National Security Archive, June 11, 2019, https://nsarchive.gwu.edu/briefing-book/nuclear-vault/2019-06-11/launch-warning-nucl ear-strategy-its-insider-critics.
79. "Military and Security Developments Involving the People's Republic of China 2022," 95; "Frequently Asked Questions About Hair-Trigger Alert," Union of Concerned Scientists, January 15, 2015, https://www.ucsusa.org/resources/frequently-asked-questions-about-hair-trigger-alert.
80. "Fact Sheet: China's Nuclear Inventory," Arms Control Association, April 2, 2020, https://armscontrolcenter.org/fact-sheet-chinas-nuclear-arsenal/.
81. "Military and Security Developments Involving the People's Republic of China 2022," 99; "Chinese Ballistic Missile Early Warning," Global Security, May 3, 2020, https://www.globalsecurity.org/space/world/china/warning.htm; Peter Wood et al., "China's Ground Segment: Building the Pillars of a Great Space Power," China Aerospace Studies Institute, September 2020, https://www.airuniversity.af.edu/Portals/10/CASI/documents/Research/Space/2021-03-01%20Chinas%20Ground%20Segment. pdf?ver=z4ogY_MrxaDurwVt-R9J6w%3d%3d.
82. Cameron M. Keys, "FY2024 Defense Budget Request: Space-Based Satellite Programs," Congressional Research Service, June 13, 2023, https://crsreports.congr ess.gov/product/pdf/IN/IN12176.
83. About 43 percent of the Russian force is land-based. See ChinaPower Team, "How Is China Modernizing Its Nuclear Forces?," ChinaPower, updated October 28, 2020, https://chinapower.csis.org/china-nuclear-weapons/.
84. "Military and Security Developments Involving the People's Republic of China 2022," 60.
85. Yu Jixun [于际训], The Science of Second Artillery Campaigns [第二炮兵战役学] (Beijing: PLA Publishing House [解放军出版社], 2004), 42-43.
86. Gerald C. Brown, "Understanding the Risks and Realities of China's Nuclear Forces," Arms Control Association, June 2021, https://www.armscontrol.org/act/2021-06/features/understanding-risks-realities-chinas-nuclear-forces.
87. "Missiles of the United States," Missile Threat, Center for Strategic and International Studies, March 3, 2021, https://missilethreat.csis.org/country/united-states/.
88. Kristensen, Korda, and Reynolds, "Chinese Nuclear Weapons, 2023," 109.
89. "Military and Security Developments Involving the People's Republic of China 2020," 55.
90. Zhang Jiadong [张家栋], "Why Would America Hype Up 'China's Hypersonic Weapon'? [美国为何热炒 ' 中国高超音速武器 ']," Global Times [环球时报], October 22, 2021, https://opinion.huanqiu.com/article/45GcOxgUZmq.
91. Matt Korda and Hans M. Kristensen, "China Is Building a Second Nuclear Missile Silo Field," Federation of American Scientists, July 26, 2021, https://fas.org/publicat ion/china-is-building-a-second-nuclear-missile-silo-field/.
92. Robert S. Norris and Hans M. Kristensen, "Global Nuclear Weapons Inventories, 1945-2010," Bulletin of the Atomic Scientists 66, no. 4 (July 2010): 77-83.
93. Exact estimates of the size of the US nuclear arsenal vary slightly across sources. Most accounts refer back to two authoritative sources: an estimate of 5,800 from Hans M. Kristensen, "World Nuclear Forces," Stockholm International Peace Research Institute, 2020, https://

sipri.org/yearbook/2020/10, and one of 5,244 from Hans M. Kristensen and Matt Korda, "Status of World Nuclear Forces," Federation of American Scientists, March 2023, https://fas.org/initiative/status-world-nuclear-forces/. Analysts agree that there are about 3,800 active warheads in the military stockpile but put the number of retired warheads awaiting dismantlement between 1,750 and 2,000, which explains the variance in the total number.

94. Kristensen and Korda, "Status of World Nuclear Forces."
95. Eric Heginbotham et al., "The U.S.-China Military Scorecard," RAND Corporation, 2015, https://www.rand.org/content/dam/rand/pubs/research_reports/RR300/RR392/RAND_RR392.pdf.
96. "2023 Report on the Military and Security Developments Involving the People's Republic of China," U.S. Department of Defense, 2023. https://media.defense.gov/2023/Oct/19/2003323409/-1/-1/1/2023-MILITARY-AND-SECURITY-DEVEL OPMENTS-INVOLVING-THE-PEOP LES-REPUB LIC-OF-CHINA.PDF; Heginbotham et al., The US-China Military Scorecard.
97. Jessie Yeung, "China Claims Successful Anti-Ballistic Missile Interceptor Test," CNN, 2022, https://www.cnn.com/2022/06/19/china/china-anti-ballistic-missile-test-intl-hnk/index.html.
98. Anthony H. Cordesman and Joseph Kendall, "Chinese Space Strategy and Developments," in Chinese Strategy and Military Modernization in 2016: A Comparative Analysis (Washington, DC: Center for Strategic and International Studies, 2016), 427-453.
99. Headquarters of the Second Artillery, The Science of Military Strategy of the Second Artillery, 112-117, 152-161.
100. "U.S. Experts: America Expands Network of Missile Defense in Asia, Targeting North Korea Explicitly and China Implicitly [美专家：美扩展亚洲导弹防御网明指朝鲜暗指中国]," iFeng News [凤 凰 网], August 24, 2012, http://phtv.ifeng. com/program/comment/detail_2012_08/24/17064804_0.shtml; "U.S. Attempts to Increase Deployment of 'Territorial Defense Radars' in Asia-Pacific; Sharp Comment: This Is Planting Mines for Regional Security [美国欲在亚太增加部署 ' 国土防御雷达 ' 锐评：这是借机为地区安全埋雷]," 81.cn [中国军网], March 15, 2019, http://www.81.cn/gjzx/2019-03/15/content_9451030.htm.
101. All statistics taken from "Trade Statistics by Country/Region," World Integrated Trade Solution, accessed December 15, 2022, https://wits.worldbank.org/countryst ats.aspx?lang=en.
102. "General Profile: China," UNCTADSTAT, October 20, 2022, https://unctadstat. unctad.org/CountryProfile/GeneralProfile/en-GB/156/index.html; "General Profile: United States," UNCTADSTAT, October 20, 2022, https://unctadstat.unc tad.org/CountryProfile/GeneralProfile/en-GB/842/index.html.
103. ChinaPower Team, "How Is China Feeding Its Population of 1.4 Billion?," ChinaPower, January 25, 2017, updated August 26, 2020, https://chinapower.csis. org/china-food-security/.
104. Zheng Xin, "China's Oil Dependence on Imports Sees Drop," State Council of the People's Republic of China, February 24, 2022, http://english.www.gov.cn/news/topnews/202202/24/content_WS6216e221c6d09c94e48a569e.html.
105. "2021 Customs Statistics Online Data Query Platform—Integrated Circuits [2021 年海关统计数据在线查询平台—集成电路]," General Administration of Customs of the PRC [中华人民共和海关总署], http://stats.customs.gov.cn/, accessed July 5, 2023.
106. "International Tourism, Number of Departures—China," World Bank, undated, accessed November 29, 2023, https://data.worldbank.org/indicator/ST.INT. DPRT?locations=CN.
107. The above represents 2017 numbers. For more specifics, see Paul Nantulya, "Chinese Security Contractors in Africa," Carnegie Endowment for International Peace, October 8, 2020, https://carnegieendowment.org/2020/10/08/chinese-secur ity-contractors-in-africa-pub-82916;

新篡起者　　412

"Chinese Workers in Africa," China Africa Research Initiative, January 2022, http://www.saiscari.org/data-chinese-workers-in-africa;

108. Research Group of International Investment [国际投资研究室], Country-Risk Rating of Overseas Investment from China (2020) [中国海外投资国家风险评级 (2020)] (Beijing: Institute of World Economics and Politics, Chinese Academy of Social Sciences [世界经济与政治研究所 , 中国社会科学院], 2020).

109. Research Group of International Investment [国际投资研究室], Country-Risk Rating of Overseas Investment from China (2018) [中国海外投资国家风险评级 (2018)] (Beijing: Institute of World Economics and Politics, Chinese Academy of Social Sciences [世界经济与政治研究所 , 中国社会科学院], 2018); Research Group of International Investment [国际投资研究室], Country-Risk Rating of Overseas Investment from China (2021) [中国海外投资国家风险评级 (2021)] (Beijing: Institute of World Economics and Politics, Chinese Academy of Social Sciences [世界经济与政治研究所 , 中国社会科学院], 2021).

110. "The Ministry of Commerce Holds Regular Press Conference on December 2, 2015 [商务部召开例行新闻发布会 (2015 年 12 月 2 日)]," Ministry of Commerce of the People's Republic of China [中华人民共和国商务部], December 2, 2015, http://www.mofcom.gov.cn/article/ae/slfw/201512/20151201199367.shtml.

111. Wang Duanyong, "The Safety of Chinese Citizens Abroad: A Quantitative Interpretation of the Special Notices for Chinese Citizens Abroad," Journal of Current Chinese Affairs 42, no. 1 (2013): 167-198; Xia Liping [夏莉萍], "Effectiveness Evaluation and Improvement Direction of the Construction of China's Consular Protection Mechanism [中国领事保护机制建设的成效评估与改进方向]," International Forum [国际论坛], no. 1 (2023): 54-68.

112. Paul Nantulya, "Chinese Security Contractors in Africa," Carnegie Endowment for International Peace, October 8, 2020, https://carnegieendowment.org/2020/10/08/chinese-security-contractors-in-africa-pub-82916.

113. "Foreign Media: Li Keqiang's Africa Tour Brings a 'Chinese Whirlwind' [外媒：李克强非洲行掀起 ' 中国旋风 ']," CPC News [中国共产党新闻网], May 14, 2014, http://cpc.people.com.cn/2014/0514/c64095-25016609.html.

114. "Reading the Chinese Diplomacy Key Words of Wang Yi's Trip to Africa [解读王毅非洲之行的中国外交关键词]," Xinhua.com [新华网], December 4, 2021, http://www.news.cn/world/2021-12/04/c_1211474100.htm.

115. Timothy Heath, "China's Pursuit of Overseas Security," RAND Corporation, 2018, ix-x, https://www.rand.org/pubs/research_reports/RR2271.html.

116. Heath, "China's Pursuit of Overseas Security," ix-x.

117. "Quadrennial Defense Review," Historical Office of the Secretary of Defense, https://history.defense.gov/Historical-Sources/Quadrennial-Defense-Review/.

118. "Summary of the National Defense Strategy of the United States of America," US Department of Defense, https://dod.defense.gov/Portals/1/Documents/pubs/2018-National-Defense-Strategy-Summary.pdf.

119. Joshua Dewberry, "Air Force Unveils New Mission Statement," Air Force news re-lease, April 8, 2021, https://www.af.mil/News/Article-Display/Article/2565837/air-force-unveils-new-mission-statement/.

120. Daniel Immerwahr, How to Hide an Empire: A History of the Greater United States (New York: Farrar, Straus and Giroux, 2019), 516.

121. "Military and Civilian Personnel by Service/Agency by State/Country, September 2022 and September 2008," DMDC, accessed July 5, 2023, https://dwp.dmdc.osd. mil/dwp/app/dod-data-reports/workforce-reports.

122. Michael J. Lostumbo et al., "Overseas Basing of U.S. Military Forces: An Assessment of Relative Costs and Strategic Benefits," RAND Corporation, 2013, 20-30, https://www.rand.org/pubs/research_reports/RR201.html.

123. Angela O'Mahony et al., "U.S. Presence and the Incidence of Conflict," RAND Corporation, 2018, 11, https://www.rand.org/pubs/research_reports/RR1906.html; Lustumbo et al., "Overseas Basing of U.S. Military Forces," 8.

124. "Operation and Maintenance Overview Fiscal Year 2022 Budget Request," Office of the Secretary of Defense, August 2021, 187-190, 267-269, https://comptroller.defe nse.gov/Portals/45/Documents/defbudget/FY2022/FY2022_OM_Overview.pdf.

125. Jennifer Kavanagh et al., "Characteristics of Successful U.S. Military Interventions," RAND Corporation, 2019, 30-32, https://www.rand.org/pubs/research_repo rts/RR3062.html; Jennifer Kavanagh et al., "The Past, Present, and Future of U.S. Ground Interventions," RAND Corporation, 2017, 17, https://www.rand.org/pubs/research_reports/RR1831.html. Note that these numbers do not include covert or civilian interventions. Between 1947 and 1989, the United States attempted seventy-two regime change interventions, sixty-six of which were covert operations. Lindsey A. O'Rourke, "The U.S. Tried to Change Other Countries' Governments 72 Times During the Cold War," Washington Post, December 23, 2021.

126. "Costs of War Summary of Findings," Watson Institute for International and Public Affairs, https://watson.brown.edu/costsofwar/papers/summary.

127. "SIPRI Military Expenditure Database," Stockholm International Peace Research Institute, https://www.sipri.org/databases/milex.

128. Xi Jinping [习近平], Edited Selections of Xi Jinping's Comments on the Comprehensive National Security Concept [习近平关于总体国家安全观论述摘编] (Beijing: Central Party Literature Press [中央文献出版社], 2018), 26-27, 40-47, 55.

129. Zhen Bingxi [甄炳禧], "Is the 21st Century the Century of the US or the Century of China? Analysis on the Shift in the Sino-US Balance of Power: A Global Perspective [21世纪：美国世纪还是中国世纪——全球视野下的中美实力对比变化分析]," Frontiers [学术前沿], no. 21 (2015): 55.

130. Fu Ying [傅莹] and Wu Shicun [吴士存], "The Situation in the South China Sea and the Controversy over the Spratly Islands: A Look Back at History and Realistic Assessments [南海局势及南沙群岛争议：历史回顾与现实思考]," Xinhua.com [新华网], May 12, 2016, http://www.xinhuanet.com/world/2016-05/12/c_128977 813.htm.

131. Heath, "China's Pursuit of Overseas Security."

132. Deng Xiaoping [邓小平], The Selected Works of Deng Xiaoping, Volume III [邓小平文选（第三卷）] (Beijing: People's Publishing House [人民出版社], 1994), 49, 88, 363.

133. Mao Zedong [毛泽东], "Mao Zedong and Others Send a Telegram Congratulating the 24th Anniversary of the Independence of the Democratic Republic of Vietnam [毛泽东等祝贺越南民主共和国独立二十四周年的电报]," in The Manuscripts of Mao Zedong Since the Establishment of the PRC, Volume XIII [建国以来毛泽东文稿（第十三册）] (Beijing: Central Party Literature Press [中央文献出版社], 1998), 64; Li Qingsi [李庆四], "Twenty Years of the US in Afghanistan—with a Wave They Leave a Mess Behind [美国在阿富汗的20年：挥一挥衣袖，留下了一地鸡毛]," Guangming [光明网], September 15, 2021, https://theory.gmw.cn/2021-09/15/content_35164733.htm.

134. Wang Jisi [王缉思], "The Historical Lessons of the Soviet-US Rivalry and China's Rise to Power [苏美争霸的历史教训和中国的崛起道路]," Cfisnet.com [国际网], May 12, 2015, http://comment.cfisnet.com/2015/0512/1301371.html.

135. "Constitution of People's Republic of China [中华人民共和国宪法]," http://www.spp.gov.cn/

spp/xf/201801/t20180131_363386.shtml; Xi Jinping [习 近 平], "Establish a Comprehensive Well-Off Society, Seize the Great Victory of Socialism with Chinese Characteristics in the New Era— Report at the 19th National Congress of the Communist Party of China [决胜全面建成小康社会，夺取新时代中国特色社会主义伟大胜利—在中国共产党第十九次全国代表大会上的报告],"Xinhua.com[新 华 网],October 27, 2017, http://www.xinhuanet.com/politics/19cpcnc/2017-10/27/c_1121867 529.htm.

136. Bi Wenbo [毕文波], "On China's Military Strategic Thought in the New Period [论中国新时期军事战略思维]," Military History Research [军事历史研究], no. 2 (2004): 55.

137. Isaac B. Kardon, "China's Overseas Base, Places, and Far Seas Logistics," in The PLA Beyond Borders: Chinese Military Operations in Regional and Global Context, ed. Joel Wuthnow et al. (Washington, DC: National Defense University Press, 2021), 92, 75.

138. "The Chinese Military Has Always Been a Staunch Force in Safeguarding World Peace [中国军队始终是维护世界和平的坚定力量]," Ministry of Defense of the People's Republic of China [中 华 人 民 共 和 国 国 防 部], January 10, 2023, http://www.mod.gov.cn/gfbw/jmsd/4930331.html; "Is the Djibouti Military Base the First Step for Overseas Expansion? The Ministry of Foreign Affairs Responded [吉布提军事基地是海外扩张第 一 步？外 交 部 回 应]," China.com [中 华 网], July 12, 2017, https://3g.china.com/act/news/10000159/20170712/30960936.html.

139. Richard Gowan, "China's Pragmatic Approach to UN Peacekeeping," Brookings Institution, September 14, 2020, https://www.brookings.edu/articles/chinas-pragmatic-approach-to-un-peacekeeping/.

140. Heath, "China's Pursuit of Overseas Security," 28-32.

141. Military Balance 2022, 261; Mikko Huotari et al., "China's Emergence as a Global Security Actor," Mercator Institute for China Studies, July 2017, 59, https://mer ics.org/sites/default/files/2020-04/China%27s%20Emergence%20as%20a%20Glo bal%20Security%20Actor.pdf.

142. Huotari et al., "China's Emergence as a Global Security Actor," 58.

143. Heath, "China's Pursuit of Overseas Security."

144. Task Force 88, which was formed from the Pakistani Navy in 2016, is composed of approximately 400 marines specializing in port defense, outfitted with gunboats, frigates, fast-attack craft, aircraft, and drones. Siegfried Wolf, "The Growing Security Dimension of the China-Pakistan Economic Corridor," Italian Institute for International Political Studies, March 10, 2020, https://www.ispionline.it/en/pubbli cazione/growing-security-dimension-china-pakistan-economic-corridor-25316.

145. "China May Deploy Marines to Gwadar Port," Maritime Executive, March 17, 2017, https://www.maritime-executive.com/article/china-may-deploy-marines-to-gwadar-port; "Pakistan Military Raises New Security Division: Report," Times of Islamabad, October 15, 2019, https://timesofislamabad.com/15-Oct-2019/pakis tan-military-raises-new-security-division-report.

146. "Timeline: China-Myanmar Relations," The Irawaddy, January 13, 2020, https://www.irrawaddy.com/specials/timeline-china-myanmar-relations.html.

147. "China, Ethiopia Ink Accord on Establishing Security Safeguarding Mechanism for Major Projects Under BRI," Xinhua, March 7, 2021, https://www.xinhuanet.com/english/2021-03/07/c_139792150.htm.

148. Andrea Ghiselli, "Continuity and Change in China's Strategy to Protect Overseas Interests," War on the Rocks, August 4, 2021, https://warontherocks.com/2021/08/continuity-and-change-in-chinas-strategy-to-protect-overseas-interests/.

149. Vladimir Fyodorov, "Chinese Weapons to Help Nigeria Fight Terrorism [中 国 武 器 助尼 日 利 亚 反 恐]," Sputnik [俄 罗 斯 卫 星 通 讯 社], April 10, 2020, https://sputnikn ews.

cn/20200410/1031194430.html.

150. Heath, "China's Pursuit of Overseas Security," 23.
151. "National Public Security Work Conference Held in Beijing on International Cooperation Work [全国公安国际合作工作会议在京召开]," Xinhua.com [新华网], February 7, 2017, http://www.xinhuanet.com/politics/2017-02/07/c_1120426 453.htm.
152. Shi Yang [石杨], "Raise High the Flag of Mutually Beneficial Cooperation, Protect Security and Development Interests, the MPS Is Succeeding in Its International Cooperation Efforts [高举合作共赢旗帜，维护安全发展利益，公安国际合作工作成果丰硕]," Ministry of Public Security of the People's Republic of China [中华人民共和国公安部], February 9, 2017, https://www.mps.gov.cn/n2253534/n2253 535/c5629811/content.html.
153. "China and the Interpol Begin 'One Belt, One Road' Security Cooperation [中国与国际刑警组织开展'一带一路'安保合作]," Ministry of Public Security of the People's Republic of China [中华人民共和国公安部], May 13, 2017, https://www. mps.gov.cn/n2253534/n2253535/c5697574/content.html.
154. Yuan Meng [袁猛], "Nie Furu Attends the Global Police Summit in South Korea [聂福如赴韩国出席国际警察峰会]," Ministry of Public Security of the People's Republic of China [中华人民共和国公安部], October 24, 2019, https://www.mps. gov.cn/n2253534/n2253535/c7268106/content.html; "Previous Event, International Police Summit in Seoul, 2019," International Police Summit, https://ips2021.kr/eng/sub01/event.html.
155. An agreement was also reached with France but was aborted. Thomas Eder, Bertram Lang, and Moritz Rudolf, "China's Global Law Enforcement Drive," Mercator Institute for China Studies, January 18, 2017, 2, https://merics.org/sites/default/files/2020-05/China%27s%20global%20law%20enforcement%20drive.pdf; Lindsey Ford, "Extending the Long Arm of the Law: China's International Law Enforcement Drive," Brookings Institution, January 15, 2021, https://www.brookings.edu/blog/order-from-chaos/2021/01/15/extending-the-long-arm-of-the-law-chinas-intern ational-law-enforcement-drive/.
156. "Two Arrested for Operating Illegal Overseas Police Station of the Chinese Government," US Department of Justice, April 17, 2023, https://www.justice. gov/opa/pr/two-arrested-operating-illegal-overseas-police-station-chinese-gov ernment.
157. "110 Overseas: Chinese Transnational Policing Gone Wild," Safeguard Defenders, September 12, 2022; Yuan Yang, "China's Offshore 'Police Service Stations' Spark European Alarm," Financial Times, November 14, 2022, https://www.ft.com/cont ent/147ce066-cc5b-4af6-98cd-9ba39eb29829; "Ministry of Public Security: The Number of Telecom and Network Fraud Cases Dropped Year-on-Year for Nine Consecutive Months [公安部：电信网络诈骗例案数 9 个月同比下降]," China News [中国新闻网], April 14, 2022, https://www.chinanews.com. cn/cj/2022/04-14/9728557.shtml.
158. Du Maozhi [杜懋之] and Yang Li [杨莉], "The Evolution of Chinese Overseas Counter-Terrorism Strategy [中国海外反恐战略的演进]," Social Sciences International [国外社会与科学], no. 2 (2017): 155-157.
159. Giulia Sciorati, "Not a Military Base: Why Did China Commit to an Outpost in Tajikistan?," Italian Institute for International Political Studies, November 2, 2021, https://www.ispionline.it/en/pubblicazione/not-military-base-why-did-china-com mit-outpost-tajikistan-32177.
160. Joel Wuthnow, "China's Other Army: The People's Armed Police," China Strategic Perspectives, no. 14 (April 2019): 30.
161. Matthew Southerland, Will Green, and Sierra Janik, "The Shanghai Cooperation Organization: A Testbed for Chinese Power Projection," US-China Economic and Security Review Commission, November 12, 2020, https://www.uscc.gov/sites/defa ult/files/2020-11/Shanghai_

Cooperation_Organization-Testbed_for_Chinese_P ower_Projection.pdf.

162. Max Markusen, "A Stealth Industry: The Quiet Expansion of Chinese Private Security Companies," Center for International and Strategic Studies, January 2022, https://csis-website-prod.s3.amazonaws.com/s3fs-public/publication/220112_ Markusen_StealthIndustry_ ChinesePSCs.pdf?VersionId=agENkxBjcx0dJsycS rvu_Y_AmBObnHNk.

163. Paul Goble, "Beijing Expanding Size and Role of Its 'Private' Military Companies in Central Asia," Jamestown Foundation, July 20, 2021, https://jamestown.org/prog ram/beijing-expanding-size-and-role-of-its-private-military-companies-in-cent ral-asia/; Meia Nouwens, "Guardians of the Belt and Road," International Institute for Strategic Studies, August 17, 2018, https://www.iiss.org/blogs/research-paper/2018/08/guardians-belt-and-road.

164. Sergey Sukhankin, "Chinese Private Security Contractors: New Trends and Future Prospects," China Brief 20, no. 9 (2020).

165. Courtney Weinbaum et al., "China's Weapons Exports and Private Security Contractors," RAND Corporation, 2022, https://www.rand.org/pubs/tools/TLA2 045-1.html.

166. Nantulya, "Chinese Security Contractors in Africa"; "About Us [关于我们]," DeWei Security Service [德威安保], http://www.dewesecurity.com/gywm.

167. Lucy Best, "What Motivates Chinese Peacekeeping?," Council on Foreign Relations, January 7, 2020, https://www.cfr.org/blog/what-motivates-chinese-peacekeeping.

168. Joel Wuthnow, "PLA Operation Lessons from UN Peacekeeping," in The PLA Beyond Borders: Chinese Military Operations in Regional and Global Context, ed. Joel Wuthnow et al. (Washington, DC: National Defense University Press, 2021), 252.

169. Lucy Poni, "South Sudan Opposition Against UNMISS Guarding Oil Facilities," VOA News, May 29, 2014, https://www.voanews.com/a/south-sudan-opposition-against-unmiss-guarding-oil-facilities/1925529.html; Okech Francis, "China Gets a Sixth of South Sudan Oil Output to Build Highways," Bloomberg, April 5, 2019, https://www.bloombergquint.com/global-economics/china-gets-a-sixth-of-south-sudan-oil-output-to-build-highways#:~:text=(Bloomberg)%20%2D%2D%20So uth%20Sudan%20tripled,nation's%20 biggest%20infrastructure%2Ddevelopm ent%20project.

170. John Hudson, Ellen Nakashima, and Liz Sly, "Buildup Resumed at Suspected Chinese Military Site in UAE, Leak Says," Washington Post, April 26, 2023, https://www.was hingtonpost.com/national-security/2023/04/26/chinese-military-base-uae/.

171. Liang Fang [梁芳], "What Are the Risks to the 'Maritime Silk Road' Sea-Lanes? [今日 ' 海上丝绸之路 ' 通道风险有多大？]," Defense Reference [国防参考], March 13, 2015, http:// www.81.cn/jwgd/2015-02/11/content_6351319.htm.

172. Pan Shanju [潘 珊 菊], "Released White Paper on China's Military Strategy Is the First to Put Forward 'Overseas Interests Area,' Struggle for Rights Will Persist [国防白皮书首提海外利益攸关区 维权斗争将长期存在]," Jinghua Times [京华时报], May 27, 2015, http:// military.people.com.cn/n/2015/0527/c1011-27061467.html.

173. "China's National Defense in the New Era," State Council Information Office of the People's Republic of China, July 24, 2019, http://www.chinadaily.com.cn/specials/whitepaperonnationa ldefenseinnewera.pdf.

174. Isaac B. Kardon and Wendy Leutert, "Pier Competitor: China's Power Position in Global Ports," International Security 46, no. 4 (Spring 2022): 9-47, 12.

175. Umesh Moramudali, "The Hambantota Port Deal: Myths and Realities," The Diplomat, January 1, 2020, https://thediplomat.com/2020/01/the-hambantota-port-deal-myths-and-realities/.

176. Jennifer Hillman and David Sacks, "How the US Should Respond to China's Belt and Road," Council on Foreign Relations, March 2021, https://www.cfr.org/report/chi nas-belt-and-road-implications-for-the-united-states/.
177. Every Chinese white paper issued from 1995 to 2019 has opposed overseas basing.
178. Li Jian [李剑], Chen Wenwen [陈文文], and Jin Jing [金晶], "Indian Ocean Seapower Structure and the Expansion of China's Sea Power into the Indian Ocean [印度洋海权格局与中国海权的印度洋拓展]," Pacific Journal [太平洋学报] 22, no. 5 (2014); Andrew Scobell, David Lai, and Roy Kamphausen, eds., Chinese Lessons from Other People's Wars (Carlisle, PA: Strategic Studies Institute, 2011).
179. Zheng Chongwei [郑崇伟], Gao Zhansheng [高占胜], and Gao Chengzhi [高成志], "The Strategy of Maritime Silk Road in the 21st Century: Construction of Strategic Strong Points [经略 21 世纪海上丝路：战略支撑点的构建]," in Proceedings from the 8th Maritime Power Strategy Forum [第八届海洋强国战略论坛论文集], October 21, 2016; Li Qingsi [李庆四] and Chen Chunyu [陈春雨], "Analysis of China's Overseas Port Chain Basing Strategy [试析中国的海外港链基地战略]," Area Studies and Global Development [区域与全球发展] 3, no. 2 (2019): 131-132.
180. Li and Chen, "Analysis of China's Overseas Port Chain Basing Strategy."
181. Liang, "What Are the Risks to the 'Maritime Silk Road' Sea-Lanes?"; Li Jian [李剑], Chen Wenwen [陈文文], and Jin Jing [金晶], "Overall Situation of Sea Power in the Indian Ocean and the Expansion in the Indian Ocean of Chinese Seapower [印度洋海权格局与中国海权的印度洋扩展]," Pacific Journal [太平洋学报] 22, no. 5 (2014), 74-75.
182. Li, Chen, and Jin, "Overall Situation of Sea Power in the Indian Ocean," 75.
183. Isaac Kardon, "China's Military Diplomacy and Overseas Security Activities," Carnegie Endowment for International Peace, January 26, 2023.
184. John Mearsheimer, The Tragedy of Great Power Conflicts (New York: W. W. Norton, 2001), 213.
185. Rush Doshi, The Long Game: China's Grand Strategy and the Displacement of American Order (New York: Oxford University Press, 2021), 645-646.
186. Military Balance 2018 (London, UK: International Institute for Strategic Studies, 2018), 209.
187. "Military Transport Aircraft Strength by Country," Global Firepower, 2022, https://www.globalfirepower.com/aircraft-total-transports.php.
188. Dingding Chen, "China Is No International Security Free Rider," The Diplomat, August 13, 2014, https://thediplomat.com/2014/08/china-is-no-international-secur ity-free-rider/.
189. Yan Xuetong [阎学通], "Yan Xuetong: The Overall 'Periphery' Is More Important than the United States [阎学通：整体的'周边'比美国更重要]," Carnegie Endowment for International Peace, January 13, 2015, https://carnegieendowment. org/2015/01/13/zh-pub-57696.

第六章

1. "GDP per Capita (Current US$) | Data," World Bank, 2015, https://data.worldbank. org/indicator/NY.GDP.PCAP.CD; "Overview of the Food and Agriculture Situation in China," in Innovation, Agricultural Productivity and Sustainability in China (Paris, France: Organization for Economic Cooperation and Development, 2018).
2. UN Comtrade Database, https://comtradeplus.un.org/, accessed April 6, 2023.
3. "China: A Development Partner to the Pacific Region," Ministry of Foreign Affairs of the

People's Republic of China, March 11, 2022, https://www.fmprc.gov.cn/mfa_eng/wjb_663304/zwjg_665342/zwbd_665378/202203/t20220311_10650946. html; "World Integrated Trade Solution," World Bank, https://wits.worldbank.org/Default.aspx?lang=en#, accessed April 19, 2023.

4. China likely owns more, but it can be difficult to track, especially if procured through third parties. These holdings demonstrate the interconnectivity of the economies but do not give China significant leverage over the United States as long as US debt re-mains a highly desired asset. "Table 5: Major Foreign Holders of Treasury Securities," US Department of the Treasury, undated, https://ticdata.treasury.gov/resource-cen ter/data-chart-center/tic/Documents/slt_table5.html, accessed November 29, 2023; Brad W. Setser, "A Bit More on Chinese, Belgian and Saudi Custodial Holdings," Council on Foreign Relations, June 20, 2016, https://www.cfr.org/blog/bit-more-chinese-belgian-and-saudi-custodial-holdings.

5. "International Trade in Goods and Services," US Department of Commerce, Bureau of Economic Analysis, https://www.bea.gov/data/intl-trade-investment/internatio nal-trade-goods-and-services, accessed July 25, 2023.

6. Edgar Crammond, "The Economic Relations of the British and German Empires," Journal of the Royal Statistical Society 77, no. 8 (1914): 777-824.

7. "U.S. Direct Investment Abroad: Balance of Payments and Direct Investment Position Data," US Department of Commerce, Bureau of Economic Analysis, https://www.bea.gov/international/di1usdbal, accessed July 25, 2023; Derek Scissors, "China's Global Investment Tracker," American Enterprise Institute, July 24, 2023, https://www.aei.org/research-products/report/chinas-global-investment-surges-finally/.

8. Scott L. Kastner and Margaret M. Pearson, "Exploring the Parameters of China's Economic Influence," Studies in Comparative International Development 56, no. 1 (March 2021): 18-44, https://doi.org/10.1007/s12116-021-09318-9.

9. Wang Jisi, "The Plot Against China? How Beijing Sees the New Washington Consensus," Foreign Affairs, June 22, 2021, https://www.foreignaffairs.com/print/node/1127545; "GDP (Current $)—China," World Bank, https://data.worldbank.org/indicator/NY.GDP.MKTP.CD?locations=CN, accessed March 31, 2023.

10. "Increasingly Negative Evaluations of China Across Advanced Economies," Pew Research Center, October 5, 2020, https://www.pewresearch.org/global/wp-content/uploads/sites/2/2020/10/PG_2020.10.06_Global-Views-China_0-01.png.

11. "America's Economic Outperformance Is a Marvel to Behold," The Economist, April 13, 2023, https://www.economist.com/briefing/2023/04/13/from-strength-to-strength.

12. G. John Ikenberry, "American Power and the Empire of Capitalist Democracy," Review of International Studies 27 (December 2001): 191-212.

13. Pan Yichen [潘怡辰], Yuan Bo [袁波], and Wang Qingchen [王清晨], "Interpretation of 'The 20th Anniversary of China's Free Trade Zone Construction and RCEP Implementation Progress Report' ["中国自由贸易区建设20周年暨RCEP实施进展报告"解读]," Foreign Investment in China [中国外资], no. 23 (2022): 14.

14. Jiang Hong [江 虹], "The Economic Advantages of Building the Sino-ASEAN Free Trade Zone [建设中国—东盟自由贸易区的经济效益分析]," International Trade Journal [国际贸易问题], no. 4 (2005): 52.

15. He Ping [贺 平], "China's Economic Diplomacy in 70 Years: Overall Evolution, Strategic Intentions and Contributory Factors [70年中国经济外交的整体演变、战略意图和影响因素]," World Economic Studies [世界经济研究], no. 11 (2019): 9; Peng Xingzhi [彭兴智] and Zhang Lixiang [张礼祥], "A Study on Measures of the Construction of the Hainan Free

Trade Port Promoting Regional Economic Cooperation in the South China Sea [海南自由贸易港建设推动南海区域经济合作的策略研究]," International Trade [国际贸易], no. 1 (2023): 3-10.

16. Sun Xue [孙雪], Chou Huafei [仇华飞], "Interests, Relative Strength, and Strategic Choices of China's Economic Diplomacy [利益、相对实力与中国经济外交的策略选择]," Journal of International Relations [国际关系研究], no. 1 (2019): 127-141.
17. James Reilley, "China's Economic Statecraft: Turning Wealth into Power," Lowy Institute, November 2013.
18. Li Wei [李巍] and Sun Yi [孙忆], "Understanding China's Economic Diplomacy [理解中国经济外交]," Foreign Affairs Review [外交评论], no. 4 (2014): 1-24.
19. Liu Guangxi [刘光溪], "Analysis of the Cost of China's Pending Accession to the 'Economic UN' [简析我国加入'经济联合国'久拖不决的代价]," International Trade [国际贸易], no. 1 (1998): 6-9.
20. Long Yongtu [龙永图], "The Core Interest of China's Accession to WTO and Existing Problems [中国入世的核心利益及发展中存在的问题]," International Economic Review [国际经济评论], no. 5 (2011): 17.
21. Zhu Rongji [朱镕基], Zhu Rongji Meets the Press [朱镕基答记者问] (Beijing: People's Press [人民出版社], 2009), 105.
22. Aaron L. Friedberg, Getting China Wrong (Cambridge, UK: Polity Press, 2022), 23-46.
23. Shivshankar Menon, "How China Bucked Western Expectations and What It Means for World Order," Brookings Institution, March 10, 2016, https://www.brookings.edu/articles/how-china-bucked-western-expectations-and-what-it-means-for-world-order/; Hui Feng, The Politics of China's Accession to the World Trade Organization (London: Routledge, 2006), 91-92.
24. Joo-Youn Jung, "Retreat of the State? Restructuring the Chinese Central Bureaucracies in the Era of Economic Globalization," China Review 8, no. 1 (Spring 2008): 105-125.
25. Zhang Yi [章冀], "Research on the Comparative Advantages of China's Foreign Trade Under the New Environment of International Trade [国际贸易新环境下中国外贸比较优势研究]," China Circulation Economy [全国流通经济], no. 32 (2020): 18-20.
26. Wayne Morrison, "China's Economic Rise: History, Trends, Challenges, and Implications for the United States," Congressional Research Service, February 5, 2018, 18.
27. "GDP Growth (Annual %)," World Bank, https://data.worldbank.org/indicator/NY.GDP.MKTP.KD.ZG, accessed July 25, 2023.
28. The PRC gained China's seat in the IMF and World Bank in 1980 after the normaliza-tion of relations with the United States.
29. "China Signed Its First FTA with a Developed Country," Chinese Ministry of Commerce, April 10, 2008, http://fta.mofcom.gov.cn/enarticle/enrelease/200911/1699_1.html; "China-Singaporean FTA Signed in Beijing," Chinese Ministry of Commerce, October 29, 2008, http://fta.mofcom.gov.cn/enarticle/chinasingaporeen/chinasingaporeennews/200910/51186_1.html; Song Guoyou [宋国友], "Global FTA Competition and China's Strategic Choices [全球自由贸易协定竞争与中国的战略选择]," Contemporary International Relations [现代国际关系], no. 5 (2013): 30-35.
30. Jiang, "The Economic Advantages of Building the Sino-ASEAN Free Trade Zone," 50.
31. Zhang Yunling [张蕴岭], "RCEP Is a Good Platform [RCEP 是个好平台]," World Affairs [世界知识], no. 16 (2019): 72.
32. Wang Yizhou [王逸舟], Global Politics and Chinese Diplomacy [全球政治和中国外交] (Beijing: World Knowledge Press [世界知识出版社], 2003), 143.

33. See database on China's leadership positions in international institutions.
34. The author was talking about APEC, but this applies to China's approach more broadly. Wang Yusheng [王嵎生], "Personally Experiencing APEC: A Chinese Official's Observations and Experiences [亲历 APEC: 一个中国高官的体察]" (Beijing: World Knowledge Press [世界知识出版社], 2000), 117, 155, 173-176.
35. Li Wei and Sun Yi, "Understanding China's Economic Diplomacy."
36. Feng Yanli [冯 颜 利] and Liao Xiaoming [廖 小 明], "Being Good at Grasping China's Development Opportunities Brought About by Global Financial Crisis and Economic Crisis [要善于把握全球金融危机与经济危机给中国发展带来的机遇]," Journal of China University of Mining and Technology (Social Sciences) [中国矿业大学学报 (社会科学版)], no. 1 (2014): 5-14.
37. Ma Hongfan [马洪范], "Trump's 'America First Strategy' Will Bring China New Chances [特朗普 ' 美国优先 ' 战略带给中国新机遇]," Fiscal Science [财政科学], no. 3 (2017): 126-130.
38. Michael J. Green, By More than Providence: Grand Strategy and American Power in the Asia Pacific Since 1783 (New York: Columbia University Press, 2017), 535-539.
39. Xi Jinping [习 近 平], "Keynote Speech at the Opening Ceremony of the World Economic Forum Annual Meeting 2017 [在世界经济论坛 2017 年年会开幕式上的主旨演讲]," Xinhua, January 17, 2017, http://www.xinhuanet.com/politics/2017-01/18/c_1120331545.htm.
40. Yuan Peng [袁鹏], "The Coronavirus Pandemic and the Great Changes Unseen in a Century [新冠疫情与百年变局]," Contemporary International Relations [现代国际关系], no. 5 (2020).
41. "A World Divided: Russia, China and the West," Bennett Institute for Public Policy, October 20, 2022, 18, https://www.bennettinstitute.cam.ac.uk/wp-content/uploads/2023/01/A_World_Divided.pdf.
42. Data on China's free trade agreements taken from "China Free Trade Network," Chinese Ministry of Commerce, http://fta.mofcom.gov.cn/english/fta_qianshu.shtml, accessed January 25, 2024; US data taken from "Free Trade Agreements," Office of the US Trade Representative, https://ustr.gov/trade-agreements/free-trade-agreements, accessed January 25, 2024.
43. Peter A. Petri and Michael Plummer, "RCEP: A New Trade Agreement That Will Shape Global Economics and Politics," Brookings Institution, November 16, 2020, https://www.brookings.edu/articles/rcep-a-new-trade-agreement-that-will-shape-global-economics-and-politics/; "A New Centre of Gravity: The Regional Comprehensive Economic Partnership and Its Trade Effects," UNCTAD, December 15, 2021, https://unctad.org/system/files/official-document/ditcinf2021d5_en_0.pdf.
44. Jill Jermano, "Economic and Financial Sanctions in U.S. National Security Strategy," PRISM 7, no. 4 (2018): 64-73.
45. Data taken from Center for a New American Security's Sanctions by the Numbers project, https://www.cnas.org/sanctions-by-the-numbers, accessed November 29, 2023. Data on the Biden administration's sanctions following Russia's inva-sion from Emily Kilcrease, Jason Bartlett, and Mason Wong, "Sanctions by the Numbers: Economic Measures Against Russia Following Its 2022 Invasion of Ukraine," Center for a New American Security, June 16, 2022, https://www.cnas.org/publications/reports/sanctions-by-the-numbers-economic-measures-against-rus sia-following-its-2021-invasion-of-ukraine.
46. "Treasury Sanctions Impede Russian Access to Battlefield Supplies and Target Revenue Generators," US Treasury Department, July 20, 2023, https://home.treasury.gov/news/press-releases/jy1636.

47. For a discussion of the logic behind the strategy, see Bai Lianlei [白 联 磊], "Why China Is Reluctant in Using Economic Sanctions [中 国 为 何 不 愿 使 用 经 济 制 裁]," Fudan International Relations Review [复旦国际关系评论], no. 18 (2016): 150-166.
48. James Reilly, "China's Unilateral Sanctions," Washington Quarterly 35, no. 4 (2012): 121-133.
49. "Foreign Ministry Spokesperson Hua Chunying's Regular Press Conference on March 25, 2021," Ministry of Foreign Affairs of the People's Republic of China, March 25,2021, https://www.fmprc.gov.cn/mfa_eng/xwfw_665399/s2510_665401/2511_665403/202103/t20210325_9170713.html.
50. Victor Cha, "How to Stop Chinese Coercion: The Case for Collective Resilience," Foreign Affairs, December 14, 2022, https://www.foreignaffairs.com/world/how-stop-china-coercion-collective-resilience-victor-cha.
51. Marcin Szczepański, "China's Economic Coercion: Evolution, Characteristics and Countermeasures," European Parliamentary Research Service, 2022, 5-6, https://www.europarl.europa.eu/RegData/etudes/BRIE/2022/738219/EPRS_BRI(2022)738219_EN.pdf.
52. Ethan Meick and Nargiza Salidjanova, "China's Response to U.S.-South Korean Missile Defense System Deployment and Its Implications," US-China Economic and Security Review Commission, July 26, 2017, https://www.uscc.gov/sites/default/files/Research/Report_China%27s%20Response%20to%20THAAD%20Deployment%20 and%20its%20Implications.pdf.
53. "Tourism Statistics," Ministry of Transportation and Communications of the Republic of China, https://admin.taiwan.net.tw/English/FileUploadCategoryList E003130.aspx?CategoryID=b54db814-c958-4618-9392-03a00f709e7a&appname= FileUploadCategoryListE003130, accessed March 31, 2023.
54. Laura He, "China Suspends Business Ties with NBA's Houston Rockets over Hong Kong Tweet," CNN Business, October 7, 2019, https://www.cnn.com/2019/10/07/business/houston-rockets-nba-china-daryl-morey/index.html; Owen Poindexter, "Silver: China Blackout Cost NBA 'Hundreds of Millions,'" Front Office Sports, June 6, 2022, https://frontofficesports.com/silver-china-blackout-cost-nba-hundreds-of-millions/.
55. Viking Bohman and Hillevi Pårup, "Purchasing with the Party: Chinese Consumer Boycotts of Foreign Companies, 2008-2021," Swedish National China Center, no. 2 (2022): 2.
56. Vanessa Friedman and Elizabeth Paton, "What Is Going on with China, Cotton and All of These Clothing Brands?," New York Times, March 29, 2021, https://www.nyti mes.com/2021/03/29/style/china-cotton-uyghur-hm-nike.html.
57. Josh Horwitz, "A 16-Year-Old Pop Star Was Forced to Apologize to China for Waving Taiwan's Flag," Quartz, January 16, 2016, https://qz.com/596261/a-16-year-old-pop-star-was-forced-to-apologize-to-china-for-waving-taiwans-flag; Lucas Niewenhuis, "All the International Brands That Have Apologized to China," SupChina, October 25, 2019, https://signal.supchina.com/all-the-international-brands-that-have-apologi zed-to-china/.
58. Daniel Victor, "John Cena Apologizes to China for Calling Taiwan a Country," New York Times, May 25, 2021, https://www.nytimes.com/2021/05/25/world/asia/john-cena-taiwan-apology.html.
59. Xi Jinping [习近平], "Xi Jinping: Several Major Issues in the National Medium-and -Long-Term Economic and Social Development Strategy [习 近 平： 国 家 中 长 期 经 济 社 会 发 展 战 略 若 干 重 大 问 题]," Qiushi [求 是], November 3, 2020, http://www.qsthe ory.cn/zhuanqu/2020-11/03/c_1126690768.htm.
60. "Wen Jiabao: China Regulates and Controls Rare Earth but Never Blocks It [温家宝：中国对稀土加以管理和控制 但决不封锁]," China News [中国新闻网], October 7, 2010, https://

www.chinanews.com.cn/cj/2010/10-07/2570433.shtml; Li Yu [李煜], "Xi Jinping Mentioned Supply Chains 20 Times in His Supply Chain Diplomacy Around the 20th National Congress of the CCP [二十大前后，习近平的" 供应链外交 "20 次谈供应链]," CN156.com [第一物流网], November 18, 2022, http://www.cn156.com/cms/scm/111512.html.

61. Ren Hongbin [任 鸿 斌], "Working Together to Maintain the Security and Stability of the Global Industrial Chain Supply Chain [携手维护全球产业链供应链安全稳定]," Chinese People's Institute of Foreign Affairs [中 国 人 民 外 交 学 会], http://www.cpifa.org/cms/book/225; Wei Jianhua [魏 建 华] et al., "From 'Decoupling' from China to 'De-risking'— Reveal the 'Risk Control' Lies of US 'Political Crooks' [从对华 ' 脱钩 ' 到 ' 去风险 '——起底美⸺政治骗子 ' 的 ' 风控 ' 谎言]," Xinhua News Agency [新华网], July 5, 2023, http://www.news.cn/world/2023-07/05/c_1129733026.htm.

62. Jonas Gamso, "Is China Exporting Media Censorship? China's Rise, Media Freedoms, and Democracy," European Journal of International Relations 27, no. 3 (May 22, 2021): 135406612110157, https://doi.org/10.1177/13540661211015722.

63. Li Xiangyang [李 向 阳], "The Idea, Organization and Implementation Mechanisms of Economic Diplomacy with Chinese Characteristics: On the Economic Diplomatic Attributes of 'One Belt, One Road' [中国特色经济外交的理念、组织机制与实施机制—— 兼论 " 一带一路 " 的经济外交属性]," World Economics and Politics [世界经济与政治], no. 3 (2021): 28.

64. Li, "The Idea, Organization and Implementation Mechanisms of Economic Diplomacy with Chinese Characteristics," 30.

65. Peter Harrell et al., "China's Use of Coercive Economic Measures," Center for a New American Security, June 2018, 31, https://www.cnas.org/publications/reports/chi nas-use-of-coercive-economic-measures.

66. "Economic Consequences of War on the US Economy," Institute for Economics and Peace, https://www.economicsandpeace.org/wp-content/uploads/2015/06/The-Economic-Consequences-of-War-on-US-Economy_0.pdf; "Post-World War II Debt Reduction," Office for Budget Responsibility, July 2013, https://obr.uk/box/post-world-war-ii-debt-reduction/.

67. Michael D. Bordo, "The Bretton Woods International Monetary System: A Historical Overview," in A Retrospective on the Bretton Woods System: Lessons for International Monetary Reform, ed. Michael D. Bordo and Barry Eichengreen (Chicago: University of Chicago Press, 1993), 3-108.

68. "World Trade Summary 2020 Data," World Integrated Trade Solution, undated, https://wits.worldbank.org/countryprofile/en/country/wld/year/ltst/summary; Rebecca M. Nelson and Martin A. Weiss, "The US Dollar as the World's Dominant Reserve Currency," Congressional Research Service, September 15, 2022, https://crsreports.congress.gov/product/pdf/IF/IF11707#:~:text=Because%20many%20 central%20banks%20and,rates)%20than%20it%20would%20otherwise, accessed January 19, 2024.

69. Nelson and Weiss, "The US Dollar as the World's Dominant Reserve Currency."

70. Li Huifen [李 惠 芬], "The Operation and Reforms of the US Dollar's Reserve Currency System [美元储备货币体系的运行及其变革]," Productivity Research [生产力研究], no. 16 (2009): 44. See also Gu Yue [顾月], Wang Ruicong [王瑞聪], and Zhu Qin [朱沁], "Pros and Cons of RMB Internationalization [人民币国际化的利与弊]," Modern Business [现代商业], no. 36 (2020): 67.

71. Emily Jin, "Why China's CIPS Matters (and Not for the Reasons You Think)," Lawfare, April 5, 2022, https://www.lawfareblog.com/why-chinas-cips-matters-and-not-reas ons-you-think.

72. Zhang Ming [张 明], "Strategic Expansion of RMB Internationalization Against the

Background of New Global Changes [全球新变局背景下人民币国际化的策略扩展——从新 '三位一体' 到新新 '三位一体 ']," National Institution for Finance and Development [国家金融与发展实验室], December 20, 2022, http://www.nifd.cn/Uploads/Paper/19d3ea6b-6dd0-422d-8631-a002cc65eca9.pdf; "Foreign Minister Qin Gang Meets the Press," Ministry of Foreign Affairs of the People's Republic of China, March 7, 2023, https://www.fmprc.gov.cn/mfa_eng/zxxx_662805/202303/t20230307_11037190.html.

73. Gu Yue [顾月], Wang Ruicong [王瑞聪], and Zhu Qin [朱沁], "Pros and Cons of RMB Internationalization [人民币国际化的利与弊]," Modern Business [现代商业], no. 36 (2020): 66.

74. Zhou Lanxu, "RMB Internationalization Gets More Attention," China Daily [中国日报], December 28, 2022, https://global.chinadaily.com.cn/a/202212/28/WS63aba467a31057c47eba68f9.html.

75. ChinaPower Team, "Is China the World's Top Trader?," ChinaPower, March 28, 2019, https://chinapower.csis.org/trade-partner/.

76. Feng and Liao, "Being Good at Grasping China's Development Opportunities Brought About by Global Financial Crisis and Economic Crisis."

77. In 2005, under pressure from trading partners, China allowed its currency to appre-ciate against the dollar and other currencies. The yuan appreciated until 2008, when China reinstated the peg following the global financial crisis. After two years, China again allowed the yuan to "float," that is, investors could buy and sell it on the open market at the price they saw fit. However, this is a "managed float" system, meaning China does not allow the rate to change too drastically on a given day.

78. "Trade Data," UN Comtrade Database, https://comtradeplus.un.org/TradeF low?Frequency=A &Flows=X&CommodityCodes=TOTAL&Partners=0&Report ers=all&period=2022&Aggrega teBy=none&BreakdownMode=plus, accessed July 24, 2023.

79. Jiang Mengying [蒋梦莹], "Yi Gang: RMB's Path to SDR Is Also China's Path to Economic Reform and Opening Up [易纲：人民币加入 SDR 之路也是中国经济改革开放之路]," The Paper [澎湃新闻], December 21, 2017, https://www.thepaper.cn/newsDetail_forward_1914606.

80. Peng Bingqi [彭冰琪], "A Brief Discussion on China's Opportunities After the Financial Crisis [浅议后金融危机的中国机遇]," Modern Economic Information [现代经济信息], no. 21 (2013): 5.

81. Yuan Peng [袁鹏], "Financial Crisis and US Economic Hegemony: An Interpretation of History and Politics [金融危机与美国经济霸权：历史与政治的解读]," Contemporary International Relations [现代国际关系], no. 5 (2009): 3-5.

82. Zhou Xiaochuan, "Reform the International Monetary System," speech delivered March 23, 2009, https://www.bis.org/review/r090402c.pdf.

83. "International Monetary System Reform and RMB Officially Joining in SDR [国际货币体系改革与人民币正式加入 SDR——人民币加入 SDR 系列文章之一]," Xinhua.com [新华网], September 21, 2016, http://www.pbc.gov.cn/goutongjiaoliu/113456/113469/3145762/index.html.

84. "China's Financial Reform and Opening-Up in RMB Joining SDR: Series on RMB Joining SDR No. 4 [人民币加入 SDR 过程中的中国金融改革和开放——人民币加入 SDR 系列文章之四]," Xinhua.com [新华网], September 26, 2016, http://www.pbc.gov.cn/goutongjiaol iu/113456/113469/3149490/index.html.

85. "Member Newsletter, 2009 Issue 2 [会员通讯 2009 第二期]," China Center for International Economic Exchanges [中国国际经济交流中心], June 3, 2009, http://www.cciee.org.cn/

Detail.aspx?newsId=58&TId=106; Zhou, "Reform the International Monetary System."
86. "Q and A on 2015 SDR Review: IMF's Executive Board Completes Review of SDR Basket, Includes Chinese Renminbi," International Monetary Fund, November 30, 2015, https://www.imf.org/external/np/exr/faq/sdrfaq.htm#four.
87. Jue Wang, "China-IMF Collaboration: Toward the Leadership in Global Monetary Governance," Chinese Political Science Review, no. 3 (2018): 75-76.
88. Zhang Ce [张 策], He Qing [何 青], and Tang Bowen [唐 博 文], "Who Will Ultimately Benefit from the RMB Currency Swap Agreements? A Bilateral Trade Perspective [人民币货币互换协议，谁最终获益？—基于双边贸易的视角]," International Currency Institute of the Renmin University of China [中国人民大学国际货币研究所], http://www.imi.ruc.edu.cn/docs/2020-12/357eec6ffcc84c519909cd7cf81bf632.pdf.
89. Zhang, He, and Tang, "Who Will Ultimately Benefit from the RMB Currency Swap Agreements?"
90. See online appendix of its swap agreements at www.orianaskylarmastro.com/upstart.
91. Zhou, "RMB Internationalization Gets More Attention."
92. Yuan Man [袁 满] and Han Xiao [韩 笑], "Zhou Xiaochuan on RMB Joining SDR: Historical Development of Opening-Up [周小川谈人民币入篮 SDR：对外开放进程的历史性进展]," Caijing [财经], October 9, 2017, https://finance.sina.cn/2017-10-10/detail-ifymrcmm9684931.d.html.
93. "What Does It Mean That the 'Scale of RMB Exchange Is Already the Largest in the World'? [人民币在全球的 ' 互换规模已是第一 ' 意味着什么？]," Sina Finance [新浪财经], March 16, 2021, https://finance.sina.com.cn/money/forex/forexroll/2021-03-17/doc-ikkntiam3169592.shtml.
94. Xu Mingqi [徐明棋], "Central Bank Currency Swaps: Impact on the International Monetary System [央行货币互换：对国际货币体系的影响]," Social Sciences [社会科学], no. 3 (2016): 64.
95. "The Impacts and Implications of RMB Joining SDR: Series on RMB Joining SDR No. 5 [人民币加入 SDR 的影响和意义—人民币加入 SDR 系列文章之五],"Xinhua.com [新华网], September 27, 2016, http://www.pbc.gov.cn/goutongjiaoliu/113456/113469/3150428/index.html; People's Bank of China [中国人民银行], 2016 RMB Internationalization Report [2016 年人民币国际化报告], July 2016, 43.
96. People's Bank of China [中国人民银行], 2019 RMB Internationalization Report [2019 年人民币国际化报告], August 2019, 71-72.
97. Gu Yue[顾 月], Wang Ruicong [王 瑞 聪], and Zhu Qin[朱 沁],"Prosand Consof RMB Internationalization [人民币国际化的利与弊]," Modern Business [现代商业], no. 36 (2020): 66; Zhu Sichang [朱四畅], "Importance of RMB Internationalization [人民币国际化的重要性]," Fortune Today [今日财富], no. 16 (2019): 215; Yu Xugang [余旭港], "Research on the Impact of RMB Internationalization on 'One Belt, One Road'—Based on the Perspective of the Impact of Exchange Rate on Export Trade [人民币国际化对 ' 一带一路 ' 的影响研究—基于汇率对出口贸易影响的视角]," National Economic Circulation [全国流通经济], no. 22 (2018): 4.
98. Cao Yuanzheng [曹远征], "China's Reform and Opening Up in Dynamic Evolutions [动态演进的中国改革开放]," BOCI Group [中银国际], 2017, https://www.bocigroup.com/wap/Inner/NewsDetail/2079.
99. "Official Foreign Exchange Reserves (COFER)," International Monetary Fund, https://data.imf.org/?sk=E6A5F467-C14B-4AA8-9F6D-5A09EC4E62A4, accessed November 29, 2023.

100. Joe Guastella and Ken DeWoskin, "China Dispatch: Can the RMB Achieve Global Currency Status?," Deloitte and Wall Street Journal, May 9, 2022, https://deloitte.wsj. com/cfo/china-dispatch-can-the-rmb-achieve-global-currency-status-01652106334. .

101. "2022 Renminbi Internationalization Report [2022 年人民币国际化报告]," People's Bank of China [中 国 人 民 银 行], September 24, 2022, http://www.gov.cn/xinwen/2022-09/24/content_5711660.htm.

102. Eswar S. Prasad, The Dollar Trap: How the U.S. Dollar Tightened Its Grip on Global Finance (Princeton, NJ: Princeton University Press, 2014), 240-241.

103. For more Chinese thinking on the trade-offs and the need for a strong govern-ment, see Zhang Liqing [张礼卿], Chen Weidong [陈卫东], and Xiao Geng [肖耿], "Further Promoting RMB Internationalization in an Orderly Manner [如何进一步有序推进人民币国际化？]," International Economic Review [国际经济评论], no. 3 (2023): 38-50; Zhang Huimin [张慧敏], "The Practical Significance and Advancement Path of RMB Internationalization [人民币国际化的现实意义与推进路径]," Northern Economy [北方经济], no. 11 (2020): 75; Shao Yutong [邵 雨 桐], "Research on the Role of RMB Internationalization in Promoting International Trade under 'One Belt, One Road' [' 一带一路 ' 倡议下人民币国际化对国际贸易的支撑作用研究], China Journal of Commerce [中国商论], no. 3 (2023): 61-63.

104. "China Wants to Make the Yuan a Central-Bank Favourite," The Economist, May 7, 2020, https://www.economist.com/special-report/2020/05/07/china-wants-to-make-the-yuan-a-central-bank-favourite.

105. Prasad, The Dollar Trap, 268.

106. Eswar Prasad, Gaining Currency: The Rise of the Renminbi (Oxford: Oxford University Press, 2017), 132.

107. Huang Yiping [黄益平], "The Past, Present, and Prospective of RMB Internationalization [人民币国际化的历史、现在和未来]," Caixin [财新], December 29, 2022, https://opinion.caixin.com/2022-12-29/101983326.html.

108. He Liping [贺 力 平], Zhao Xueyan [赵 雪 燕] and Wang Jia [王 佳], "On the Relation Between Economic Scale and Currency's International Position: An Interpretation of Determination of the US Dollar as an International Reserve Currency [经济规模与货币国际地位的关系—兼论美元国际储备货币地位的决定]," Academic Research [学术研究], no. 8 (2018): 95-105; Gao Haihong [高海红], "The Deep Conflict of the US Dollar's Reserve Status [美元储备地位的深层次矛盾]," China Finance [中国金融], no. 4 (2022): 83-84.

109. Xi Jinping, "20th Party Congress Work Report," October 16, 2022, https://www. fmprc.gov.cn/eng/zxxx_662805/202210/t20221025_10791908.html.

110. Zhou, "RMB Internationalization Gets More Attention."

111. People's Bank of China [中国人民银行], 2021 RMB Internationalization Report [2021 年人民币国际化报告], September 2021, 4-5.

112. Yi Gang [易纲], "Report by the State Council on the Financial Work [国务院关于金融工作情况的报告]," October 29, 2022, https://www.safe.gov.cn/hainan/2022/1109/1686.html.

113. Xi Jinping [习 近 平], "Keynote Speech on the Opening Ceremony of the World Economic Forum Annual Meeting 2017 [在世界经济论坛 2017 年年会开幕式上的主旨演讲]," Xinhua News Agency [新 华 社], January 18, 2017, http://www. xinhuanet.com/politics/2017-01/18/c_1120331545.htm.

114. Xi Jinping [习近平], "Speech at the Meeting with Hong Kong and Macau Visiting Missions to the 40 Years Anniversary Celebration of China's Reform and Opening Up [会见香港澳门各界庆祝国家改革开放 40 周年访问团时的讲话]," People's Daily [人民日报], November 12, 2018, https://www.gov.cn/gongbao/content/2018/content_5343727.htm.

115. Zhang Yuyan [张宇燕], "Understanding the Great Changes Unseen in a Century [理解百年未有之大变局]," International Economic Review [国际经济评论], no. 5 (2019): 14.
116. Tu Yonghong [涂 永 红], "Promoting RMB Internationalization in an Orderly Manner [有序推进人民币国际化]," Economic Daily [经济日报], December 16, 2022, http://finance.people.com.cn/n1/2022/1216/c1004-32588241.html.
117. Muhammad Tayyab Safdar and Joshua Zabin, "Pakistan and the Belt and Road: New Horizons for a Globalized RMB," The Diplomat, September 4, 2020, https://thediplo mat.com/2020/09/pakistan-and-the-belt-and-road-new-horizons-for-a-globali zed-rmb/.
118. "PBC and SBP Sign MOU on Establishing RMB Clearing Arrangements in Pakistan," People's Bank of China, November 2, 2022, http://www.pbc.gov.cn/en/3688110/3688172/4437084/4700940/index.html.
119. Summer Said and Stephen Kalin, "Saudi Arabia Considers Accepting Yuan Instead of Dollars for Chinese Oil Sales," Wall Street Journal, March 15, 2022, https://www.wsj.com/articles/saudi-arabia-considers-accepting-yuan-instead-of-dollars-for-chinese-oil-sales-11647351541.
120. Maha Kamel and Hongying Wang, "Petro-RMB? The Oil Trade and the Internationalization of the Renminbi," International Affairs 95, no. 5 (2019): 1131-1148; John Geddie, "Myanmar Seeks Closer China Ties with Renminbi Trade Project," Reuters, December 22, 2021, https://www.reuters.com/markets/currenc ies/myanmar-says-accept-renminbi-settlements-stresses-china-ties-2021-12-22/.
121. "HKEX to Introduce HKD-RMB Dual Counter Model and Dual Counter Market Making Programme in Hong Kong Securities Market," HKEX, December 13, 2022, https://www.hkex.com.hk/News/News-Release/2022/221213news?sc_lang=en.
122. Guastella and DeWoskin, "China Dispatch: Can the RMB Achieve Global Currency Status?"
123. "China Wants to Make the Yuan a Central-Bank Favourite," The Economist, May 7, 2020. https://www.economist.com/special-report/2020/05/07/china-wants-to-make-the-yuan-a-central-bank-favourite. For more detailed statistics on Chinese foreign trade, see: People's Bank of China [中国人民银行], 2022 Renminbi Internationalization Report ['2022 年人民币国际化报告 '], September 24, 2022, http://www.gov.cn/xinwen/2022-09/24/content_5711660.htm.
124. "China Expands Cross-Border RMB Use," State Council Information Office of the People's Republic of China [中 华 人 民 共 和 国 国 务 院 新 闻 办 公 室], March 6, 2023, http://english.scio.gov.cn/pressroom/2023-03/06/content_85146981.htm#:~:text= China's%20cross%2Dborder%20receipts%20and,to%20a%20press%20confere nce%20Friday.
125. Li Ruohan [李若菡] and Cai Hongbo [蔡宏波], "Lessons on National Financial Security Drawn from the US and Western Sanctions for the Russia-Ukraine Crisis [俄 乌 冲 突 美西方对俄金融制裁对我国金融安全的启示]," January 15, 2023, https://www.gmw.cn/xueshu/2023-01/15/content_36304300.htm.
126. Barry Eichengreen, "Sanctions, SWIFT, and China's Cross-Border Interbank Payments System," Center for Strategic and International Studies, May 20, 2022, https://www.csis.org/analysis/sanctions-swift-and-chinas-cross-border-interbank-payments-system.
127. "Compliance," Society for Worldwide Interbank Financial Transactions, https://www.swift.com/about-us/legal/compliance-0/swift-and-sanctions#how-is-swift-governed?, accessed February 21, 2023.
128. "China Wants to Make the Yuan a Central-Bank Favourite."
129. "Knowledge Base: Digital Currency Research Institute (数 字 货 币 研 究 所) of the People's Bank of China—DigiChina," DigiChina, June 8, 2022, https://digichina. stanford.edu/work/knowledge-base-digital-currency-research-institute-of-the-peoples-bank-of-china/.

130. "The Digital Yuan Offers China a Way to Dodge the Dollar," The Economist, September 5, 2022, https://www.economist.com/finance-and-economics/2022/09/05/the-digital-yuan-offers-china-a-way-to-dodge-the-dollar.
131. Darrell Duffie and Elizabeth Economy, Digital Currencies: The US, China, and the World at a Crossroads (Stanford, CA: Hoover Institution Press, 2022), 38.
132. "Lexicon: 'Controllable Anonymity' or 'Managed Anonymity' (可控匿名) and China's Digital Yuan," DigiChina, March 8, 2022, https://digichina.stanford.edu/work/lexicon-controllable-anonymity-or-managed-anonymity-and-chinas-digital-yuan/.
133. Pang Dongmei [庞 冬 梅], "The Value, Challenges and System Construction of Developing Digital RMB Cross-Border Transactions [发展数字人民币跨境交易的价值，挑战及制度构建]," Shanghai Law Journal [上海法学研究], no. 5 (2022): 271.
134. Prasad, The Dollar Trap, xvii.
135. Nicholas R. Lardy, China's Unfinished Economic Revolution (Washington, DC: Brookings Institution Press, 1998); Gordon Chang, The Coming Collapse of China (New York: Random House, 2001).
136. James R. Gorrie, The China Crisis: How China's Economic Collapse Will Lead to a Global Depression (Hoboken, NJ: John Wiley & Sons, 2013).
137. Simon X. B. Zhao et al., "How Big Is China's Real Estate Bubble and Why Hasn't It Burst Yet?," Land Use Policy 64 (2017): 153-162; Xu Jianguo, "China: Collapse of Threat?," New Zealand International Review 36, no. 6 (2011): 13-16.

第七章

1. Chang Lulu [常璐璐] and Chen Zhimin [陈志敏], "The Use of Attractive Economic Power in Chinese Diplomacy [吸引性经济权力在中国外交中的运用]," Foreign Affairs Review [外交评论], no. 3 (2014): 1-16; Dou Xiaobo [窦晓博], "Economic Diplomacy and Chinese Soft Power [经济外交与中国软实力]," Theory Research [学理论], no. 26 (2012): 6.
2. Wang Changlin [王 昌 林], "The Main Process, Important Role, Valuable Experience and Suggestions of the Formulation and Implementation of the Five-Year Plan (Plan) for National Economic And Social Development [国民经济和社会发展五年规划(计划)制定和实施的主要历程、重要作用、宝贵经验与建议]," The National People's Congress of the People's Republic of China [全 国 人 民 代 表 大 会], October 20, 2020, https://www.ndrc.gov.cn/wsdwhfz/202010/t20201021_1248 571.html.
3. Li Xiangyang [李 向 阳], "The Idea, Organization and Implementation Mechanisms of Economic Diplomacy with Chinese Characteristics: On the Economic Diplomatic Attributes of BRI [中国特色经济外交的理念、组织机制与实施机制——兼论 ' 一带一路 ' 的经济外交属性]," World Economics and Politics [世界经济与政治], no. 3 (2021): 28.
4. Alastair Iain Johnston, "China in a World of Orders: Rethinking Compliance and Challenge in Beijing's International Relations," International Security 44, no. 2 (2019): 9-60.
5. See, for example, Stephen M. Walt, "China Wants a 'Rules-Based International Order,' Too," Foreign Policy, March 31, 2018, https://foreignpolicy.com/2021/03/31/china-wants-a-rules-based-international-order-too/.
6. National Academy of Engineering, Mastering a New Role: Shaping Technology Policy for National Economic Performance (Washington, DC: National Academies Press, 1993), 7.
7. Lauri Scherer, "World War II R&D Spending Catalyzed Post-War Innovation Hubs," NBER Digest, no. 9 (2020): 2.

8. Mick Ryan, "An Evolving Twentieth-Century Profession: Technology After World War II," *Modern War Institute*, July 1, 2021, https://mwi.westpoint.edu/an-evolving-twentieth-century-profession-technology-after-world-war-ii/.
9. "American Competitiveness Initiative," Domestic Policy Council, Office of Science and Technology Policy, February 2006, https://georgewbush-whitehouse.archives. gov/stateoftheunion/2006/aci/aci06-booklet.pdf.
10. "Largest Tech Companies by Market Cap," Companiesmarketcap.com, https://com paniesmarketcap.com/tech/largest-tech-companies-by-market-cap/, accessed August 4, 2023.
11. "U.S. R&D Expenditures, by Performing Sector and Source of Funds: 2010-20," National Center for Science and Engineering Statistics, June 1, 2022, https://ncses. nsf.gov/pubs/nsf22330#:~:text=New%20data%20from%20the%20National,in%202 019%20(table%201).
12. "Xi Jinping on Vigorously Promoting Scientific and Technological Innovation [习近平谈大力推进科技创新]," Xinhua.com [新华网], September 29, 2021, http://www. xinhuanet.com/politics/leaders/2021-09/29/c_1127917942.htm; "Introduction to Main Chapters of Xi Jinping's On Self-Reliance and Self-Improvement in Science and Technology [习近平同志 ' 论科技自立自强 ' 主要篇目介绍]," State Council of the People's Republic of China [中华人民共和国中央人民政府], May 28, 2023, https://www.gov.cn/yaowen/liebiao/202305/content_6883464. htm?eqid=d8b7a77c009f4 6fd00000003647cb09b.
13. Huang Ning [黄宁], "Is China's Technological Opening Lagging Behind Economic Opening? [中国的科技开放落后于经济开放吗 ?]," China Scitechnology Think Tank [科技中国], no. 11 (2020): 29-32.
14. "The Political Bureau of the CPC Central Committee Held Its Ninth Collective Study Session, Chaired by Xi Jinping [中共中央政治局举行第九次集体学习 习近平主持]," Xinhua News Agency [新华社], October 1, 2013, https://www.gov.cn/ldhd/2013-10/01/content_2499370. htm.
15. "Xi Jinping: Accelerate the Construction of an S&T Great Power to Achieve High-Level S&T Self-Reliance and Self-Improvement [习近平：加快建设科技强国 实现高水平科技自立自强]," State Council of the People's Republic of China [中华人民共和国中央人民政府], April 30, 2022, https://www.gov.cn/xinwen/2022-04/30/content_5688265.htm.
16. "Introduction to Main Chapters of Xi Jinping's On Self-Reliance and Self-Improvement in Science and Technology [习近平同志 " 论科技自立自强 " 主要篇目介绍]."
17. "Watch Xi Jinping's Important Speeches to Understand the 'Big Circulation' and 'Dual Circulation' [看习近平这几次重要讲话，弄懂 " 大循环 "" 双循环 "]," Xinhua.com [新华网], September 5, 2020, http://www.xinhuanet.com/politics/xxjxs/2020-09/05/c_1126455277. htm.
18. Xi Jinping [习近平], "Remarks on the Second Plenary Session of the Fifth Plenary Session of the 18th Central Committee of the Party [在党的十八届五中全会第二次全体会议上的讲话]," CPC News [中国共产党新闻网], January 1, 2016, http://cpc. people.com.cn/n1/2016/0101/c64094-28002398.html.
19. "Outline of the National Innovation-Driven Development Strategy," Central Committee of the Chinese Communist Party and the State Council of the People's Republic of China, May 19, 2016, trans. Georgetown Center for Security and Emerging Technology, https://cset.georgetown.edu/publication/outline-of-the-natio nal-innovation-driven-development-strategy/.
20. "Outline of the National Innovation-Driven Development Strategy."
21. For instance, Ant Financial (an affiliate of Alibaba) threatened the Party's grip on the financial system by providing consumers with access to loans (although there may have been reasons

to curb Ant's lending outside political concerns alone). "Is China Right to Tame Ant?," The Economist, January 2, 2021, https://www.economist.com/finance-and-economics/2021/01/02/is-china-right-to-tame-ant.

22. Li Yuan, "Why China Turned Against Jack Ma," New York Times, December 24, 2020, https://www.nytimes.com/2020/12/24/technology/china-jack-ma-alibaba.html.
23. Carl Benedikt Frey, "How Culture Gives the US an Innovation Edge over China," MIT Sloan Management Review, February 8, 2021, https://sloanreview.mit.edu/article/how-culture-gives-the-us-an-innovation-edge-over-china/.
24. Gerard DiPippo et al., "Red Ink: Estimating Chinese Industrial Policy Spending in Comparative Perspective," Center for Strategic and International Studies, May 23, 2022, 17-18, https://csis-website-prod.s3.amazonaws.com/s3fs-public/publicat ion/220523_DiPippo_Red_Ink.pdf?VersionId=LH8ILLKWz4o.bjrwNS7csuX_C 04FyEre.
25. "What Is a Government Guidance Fund? What Is the Difference Between Government Guidance Funds and Industry Funds? [什么是政府引导基金?政府引导基金和产业基金的区别在哪?]," Sha'an Xi Net [中陕网], May 26, 2023, http://zx.dsww.cn/zixun/2023/0526/122797.html.
26. Barry Naughton, The Rise of China's Industrial Policy: 1978 to 2020 (Mexico City: Catedra Mexico-China, 2021), 19.
27. Naughton, The Rise of China's Industrial Policy, 44.
28. "Medium-and Long-Term Program of Science and Technology (2006-2020) [国家中长期科学和技术发展规划纲要 (2006-2020年)]," State Council of the People's Republic of China [中华人民共和国中央人民政府], http://www.gov.cn/gongbao/content/2006/content_240244.htm.
29. "Medium-and Long-Term Program of Science and Technology."
30. Sebastian Heilmann and Lea Shih, "The Rise of Industrial Policy in China, 1978-2012," China Analysis, no. 100 (2013): 1-25.
31. Naughton, The Rise of China's Industrial Policy, 59-64.
32. "China in Focus: Lessons and Challenges," Organization for Economic Cooperation and Development, 2012, 76-77, https://www.oecd.org/china/50011051.pdf.
33. Like the Innovation-Driven Development Strategy (IDDS); Naughton, Rise of Chinese Industrial Policy.
34. "'Made in China 2025' Plan Issued," State Council, May 19, 2015, http://english.www.gov.cn/policies/latest_releases/2015/05/19/content_281475110703534.htm; Xi Jinping [习近平], "The 20th National Congress of the Communist Party of China Opens in Beijing Xi Jinping Reports to the Congress on Behalf of the 19th Central Committee [(二十大受权发布)中国共产党第二十次全国代表大会在京开幕习近平代表第十九届中央委员会向大会作报告]," Xinhua.com [新华网], October 16, 2022, http://www.news.cn/politics/leaders/2022-10/16/c_1129067252.htm.
35. Li Keqiang [李克强], "Government Work Report [政府工作报告]," March 5, 2023, http://www.gov.cn/zhuanti/2023lhzfgzbg/index.htm.
36. "35 Key 'Stranglehold' Technologies ['卡脖子'的35项关键技术]," Ministry of Education of the People's Republic of China [中华人民共和国教育部], September 24, 2020, https://www.edu.cn/rd/zui_jin_geng_xin/202009/t20200924_2016 138.shtml; Xi Jinping [习近平], "Accelerate the Construction of a Scientific and Technological Power to Achieve High-Level Self-Reliance and Self-Reliance in Science and Technology [加快建设科技强国 实现高水平科技自立自强]," Qiushi [求是], April 30, 2022, speech delivered May 28, 2021, http://www.

qstheory.cn/dukan/qs/2022-04/30/c_1128607366.htm.

37. Xi Jinping [习 近 平], "Major Issues Concerning China's Strategies for Mid-to Long-Term Economic and Social Development [国家中长期经济社会发展战略若干重大问题]," Qiushi [求是], October 31, 2020, http://www.qstheory.cn/dukan/qs/2020-10/31/c_1126680390.htm.

38. "Watch Xi Jinping's Important Speeches to Understand the 'Big Circulation' and 'Dual Circulation.'"

39. Gerard DiPippo et al., "Red Ink: Estimating Chinese Industrial Policy Spending in Comparative Perspective," Center for Strategic and International Studies, May 23, 2022, 10-11, 33.

40. "China's Increasingly Cheap Wind Turbines Could Open New Markets," S&P Global, September 26, 2022, https://www.spglobal.com/marketintelligence/en/news-insig hts/latest-news-headlines/china-s-increasingly-cheap-wind-turbines-could-open-new-markets-72152297.

41. For example, Liu Shejian [刘社建], "Inspiration from the Four Asian Tigers [亚洲四小龙的启示]," South Reviews [南风窗], no. 3 (2006): 43-44; Peng Xingzhi [彭兴智], "Examining the Purpose of East Asian Authoritarian Regimes from the Economic Take-off of 'Four Asian Tigers' [从 " 亚洲四小龙 " 经济的腾飞看东亚威权政体的存在意义]," Business [商], no. 11 (2016): 123.

42. DiPippo et al., "Red Ink," 9, 31.

43. Sean O'Connor, "How Chinese Companies Facilitate Technology Transfer from the United States," US-China Economic and Security Review Commission, May 6, 2019, 7-8, https://www.uscc.gov/sites/default/files/Research/How%20Chinese%20Co mpanies%20Facilitate%20Tech%20Transfer%20from%20the%20US.pdf.

44. Keith Bradsher, "How China Obtains American Trade Secrets," New York Times, January 15, 2020, https://www.nytimes.com/2020/01/15/business/china-technology-transfer.html.

45. Kathrin Hille and Richard Waters, "Washington Unnerved by China's 'Military-Civil' Fusion," Financial Times, November 8, 2018, https://www.ft.com/content/8dcb534c-dbaf-11e8-9f04-38d397e6661c.

46. US Department of State, "The Chinese Communist Party on Campus: Opportunities and Risks," September 2020.

47. "APT1: Exposing One of China's Cyber Espionage Units," Mandiant, February 2013, https://www.mandiant.com/sites/default/files/2021-09/mandiant-apt1-report.pdf.

48. Office of the US Trade Representative, "Findings of the Investigation into China's Acts, Policies, and Practices Related to Technology Transfer, Intellectual Property, and Innovation Under Section 301 of the Trade Act of 1974," March 22, 2018, 153, https://ustr.gov/sites/default/files/Section%20301%20FINAL.PDF.

49. Office of the US Trade Representative, "Findings of the Investigation into China's Acts, Policies, and Practices," 6-7.

50. IP Commission, "The Report of the Commission on the Theft of American Intellectual Property," National Bureau of Asian Research, 2013, 2-3, https://www.nbr.org/wpcontent/uploads/pdfs/publications/IP_Commission_Report.pdf.

51. "2022 American Business in China White Paper," American Chamber of Commerce in the People's Republic of China, 2022, https://www.amchamchina.org/wp-content/uplo ads/2022/05/WP2022-Final.pdf.

52. Robert Atkinson and Ian Clay, "Wake Up, America: China Is Overtaking the United States in Innovation Output," Hamilton Center on Industrial Strategy, November 2022, 1, https://www2.

itif.org/2023-us-v-china-innovation.pdf.

53. Soumitra Dutta, INSEAD, and Simon Caulkin, "The World's Top Innovators," World Business, January-February 2007, 26-37; "China Ranks 11th Among the 132 Economies Featured in the GII 2022," Global Innovation Index, 2022, https://www. wipo.int/edocs/pubdocs/en/wipo_pub_2000_2022/cn.pdf.
54. "Foreign Direct Investment Statistics: Data, Analysis and Forecasts," OECD, https://www.oecd.org/investment/statistics.htm, accessed July 26, 2023; "Global Foreign Direct Investment Flows over the Last 30 years," United Nations Conference on Trade and Development, May 5, 2023, https://unctad.org/data-visualization/global-fore ign-direct-investment-flows-over-last-30-years.
55. "Digest of Japanese Science and Technology Indicators 2022—Executive Summary," National Institute of Science and Technology Policy, August 2022, https://www.nis tep.go.jp/en/wp-content/uploads/NISTEP-RM318-SummaryE_R.pdf.
56. "Japanese Science and Technology Indicators 2010," National Institute of Science and Technology Policy, January 2011, https://www.nistep.go.jp/en/wp-content/uploads/Indicator2010_tex.pdf.
57. "China Pathfinder: Annual Scorecard," Rhodium Group and Atlantic Council Geoeconomics Centers, October 2022, 4, https://www.atlanticcouncil.org/in-depth-research-reports/report/china-pathfinder-2022-annual-scorecard/.
58. Soumitra Dutta et al., eds., Global Innovation Index 2022: What Is the Future of Innovation-Driven Growth?, 15th ed. (Geneva: World Intellectual Property Organization, 2022), https://www.wipo.int/edocs/pubdocs/en/wipo-pub-2000-2022-en-main-report-global-innovation-index-2022-15th-edition.pdf.
59. "China Daily: China's Photovoltaic Industry Has Entered a Period of High-Quality Development [中国光伏产业不如高质量发展期]," China Daily [中国日报], December 24, 2019, https://cn.chinadaily.com.cn/a/201912/24/WS5e01bd77a3109 9ab995f3640.html.
60. "Fact Sheet: Commerce Finds Dumping and Subsidization of Crystalline Silicon Photovoltaic Cells, Whether or Not Assembled into Modules from the People's Republic of China," International Trade Administration, Department of Commerce, October 10, 2012, https://enforcement.trade.gov/download/factsheets/factsh eet_prc-solar-cells-ad-cvd-finals-20121010.pdf.
61. "Executive Summary—Solar PV Global Supply Chains—Analysis," IEA, 2022, https://www.iea.org/reports/solar-pv-global-supply-chains/executive-summary.
62. Rachel Tang, "China's Auto Sector Development and Policies: Issues and Implications," Congressional Research Service, June 25, 2012.
63. "Global Electric Car Stock, 2010-2021," International Energy Agency, October 26, 2022, https://www.iea.org/data-and-statistics/charts/global-elect ric-car-stock-2010-2021.
64. Christoph Nedopil Wong, "China Belt and Road Initiative (BRI) Investment Report 2023 H1," Fudan University Green Finance and Development Center, August 1, 2023, https://greenfdc.org/china-belt-and-road-initiative-bri-investment-report-2023-h1/.
65. "A Battery Supply Chain That Excludes China Looks Impossible," The Economist, July 17, 2023, https://www.economist.com/asia/2023/07/17/a-battery-supply-chain-that-excludes-china-looks-impossible.
66. Naughton, The Rise of China's Industrial Policy, 60-61.
67. Graham Allison and Eric Schmidt, "China's 5G Soars over America's," Wall Street Journal, February 16, 2022, https://www.wsj.com/articles/chinas-5g-america-stream ing-speed-

midband-investment-innovation-competition-act-semiconductor-biot ech-ai-11645046867.

68. "The 5G Ecosystem: Risks and Opportunities for DoD," Defense Innovation Board, April 2019, 13, https://media.defense.gov/2019/Apr/03/2002109302/-1/-1/0/DIB_5G_STUDY_04.03.19.PDF.

69. Financial Research Center of the Fudan Development Institute, "Frontiers of Financial Academics: Talking About the Difficulties of the Development of China's Semiconductor Industry and the Way Out [金融学术前沿：浅谈中国半导体产业发展的困境和出路]," Fudan Development Institute [复旦发展研究院], April 23, 2022, https://fddi.fudan.edu.cn/bc/f0/c18985a441584/page.htm.

70. Yu Huimin [余惠敏], "Seize the Must-Have for the Development of High Technology [抢占高科技产业发展必争之地]," People's Daily [人民网], January 8, 2023, http://theory.people.com.cn/n1/2023/0108/c40531-32601964.html.

71. "Made in China 2025 Technical Area Roadmap ['中国制造2025'重点领域技术路线图]," National Manufacturing Power Construction Strategy Advisory Committee [国家制造强国建设战略咨询委员会], September 29, 2015, https://www.cae.cn/cae/html/files/2015-10/29/20151029105822561730637.pdf.

72. "State Council Notice on the Publication of the National 13th Five-Year Plan for S&T Innovation [国务院关于印发'十三五'国家科技创新规划的通知]," State Council of the People's Republic of China [中华人民共和国中央人民政府], August 8, 2016, http://www.gov.cn/zhengce/content/2016-08/08/content_5098072.htm.

73. Financial Research Center of the Fudan Development Institute, "Frontiers of Financial Academics"; Yu, "Seize the Must-Have for the Development of High Technology."

74. Wei Zhongyuan [魏中原], "The Science and Technology Innovation Board Promotes the 'Evolution' of Domestic Semiconductors, and the Trend of the Third Transfer of the Semiconductor Industry to China Will Not Change [科创板推动国产半导体'进化'，第三次半导体产业转移向中国趋势不改]," Yicai [第一财经], August 22, 2022, https://m.yicai.com/news/101513312.html.

75. "Measuring Distortions in International Markets: The Semiconductor Value Chain," OECD, December 2019, OECD Trade Policy Papers no. 234, doi:10.1787/8fe4491d-en. China's State Council explicitly instructs Chinese state-owned banks to provide capital to Chinese semiconductor firms. China's State Council, "Guideline for the Promotion of the Development of the National Integrated Circuit Industry," June 2014, https://members.wto.org/CRNAttachments/2014/SCMQ2/law47.pdf.

76. John VerWey, "Chinese Semiconductor Industrial Policy: Past and Present," Journal of International Commerce and Economics, July 2019, 13, https://www.usitc.gov/publications/332/journals/chinese_semiconductor_industrial_policy_past_and_present_jice_july_2019.pdf.

77. Julie Zhu, "Exclusive: China Readying $143 Billion Package for Its Chip Firms in Face of U.S. Curbs," Reuters, December 13, 2022, https://www.reuters.com/technology/china-plans-over-143-bln-push-boost-domestic-chips-compete-with-us-sources-2022-12-13/.

78. Debby Wu, "Engineers Found Guilty of Stealing Micron Secrets for China," American Journal of Transportation, June 12, 2020, https://ajot.com/news/engineers-found-guilty-of-stealing-micron-secrets-for-china; Chris Miller, Chip War: The Fight for the World's Most Critical Technology (London: Simon & Schuster Ltd, 2023), 305-310.

79. "SIA Whitepaper: Taking Stock of China's Semiconductor Industry," Semiconductor Industry Association, July 2021, https://www.semiconductors.org/wp-content/uplo ads/2021/07/Taking-Stock-of-China%E2%80%99s-Semiconductor-Industry_fi nal.pdf.

80. Gregory C. Allen, "Choking off China's Access to the Future of AI," Center for Strategic and International Studies, October 11, 2022, https://www.csis.org/analysis/choking-chinas-access-future-ai.
81. "How Military-Civil Fusion Steps Up China's Semiconductor Industry—DigiChina," DigiChina, April 1, 2022, https://digichina.stanford.edu/work/how-military-civil-fusion-helps-chinas-semiconductor-industry-step-up/.
82. Helen Toner, Jenny Xiao, and Jeffrey Ding, "The Illusion of China's AI Prowess," Foreign Affairs, June 2, 2023, https://www.foreignaffairs.com/china/illusion-chinas-ai-prowess-regulation?gad=1&gclid=Cj0KCQjw8NilBhDOARIsAHzpbLBqdnZAlv l4ZQA0GC8L6CSTEuXKBf7dtpS5UlwpykqSrXS9uAm13MMaAguQEALw_wcB.
83. Tan Tieniu [谭 铁 牛], "Lecture 7 of the Special Lectures of the Standing Committee of the Thirteenth National People's Congress: Innovative Development and Social Impact of Artificial Intelligence [十三届全国人大常委会专题讲座第七讲：人工智能的创新发展与社会影响]," The National People's Congress of the People's Republic of China [全国人民代表大会], October 29, 2018, http://www.npc.gov.cn/c12434/c541/201905/t20190521_268525.html.
84. "Xi Jinping on Artificial Intelligence [习近平谈人工智能]," CASIA [中国科学院自动化研究所], December 23, 2020, http://www.ia.cas.cn/dqyd/xxyd/202012/t20201 223_5837241.html.
85. Jia Zhenzhen [贾珍珍], Ding Ning [丁宁], and Chen Fangzhou [陈方舟], "The Advent of Intelligent Warfare Is Accelerating [智能化战争加速到来]," PLA Daily [解放军报], March 17, 2022.
86. Gregory C. Allen, "Understanding China's AI Strategy: Clues to Chinese Strategic Thinking on Artificial Intelligence and National Security," Center for a New American Security, February 2019.
87. Elsa B. Kania and Lorand Laskai, "Myths and Realities of China's Military-Civil Fusion Strategy," Center for a New American Security, January 28, 2021, https://www. cnas.org/publications/reports/myths-and-realities-of-chinas-military-civil-fusion-strategy.
88. "Communiqué on National Expenditures on Science and Technology in 2021," National Bureau of Statistics in China, September 1, 2022, http://www.stats.gov.cn/english/PressRelease/202209/t20220901_1887829.html.
89. "The Central Committee of the Communist Party of China and the State Council Issued the 'Party and State Institutional Reform Plan' [中共中央国务院印发'党和国家机构改革方案']," Xinhua.com [新华网], March 16, 2023, http://www.news.cn/politics/zywj/2023-03/16/c_1129437368.htm.
90. "35 Key 'Stranglehold' Technologies."
91. Regina M. Abrami, William C. Kirby, and F. Warren McFarlan, "Why China Can't Innovate," Harvard Business Review, March 2014, https://hbr.org/2014/03/why-china-cant-innovate.
92. Chang Sheng [常盛], "Don't Just Worry About a Few Bundles of Cabbage, the 'Sea of Stars' and Technological Innovation Is Even More Exciting [别只惦记着几捆白菜，科技创新的星辰大海更令人心潮澎湃]," People's Daily [人民日报], December 12, 2020, https://www.sohu.com/a/438055555_650579.
93. Cat Tarnoff, "The Marshall Plan: Design, Accomplishments, and Significance," Congressional Research Service, January 18, 2018, 2, https://sgp.fas.org/crs/row/R45079.pdf; George S. Marshall, "The 'Marshall Plan' Speech Delivered at Harvard University, 5 June 1947," OECD, accessed April 6, 2023, https://www.oecd.org/gene ral/themarshallplanspeechatharvarduniversity5june1947.htm.

94. Ilyana Kuziemko and Eric Werker, "How Much Is a Seat on the Security Council Worth? Foreign Aid and Bribery at the United Nations," Journal of Political Economy 114, no. 5 (2006): 905-930.
95. "U.S. Agency for International Development: An Overview," Congressional Research Service, January 3, 2023, https://crsreports.congress.gov/product/pdf/IF/IF10261.
96. "U.S. Agency for International Development: An Overview."
97. Many countries labeled both as "not free" and/or a "consolidated authoritarian re-gime" by Freedom House received over $500 million in USAID funds in FY2022, in-cluding Ethiopia, Somalia, Syria, Uganda, and Yemen. "Democracy, Human Rights, and Governance," US Agency for International Development, https://www.usaid. gov/democracy, accessed November 29, 2023; "Countries and Territories," Freedom House, https://freedomhouse. org/countries/nations-transit/scores, accessed November 29, 2023; "U.S. Foreign Assistance by Country," Foreign Assistance, https://www.foreignassistance.gov/cd/ethiopia/, accessed November 29, 2023.
98. "Poverty Headcount Ratio at $2.15 a Day (2017 PPP) (% of Population)—China," World Bank, https://data.worldbank.org/indicator/SI.POV.DDAY?locations=CN, accessed July 18, 2023.
99. Sun Yun [孙云], "Why Is China's Foreign Aid So Secretive [中国对外援助为何神神秘秘]," China-US Focus [中美聚焦], December 27, 2017, http://cn.chinausfocus.com/foreign-policy/20171027/22213.html.
100. For China's most recent white paper on foreign aid and development, see "China's International Development Cooperation in the New Era," PRC State Council Information Office, January 2021, http://english.scio.gov.cn/whitepapers/2021-01/10/content_77099782_3.htm.
101. Gu Guan-Fu, "Soviet Aid to the Third World: An Analysis of Its Strategy," Soviet Studies 35, no. 1 (January 1983): 71-89.
102. Norman A. Graebner, "Foreign Aid: A Strategy in the Cold War," paper presented at the Farm Foundation's conference "Increasing Understanding of Public Problems and Policies," 1959, 21.
103. Dennis T. Yasutomo, "Why Aid? Japan as an 'Aid Great Power,'" Pacific Affairs 62, no. 4 (Winter 1989): 490-503; Robert M. Orr Jr., "The Aid Factor in U.S-Japan Relations," Asian Survey 28, no. 7 (1988): 740-756.
104. Robert D. Blackwill and Ashley J. Tellis, "A New U.S. Grand Strategy Towards China," National Interest, April 13, 2015, https://nationalinterest.org/feature/wake-america-china-must-be-contained-12616.
105. Michael J. Green, By More than Providence: Grand Strategy and American Power in the Asia Pacific since 1783 (New York: Columbia University Press, 2017), 538.
106. Li-Han Chan, "Soft Balancing Against the US 'Pivot to Asia,'" Australian Journal of International Affairs 71, no. 6 (2017): 569.
107. "Lou Jiwei Answers Reporters' Questions on the Establishment of AIIB [楼继伟就筹建亚洲基础设施投资银行答记者问]," Ministry of Finance of the People's Republic of China [中华人民共和国财政部], March 7, 2014, http://www.mof.gov. cn/zhengwuxinxi/caizhengxinwen/201403/t20140307_1053025.htm .
108. "AIIB Welcomes Mauritania as New Prospective Member," Asian Infrastructure Investment Bank, January 9, 2023, https://www.aiib.org/en/news-events/news/2023/AIIB-Welcomes-Mauritania-as-New-Prospective-Member.html.
109. Tang Lixia [唐丽霞], "Practices and Experiences of China's 70 Years of Foreign Assistance [新中国 70 年对外援助的实践与经验]," Frontiers [学术前沿], no. 2 (2020): 75-77.
110. Receiving Chinese aid in 2000-2014 brought recipient countries more in line with Beijing's

voting patterns at the United Nations, leading to an increase in local residents' favorable views of China. Che Yi [车翼], He Xiaoyu [贺晓宇], and Zhang Yan [张燕], "Foreign Aid and International Influence: Evidence from the Economic Rise of China [对外援助与国际影响力：来自中国经济复兴的证据]," Journal of Finance and Economics [财经研究], no. 7 (2023): 122-137.

111. Nadege Rolland, China's Eurasian Century: Political and Strategic Implications of the Belt and Road Initiative (Seattle, WA: National Bureau of Asian Research, 2017), 93-109.

112. ChinaPower Team, "How Will the Belt and Road Initiative Advance China's Interests?," ChinaPower, May 8, 2017, updated August 26, 2020, https://chinapower.csis.org/china-belt-and-road-initiative/.

113. Liu Xiangfeng [刘翔峰], "AIIB and 'One Belt, One Road' [亚投行与一带一路战略]," China Finance [中国金融], no. 9 (2015): 41-42, http://www.cqvip.com/QK/96434X/20159/664541240.html.

114. Liu Xiangfeng [刘翔峰], "AIIB and the Belt and Road Strategy" [亚投行与一带一路战略], China Finance [中国金融], no. 9 (2015): 41-42

115. Yougang Chen, Stefan Matzinger, and Jonathan Woetzel, "Chinese Infrastructure: The Big Picture," McKinsey and Co., June 1, 2013, https://www.mckinsey.com/featured-insights/winning-in-emerging-markets/chinese-infrastructure-the-big-picture.

116. ChinaPower Team, "How Are Foreign Rail Construction Projects Advancing China's Interests?," ChinaPower, November 12, 2020, https://chinapower.csis.org/rail-construction/.

117. Huang Meibo [黄梅波] and Wang Jiejia [王婕佳], "International Aid Evaluation System and China's Foreign Aid [国际援助评价体系及中国的对外援助]," Overseas Investment and Export Credits [海外投资与出口信贷], no. 6 (2022): 9.

118. Li Xiaoyun [李小云], The Future of Development Assistance: The Dilemma of Western Model and China's New Role [发展援助的未来：西方模式的困境和中国的新角色] (Beijing: CITIC Press [中信出版集团], 2019), chap. 3.

119. Li Xiaoyun [李小云], "Global Poverty Reduction Needs More of China's Voices [世界减贫需要更多中国声音]," in Li Xiaoyun [李小云], The Future of Development Assistance: The Dilemma of Western Model and China's New Role [发展援助的未来：西方模式的困境和中国的新角色] (Beijing: CITIC Press [中信出版集团], 2019).

120. Li, "Global Poverty Reduction Needs More of China's Voices"; Wang Zhao [王钊], "The Symbiosis Between China's Infrastructure Aid and International Development System [中国的基础设施建设援助与国际发展援助的"共生"]," Foreign Affairs Review [外交评论], no. 2 (2020): 51-81.

121. Rolland, China's Eurasian Century, 93-109.

122. "Official Development Assistance (ODA)," OECD, https://www.oecd.org/dac/financing-sustainable-development/development-finance-standards/official-deve lopment-assistance.htm, accessed July 18, 2023.

123. Ammar A. Malik et al., "Banking on the Belt and Road: Insights from a New Global Dataset of 13,427 Chinese Development Projects," AidData, September 29, 2021, 37, https://docs.aiddata.org/ad4/pdfs/Banking_on_the_Belt_and_Road_Insights_from_a_new_global_dataset_of_13427_Chinese_development_projects.pdf.

124. Zhou Shangsi [周尚思] and Xu Zhiming [徐之明], "Comparative Analysis of China's and US Official Development Assistance to Africa [中国与美国对非洲官方发展援助模式的比较分析]," Shandong Social Sciences [山东社会科学], no. 12 (2021): 160.

125. Malik et al., "Banking on the Belt and Road."

126. Malik et al., "Banking on the Belt and Road," 18-19.
127. Malik et al., "Banking on the Belt and Road," 3.
128. "China Rethinks Developing World Largesse as Deals Sour," Financial Times, October 13, 2016, https://www.ft.com/content/5bf4d6d8-9073-11e6-a72e-b428c b934b78, quoted in Malik et al., "Banking on the Belt and Road," 37.
129. China's Foreign Assistance (2014) [中 国 的 对 外 援 助 (2014)], State Council Information Office of the People's Republic of China [中华人民共和国国务院新闻办公室], July 2014. From 2007 to 2015, Chinese companies won contracts for 30 percent of the World Bank's infrastructure projects. In the ranking of global construction contractors in 2017, seven of the top ten were Chinese companies. Li Xiaoyun [李小云], "How to Understand China's Foreign Aid [如何理解中国的对外援助]," in Li Xiaoyun [李小云], The Future of Development Assistance: The Dilemma of Western Model and China's New Role [发展援助的未来：西方模式的困境和中国的新角色] (Beijing: CITIC Press [中信出版集团], 2019).
130. "Does China Dominate Global Investment?," ChinaPower, https://chinapower.csis. org/china-foreign-direct-investment/#breakdown-of-chinese-outbound-fdi-by-sector.
131. "Budget Dataset," US Department of State and USAID, https://www.foreignassista nce.gov/data, accessed March 17, 2023.
132. "Fiscal Year (FY) 2023 President's Budget Request for the United States Agency for International Development (USAID)," USAID, 2022, https://www.usaid.gov/sites/default/files/2022-05/USAID_FY_2023_BudgetRequest_FactSheet.pdf.
133. Zhou and Xu, "Comparative Analysis of China's and US Official Development Assistance to Africa," 160.
134. "China and the World in the New Era [新时代的中国与世界]," State Council Information Office of the People's Republic of China [中华人民共和国国务院新闻办公室], September 27, 2019, http://www.gov.cn/zhengce/2019-09/27/cont ent_5433889.htm; "Xi Jinping: Promoting 'One Belt, One Road' Cooperation to Deeply Benefit the People [习近平：推动共建'一带一路'走深走实造福人民]," Xinhua News Agency [新华社], August 27, 2018, http://www.xinhuanet.com/polit ics/2018-08/27/c_1123336562.htm.
135. Ana Horigoshi et al., "Delivering the Belt and Road: Decoding the Supply of and Demand for Chinese Overseas Development Projects," AidData, October 2020, 20, https://www.aiddata.org/publications/delivering-the-belt-and-road.
136. Malik et al., "Banking on the Belt and Road," 1.
137. Yufan Huang and Deborah Brautigam, "Putting a Dollar Amount on China's Loans to the Developing World," The Diplomat, June 24, 2020, https://thediplomat.com/2020/06/putting-a-dollar-amount-on-chinas-loans-to-the-developing-world/.
138. "Belt and Road Initiative," European Bank for Reconstruction and Development, n.d., https://www.ebrd.com/what-we-do/belt-and-road/overview.html.
139. Lingling Wei, "China Reins In Its Belt and Road Program, $1 Trillion Later," Wall Street Journal, September 26, 2022, https://www.wsj.com/articles/china-belt-road-debt-11663961638?mod=article_inline; Malik et al., "Banking on the Belt and Road," 2.
140. Malik et al., "Banking on the Belt and Road," 2.
141. Christopher Balding, "Why Democracies Are Turning Against Belt and Road: Corruption, Debt, and Backlash," Foreign Affairs, October 24, 2018, https://www.foreignaffairs.com/articles/china/2018-10-24/why-democracies-are-turning-against-belt-and-road.
142. "Xi Jinping: Promoting Belt and Road Cooperation to Deeply Benefit the People."
143. François de Soyres et al., "How Much Will the Belt and Road Initiative Reduce Trade Costs?,"

Federal Reserve Board of Governors, International Finance Discussion Papers 1274, 2020, https://doi.org/10.17016/IFDP.2020.1274; Belt and Road Economics: Opportunities and Risks of Transport Corridors (Washington, DC: World Bank, 2019), 5.

144. Maryla Maliszewska and Dominique van der Mensbrugghe, "The Belt and Road Initiative: Economic, Poverty and Environmental Impacts," World Bank Policy Research Working Paper 8814, April 2019, 3.

145. Sebastian Horn, Carmen M. Reinhart, and Christoph Trebesch, "China' Overseas Lending," NBER, July 2019, https://www.nber.org/system/files/working_papers/w26050/revisions/w26050.rev0.pdf.

146. Ren Xiao [任晓] and Guo Xiaoqin [郭小琴], "Interpreting China's Foreign Assistance: A Preliminary Theoretical Analysis [解析中国对外援助：一个初步的理论分析]," Fudan Journal [复旦学报], no. 4 (2016).

147. Axel Dreher et al., "Apples and Dragon Fruits: The Determinants of Aid and Other Forms of State Financing from China to Africa," International Studies Quarterly 62, no. 1 (2018): 182-194.

148. Wang Da [王达], "AIIB: China's Considerations and Global Significance [亚投行的中国考量与世界意义]," Northeast Asia Forum [东北亚论坛], no. 3 (2015): 63; see appendix on Development Finance Institutions at www.orianaskylarmastro.com/upstart; Zhang Monan [张茉楠], "The Multiple Implications of AIIB on the Transition of Global Financial Governance [亚投行之于全球金融治理变革的多重意义]," China.com.cn [中国网], January 25, 2016, http://finance.china.com.cn/news/special/zgjjqjzw/20160125/3561348.shtml.

149. "China's Global Development Initiative Is Not as Innocent as It Sounds," The Economist, June 9, 2022, https://www.economist.com/china/2022/06/09/chinas-glo bal-development-initiative-is-not-as-innocent-as-it-sounds.

150. Marek Jochec and Jenny Jenish Kyzy, "China's BRI Investments, Risks, and Opportunities in Kazakhstan and Kyrgyzstan," in China's Belt and Road Initiative and Its Impact in Central Asia, ed. Marlene Laruelle (Washington, DC: George Washington University, Central Asia Program, 2018), 69.

151. "The Central Committee of the Communist Party of China and the State Council Issued the 'National Standardization Development Outline' [中共中央国务院印发'国家标准化发展纲要']," Xinhua News Agency [新华社], October 10, 2021, https://www.gov.cn/zhengce/2021-10/10/content_5641727.htm; "Notice on Issuing the Action Plan for Implementing the 'Outline of National Standardization Development' [关于印发贯彻实施'国家标准化发展纲要'行动计划的通知]," State Council of the People's Republic of China [中华人民共和国国务院], July 8, 2022, https://www.gov.cn/zhengce/zhengceku/2022-07/09/content_5700171.htm.

152. Yi Wu, "China Standards 2035 Strategy: Recent Developments and Implications for Foreign Companies," China Briefing, July 26, 2022, https://www.china-briefing.com/news/china-standards-2035-strategy-recent-developments-and-their-impli cations-foreign-companies/.

153. Malik et al., "Banking on the Belt and Road," 19; "UN Comtrade Database," United Nations Comtrade, https://comtrade.un.org/data/, accessed April 3, 2023.

154. Malik et al., "Banking on the Belt and Road," 3.

155. Liang Fang [梁芳], "What Are the Risks to the 'Maritime Silk Road' Sea-Lanes? [今日'海上丝绸之路'通道风险有多大？]," Defense Reference [国防参考], March 13, 2015, http://www.81.cn/jwgd/2015-02/11/content_6351319.htm.

156. China has supplemented these strategies with foreign direct investment. According to the American Enterprise Institute and the Heritage Foundation's China Global Investment

Tracker, between 2005 and 2019 China invested just over $130 billion in European and North American energy projects—about one-fifth of its total FDI during that period. ChinaPower Team, "Does China Dominate Global Investment?," ChinaPower, September 26, 2016, updated January 28, 2021, https://chinapower.csis.org/china-foreign-direct-investment/.

157. "Blue Dot Network," US Department of State, https://www.state.gov/blue-dot-netw ork/, accessed July 31, 2023.

158. "FACT SHEET: Roadmap for a 21st-Century U.S.-Pacific Island Partnership," The White House, September 29, 2022, https://www.whitehouse.gov/briefing-room/sta tements-releases/2022/09/29/fact-sheet-roadmap-for-a-21st-century-u-s-pacific-island-partnership/.

159. "Real and Heavy Achievements—A Side Note of General Secretary Xi Jinping's Attendance at the Third 'One Belt, One Road' Construction Symposium [实打实、沉甸甸的成就——习近平总书记出席第三届'一带一路'建设座谈会侧记]," Xinhua.com [新华网], November 21, 2021, http://www.news.cn/2021-11/21/c_112 8084028.htm.

160. Luo Zhaohui [罗照辉], "China's Foreign Aid and International Development Cooperation in a COVID-19 Pandemic World [大疫情背景下中国对外援助和国际发展合作]," China International Studies [国际问题研究], no. 1, January 15, 2022, 18.

161. Jane Nakano, "Greening or Greenwashing the Belt and Road Initiative?," Center for Strategic and International Studies, May 1, 2019, https://www.csis.org/analysis/greening-or-greenwashing-belt-and-road-initiative.

162. Chinese media articulates that GDI is still primarily a conceptual framework, while the BRI is a concrete means of realizing it. Another interpretation is that GDI has a global focus and corresponds directly to the United Nations Sustainable Development Goals and is considered to express the Chinese government's over-arching understanding and policy agenda for global development, whereas the BRI focuses on specific regions and issue areas. Wang Junsheng [王俊生], "Implementing 'One Belt, One Road' and Global Development Initiative [落实'一带一路'倡议与全球发展倡议]," Guangming Daily [光明日报], April 26, 2023, http://cn.chinadi plomacy.org.cn/2023-04/26/content_85255281.shtml.

163. Joseph Lemoine and Yomna Gaafar, "There's More to China's New Global Development Initiative than Meets the Eye," Atlantic Council, August 18, 2022, https://www.atlanticcouncil.org/blogs/new-atlanticist/theres-more-to-chinas-new-global-development-initiative-than-meets-the-eye/. GDI seems to be a smaller effort than BRI—China's National Development and Reform Commission is the main coordinating body behind the BRI, whereas the GDI is run by the Ministry of Foreign Affairs and the China International Development Cooperation Agency. "Xi's New Global Development Initiative," Center for Strategic and International Studies event, September 12, 2022, https://www.csis.org/events/xis-new-global-development-initiative.

164. Michael Schuman, Jonathan Fulton, and Tuvia Gering, "How Beijing's Newest Global Initiatives Seek to Remake the World Order," Atlantic Council, June 21, 2023, https://www.atlanticcouncil.org/in-depth-research-reports/issue-brief/how-beiji ngs-newest-global-initiatives-seek-to-remake-the-world-order/.

165. Andrew Scobell et al., "At the Dawn of Belt and Road," RAND Corporation, 2018, 215.

結論

1. For examples, see Fang Cai, The China Miracle: Development Strategy and Reform (Hong Kong: Chinese University of Hong Kong Press, 2003); Nicholas L. Lardy, China's Unfinished Economic Revolution (Washington, DC: Brookings Institution Press, 1998); and Barry Naughton and Kellee S. Tsai, State Capitalism, Institutional Adaptation, and the Chinese

Miracle (Cambridge, UK: Cambridge University Press, 2015).

2. Xi Jinping, "20th Party Congress Work Report," Ministry of Foreign Affairs of the People's Republic of China, October 16, 2022, https://www.fmprc.gov.cn/eng/zxxx_ 662805/202210/t20221025_10791908.html.

3. Pei Changhong [裴长洪], and Liu Hongkui [刘洪愧], "How China Can Become a Powerful Country in International Trade: A New Analysis Framework [中国怎样迈向贸易强国：一个新的分析思路]," Economic Studies [经济研究], no. 5 (2017): 26-43.

4. Li Gang [李 钢], "China's Strategic Path Toward Becoming a Trade Great Power [中 国 迈 向贸易强国的战略路径]," Journal of International Trade [国际贸易问题], no. 2 (2018): 11-15; Alicia García-Herrero, "Could the RMB Dislodge the Dollar as a Reserve Currency?," MarshMcLennan, BrinkNews, July 8, 2021.

5. Mu Rongping [穆 荣 平], Fan Yonggang [樊 永 刚], and Wen Hao [文 皓], "Innovation Development: Way to Build China a Major S&T Power [中国创新发展：迈向世界科技强国之路]," Journal of Chinese Academy of Sciences [中国科学院院刊] 32, no. 5 (May 15, 2017): 512-520, https://doi.org/10.16418/j.issn.1000-3045.2017.05.010.

6. "Jin Yinan: They Are Afraid Because the Cost Is High [美国永不与中国开战？金一南：代价太大，自然会怕]," Huanqiu.com [环 球 网], September 17, 2021, https://mil.huanqiu.com/article/44oDAJnRaiX; Luo Fuqiang [罗富强], "What Are the Costs and Conditions for Foreign Countries if They Dare to Intervene in China's Unification by Force [统一之战，外国若敢干预会付出怎样的代价和条件]," Sina News [新浪新闻], August 16, 2018, https://jmqmil.sina.cn/dgby/doc-ihhtfwqs0284 397.d.html?vt=4.

7. "Not the Partner You Were Looking For," The Economist, March 1, 2018, https://www.economist.com/leaders/2018/03/01/how-the-west-got-china-wrong.

8. Da Wei [达 巍] and Cai Hongyu [蔡 泓 宇], "50 Years of China-US Relations Under US National Security Strategies [美国国家安全战略视阈下的中美关系 50 年]," Journal of International Security Studies [国际安全研究], no. 2 (2022): 38.

9. Chun Han Wong, Keith Zhai, and James T. Areddy, "China's Xi Jinping Takes Rare Direct Aim at U.S. in Speech," Wall Street Journal, March 6, 2023, https://www.wsj.com/articles/chinas-xi-jinping-takes-rare-direct-aim-at-u-s-in-speech-5d8fde1a.

10. Yuan Peng [袁鹏], "The Coronavirus Pandemic and the Great Changes Unseen in a Century [新冠疫情与百年变局]," Contemporary International Relations [现代国际关系], no. 5 (2020): 1-2.

11. Hal Brands and Michael Beckley, Danger Zone: The Coming Conflict with China (New York: W. W. Norton, 2022).

12. Jonathan Fenby, Will China Dominate the 21st Century (Medford, MA: Polity Press, 2014); Melvin Gurtov, Will This Be China's Century? A Skeptic's View (Boulder, CO: Lynne Rienner, 2013); David Shambaugh, China Goes Global: The Partial Power (New York: Oxford University Press, 2013); David Shambaugh, ed., China and the World (New York: Oxford University Press, 2020); Robert Sutter, Chinese Foreign Relations: Power and Policy Since the Cold War (Lanham, MD: Rowman and Littlefield, 2007).

13. Kenneth Waltz, Theory of International Politics (Long Grove, IL: Waveland Press, 1979), 195.

14. Andy W. Marshall, Long-Term Competition with the Soviets: A Framework for Strategic Analysis (Santa Monica, CA: RAND Corporation, 1972), viii.

15. Jan-Michael Ross and Dmitry Sharapov, "When the Leader Follows: Avoiding Dethronement Through Imitation," Academy of Management Journal 58, no. 3 (2015): 658-679.

16. Michael E. Porter, "Stop Imitating, and Get to the Real Strategy," Bank Advertising News,

January 12, 1998, 6.
17. I would like to thank Thomas Fingar for encouraging me to emphasize this point.
18. Walter Russell Mead, "The Return of Geopolitics," Foreign Affairs, April 17, 2014, https://www.foreignaffairs.com/articles/china/2014-04-17/return-geopolitics.
19. Paul Scharre, "America Can Win the AI Race," Foreign Affairs, April 4, 2023, https://www.foreignaffairs.com/united-states/ai-america-can-win-race.
20. Oriana Skylar Mastro, "Conflict and Chaos on the Korean Peninsula: Can China's Military Help Secure North Korea's Nuclear Weapons?," International Security 40, no. 3 (Winter 2015-2016): 7-53.
21. G. John Ikenberry, After Victory: Institutions, Strategic Restraint, and the Rebuilding of Order after Major Wars (Princeton: Princeton University Press, 2001); Stephen G. Brooks and William C. Wolfforth, "The Rise and Fall of the Great Powers in the Twenty-First Century: China's Rise and the Fate of America's Global Position," International Security 40, no. 3 (Winter 2015-2016): 7-53; Michael C. Beckley, "China's Century? Why America's Edge Will Endure," International Security 36, no. 3 (Winter 2012): 41-78.
22. Yuan, "The Coronavirus Pandemic and the Great Changes Unseen in a Century."
23. Mary E. Lovely, "The Trouble with Trans-Pacific Trade," Foreign Affairs, January 23, 2023, https://www.foreignaffairs.com/united-states/trouble-trans-pacific-trade.
24. "Economic Power Play: Assessing China's Trade Policies," The Economist Intelligence Unit, 2021, https://impact.economist.com/perspectives/sites/default/files/eco-nomic_power_play_assessing_chinas_trade_policies_0608.pdf.
25. André Sapir and Petros C. Mavroidis, "China and the WTO: An Uneasy Relationship," Center for Economic Policy Research, April 29, 2021, https://cepr.org/voxeu/colu mns/china-and-wto-uneasy-relationship.
26. Matthew Reynolds and Matthew P. Goodman, "Deny, Deflect, Deter: Countering China's Economic Coercion," Center for Strategic and International Studies, March 2023, https://csis-website-prod.s3.amazonaws.com/s3fs-public/2023-03/230 321_Goodman_CounteringChina%27s_EconomicCoercion.pdf?VersionId=UnF29 IRogQV4vH6dy6ixTpfTnWvftd6v.
27. Arzan Tarapore et al., "Minilateral Deterrence in the Indo-Pacific," Asia Policy 17, no. 4 (2022).
28. Oriana Skylar Mastro, "Testimony of Dr. Oriana Skylar Mastro," testimony before the Senate Foreign Relations Committee Hearing on a New Approach for an Era of US-China Competition, March 13, 2019, https://www.foreign.senate.gov/imo/media/doc/031319_Mastro_Testimony.pdf.
29. Duncan Hollis, "China and the US Strategic Construction of Cybernorms: The Process Is the Product," Hoover Working Group on National Security, Technology, and Law, Aegis Paper Series No. 1704, July 7, 2017; Ines Kagubare, "Cyberspace Plays Key Role in Growing US-China Tension," The Hill, June 6, 2023, https://thehill.com/policy/cybersecurity/4032479-cyberspace-plays-key-role-in-growing-us-china-tension/.
30. James A. Lewis, "Creating Accountability for Global Cyber Norms," Center for Strategic and International Studies, February 23, 2022, https://www.csis.org/analysis/creating-accountability-global-cyber-norms.
31. Ankit Panda and Benjamin Silverstein, "The U.S. Moratorium on Anti-Satellite Missile Tests Is a Welcome Shift in Space Policy," Carnegie Endowment for International Peace, April 20, 2022, https://carnegieendowment.org/2022/04/20/u.s.-moratorium-on-anti-satellite-missile-tests-is-welcome-shift-in-space-policy-pub-86943.

32. "New Generation Artificial Intelligence Development Plan [国务院关于印发新一代人工智能发展规划的通知]," State Council of the People's Republic of China [中华人民共和国中央人民政府], September 20, 2017, https://www.gov.cn/zhengce/content/2017-07/20/content_5211996.htm.
33. Adrian Pecotic, "Whoever Predicts the Future Will Win the AI Arms Race," Foreign Policy, March 5, 2019, https://foreignpolicy.com/2019/03/05/whoever-predicts-the-future-correctly-will-win-the-ai-arms-race-russia-china-united-states-artificial-intelligence-defense/.
34. Walter J. Ferrier, Ken. G. Smith, and Curtis M. Grimm, "The Role of Competitive Action in Market Share Erosion and Industry Dethronement: A Study of Industry Leaders and Challengers," Academy of Management Journal 42, no. 4 (August 1999): 376.
35. Kenneth Arrow, "Economic Welfare and the Allocation of Resources for Invention," in The Rate and Direction of Innovative Activity, ed. R. R. Nelson (Princeton, NJ: Princeton University Press, 1962).
36. Richard N. Foster, Innovation: The Attacker's Advantage (New York: Summit Books, 1986), 21.
37. Yun Jiang and Jordan Schneider, "The United States Needs More Wine to Stand Up to Chinese Bullying," Foreign Policy, December 10, 2020, https://foreignpolicy.com/2020/12/10/united-states-australian-wine-chinese-bullying-strategic-shiraz-reserve/.
38. For example, see Oriana Skylar Mastro and Sungmin Cho, "How South Korea Can Contribute to the Defense of Taiwan," Washington Quarterly 45, no. 3 (2022): 109-129; Oriana Skylar Mastro, "The Taiwan Temptation," Foreign Affairs, June 3, 2021, https://www.foreignaffairs.com/articles/china/2021-06-03/china-taiwan-war-tem ptation; Oriana Skylar Mastro, "Reassurance and Deterrence in Asia," Security Studies 31, no. 4 (2022): 743-750.
39. "Philippines Announces Four More Military Bases US Troops Can Use," Straits Times, April 4, 2023, https://www.straitstimes.com/asia/se-asia/philippines-announ ces-four-more-military-bases-us-troops-can-use.
40. Seth G. Jones, "America's Looming Munitions Crisis," Foreign Affairs, March 31, 2023, https://www.foreignaffairs.com/united-states/americas-looming-munitions-crisis; Michael Brown, "Taiwan's Urgent Task," Foreign Affairs, January 25, 2023, https://www. foreignaffairs.com/china/taiwan-urgent-task-new-strategy-to-keep-china-away.
41. Jake Sullivan, "Remarks by National Security Advisor Jake Sullivan at the Special Competitive Studies Project Global Emerging Technologies Summit," White House, September 16, 2022, https://www.whitehouse.gov/briefing-room/speeches-rema rks/2022/09/16/remarks-by-national-security-advisor-jake-sullivan-at-the-special-competitive-studies-project-global-emerging-technologies-summit/.
42. For more recommendations, see Oriana Skylar Mastro, The Costs of Conversation: Obstacles to Peace in Wartime (Ithaca, NY: Cornell University Press, 2019), 126-142.
43. Men Honghua [门洪华] and Li Ciyuan [李次园], "Great Power Competition in International Relations: A Strategic Research Agenda [国际关系中的大国竞争：一项战略研究议程]," Journal of Contemporary Asia-Pacific Studies [当代亚太], no. 6 (2021): 41-42.
44. Rohan Mukherjee, "Rising Powers and the Quest for Status in International Security Regimes" (PhD dissertation, Princeton University, May 2016), 140.
45. See Oriana Skylar Mastro, "In the Shadow of the Thucydides Trap: International Relations Theory and the Prospects for Peace in U.S.-China," Journal of Chinese Political Science, no. 24 (2019): 25-45.
46. Ikenberry, After Victory.
47. For example, see Evan Montgomery, In the Hegemon's Shadow: Leading States and the Rise of

Regional Powers (Ithaca, NY: Cornell University Press, 2016); Dale Copeland, The Origins of Major Wars (Ithaca, NY: Cornell University Press, 2000).

48. Another point of intense debate is the source of these intentions. Those with a pre-disposition toward Sinology and cultural essentialism argue that China's ancient his-tory and political culture have set it toward a modern iteration of its ancient Middle Kingdom tributary system. Henry Kissinger, On China (New York: Penguin Books, 2011); Martin Jacques, When China Rules the World: The Rise of the Middle Kingdom and the End of the Western World (New York: Penguin Books, 2009). Others point to grand strategy as the result of rational conclusions drawn through rational decision-making by Communist Party leaders who want to maintain and expand domestic power and legitimacy—and foreign policy is thus a tool of domestic politics. Bates Gill, Daring to Struggle: China's Global Ambitions Under Xi Jinping (New York: Oxford University Press, 2022); Suisheng Zhao, The Dragon Roars Back: Transformational Leaders and Dynamics of Chinese Foreign Policy (Stanford, CA: Stanford University Press, 2022).

49. Avery Goldstein demonstrates that Chinese grand strategy is largely an attempt to shape and respond to US strategy when he argues that Xi Jinping is reassuring, reforming, and resisting. Avery Goldstein, "China's Grand Strategy Under Xi Jinping: Reassurance, Reform, and Resistance," International Security 45, no. 1 (2020). Rush Doshi argues that China engaged in blunting (that is, impeding US power) be-ginning at the end of the Cold War, and later commenced building (that is, actively strengthening a regional presence) in the early twenty-first century. Rush Doshi, The Long Game: China's Grand Strategy to Displace American Order (Oxford: Oxford University Press, 2021). See chaps. 3 through 6 on blunting and chaps. 7 through 10 on building. M. Taylor Fravel argues that the degree of internal consensus as well as assessments of the changing nature of warfare determine when and how China changes its military strategy. Taylor Fravel, Active Defense: China's Military Strategy Since 1949 (Princeton: Princeton University Press, 2019).

50. "In Their Own Words: Foreign Military Thought—Science of Military Strategy (2013)," China Aerospace Studies Institute, February 8, 2021, https://www.airunivers ity.af.edu/CASI/Display/Article/2485204/plas-science-of-military-strategy-2013/, 303-306; translated from Shou Xiaosong [寿晓松], The Science of Military Strategy [战略学] (Beijing: Military Science Press [军事科学出版社], 2013), 241-244.

Horizon 視野 019

新竄起者：破解中國巧妙的霸權之路
Upstart: How China Became a Great Power

作者	梅慧琳（Oriana Skylar Mastro）
譯者	邱鐘義

明白文化事業有限公司

社長暨總編輯	林奇伯
責任編輯	楊鎮魁
文字編輯	高仲良
文稿校對	高仲良、楊鎮魁
封面設計	兒日設計
內文排版	大光華印務部
出版	明白文化事業有限公司 地址：231 新北市新店區民權路 108-3 號 6 樓 電話：02-2218-1417　傳真：02- 8667-2166
發行	遠足文化事業股份有限公司（讀書共和國出版集團） 地址：231 新北市新店區民權路 108-2 號 9 樓 郵撥帳號：19504465　遠足文化事業股份有限公司 電話：02-2218-1417 讀書共和國客服信箱：service@bookrep.com.tw 讀書共和國網路書店：https://www.bookrep.com.tw 團體訂購請洽業務部：02-2218-1417 分機 1124
法律顧問	華洋法律事務所　蘇文生律師
印製	中原造像股份有限公司
出版日期	2025 年 8 月初版
定價	650 元
ISBN	978-626-99653-5-9（平裝） 978-626-99653-4-2（EPUB）
書號	3JHR0019

© Oriana Skylar Mastro 2024
Upstart: How China Became a Great Power was originally published in 2024. This translation is published by arrangement with Oxford University Press. Crystal Press Ltd. is solely responsible for this translation from the originally work and Oxford University Press shall have no liability for any errors, omissions or inaccuracies or ambiguities in such translation or for any loses caused by reliance thereon.
This publication is arranged through Andrew Nurnberg Associates International Limited.
Complex Chinese translation copyright © 2025 by Crystal Press Ltd.
All rights reserved.

著作權所有・侵害必究 All rights reserved
特別聲明：有關本書中的言論內容，不代表本公司 / 出版集團之立場與意見，文責由作者自行承擔。

國家圖書館出版品預行編目 (CIP) 資料

```
新竄起者：破解中國巧妙的霸權之路 / 梅慧琳 (Oriana Skylar Mastro) 著；邱鐘義譯. -- 初版. --
新北市：明白文化事業有限公司出版：遠足文化事業股份有限公司發行, 2025.08
    面；　公分. -- (Horizon 視野；19)
    譯自：Upstart : how China became a great power
    ISBN 978-626-99653-5-9( 平裝 )

1.CST: 中國大陸研究 2.CST: 外交政策 3.CST: 軍事戰略 4.CST: 國際關係

574.1                                                              114005004
```

Upstart
How China Became a Great Power

ISBN 978-626-99653-5-9 | 3JHR0019 | NTD 650
建議書區：社會科學、國際關係、外交